No Stranger to Kindness

MUKESH KAPILA

© Mukesh Kapila 2019.

Mukesh Kapila has asserted his rights under the Copyright, Design and Patents Act, 1988, to be identified as the author of this work.

First published in 2019 by Sharpe Books.

*If left unpolished
The glow of precious stones
Will not lustre forth;
Surely this is also true
Of these human hearts of ours.*

- The Empress Shōken of Japan, 1849-1914.

CONTENTS

Author's Note
List of Abbreviations
Prologue
Chapter One
Chapter Two
Chapter Three
Chapter Four
Chapter Five
Chapter Six
Chapter Seven
Chapter Eight
Chapter Nine
Chapter Ten
Chapter Eleven
Chapter Twelve
Chapter Thirteen
Chapter Fourteen
Chapter Fifteen
Chapter Sixteen
Chapter Seventeen
Chapter Eighteen
Chapter Nineteen
Chapter Twenty
Chapter Twenty-One
Chapter Twenty-Two
Chapter Twenty-Three
Chapter Twenty-Four
Chapter Twenty-Five
Chapter Twenty-Six
Chapter Twenty-Seven
Epilogue

AUTHOR'S NOTE

When you are living in the middle of history as it is being made, and especially if chance or fate has given you a small role to play, you are not actually conscious of it. On the good days you may catch yourself in the brief thought that you are making a real difference. Mostly however, you are too busy navigating reality; trying to stay afloat.

It's only afterwards - in Shakespeare's words, *"when the hurly-burly's done, when the battle's lost and won,"* - that events find their rightful place in the helter-skelter of your mind and the confusion in your heart. It is only then that you can properly assess the significance of what you have experienced.

This book is written from my personal recollections, supported by forty years' worth of archival notes and documents, that have survived transits through many organisations and several relocations across continents. I have also been helped in my reminiscences by many kind colleagues who shared these experiences and refreshed my recall of distant times. I have changed many of their names to protect them or to preserve their privacy.

I am indebted to my co-writer Ennis M Ganinick who was instrumental in giving shape and form to this narrative, and to Damien Lewis who provided critical improvements. Without them, this book would not have seen the light of day. Any errors are, of course, my own responsibility, and I will be happy to correct them in future editions.

This book is intended as both a complement as well as a counter-blast to my first memoir, *Against A Tide Of Evil*. It is my attempt at making sense of my own life as I have lived it. The events that have happened to me, how I've been shaped by them, and ultimately the ways I have chosen to move forward through the inevitable false starts, wrong turns, pitfalls and stumbles, many failures and some triumphs.

Yet most of all this is the story of the people I have met along the way whose humanity and kindness has given me strength. Our world is full of evils like the Rwanda and Darfur genocides - horrors that I witnessed at first hand. Yet, it is also full of valiant survivors, human rights defenders, and ordinary people possessed of an unfaltering spirit who, despite the odds, do not stop working for the good of humankind.

This book is dedicated to them.

Mukesh Kapila,
Geneva, 2019.

List of Abbreviations

AIDS	Acquired Immune Deficiency Syndrome
BBC	British Broadcasting Corporation
CHAD	Conflict and Humanitarian Affairs Department (of DFID)
OCHA	Office for the Coordination of Humanitarian Affairs (of UN)
ODA	Overseas Development Administration (of FCO)
OHCHR	Office of the High Commissioner for Human Rights (of UN)
DFID	Department for International Development (of UK Government)
DIHAD	Dubai International Humanitarian Aid & Development Conference & Exhibition
DPRK	Democratic People's Republic of Korea
FCO	Foreign and Commonwealth Office (of UK Government)
GCSE	General Certificate of Secondary Education
GDP	Gross Domestic Product
HIV	Human Immunodeficiency Virus
ICC	International Criminal Court
ICRC	International Committee of the Red Cross
IDPs	Internally Displaced Persons
IFRC	International Federation of Red Cross and Red Crescent Societies
ILO	International Labour Organization
IMC	International Medical Corps
JCR	Junior Common Room
NCDs	Non-communicable diseases
NGOs	Non-governmental organisations
RPF	Rwandan Patriotic Front
SEARO	South-East Asia Regional Office (of WHO)
SLM	Sudan Liberation Movement
SPLM	Sudan People's Liberation Movement
TB	Tuberculosis
UK	United Kingdom
UN	United Nations
UNAMA	United Nations Assistance Mission in Afghanistan
UNDRO	UN Disaster Relief Organisation

UNFPA	United Nations Population Fund
UNGA	UN General Assembly
UNHCR	UN High Commissioner for Refugees
UNICEF	United Nations Children's Fund
USA	United States of America
WFP	World Food Programme
WHO	World Health Organization

Prologue
On the Road to Damascus

I feel people will tend toward universal mutual aid like fire tending upward and water downwards — it will be unpreventable in the world.
Mo Tzu, 470-391 BC

THIS BOOK WAS BORN IN LEBANON IN A REFUGEE CAMP midway between Beirut and Damascus. More precisely, it was inspired by a woman named Fatima who I met in a freezing ramshackle shelter in the Bekaa Valley, close to the Syrian border. It was the fifth year of the vicious Syrian war and I was examining the living costs the conflict had created for refugees on the ground, as a guest of the British charity Islamic Relief.

As Fatima squatted on the threadbare carpet, coaxing heat out of the simple paraffin burner to boil water for tea, the wind howled outside the tent and flakes of snow pierced the torn canvas. In stark contrast to the icy weather outside, Fatima's smile was warm and her toothless face beamed with love as she lifted a baby out of harm's way from the smoking stove. There, surrounded by her seven grandchildren aged between nine months and thirteen years, Fatima told me her story.

"We had a nice life near Damascus but when the plane destroyed our house and killed my husband, I ran," she said. Fleeing the country that had been her home for fifty years she slipped across the border into Lebanon.

Her smiling face now solemn, Fatima served the steaming tea and continued her difficult story.

"I had two sons. The elder and his wife died in an air attack on Aleppo; luckily the children were at school. The younger was press-ganged into a militia and killed somewhere. I don't know what happened to my second daughter-in-law."

Fatima described how she had gone back and forth across the border, darting over the frontlines repeatedly and putting herself in grave danger, until she had rescued each of her scattered grandchildren. Against all the odds she had saved them, but everything else in their lives had been ripped apart by the war.

"You must be very, very angry at the people who did this to your family. You must be wanting revenge," I commented when I thought of all she had lost.

Fatima paused for a long moment, cupping her hot mug of tea and regarding the children clustered near her like chicks around a mother hen.

"Enough blood has been spilt," she said after a time. "I want my grandchildren to have a better life. They must be educated and get good jobs." She gestured proudly at the eldest. "He is good at maths and wants to be an engineer. We will need many to rebuild our country."

I could not help but smile as I regarded the boy, for though he would undoubtedly face many hardships on his path to qualifying as an engineer, in that moment I felt great faith in him. Fatima's optimism was truly contagious.

"And really we are the lucky ones," Fatima added. "Allah be praised, a kind man let us stay on his field and helped me build this home."

***

This kind Samaritan was Elias, a small-scale Lebanese businessman who owned the field on which Fatima had pitched her tent, together with around two-hundred other Syrian refugees. Elias showed me around the camp.

"These are our own brothers and sisters and the field was lying empty, anyway," he said modestly as we walked along the icy pathways between the tents. This was not an UN-recognised refugee camp and so was not eligible for official help. But seeing the needs of the Syrians, Elias had mobilised his local church to provide the necessities for living, and other local NGOs had also pitched in.

Humbled by all I had seen, I prepared to leave. But Elias asked for my help with one final job before parting. It was almost Christmas Day and he had a huge bag of chocolates gifted by the surrounding community.

"Will you do us the honour to give them out?" He asked me.

Under a corrugated tin shed, which served as a school for the refugee children, several dozen kids did their best to keep warm. Elias had helped the refugees construct this school where anyone with skills to share could impart their wisdom to the younger generation as a way of investing in their future. These shivering children were Syria's future engineers, teachers, nurses and doctors. Perhaps they would also grow up to be peace builders if Fatima had her wish.

I shared the chocolates out between them but they insisted that the last one was for me to keep.

"Thanks for coming and have a happy new year," said Elias as he and the children waved me off.

***

On the drive back to Beirut, I marvelled at Fatima's remarkable courage in facing the dangers she had encountered and her tenacious optimism for the future of her grandchildren and the refugee community, despite the odds stacked against them. Fatima refused to become a victim of misfortune or to be bitter about the injustices inflicted upon her. She was busy planning for the future and I learnt from her the true meaning of resilience - a much-used buzzword in the humanitarian business that has become my life's vocation. She also brought hope, conveyed a vision of the future she wanted, and expressed determination to shape it, exhibiting true leadership skills. Really, she merited a book of her own.

So too did Elias whose generous response to the needs of the refugees epitomised the deeply human impulse to help one's fellow man. I saw that throughout my own life's work - spanning public health, humanitarian, and human rights fields - it has been kind strangers like Elias whose actions have impacted me the most, particularly in the darkest of times when all had seemed hopeless.

The very darkest of these had been without a doubt my experiences of the Darfur genocide. I knew that in truth, a part of me was still very much immersed in the horrors of Darfur. Although a decade had gone by since I had witnessed the first genocide of the Millennium, my failure to stop it, despite being the Head of the United Nations in Sudan, had crushed me, professionally and personally. I have spoken on this in my earlier memoir, *Against A Tide of Evil,* and for a while that narrative had felt all-consuming.

Since Darfur however, I have managed to find some accommodation with myself, through burying myself in all types of work hoping that I could still prove useful to the world, and finally I felt myself wanting to give space to the other stories of my life – ones that had been punctuated by brave women like Fatima and kind men like Elias, whose human spirit shone brightly despite the grave challenges they faced.

***

The following morning, I visited a Palestinian Red Crescent hospital near Saida, in the centre of Lebanon. In the rehabilitation section, a Syrian mother recounted how she and her family had fled from Homs. Her four-year-old son, Qasim, had autism and the constant bombardments had made it impossible to manage his disruptive behaviour. I could see that that was true, for the little boy cowered between his mother's legs but lashed out at anyone who came near.

I watched mesmerised as Bushra - Qasim's therapist - calmly cajoled him to sit still and take a green toy from her outstretched hand. An hour later he could do this without scratching and snatching, and was duly rewarded with an apple. This was the culmination of two months of therapy where Bushra had spent many patient hours each week with the severely disturbed child. A true labour of love.

Over tea, Bushra told me about herself. She was a highly-trained speech therapist but, as a Palestinian refugee, she was not allowed formal employment in the national health system, and so she worked in the Red Crescent hospital instead. She was in her late twenties born in Burj El-Barajneh, Lebanon's oldest refugee camp for Palestinians, established in 1948.

"I had the chance to go to Canada as they need speech therapists but I want to help my own people," she said simply. Now her skills were much needed by Syrian refugees and Palestinians alike.

Bushra described for me what it was like to be a refugee. Despite being born on Lebanese soil and never having seen her Palestinian "home", her refugee status meant her options were severely limited. She and her people were unable to live in dignity, could not travel freely, and were not permitted to make a proper living from their precious skills - even as the trained, talented, dedicated therapist that Bushra clearly was.

She was quite matter-of-fact about all of this and I marvelled at her accepting attitude and the compassionate professionalism with which she went about her duties - treating Palestinian, Syrian, Sudanese, and Iraqi refugees as well as the local Lebanese poor, without distinction. Bushra even bought apples with her own meagre income to give out to the little ones!

Her shift at an end, and readying herself to return to her own refugee home, Bushra turned to me and asked, "Do you want to see how the Syrians live here?"

***

Under Bushra's directions, my Islamic Relief driver transported us a short distance to a dilapidated old building, which I was told had formerly been a college. A United Nations flag fluttered atop its roof, for unlike the camp in Elias's field, this was an official refugee centre under the protection of the UN High Commissioner for Refugees (UNHCR).

Some eight-hundred recent arrivals were housed in the cramped classrooms. As Bushra showed me around, I saw that two or three families - often upwards of fifteen people - shared each room. Rivulets of filthy water meandered through the corridors and smoky fires glowed under the sheltered stairwells as people cooked the rations received from the UN.

In one room we met up again with the Syrian mother and her autistic son Qasim, and were introduced to the rest of their family. They all sat huddled together under a quilt as heaters were not allowed in these living rooms due to the risk of fire. A tattered bedsheet and a few pieces of cardboard were nailed to the broken windows in feeble defence against the icy wind that blew in from the street outside.

"Why hasn't the glass been replaced in the windows?" I asked in astonishment. "It's easy and cheap to do, and would make a big difference here."

I was informed that the officials in charge had decreed otherwise. "The powers-that-be say that this is only a temporary camp," Bushra reported sadly. "They say they don't want the refugees getting too comfortable, for they may never leave…"

I was appalled. In a lifetime spent at the humanitarian frontlines of the world's worst crises, I have never come across anyone who had become a refugee out of choice. Nobody willingly flees their own homes. In my experience, those who were forced out to become refugees either went back as soon as they could or toiled hard to make a better life for themselves elsewhere. Yes, they could be stuck like the Palestinians in this region, or the Darfuris in neighbouring Chad - sometimes for many, many years - due to circumstances outside their control. But nobody tarried longer than necessary in second-class limbo as a dependent refugee in a foreign land.

The limits and restrictions enforced upon Bushra as a second or third generation refugee - despite her many talents, dedication to her patients and strong desire to work - was clear proof of this.

I felt angry at the mindless bureaucrats who forced an uncomprehending autistic child to shiver in the bitter depths of winter when they could easily bring a modicum of the comfort that their humanitarian mission demanded. I was myself one of the prime architects of the global humanitarian system constructed to help the tens of millions of vulnerable survivors of the disasters and conflicts that occur across the globe. I saw now more than ever the problems rife within the international humanitarian business - for unfortunately yes, that is what it has become: valued at billions of dollars, providing employment to thousands of workers from countless organisations, and reaching millions of beneficiaries in all continents.

***

Throughout my life I have been inexplicably entwined with this leviathan system of migration, donorship, humanitarianism, health, and aid that make up this business of kindness.

My father had fled Pakistan in his youth as a refugee himself during the violent partition of India. I received a first-rate education as a small boy in India thanks to Irish missionary teachers at the excellent Christian Brothers' School in Chandigarh, North West India, where my family had settled. At sixteen I migrated to England to continue my education at a first-rate boarding school on a charitable scholarship. This enabled me to go on to study medicine at Oxford University and public health at Cambridge, with a view of giving something back to my fellow men and women.

This training had begun a career in the British government where I was able to affect policy and make real changes for the good of some of Britain's most at-risk people, starting with victims of the HIV and AIDS crisis. This point had tipped the scales and began my many, many long years as a benefactor of aid, rather than a grateful recipient.

From there, I went on to head the conflict and humanitarian affairs wing of the UK Government's Department for International Development (DFID). I had used my position aggressively to help boost the UK's global ranking to become the second largest bilateral humanitarian donor, and my work as a humanitarian advisor had taken me to the heart of some of the world's worst disasters as they unfolded, including the Rwandan genocide.

From DFID I had been seconded to the United Nations in a range of roles culminating in my appointment in 2003 as the UN Resident and Humanitarian Coordinator for Sudan. That was a leadership position which made me the head of the world's biggest humanitarian operation at that time.

The Darfur genocide would soon fell me but I survived by being parachuted into the World Health Organisation (WHO) where, as a director for emergencies, I combined my medical and humanitarian skillsets to play a central role in the biggest disaster response of the age, the Indian Ocean Tsunami.

A couple of years later I was to find myself in a new career at the International Federation of Red Cross and Red Crescent Societies (IFRC) where, as Undersecretary General by 2010, I was near the apex of the world's largest humanitarian network.

More recently I have taken on the role of teacher - as professor of global health and humanitarian affairs at the University of Manchester - where I now impart what I have learned to the brightest young minds of today who will go on to play their part in developing the world of tomorrow.

The largest... the biggest... at the head... in the centre... at the

apex.... the brightest... What did all that really mean?
***

As I drove back from Saida refugee camp to Beirut along the road that continued on to Damascus via the sodden fields of Bekaa, I had an uncomfortable self-realisation.

Yes, I had indeed made a successful career out of the misfortune and misery of others, and while there is no doubt that this global humanitarian system is doing much good in the world, there is clearly much more still to do, for it is now failing those refugees like vulnerable Qasim and his mother.

Despite the growth of the international humanitarian system and the parallel advancement of my own career, it was still the ordinary kind-hearted people - those who official statistics ignore nor record the value their invisible work - who were making a real difference to the people on the ground where it counted.

No one had thought it worthwhile to plant any flag on Elias's muddy field. The two-hundred refugees there had no formal status and relied entirely on their own wits and the random kindness of strangers - as they were not entitled to official assistance and protection as mandated by the 1951 Refugee Convention. Yet, when I had seen them yesterday, they had looked as happy and hopeful as anyone could be under the circumstances. I had felt good to be with them.

In contrast, the eight-hundred people in the old college building, including Qasim and his family, were officially recognised as refugees and were being cared for, after a fashion. But they were also subject to the random meanness of the humanitarian system, and looked miserable and hopeless. I had felt bad to be among them.
***

My visit to Lebanon had turned out to be a crash course in the paradoxes of modern humanitarianism. On one hand, I saw that the milk of human kindness was still flowing, warm and consoling - from people like Elias and Bushra. But, on the other hand, was the humanitarian instinct being frittered away, or worse still, getting stifled by the bureaucracy of modern humanitarian institutions? I could see that there was still much work to be done to overcome these problems, before these institutions can also learn to make real use of the kindness that is present in every human heart.

As I have moved through these many institutions, from one well-respected organisation to another, I have come to realise that it is not the wealthy philanthropists, nor the powerful donor governments who exemplify the altruistic instinct best, but the everyday people helping to raise themselves and others out of poverty and suffering.

In spite of the many grave situations I have witnessed over the years, like Fatima, I have always been possessed of a fundamentally optimistic nature. Encounters with people like her who exemplify the resilience of the human spirit and its ceaseless capacity for kindness has been my impetus to keep moving through my professional life. The stories that follow between these pages are a record of that journey - not just my own tale, but also those of all the remarkable individuals I have met in different guises along my way, who have inspired me to keep going.

Chapter One

Yesterday is gone. Tomorrow has not yet come. We have only today. Let us begin.
Mother Teresa

I STRAINED AGAINST THE HELICOPTER HARNESS TO TAKE in the view all around me - a sea of endless green. It was the deep, vibrant green of the Cameroonian rainforest stretching from horizon to horizon. From this high up, it looked as if a mossy blanket had been flung over the undulating mountain terrain. Mist pooled in the deep valleys and occasionally the muddy brown of a meandering river or glistening crater-lake came into view, briefly interrupting the verdant scene.

One of these crater lakes was my intended destination: Lake Nyos in the north-western region of Cameroon, an incredibly deep body of water, formed in the gullet of an extinct volcano. When news came from the local people of an unexplained disaster that was both macabre and mysterious, the government of Cameroon had reached out to Britain for help. Over one-and-a-half thousand people had been found dead from unidentified causes, and nobody knew how or why. That was how I - a junior public health specialist at Cambridge University - came to be soaring over the vastness of the jungle, hitching a ride in a tiny - and worryingly temperamental - missionary helicopter.

I had flown to Cameroon from London the day before with two other colleagues assigned to solve this enigma: Peter Baxter, a senior colleague at the university specialising in occupational health, and Sam Freeth from the British Geological Society. As an epidemiologist - someone who deals with the spread and control of diseases and health hazards - I had been asked by Peter to come along to complete the team.

I was by far the most inexperienced of the group but hoped that my training could still make a contribution. Together, we'd travelled to Bamenda, the capital of the region, but I desperately needed to get to the site of the disaster to see it at first hand.

It would have been possible to drive a four-by-four through the tight-knit brooding jungle, but that would have taken days. Time was of the essence, so when we had the good luck to come upon some Christian evangelists working in the area, with the means to transport one of our number by helicopter, I jumped at the chance.

One of these missionaries sat beside me now. A huge man, he seemed to dwarf the miniature helicopter cabin even further and, with his white hair and beard, and jungle-toughened skin, he seemed as old as God, and almost as formidable. He frowned at the terrain below us, his gaze reaching far past the plastic crucifix pinned to the helicopter's console, reading the seemingly featureless countryside like a map. I tried my best to follow his gaze. We had been flying for almost an hour now, so I guessed we must be getting close.

Sure enough we soon began a staggered descent. The missionary-cum-pilot deftly manoeuvred the helicopter down through the tree canopy towards a hilltop clearing.

"I can't turn off the engine." He shouted to me over the noisy thrum of the blades overhead.

"What?" I called back, straining closer to hear.

"I can't turn off the engine. I had to jump-start it this morning, so if I turn it off there is no guarantee I'll be able to get it running again." He explained over the noise, "I'll have to drop you off, fly back to base, and try to get it sorted. I'll come back for you this evening before sundown."

I was less than thrilled by this unexpected turn of events, but there was not much I could do about it now. He set the helicopter down lightly. It gently bumped and buffeted the mountaintop as he tried to keep it steady. I unbuckled myself from the harness at my chest, grabbed my small backpack, flung open the cabin door and half-tripped out onto the soft, peaty ground.

I looked up to see the helicopter already beginning its ascent, clawing its way into the sky.

"God Bless You!" I heard the missionary-pilot yell, as the aircraft shrunk against the African sky, leaving me utterly alone in the jungle.

***

The sound of the rotor blades receded into the distance and the quiet of the mountains settled around me. I hauled myself to my feet, brushed the mud from my light cotton trousers, and peered into the shadows. Though it was still early in the day, the forest was dark and somewhat gloomy thanks to a heavy canopy of ferns and creepers.

A couple of overgrown paths wound out of the clearing in different directions. I looked from one to the other, weighing up which seemed the most promising, when I heard a twig snap in the undergrowth. I span around. I saw immediately that I wasn't alone. Out of the leafy shadows, tall figures emerged from all sides, moving softly through the trees. I was surrounded by a group of about a dozen tall, dark strangers.

I looked from one man to the next. "Hello!" I called, in an effort to break the ice. "Am I pleased to see you!"

The welcoming committee - for that's what they turned out to be - wore long, white robes and skull caps. They were a mix of local elders and a few younger men who had been brought along to aid in translation. With their help I explained who I was and my purpose in visiting. They said they had been expecting me and would show me whatever I needed to see.

I requested to meet with some of the survivors and they escorted me to a nearby village. As I trudged along the winding paths, dampness seeping into my canvas gym shoes, I listened to their account of what had occurred.

A tall young man with ebony skin and high cheekbones, named Loïc, was a good English speaker and acted as my interpreter. While we walked, he helped me understand what the local men had seen and heard.

"One morning whole villages of people and animals were found dead," Loïc explained. "Some seemed as though they died running away from their homes in the night, others passed away peacefully in their beds without waking. Many were unblemished and perfect, but many more appeared covered with burns and blisters, although there were no fires left alight.

"Those who awoke found themselves struggling to breathe and ran from their homes. The survivors seemed to be unharmed but sometimes fell into sudden deep sleep and could not be roused. Nobody understands why or how this happened. People are afraid that whatever is causing it will strike us again."

I listened intently and nodded in a thoughtful-yet-knowing fashion. I hoped I seemed more clued in than I felt. I had hoped that arriving in the rainforest and talking to the villagers in person would clarify the situation, but so far things appeared even more mysterious than ever.

Before long the dense trees thinned out and made way for more open grassland. I was taken to a typical Cameroonian mountain settlement, consisting of several *tukuls* - huts - with clay walls and conical roofs thatched with dried grasses. The men led me into one that was acting as a hospital for some of the survivors.

"This is doctor Salomon," Loïc announced. "Most of the survivors went to the nearest hospital, but he's been treating the people who came here instead."

I shook hands with the doctor and asked him if I might be permitted to take a look at his patients. He assured me this was fine and showed me around the ward. It was very basic. Most of the beds looked as if they had been thrown together in a hurry to accommodate the influx of patients. The mismatched bedding that covered the improvised cots was all spotlessly clean, and the patients looked as comfortable as possible considering the shocking state they were in.

The men, women and children who lay about the hut looked like the survivors of a terrible biblical plague. Huge welts and skin lesions blistered their bodies. Some small children had suffered such dreadful disfigurements they looked as if they had been caught in a fire or burned with acid, their small bodies mottled brown and pink with weeping open sores.

Their eyes were swollen and inflamed, some so badly they could barely see. All around came the disquieting rasps of laboured breathing, and the hacking of chesty coughs reverberated across the sombre room.

I had trained as a medical doctor before branching into public health, so could recognise most of the symptoms. The doctor must have sensed my shock at the severity of the suffering. As we left the *tukul* to find ourselves once more in the fresh mountain air, he confided in me that these were the very worst of the casualties that had come to the village.

"Those who could be treated at home by relatives I sent back as soon as possible. These were the ones I wanted to keep close by for observation, the very worst. Many of the victims simply woke from deep comas as if they had been asleep, and some were unaffected entirely."

"Was there anything unusual about that night to give a clue of what happened?" I asked.

"Nothing out of the ordinary," Dr. Salomon told me. "That's what makes it so strange. Some of the survivors reported smelling the stench of sulphur on the air, but that's only in a few cases."

"Interesting." I said, though I had no idea what this might mean.

"Are the corpses here too? Of the people who died?"

The doctor shook his head.

"There were too many and the people were afraid of contagion."

"Can I see where they're buried?" I asked. "Or see the place in question? I'd like to see where it all happened."

"Someone can show you the way," the doctor replied.

Loïc and some of the others volunteered to take me further down the mountain towards the village of Nyos. We skirted the pale brown crater lake from which the small town took its name and made our way across muddy terrain.

Rounding a small hillock, I stopped dead in my tracks. Ahead of me the ground was littered with the bloated bodies of dead cattle. Hundreds of the ghostly white animals were lying there, legs stuck out awkwardly, necks distended, heads thrown back, their bodies flecked with mud from where they had fallen.

I approached the beast nearest to me cautiously, aiming for a closer look. There seemed to be nothing wrong with it apart from the obvious problem that it was dead. No blistered skin or weeping eyes. It lay with its legs akimbo, and its tongue lolled out of his mouth giving it a distinctly unsettling expression of death-by-surprise. The other animals were the same. They seemed to literally have dropped down dead on the spot.

Curiosity pulled me onwards through this surreal landscape, before I realised with a start I was no longer accompanied by Loïc and his friends. Turning, I saw them bunched together further up the hillside, unwilling to walk among the ghostly herd.

"We'll wait for you here," Loïc called down to me, "the village is further along, beyond the next bend in the path."

I was surprised. Perhaps these Cameroonians were more worried than they had at first seemed? But I nodded and continued along, weaving my way between the prostrate cattle, until another village of grass-roofed *tukuls* came into view.

The sight of the first human body stopped me in my tracks. Lying face down with his hands spread out as if to catch his fall, the figure seemed merely to have tripped over in the long grass, though I knew instinctively that he would never get up again.

I approached cautiously and crouched down beside him. There were none of the skin lesions that I had seen on the survivors. The arms and legs that extended from his loose white robe were smooth, warm-brown and perfect. Gingerly I took hold of his shoulder and pulled him gently onto his back.

I instantly regretted doing so. Bile rose in my throat. Two days lying face down in the wet grass had not been kind to this body, and decomposition had already set in. Reeling backwards, I lurched clumsily to my feet. More disturbing even than the putrid smell and sight of rotting human flesh was the expression on the man's face: the unmistakable wild-eyed look of fear distorting what had once been handsome, youthful features.

I gasped for breath, trying to compose myself. Focusing on steadying my racing pulse, I stared all around at the leafy countryside.

That's when I noticed the others.

The whole area was littered with bodies. Human bodies. Men, women and children lay where they'd fallen on the ground, slumped clumsily against the walls of the *tukuls* or in the doorways. Some had blistered skin; many more appeared unblemished. But everywhere I looked I saw the same expression of confusion and horror on their tortured faces.

I wanted to turn around right there and then and get the hell out of there, but I knew I had a job to do, so I continued.

All the corpses wore the same look of wide-eyed terror, that was so until I stepped into one of the *tukuls*. There I found a very different story. Inside was a picture of apparent quiet and calm. The bodies of the man, woman and three children within appeared as if asleep in their beds. They were dead, still, but they looked as if they had passed-away peacefully in the night.

Somehow, this eerie sight was even more unnerving than the expressions of those who had died in terror. I fumbled for my camera, quickly snapping off a few photographs with trembling hands, before stepping back out into the bright light of day. I had seen enough. My nerves could take no more, not to mention my stomach. Pausing only to photograph some of the other bodies, I retreated up the mountainside without looking back.

After seeing all this I felt utterly shaken and perplexed. What evil could have caused some people such blatant agony, while killing others silently - peacefully - in their sleep?

Picking my way back through the herd of dead cows, I caught sight of Loïc and his friends waiting for me. Their eyes conveyed their concern - I must have looked a lot paler than when they had last seen me. I understood now why they had not wanted to accompany me into the ghost-village.

We walked back to their homes in silence. The gravity of what I had just witnessed mingled with the local collective grief, hanging heavy in the air between us.

On our arrival, the sombre atmosphere lifted somewhat. Other villagers had been busy preparing a meal and we were invited to sit around and talk. I didn't feel like eating ever again after what I had just seen, but it would have been rude to decline their kind hospitality, so I accepted the flatbreads and small cubes of lamb. They turned out to be delicious and cooked to perfection.

Afterwards I shared out the packet of digestive biscuits I had bought with me from England, and we ate those for dessert.

As the warm food in my belly soothed my ragged nerves, a new anxiety overtook me. The sun was edging ever closer to the mountain horizon, tinging the treetops a flaming orange. Soon it would be nightfall and there was no sign of my helicopter saviour.

Just as the last rays of the sun turned the clouds from white to rich pink, I heard it; the steady thrumming of the helicopter - my ticket out of the jungle. The kind locals accompanied me back to the mountaintop clearing, as the rotor blades buffeted the tree canopy all around.

The missionary pilot had still not managed to fix his helicopter, so it was a swift scramble inside for me as he hovered as close to the ground as he dared.

I had never been so relieved to see anyone in my life. I waved goodbye to Loïc and the others as we lifted off into the peach-coloured sky. Before long Lake Nyos receded into the distance and we headed back to Bamenda.

***

Our hotel there was a handsome colonial-style building. On my return, I found Peter and Sam waiting for me on the terrace. I ordered a Beaufort lager from the well-stocked bar and joined them.

"Mukesh!" exclaimed Sam, "You look like you've had a hell of a day."

"Yes Mukesh, you're incredibly pale. Was it rough out there?" Peter asked.

"Oh, I'm fine" I assured them, not wanting to look soft. They were both older than me and I wanted to prove myself tough, and not a scared boy who almost spewed his guts out at the sight of a few corpses. "It was that helicopter ride more than anything else - pretty hair-raising stuff." I told them. I took a swig from my beer and recounted the rest of the day's events, hoping that together we could untangle this conundrum.

They had each been busy too. Peter had been inspecting the bodies of the villagers who had initially survived the disaster, but died later in Bamenda hospital.

"Autopsy showed they died of pneumonia," he told us, "perfectly healthy other than that. It's a real puzzle."

"The survivors I saw all had terrible coughs" I told them.

"That points to the most likely killer being asphyxiation, probably by some kind of gas, but is that possible?" said Peter.

"I guess it's possible," Sam answered. He had been making assessments of the area's physical terrain, from records held at Bamenda University, getting a feel for the lie of the land. "The whole area is volcanic, so there's potential for earthquakes or gas emissions - there always are with volcanos, even inactive ones like this one."

"But what could account for all the blistering we saw on the skin?" I asked.

"No idea," he said, taking a swig of his beer. "Volcanoes can throw up a whole cocktail of nasty gases though. Could that cause blistering, d'you think?"

"Depends if the gases were corrosive or not, and in what consistency. Isn't blistered skin one of the effects of mustard gas? I guess it's not impossible..." Peter pondered out loud.

"Mustard gas is a sulphide," Sam interjected excitedly, "and Mukesh said some of the survivors reported smelling sulphur in the air."

"But mustard gas is supposed to smell sweet, isn't it?" I asked, recalling a half-remembered fact from my school days.

"Maybe not mustard gas...' Sam pondered. "But maybe some kind of sulphurous gas cloud that suffocates some people and causes others to blister, that leaks from the ground in the volcanic area... from a fissure in the rock somewhere? And then what? Evaporates?"

"Sounds utterly bizarre to me!" Peter announced, "but it's the best theory we've got so far!"

***

As they continued to throw wild possibilities around I sat back in my chair, sipped my beer and considered all of this. It felt exciting to be part of a collaboration and, as I listened to their discussion, I saw the true importance of uniting skill sets and methods of thinking from across different branches of learning.

Peter and Sam were both men of science, so they came at challenges with a strictly logical, fact-based perspective. While I thought they were brilliant, and was more than a little in awe of them, my population health background meant I had to solve problems more holistically, by looking at the bigger picture. By combining our disciplines I reckoned we could understand far more than by looking at scientific facts alone.

"What's on your mind, Mukesh?" Peter inquired. "You look deep in thought."

"Nothing in the world is ever new." I told him after a second or two - somewhat cryptically I realised, so I elaborated. "I feel that this must have taken place before somehow. We are in a remote spot without much of a written tradition, so it might have gone undocumented, but it's likely that funny stuff like this has probably happened before.

Tomorrow I am going to find the oldest person I can, and ask them about it. Maybe that will shed some light on our poisonous-suffocating-volcanic-gas-idea."

***

The next morning Sam set off to the university to assess whether there had been any earthquakes or tremors in the area capable of leaking poisoned gases into the air; Peter returned to the hospital to investigate our corrosive gas theory; and I set off to find the most senior citizen to talk to.

I had grown up in India surrounded by the ancient legends of my culture, so seeking such wisdom from elders came naturally to me. My grandmother was a wonderful storyteller and would read to us the great tales of our past. While these were fantastical myths of good and evil, they also offered much practical wisdom passed down by generations, on how to lead a virtuous and fruitful life. Despite featuring powerful gods and mystical creatures, these fables were often full of hard facts, colourfully embroidered over the years.

I felt sure that this area of Cameroon must have similar folk-tales offering advice to the people on how to stay safe and to lead a good life, and maybe there was one that might feature unexplained deaths like those we had seen.

I figured the oldest person I'd met so far had to be the missionary helicopter pilot. Maybe he had been prematurely bleached and wrinkled by the sun, but I knew that his religious community had been in this area for at least one hundred years, so I figured that was as good a place as any to start.

The missionary complex consisted of a few small red brick buildings with thatched roofs, a communal dining hall, a little school and a whitewashed church. Cameroon is a predominantly Christian nation and this mission was home to both foreigners and locals alike, all of whom had dedicated their lives to serving their community.

The helicopter pilot greeted me warmly and took me to meet the oldest man in residence. He was a local from the region, with a serene and open face, dark skin, and kind eyes. He struck me as having a calm, saintly appearance, in his long robe and wispy white beard. Although he was at least eighty years old he had a spirit of youthful vitality about him. Perhaps this was down to the fresh mountain air, or maybe he had simply discovered the true meaning of happiness by dedicating his life to the selfless care of others.

He moved with a lightness of foot surprising for someone his age. He busied himself with his daily tasks as we talked, but when I questioned him about the local folklore he fixed me with ink-black eyes that seemed as deep as Lake Nyos itself.

"The old stories say that if people do not lead good lives they could go to sleep and never awaken. It was lore that while you could graze your animals in the valley by day, you must always return to the hilltop villages by night, for if you were lazy and fell asleep in the lower fields, there was a chance that evil spirits might get hold of you and you would never wake again."

This felt like a eureka moment for me. "Do you remember if there have been deaths reported like this before?"

"Certainly," he confirmed. "There have been countless incidents of such deaths. People going to sleep in the valleys and not waking up again - but never on the mountaintops. It's been occurring for hundreds of years. That's where the fairytale comes from."

I thanked the old man many, many times for his help and set off with a sense of triumph. This had been occurring for centuries, for so long that it had become embedded in the local folklore, and through engaging with the native people and their oral tradition I'd discovered a vital piece of the puzzle.

I returned to the hotel that night elated by the elderly missionary's insight, though I tried to maintain an air of professional composure in front of Peter and Sam. I ordered another lager and it turned out their day's findings were somewhat less illuminating than my own.

Peter's study of the victims of gas poisoning was inconclusive. Sam's communications within the international seismic measurement community had revealed there *was* a small tremor in the area on the night of the disaster. Yet it was no way big enough for what Sam was hoping to find; to rent a fissure in the landscape to support his volcanic gas emission idea.

Excitedly, I presented my day's findings. After a while Peter interjected, "So the hills are safe, but not the valleys - that would suggest that whatever our gas cloud is made from, it's denser than air, so it would flow downhill and form pools, suffocating people."

"Exactly!" I said, "and I bet that historically they probably didn't build their settlements in the valleys, but with population increase people forgot these old stories or dismissed them as superstitious mumbo-jumbo. They began building houses and raising animals down below in spite of the old warnings."

"That's why a catastrophe like this has never taken place before," Sam extrapolated. Previously there was only the odd lazy shepherd asleep down there. Now there are villages full of people."

"So that means whatever is creating this gas must be at the top of the mountain somewhere" Peter said. "But what's up there that could be producing it?"

We sat in silent contemplation for a while. "The lake?" I ventured.

"The lake!" Sam exclaimed. "Lake Nyos is a crater lake, which means it's incredibly deep. Hundreds of metres I'd guess. There are probably lava tunnels feeding into it, potentially leaking all kinds of strange gases from the earth's core into the lake water."

"Could those release to kill all these people?" I asked, my mind somewhat irreverently imagining malodorous farts rising in the bath.

"It's possible" Sam confirmed, "and what's more they could probably release all at once, if say, a small earth tremor shook up the water at the bottom of the lake and unleashed the pressurised gas in one massive explosion. It must be very rare."

It was the closest thing to a hypothesis we had, so we celebrated with more beers all around.

***

The next morning was Sam's turn to brave the helicopter journey across the wild terrain to take water samples from Lake Nyos. We waited with bated breath for the results. If our hunch was wrong and they came back inconclusive then it would be back to the drawing board.

The results showed a huge percentage of carbon dioxide dissolved in the water. From this we deduced that, due to the incredible depth of the lake, the gas at the bottom must have been under stupendous pressure. We hypothesised that when the tremor hit, it shook up the water causing the carbon dioxide within to erupt from the lake in huge quantities. Carbon dioxide is denser than air and so when the released gas formed a cloud it rolled down the mountainside, displacing the air and suffocating any people or animals in its path. Then the gas dissipated into the air, leaving no trace.

The skin blisters were still a mystery, but volcanoes are known to emit toxic gases, which could have mingled with the carbon dioxide and caused those burns and lesions.

Sam went straight to his adopted lab in the nearby university to build a model and test this idea. Our hypothesis checked out and by morning we had a theory we were ready to share with the Cameroonian government.

As a direct result of our findings, they began developing a system to periodically vent the gas from the lake in small quantities, as a preventative measure to avoid a disaster of this magnitude from

befalling local communities in the future.
***

I returned to Cambridge in high spirits. Lake Nyos was my first experience that my work in population health could not only be life-saving, but also exciting. Never had I thought that I might be leaping into helicopters from mountain tops, nor partnering with geologists to solve mysteries of deadly lakes.

I was glad that my skills had helped us unearth the truth. Above all, I felt inspired by the success of our multi-disciplinary collaboration. By combining our skills Peter, Sam and I had reached a conclusion that none of us could have come to alone.

I had also learned to appreciate the value of reaching out to the community and respecting their accumulated wisdom. Without the folktales of the ancient missionary we may have never worked out to look into the depths of the lake for our answers.

Chapter Two

Conquering the world on horseback is easy; it is dismounting and governing that is hard.
Genghis Khan

I WAS BORN IN A MODEST CORRUGATED METAL SHACK IN Hirakud, Odisha, a rural region of eastern India. My father, a promising young engineer, was working on the construction of an earthen dam across the mighty Mahanadi river and his work had brought our family to the area.

To mark the occasion of my birth, my father knelt in the rich dirt outside our home and pressed the earth tightly around the roots of a newly planted mango sapling. As he scooped and moulded the cool soil under his skilled touch, he said a quiet prayer to Shiva, our family God, thanking him for the birth of a healthy first-born son.

Inside the house, on a giant bed that took up most of the room, my mother rested with me in her arms. As she held me close she whispered stories in my ear determined that, despite my humble beginnings, I would be instilled with the importance of my family history and the riches of our culture.

When the Hirakud dam was complete my father travelled to Germany to study. He left my mother and I in the care of her parents in the Punjab until he returned with new qualifications and the prospect of a better life for all.

When he completed his studies our family moved to Bihar, a state in eastern India that borders Nepal. I lived there with my parents until I was seven, but Bihar was one of the poorest and most corrupt regions of India, and my mother worried for the sake of my education. Before too long I was shipped off back to my grandparents.

They had built a house on land they had acquired after Partition. They, like so many Pakistani Hindus, had been sold a plot cheaply, to compensate for the home they had been forced to abandon when fleeing the bloody exodus of 1947 - Partition - that formed the separate nations of India and Pakistan, at the end of British Rule. This plot was part of the wider resettlement project that became the brand-new city of Chandigarh.

To me Chandigarh was a futuristic playground unlike anything I had seen before. Designed from scratch by the modernist master architect Le Corbusier, it was clean, tidy, safe and smart, with long straight roads, elegant municipal buildings and wide sweeping public spaces edged with graceful landscaping.

In keeping with the avant-garde, modernist values of the new city, my school provided me with the most wonderful education. St John's High School was an all-boys English-speaking school run by Irish priests, though it was not heavily religious. True, we had a gruesome statue of Christ on the wall, suffering on the cross with blood dripping from his toes and we learned to recite *The Lord's Prayer*. But that was about the extent of the Christian doctrine to which we were subjected. We had one "moral knowledge" class per week, which taught lessons from all faiths and cultures. Other than that, it followed the Cambridge-based GCSE system - so for a religious school it was very progressive.

The teachers were a mix of Irish and Indian priests, all of whom dressed in crisply starched, high-buttoned white smocks, which must have been tortuous in the heat. While they were not strict on their religious teachings they were strident advocates of the values of hard work and diligence.

I arrived at the school, feeling somewhat awkward in my fresh uniform - an orange striped tie and blazer over my white shirt and shorts. At first I found the lessons difficult. My previous studies in Bihar hadn't helped me. However, with some extra tutoring from my favourite teacher, Reverend Brother Drew - a giant of a man who appeared to be as tall and as old as a mountain - I gradually improved until I was one of the best in the class.

I loved English. So much so that I became the school librarian where I abused my position shamelessly. While the other boys were allowed to take only one book home at a time, I thought myself above this rule, and would take many away to devour hungrily at my grandparents' house, or back home in Bihar during the school holidays. I always returned them, so I didn't see any problem with this transgression, though I'm not sure my teachers would have felt the same way had they found me out.

I adored the cool quiet library with its musty smell and aura of silent concentration. I rapidly progressed from Enid Blyton to Charles Dickens and Somerset Maugham. Through these books I pieced together a rich tapestry of what life must be like in Britain. I was well aware of India's history and our overthrow of oppressive colonial rule, yet still my young brain was seduced by visions of the green English countryside, the majesty of the royal courts and the appeal of elitism, wealth and education.

***

When I stumbled upon an advertisement in the library for a

scholarship to a private school in England, I applied without a second thought. Although the ad was already six months out of date I was not deterred - I figured there was no harm in trying, as all I could lose was the price of a stamp.

Speaking from the heart I told them everything about my life, my studies, my hopes and dreams for myself, my family and my future. I cycled to the post office, mailed the letter, and swiftly forgot all about it. Little did I suspect that it would alter the path of my life forever.

A week or so later a telegram arrived. I was petrified: it was not my birthday and telegrams were often harbingers of bad news. But the message was about the scholarship. It informed me that someone had dropped out of the scheme at the last-minute, freeing up a position. There was a place for me to go to study A-Levels at a top school in the United Kingdom.

The next few weeks passed in a blur of activity. There was no doubt in my family's mind: I had to go, and the whole community sprang into action to facilitate my departure. A passport was acquired, money was borrowed, jumpers were knitted by friends of my grandmother to keep me warm in the cold British climate, and before long I was bundled onto Pan Am flight 001 headed halfway across the world. I was sixteen years old.

I sat on the plane as it taxied across the airstrip, feeling stuffy and uncomfortable in my starchy suit, for at that time it was still customary to dress up for air travel. All around me I saw what looked to my mind to be incredibly sophisticated and glamorous people. I marvelled at my own good fortune. It had been sheer luck that had led me to the scholarship advert, pure chance that someone else had dropped out, and now here I was jetting off to a new life and the best education available in the world.

As the plane rose into the air my spirits also soared. Thoughts of the gravitas of English society with its great wealth of cultured learning filled my mind. I pictured myself attending an elite centre of education and sat up a little straighter in the plane. I was ready to meet my destiny.

***

Of course, this was also the start of a chain of events that had eventually led to my adventures around Lake Nyos, in Cameroon. From Wellington College - a private school for boys in the Berkshire countryside - I went on to Oxford University. Then to postgraduate study at Cambridge and onwards to a career in public health.

After my trip to investigate the mystery of the exploding lake, I went in and out of Cameroon several times. The tragic disaster had turned the world's attention to this remote part of West Africa, and development aid had followed.

Peter and Sam had long since returned to their pre-Nyos lives, but coming from a public health background, and now with experience of the area, I was asked to help in the rehabilitation effort. New villages needed to be built to house returning survivors. Nobody wanted to go back to the homes so steeped in tragedy, where friends and family had perished all around them. What's more, better hospitals and schools were needed and the disaster had brought this gap to the attention of the international community.

I was working closely with the British High Commissioner, Kaye Oliver. She was based in Yaoundé, Cameroon's capital and, over time, we became good friends. It was Kaye who first suggested that we should visit the enigmatic traditional leader, the Fon of Bafut.

Bafut is a small kingdom - or *fondom* - in North West Cameroon. Although taken under German control during the fierce Bafut Wars in the early twentieth century, it retained many of the qualities of an independent state including its ruling monarch, the Fon. When the end of the First World War brought Cameroon under Allied rule, the Fon established a good relationship with the British, and the ancient way of life of the area was preserved.

As I was in the country on official government business, Kaye assured me that it was only right and proper that we should pay a visit to meet the fabled ruling Fon, Abumbi II.

The Union Jack fluttered on the bonnet of Kaye's ambassadorial Rover, as it purred along the highway heading northwest out of Yaoundé. The clink of beer bottles emanated from the spacious boot with every bend in the road. Decorum states that visiting guests must bring an offering to the court of the Fon, and Kaye had heard that Abumbi II was an enthusiastic beer drinker. We'd picked up two crates of the local speciality, Beaufort lager, before piling into the Rover for the long drive, Kaye's assistant, a serious young woman in her early twenties, named Cynthia, also joining us.

The driver peered around from the front seat to speak to Kaye. "We're approaching a particularly impressive waterfall up ahead ma'am. May I suggest this might be a favourable spot to break for lunch?"

"Certainly Patrick, if you think so." Kay replied, and before long the sleek black car slowed to a halt. I clambered out of the air-conditioned interior. The heat of the midday sun reminded me of opening the oven door at home in Cambridgeshire, though there was nothing like this level of natural beauty in the Fens. I gazed around at the impressive scenery, while Cynthia helped the driver to lay out our picnic lunch on the bonnet of the car.

"Champagne?" Kaye asked, and I accepted the chilled glass. "Smoked salmon?"

I couldn't ignore the obvious parallels with British colonial rule - after all here I was eating a picnic of smoked salmon sandwiches and sipping champagne with the British High Commissioner in a country which, like my native India, had been sucked into the British Empire's maw. But I had to admit, I was enjoying myself.

As we ate and drank, with ferns and palm trees gently swaying all around, Kaye glanced at me with a mischievous glint in her eye.

"You know," she announced, "the Fon has close to one hundred wives?"

"Really?" I enquired. "How fascinating. And why is that?"

"Some say it's because the Bafut culture dictates that the Fon inherit all his father's wives on his death, but I've heard it's also custom for visitors to the court to offer up their young female companions as a benefaction to his majesty."

At these words Cynthia practically choked on her sandwich.

"Really?" I continued, pretending I hadn't noticed Cynthia's sudden discomfort "I believe I've heard something similar. Isn't it true that as Fon he has the divine right to claim any woman within the *fondom's* walls as his bride?"

"That's what I heard," Kaye confirmed. "There are rumours - all very hush-hush - of him claiming young white women for his own. Terrible for diplomatic relations of course, and a real headache for us, but local customs must be respected at the end of the day, don't you think?"

"Naturally," I replied, struggling to keep a straight face. "You can't really blame him for wanting an exotic English bride to add to his collection, when he already has so many."

"Good point. It might be favourable for us to offer up Cynthia as a sacrificial gift along with the beer. Would you like that, Cynthia?"

Cynthia gulped, looking from Kaye's face to mine. After a moment of stony seriousness, I could hold back the laugher no longer, but the jokes of leaving Cynthia behind as a wife for the Fon continued long after we were back on the road.

***

We made good time through the grasslands and reached Bafut by mid-afternoon. We were greeted with a breath-taking vista. The Fon's palace sits inside a spacious walled courtyard, dotted with smart square brick buildings and surrounded by swathes of leafy greenery. In the centre stood the *Achum*, a huge ancient structure, with a pyramidal grass roof that towered over the surrounding buildings. The tall wooden pillars that supported the thatch were carved with symbolic depictions of men and animals. In front of the *Achum*, in a wide-open quadrangle, were assembled a crowd that watched our approach with interest.

The court had been forewarned that there was a diplomatic envoy on the way and were clearly out to impress. The large royal family were all assembled, with many princes, princesses and wives of all ages. It was true that the Fon inherited all his father's wives on the old man's death: the concept was that the older queens taught the younger queens, and the young Fon himself, how to behave properly according to their culture.

Presiding over all of this, enthroned on a wooden dais in front of the *Achum*, sat the Fon himself. He wore a black robe finely embroidered with a riot of colourful patterns. On his head sat a woven headdress, with fronds of black grass protruding outward to form an elaborate halo. On his face he wore nothing but a beaming smile, expressing genuine pleasure at our arrival.

Decorum states that visitors should never be higher up than the Fon, so we approached the raised platform carefully to make our introductions. He welcomed us and thanked us for the gift of beer. I shot a sidelong glance at Cynthia who seemed relieved that there had been no mention of her making a sacrificial offering.

"Would you like a tour of my kingdom?" he asked, and we assured him that we would. So we piled into the Fon's battered 1950s open-topped Land Rover for a driving tour of the district. As we negotiated the bumpy roads and overgrown tracks, he spoke of the local history and belief systems.

"The customary role of the Fons of North West Cameroon is to provide political and religious leadership for the people" he told us. "This remains our role today. I am involved in much decision-making in this region and I am the leader of our religion of ancestor worship. I am the connection between the living people of Bafut and the souls who have passed on. We are a very spiritual people, and our ancient beliefs play an active part in our modern daily lives."

This became clear as we drove, coming upon many intricately sculpted structures, standing stones and other artefacts. The significance of these remained unclear, but the whole place seemed to be steeped in a very potent mysticism, as if wandering spirits lingered just out of sight in the shades.

***

In a way it felt like my childhood home to me. As the Fon talked about the local religion, I remembered how my own upbringing was not without its form of ancestor worship. I was raised in a strict Hindu household. Hinduism is a code for life, which I learned through scriptures, rich with stories that delineate how good Hindus should conduct themselves.

Kapil Muni or 'The Sage Kapila', my direct ancestor, features in the *Vedas*, which are the very earliest of the Hindu scriptures dating back thousands of years ago. He was a wise man who advised the mighty leaders of the time. In a slightly later book, the *Mahabharata* - one of my favourites to be read from as a child - another wise Kapila appeared. This insightful man promoted the values of *Ahimsa*, which means to live a life of kind-heartedness and non-violence.

There are many more incarnations of wise Kapila men throughout the Hindu scriptures. As a child I imagined this proud lineage of ancestors stretching back to the dawn of civilisation - the extraordinary and distinguished Kapila clan, peppering the history books with their knowledge, teachings and benevolence towards mankind. I remembered my parents telling me how I was descended from a very, very special person whose name and fate is depicted in the oldest books in India and maybe even the world.

"Not many families can trace their name back so far, my boy" my father remarked, with pride.

I remembered how, with this strong sense of familial identity, my parents and I had made the journey to the Temple City of Bhubaneswar when I was a young boy. The capital of Odisha State, this city is one of the most vibrant and sacred cultural sites in the whole of India. Here stand over six hundred temples the majority built in the intricate *Kalinga* style, their walls and domes carved with ornate details illustrating tales from the ancient Hindu scriptures.

The oldest of these, hewn into natural caves in the hillsides, reach back through the millennia. Embodied within these sacred structures is a vast archive of at least a thousand years of history, preserved in a written tradition unique to the area. The records are tended by priests and record the births, marriages and deaths of Indian families. It is here that parents would bring their infants to add their names to their ancestry.

At the family temple our priest looked up the Kapila name with immense care, retrieving one of the rolls of fine silk and paper, some so old and delicate they seemed as if they might crumble into dust at any moment. My head was shaved in a simple yet solemn ceremony and my identity inked upon the Kapila scroll - the most recent in a lineage that stretched back to the days when gods still walked the earth.

When you come from a society as old as the beginning of civilisation, as India's is, it seeps into your soul. Even as a young boy, more interested in space ships and steam trains, my life was infused by this sense of my history. I felt that it set me apart somehow. It was not that I was better than anyone else, but the fact that I came from a line of wise men - advisors to kings and gods - somehow made me more obligated than most to do some good on behalf of the rest of mankind. Or so I felt.

***

Now, witnessing the beliefs of the Fon of Bafut and his people, I was reminded of all of this. The Bafut villagers also took strength from an ancestral past. By mingling the more recent memories of lost loved ones with ancient tales of their forefathers, they wove a similarly rich history.

We arrived back at the Fon's palace to find that a magnificent feast had been prepared. Roasted chicken, buttery yams, bush meat, rice, and spicy bean dishes accompanied with free-flowing beer. Everyone around the feasting table seemed very well educated. From young to old and male to female, everyone spoke with the confidence of a person who had been given the gift of free-thinking that comes from a good education.

I was a little surprised, and at this I felt a certain sense of shame. I wasn't sure what I had been expecting. Perhaps I had imagined a remote and exotic native civilisation, savage as all the clichés the West paints Africans to be: a primitive patriarch ruling over his jungle people with fear and mysticism. I hadn't been prepared for the levels of respect between ages and genders, not to mention this fusion of ancient beliefs held by enlightened, educated people.

Over dinner the Fon spoke more. I listened attentively, hoping he would explain these feelings I was experiencing but couldn't quite put into words.

"Thank you for coming to visit. It is important for me as the spiritual leader to guide my subjects, now more than ever. The best thing for our people is to combine the modern advances from the West, so we can flourish and grow, while maintaining our links to the old customs of Bafut."

"Without someone like me to guide the people and the law-making, well-meaning western interaction could overwhelm a small society like our own. My role is even more important today than in the past because if these two elements of tradition and progress are not finely balanced, our life here is under threat. We would be in danger of becoming an outdated and politically irrelevant civilisation on one hand, and on the other, of losing our time-honoured connection to our higher knowledge and cultural wealth."

"Are you afraid for your society and people in modern times?" I asked. To which the Fon threw back his head and laughed a hearty belly-laugh.

"Afraid? No. No, no. We have withstood German invasion and French occupation and British imperialism, and we have maintained our own autonomy. The modern development we see today is one in a long line of challenges the Fons here have faced for centuries. We change and we adapt where we need to, but we hold on to our own culture and our own politics, and our history."

"Anyhow, that is enough talk," he announced loudly, with another wide grin. "Now it is time for dancing."

The courtyard was filled with the sound of what looked to me to be an enormous wooden xylophone, so long it needed four men at once to play it. They beat out a rhythmic song in the warm evening air. Dancers began to cavort all around, wearing coats of black and white feathers that bristled as they moved. Some of them had anklets hung with garlands of large flat seeds, which clattered together noisily as they stamped and shuffled. Others artfully leaped and twirled across the dusty ground on high wooden stilts. Each performer wore an ancient wooden mask hewn to resemble a different animal's head, and they were so proficient in their actions it seemed that an elephant, a lion and an exotic bird were chasing each other around and around.

I was mesmerised, both by the whirling figures and the majesty of this ancient community. It seemed to me that when people are educated and treated fairly, with respect to the different genders and the young and the old, then a vital, rich lifestyle can be fostered without the need for abandoning the ancient ways.

Visiting the Fon's court had transformed my impression of what a developed society might look like. It showed me that unbending, patriarchal, limited structures are not necessary to preserve ancient ways of life. More egalitarian systems can evolve and society can adapt. If there is respect for both the new and old, the established and the progressive, all can exist in harmony.

It was already dark by the time we said goodbye to the Fon. My belly was full from feasting and my mind felt just as replete. I had come face-to-face with my innate preconceptions about "primitive" societies, and felt enlightened by my new outlook.

As the car pulled away on the moonlit road, I sensed the soft night air reverberating with the ancestral magic of this unique place. I realised there is much to learn from people everywhere and enlightened society comes in many forms.

I felt I was outgrowing my prejudices through exposure to the wider world.

Chapter Three

Many spiritual teachers - in Buddhism, in Islam - have talked about first-hand experience of the world as an important part of the path to wisdom, to enlightenment.
bell hooks

I sat on the edge of the pristine white bed covers in my room in the Intercontinental Hotel and removed my ruined Oxford brogues. Once the sturdy leather had been a pleasant tan colour, but those days were over. Now they were caked in a layer of thick grey-green mud. I half-considered asking the hotel laundry service to see if they might clean them for me, but it would be fruitless. I knew well how that mud held like glue to everything it touched.

I shook my head - how could I have forgotten? Years previously I had spent many weeks barefoot, sloshing happily through that same thick, oozing mud as a school-leaver, on a placement with *Service Civil International*. The pungent scent seeping up from the ruined shoes brought back those memories vividly.

I stood up to survey my reflection in the hotel mirror. How very different I was now from that teenage boy. I had the same round face, same russet complexion, the same patina of mud speckles sticking to my trouser legs. Only now that face was creased with lines delineating experience and authority; the complexion paler, as of someone who spent more time in offices, conference rooms and hotel suites than under the baking sun; and those trouser legs were part of a smart - if rumpled - linen suit.

After a short time working in public health in the UK, I'd soon realised that that kind of work offered no panacea to the world's ills. Beyond such work lay the wider world of politics that, in turn, dictated the deprivation and unfairness that afflict people's lives. I had decided that that was the world I needed to be part of, which had lead me to a job as a civil servant dedicated to helping developing countries.

This was my second year as Senior Health and Population Advisor for the Overseas Development Administration (ODA). This was part of the Foreign and Commonwealth Office, the branch of government that dealt with the UK's relief and development efforts overseas.

I had flown into Bangladesh direct and had been taken straight out to see one of our projects in the field, without stopping to change my clothes and footwear to something more suitable. We'd headed to some *char* islands, where the immense Ganges Delta meets the Bay of Bengal. Mud and silt washed down the Ganges form alluvial islands at the river's mouth. These are extremely fertile and excellent for cultivating rice paddy. It can be very profitable but due to the way they are formed, the islands themselves are in a constant state of flux.

In the event of a flood or a cyclone - of which there are many in this area - the entire landscape changes. Some islands can be washed away completely in one bad storm; others meander more slowly across the delta as they are moulded and shaped by the waters. As a result of this constantly shifting landscape, there are no buildings on the islands and barely any infrastructure.

The people who call this impermanent land their home live in large, sturdy boats made of local timber. When the water rises or the rains come, whole families pack up their worldly possessions and take to the water. This unique way of life has remained unchanged for generations.

From my time spent in Cameroon, I believed that aid should be used to help those people whose need was greatest, even if they were far away and hard to reach. I had seen for myself how the villages in the remote crater lake area of North West Cameroon had been largely forgotten by the outside world, while development had focussed on more visible projects in more accessible areas.

I was determined to do things differently, which had taken me to the silty sludge of the Bangladesh delta, for who needed our help more than the *char* islanders? Due to their transient lifestyle they were often left bereft of even the most basic healthcare. The solution we'd set upon was to establish mobile clinics on boats. These DIY 'hospital-ships' could go back and forth between the different islands, offering the communities of subsistence farmers basic medical treatment, even while the landscape formed and reformed all around.

***

It was one of those medical boats that I had gone to visit that morning. I'd stepped off the small motor launch onto the squelching mud of the makeshift docking station. I breathed in deeply. It was a beautiful day in Bangladesh. The sun shone high in the clear sky and the air was humid. The sharp scent of petrol from the outboard motor mingled with that earthy smell of silt and vegetation that I remembered so well.

My guide asked one of the local men for directions and together we went squelching-off to locate the floating clinic. We found it moored next to a pair of traditional islander boats. I jumped onto the deck. A young doctor moved forward to shake my hand. She had a healthy-looking, tanned complexion and lots of frizzy brown hair pinned up in a messy bun atop her head.

"Good afternoon, Dr Kapila, I am Nancy Austin," she introduced herself. "Welcome aboard."

She showed me around. Everything was beautifully designed to fit neatly within the casing of the interior bulkheads. Not an inch of space was wasted. The boat functioned like any other land-bound health centre in the area. Local people were offered treatments for aliments like scabies and malaria; children could be vaccinated against common diseases, and more troubling health complaints could be assessed and managed before the seriously ill patients were transported to a hospital somewhere on the mainland. A myriad of family planning supplies were also available.

Everything was neat and clean and perfectly well maintained, despite the humidity and pervasiveness of the mud. Over tea - augmented by a plastic lunchbox full of glucose biscuits - Dr Austin explained to me that there were two doctors working out of the boat, but that her partner was currently on call to tend to a woman in labour on the other side of the island.

"We have two local ladies and one local man who also lend a hand. They work mainly as first aiders as they have no official qualifications, but their regional knowhow is invaluable, and they are incredibly quick to learn."

"That's great to hear" I said. "I often find just because a people aren't literate doesn't mean they are unintelligent. Indeed, for people who live in marginalised and challenging environments like this, there is often no choice - if you are not clever you do not survive. I'm sure I would have folded up and died years ago if I had to survive in a place that flooded every year."

I bit on a biscuit and went on, "From what I've seen, you're doing a commendable job here at a grass roots level. But I wonder if we can talk about the broader picture for a moment?"

"Certainly, I'd be happy to," replied Dr Austin.

"One of our biggest policy concerns is around population control. The total fertility rate for Bangladesh last year was around five. It's a lot better than twenty years ago, but still means that most women are having more than five children on average. This fast-growing population creates a large strain on the infrastructure, particularly in such a fragile country, prone to natural disasters.

"The usual method for reducing birth-rates is to educate women. As I'm sure you know there is a strong correlation showing that when female literacy rises the birth rate falls. Educated women also have generally healthier children.

"However, we have a kind of chicken and egg situation in Bangladesh at the moment. It would take a generation to make women literate. But in that time the population would have close to doubled so we could never keep up."

"I see the predicament," Dr Austin nodded in agreement.

"This is why we create clinics like this one," I went on. "We offer treatment for diseases as incentives for people to come, but when they are here we can educate them about family planning and provide anything they might need for free. This creates a good opportunity for people to learn how to control the size of their families and hopefully population rates will fall. But how has that side of it been going? Have you seen much progress?"

Dr Austin paused before answering. "It is precisely because life here is so precarious that many of the women believe that it is necessary to have a lot of children. Infant mortality rates are still quite high. For this reason, education about sexual health hasn't been easy."

She looked uncomfortable for a moment, a frown creasing her forehead. I sipped my tea, waiting to hear what was on her mind. Mosquitoes buzzed around in the heavy silence.

"I'm not sure, Dr Kapila, whether what we are doing here is entirely the right thing," she ventured.

"Go on," I said. "Please don't be intimidated. I'm happy to hear any feedback. You're the one working here every day so you're really better equipped to tell me about things. I'm here to learn from you, after all."

"Well I know that it is in the best interests of everyone to bring down the fertility rate. But this kind of coercive way of doing things doesn't sit well with me. We offer genuine medical care; malaria medicine, hookworm cures and treatment of minor injuries. Yet knowing that our real *raison d'être* is ultimately to try to introduce population control feels underhand to me. I mean I know we're acting for these people's best interests, but to try to push our agenda onto them seems very much like the *West-Knows-Best* rhetoric that strips the local people of the power to decide what's right for themselves."

It was my turn to look uncomfortable.

"The policy is not to push contraception onto anyone, merely to provide the option and the education. We aim to start a conversation about family planning. That is really the key thing, because that starts a dialogue. You have peer-to-peer education. Women talking to women and men talking to men. Then hopefully, within a little while, we have people who are in a position to choose how many children to have and when, rather than leaving that up to chance."

"I know that," Dr Austin said. "I'm not denying it's important. Many of the women who come to visit us are really much too young to be starting families at all. They are only children themselves in some cases. So I don't deny it is important. But such a duplicitous policy feels like we are getting people to come under false pretences. The whole thing seems like some kind of condescending, neo-colonialism to me."

"I see your point," I mused. "It would be better if the Bangladeshis were more open to the idea of being educated about family planning. There is a lot of cultural dishonour around this still, isn't there? Can you suggest a better way to address this, one that is less "underhand" as you put it?"

"Not really," she admitted. "I know it is necessary, and you're right it can't be addressed in a more outward way without putting off people coming at all - and god knows they need healthcare."

"True." I said, glancing at my watch. "I do appreciate your point, but at the end of the day it has to be done. I think we both know we are acting for their best interests."

She nodded thoughtfully.

"Thank you so much for taking the time to talk with me and for showing me all your excellent work. I really am very impressed."

It was incredibly inspiring to see this young doctor - who was clearly in possession of an acute, critical mind - dedicating her time to treating the ailments of the *char* islanders. It takes a special kind of humanitarian to set aside the desire for personal aggrandisement, and instead dedicate one's talents to helping a needy, forgotten population on the edge of the world.

I shook her hand in thanks.

"I really must be making my way back to Dhaka. I have a meeting with government officials. I'm sure they'll be very interested to hear your thoughts on how well the project seems to be going."

She thanked me for my visit and I trekked back across the island to where my motor launch waited.

I thought about her words the way back in the comfort of the diplomatic car that had been lent to me for the duration of my trip. I guess if I really thought about it, this kind of population "control" did feel somewhat disingenuous, but really, we were giving people choices. They didn't have to use the contraception if they didn't want to, and we were providing genuine health care and education. Or, so I believed uncritically those days.

***

Back in my hotel room, I changed into a more formal, splatter-free suit and stood once more in front of the mirror. I surveyed my reflection critically. Smarter now, standing in this fancy five-star hotel room, I could not have been further away from the hardship of the *char* islanders. How curious, I thought, that in this business of eradicating inequality on a global scale I have to first become this bizarre paradox: a Lord of Poverty, driving around in fancy cars and staying in luxury hotels in order to bring help to the most destitute.

I tried to reassure myself that all this was inevitable. After all, if it was to be anyone making such decisions, why not me? This is the system that we're working with, come what may, I told myself. I am an expert. I have read all the books and know all the theory. I know that I am a good man. I am determined to do good with a good heart and I am going to do good things with the money and power the British government have entrusted in me.

True, the perks are nice, but these people need help and that is the main issue at hand. If anyone is to be a Lord of Poverty at least I know I am not corrupt and will act in the best interest of this country's most-needy.

With that decided, I straightened my tie and hurried downstairs for my meeting. I had been invited to dine with two representatives from the Bangladeshi government, Mamun Gushami and Rafi Dewan, in the hotel restaurant. It was supposed to be an informal dinner, but I suspected that this was just a front to discuss the UK's relationship with Bangladesh.

Sure enough, after the main course of succulent chicken was over, the chat turned into a discussion on the conditionality of British aid.

"What kind of aid increases are we likely to expect for the health sector, Mukesh?" Rafi asked me. "Just give us a ballpark figure for the next six months or so, to give us an idea of what we're working with."

Outwardly I maintained my expression of polite composure, but inwardly I groaned. For one thing there was no simple answer to his question, and for another I was not entirely sure that I could trust these men. Many people within the Bangladeshi government were suspected of corruption. How did I know he wasn't plotting how much he would be able to skim off the top of any figure I mentioned?

More to the point, did he really think I was going to divulge that kind of information here in the middle of the restaurant with so many eyes and ears around us? Like many other British government officials before me, I deftly evaded his question by asking one of my own.

"I think the most important question is not about an increase of foreign aid to the health sector, Mr Dewan, but rather about how much of your country's own Gross Domestic Product it is willing to invest into health? I have said before that we must aim for a sustainable way for Bangladesh to provide its own healthcare. Eventually your government must take over funding of the infrastructure that donors like the UK have put in place. Wouldn't you agree Mr Gushami?"

"Please call me Mamun; we're all friends here, after all," replied Mamun Gushami. "I would agree that ideally yes, Bangladesh must stand on her own two feet and maintain these health systems, as well as everything else. But we are still a poor country, and a relatively new country. We have many calls on our limited assets, and while cyclones and floods continue to plague the area yearly, it is a hard struggle."

"Yes there are many strains on our meagre resources," Rafi agreed. "Health is but one area of development that our country is working towards supporting by itself, but in the meantime, how much can we expect in terms of…"

"I understand that, gentlemen," I cut in. For one thing I was tired from a long day of mud slipping. For another I was unwilling to get further into the discussion of the plight of the country, with two men who sat before me enjoying first-class cuisine and fine Côtes du Rhône. "But let me ask, what can be more important to the government in Dhaka than the health of its people? Really, your government should be spending seven or eight percent of its GDP on health and at present it spends I think only about…"

But it was my turn to get cut off.

"One would think," Mamum interrupted, in a quiet yet somewhat loaded tone, "that it would be the Bangladeshis who get to decide how much of their own country's money they spend in which areas, not the diplomat from London. But I guess the UK is still determined to meddle where it doesn't belong. The imperial temperament lives on it seems."

I snorted.

Looking back now, perhaps he did have a point. But all I knew then was my own smug certainty. I was arrogant enough to believe what was right for the poor people of Bangladesh better than these fat cat government officials. For all I knew, they might be getting fatter off the cream from all the aid money they were skimming off, hence their interest.

Later, I would learn the value of long-term partnerships between donors and recipients, where both sides could be absolutely transparent about their investment and spending. I learned that if a beneficiary was aware of the income they would receive and when, they were better able to prepare for the future rather than depending on the whims of rich nations.

But back then, our help came at a price: the complicity of poor countries to bend to the will of the rich.

"Mr Gushami, please forgive me for saying this so directly, but if Bangladesh wishes to continue to receive aid from the UK, her own government needs to begin a policy of sustainability for healthcare. That is the long and the short of it."

"Of course, of course," interjected Rafi Dewan, trying to lessen the tension. "We are so very grateful for the support, of course. Without it our people would be dying in the thousands. It's just that this conditionality puts pressure on the government to act in favour with the UK.

"Many argue, like my friend Mamun here, that those decisions should be made by elected ministers, acting on behalf of the Bangladeshi people, without influence from third party donor governments. If anything, this takes away our free will and the responsibility to make decisions that are right for our nation.

"It would be better if money was paid into the government's general coffers, rather than by cherry-picking specific projects. We are a newly independent government and we have fought bravely for our freedom. If you have faith and trust in our legitimacy as a state and confidence in our systems of accountability, then really aid should come straight to us to spend in what *we* think are the most important areas."

"I agree with you to a point" I conceded, "but not when those decisions come at the expense of the very lives of the poorest and most vulnerable people. Investment in primary healthcare must be prioritised. Now if you will both please excuse me, I have had a long day and have an early flight tomorrow. Goodnight to you both."

I left the table and tramped up the stairs to my room. Of course, they had been right in some ways. I could see it from their point of view. Meddlesome donor governments using aid as a stick to beat poorer countries, desperate for support. But what else could we do? If support was given unconditionally without guidance from people like me, what would happen? Who knows whose pockets it might end up in.

***

NO STRANGER TO KINDNESS

As I slid between the cool cotton sheets my thoughts took me again to the first trip I had made to Bangladesh in my youth.

At the tender age of nineteen, fresh out of Wellington College and about to embark on my training as a medical doctor, I had my first taste of real humanitarian work providing basic healthcare on the *char* islands of newly-independent Bangladesh.

On my journey home from England to India, I had diverted to Bangladesh to help at a refugee camp, just outside the capital Dhaka, one established to help those displaced by recent cyclones. Sweating in the humidity, sleeves rolled-up, I glanced down the line of people winding out of the medical tent. The queue of young mothers, children and babies stretched on, seemingly without end. I knew, with a sinking feeling in my gut, that today, as yesterday and all the days before that, the over-stretched medical team could not hope to get through everyone who needed us.

In spite of the long, arduous hours of waiting, mothers stood quietly, wrapped in thin saris. Though they wore the fabric pulled up over their heads for modesty, their cheekbones stood out a little too sharply from the folds, their eyes seemed too large for their faces, and as they moved, repositioning babies on hips or brushing away hungry insects, the simple bangles they wore slid from bony elbows to fleshless wrists.

The Bangladeshis had seen precious little respite since the bloody and brutal war of independence in 1971, which they had fought and won at a huge cost. They had emerged from that conflict as an independent nation victorious, yet deeply traumatised by the destruction of their homes and livelihoods. I wondered what horrors these queueing women and children had already lived through. I shivered despite the day's humidity.

That war was nearly three years ago, and many had returned to their villages to try to re-build shattered lives. Yet this was a country vulnerable not only to the ravages of man, but also the devastation brought by nature. In 1974, a particularly bad cyclone season wiped out huge swathes of crops, and the famine, which had been threatening to engulf the country ever since the war, had taken a powerful stranglehold on the vulnerable population.

Starving and with their lives in ruins, the Bangladeshis had little option but to move to camps like this one. It was crowded, stretching out around me as far as I could see. An ocean of tents, shacks, and all manner of flimsy structures, which the displaced people had constructed from anything you could imagine - corrugated sheets, newly felled saplings, mats woven from jute and palm fibre - everything lashed together under roofs of canvas and plastic to provide a little shelter for the thousands of displaced souls.

Above our heads, the sun beat down through gaps in towering white clouds. These broiled menacingly against the steely grey of the monsoon sky. Mercifully it had not rained for a few days now, and the ground had solidified somewhat into a sort of thickly crusted sludge. This made life a little easier. But on rainy days, boards, mats and palm fronds had to be laid down so people could walk between the shelters, and moving around by vehicle became practically impossible.

Today the ground was firm enough to permit aid vehicles to drive around, and when I heard the unmistakable sound of an engine above the hustle and bustle of camp life, I turned to look, hoping that it would be a shipment of medical supplies from the Red Cross base in Calcutta (now called Kolkata).

It was not. Instead, I watched in fascination as an unfamiliar, old-fashioned, khaki-green Jeep drove up, its large wheels caked in mud. Perched in the vehicle's open back was an American missionary, dressed all in white with a stiffly starched collar. He didn't get down, nor did he speak to anyone. Instead he took out a stack of paper money and began throwing bills out to the gathering crowd. Everyone rushed forwards to seize the notes, snatching cash from the air and scrabbling for it on the ground. Without a word of explanation, the Jeep drove onwards a few metres to a fresh section of the crowd and repeated the whole process, and again further on, and so on through the camp.

Though the whole event had taken only a matter of minutes, the perplexing questions raised by this missionary's behaviour lingered in my mind. Back then, unseasoned and idealistic, my head filled with high-minded ideals about the correct ways to provide aid, I reasoned that the behaviour of this man was at best unusual, at worst downright irresponsible. Though the refugees were in dire need of financial assistance, his mode of relief would only benefit those who were fit enough to grab the money. What about those too weak or slow to follow the Jeep?

But years later in my luxury Dhaka hotel room - and with some of the clarity that hindsight brings - I considered that this man was, although unorthodox and far from perfect, somewhat perceptive of the plight of the Bangladeshis. He saw what they needed most: money to get the things that would be most useful for them. With money circulating they could set up little shops themselves, giving the most enterprising something to do with their time. That was a lot better than passively receiving their daily quotas of high-protein solution mixed with boiled rice.

There is that old cliché: if you give a man a fish you can feed him for a day; but if you teach a man to fish you can feed him for a lifetime. The actions of the cash-hurling missionary suggested that we should be aiming even higher. What if we could not only ensure that a man and his family were fed, but that we could give back the choice of how and what they would feed themselves? A man may not want to be a fisherman; he might suffer from seasickness; he might not even like fish. Surely, he deserved the basic right to choose for himself how to rebuild his life after a trauma, be it famine or flood or war?

***

As I lay in my hotel room the events of the day jostled for attention with such distant memories. Were Dr Austin's challenge to our morals regarding population control well-founded? It was true that education and free access to contraception would give Bangladeshi women the right to choose for themselves how, when and if they wanted children. But were we underhand in disseminating this information? Was there a more transparent way to approach this controversial problem?

If more transparency was the ideal answer, then didn't Gushami and Dewan also have a point? They argued that Bangladesh's government should have more choice and control over how aid was spent. Was my own fear of local corruption and reluctance to relinquish control just exacerbating the problem? Didn't the beneficiaries of our support deserve to be better trusted and respected by donors like me?

In truth nobody wants to be a passive recipient of aid. Most want to be an active force for bringing about their own salvation. That's what the cash throwing missionary had understood. These poor displaced people had lost everything. They no longer had control over their lives. By giving them cash to spend as they pleased, he restored their agency. Yet those who were not strong enough were left behind. Would the poor of Bangladesh be left behind in the same way if such free-flowing cash was given to their government, possibly to spend in a similarly unsupervised way? I feared they would.

The idea of giving cash to the survivors of disasters - it was a fascinating proposition. Not providing the victims of disaster with food, or grain, or even education, but instead providing cash. Might cold, hard cash be the answer that the humanitarian world has been waiting for? In many situations I didn't doubt that it really would work.

The argument for cash-based assistance was that recipients can choose what they want to spend it on, ensuring they get what they really need, while stimulating growth in the area as markets respond to demand. It's also far easier logistically to send cash, which can be transmitted across continents almost instantly, instead of wasting precious time and resources transporting large shipments of physical commodities.

Often in crisis areas, raw materials are still readily available and goods could continue to be produced. But people just don't have the ready money with which to help themselves, as they may have lost everything they own, and often much more besides. Giving cash addresses much of this.

What's more, when people know they have money coming into the family, it allows them to plan for the future. If they know they won't be forced to sell off their assets - belongings, livestock, even land - in times of real desolation, they can begin to re-build livelihoods and communities.

As I lay in my bed at the Intercontinental, mind spinning, I was beginning to make some of these connections. I rolled over and caught my reflection in the darkened mirror: the Lord of Poverty debating the moral dilemma of how to best help the world's poor, while lying between sheets of soft, fine cotton.

I rolled back onto my other side. I couldn't ignore it anymore: there appeared to be something very rotten in the aid world. I felt certain that the way we distributed help had to change. I was not sure what the answer to this question might be, but I resolved to dedicate my life working on development and try to find the answer.

Chapter Four

The question is not how to get cured, but how to live.
Joseph Conrad

MY HEART LURCHED IN MY CHEST. I'D KNOWN IT WOULD be bad when I had taken the job. But no amount of prior warning could have prepared me for what I saw now before me in the harrowing, chaotic nightmare of Lilongwe's major hospital.

The AIDS crisis had been worsening in Africa, ever since the first whispers of the deadly disease began emanating out of the Congo in the late 1970s, but nobody could have predicted an epidemic on this scale. The health system in Malawi was archaic, still operating largely on the post-colonial system left over from British rule, and was woefully ill-suited to the plague-like horrors that now besieged it.

Hospital beds lined the corridors, spilling into the waiting rooms and out into the blinding sunlight of the dusty streets. Cadaverous patients lay beneath thin blankets, their wasted limbs forming sharp angular shapes. Stains spread across the sheets, streaks of vomit, blood and excrement, and the stench confirmed that the nurses were too overworked, understaffed and overwhelmed to tend to everyone. They rushed around, frantically doing what they could, but there were simply too many patients for the overburdened staff to care for.

A nurse told me that they had run out of beds several weeks ago, and now new patients were simply laid out on the floor. "We make them as comfortable as possible, until a bed becomes available. The turnaround of beds is pretty fast, at least. None of the poor souls stick around for long. Once they're here, there's really only one way they're leaving, and it's not walking out of the front door, I'll tell you that for nothing."

Some of the patients had family members by their sides. I saw a mother sat up in a hospital bed, cradling the head of her adult son to her chest. She looked to be healthy herself, but her eyes betrayed the tragedy of a parent who has long ago realised she would outlive her child.

He was a tall man and his feet protruded from the bottom of the blanket. I tried to imagine what he used to look like before the virus took its strangle-hold on his body. Probably a strong, young man, strutting around the city, full of the vitality, curiosity and easy smiles the Malawian people are famous for. But no smile stretched his thin lips now.

Further down the corridor lay a skeletal woman with her three children perched on the edge of her bed. With a hand that was little more than skin and bone, she reached to stroke the hair of her eldest daughter. In some areas of Africa where the disease was most aggressive, entire generations were being obliterated. There were some grandparents left, but most families were headed by the children themselves. I guessed it wouldn't be long before this young girl would be the head of her family, caring for her younger siblings in one of the homes for AIDS orphans that were springing up around the city.

These were the patients who were lucky enough to have family still around. The nurse told me that many of the AIDS victims were simply abandoned into the hospital's care.

"They come with their husband or son or daughter or father. They're dumped here on the floor. Some are crying, some are silent, some have a look on their face like it's normal, like they are just taking out the trash. There is a terrible shame associated with the sickness. Everyone is afraid. Afraid that they might catch it. Afraid that neighbours think that they have it and shun them. Many don't even come to claim the bodies. Some have no family of course, as they're all sick or dead already, but many are too afraid to even give their kin a good burial. It is so sad. Whatever will become of our people? I do not know."

I didn't know either. As I drove back to my office at the British High Commission, on the far side of the city, I thought about the nurse's words.

***

After two years working at ODA in London, I had chosen to transfer to the regional office in Malawi. I was looking forward to spending more time in the field, right in the thick of things, experiencing life in the places I was trying to help. I had been curious to move to Africa; curious and excited. This was where the needs were greatest. Here were the poorest countries that urgently required development, and now that the AIDS crisis was ripping through the continent I felt that it was here that I could do the most good.

After getting my postgraduate health qualifications, I had become something of an expert in HIV and AIDS: the shame, the heart-ache and the all-too-slowly-developing treatments. My first senior position was with a new government organisation created by the Conservative Prime Minister, Margaret Thatcher - the Health Education Authority,

Britain's national institute for health promotion.

As a specialist in community medicine I had been put in charge of the National UK AIDS Programme. The disease was just beginning to be recognised as a serious problem, yet it was still a relatively minor issue. It grew into a global scourge, with all the accompanying hysteria and stigma, primarily effecting as it did homosexuals, sex workers and drug users.

I had worked closely with the afflicted, whom many termed the "dregs of society". It had been an eye opening experience for me, but my time working within London's Thatcherite underbelly during the 1980s, was nothing compared to what I was to see in Malawi.

My position here was serving as First Secretary in the British High Commission in Lilongwe. I was supervising health support across Southern Africa. As well as Malawi, my remit included Angola, Mozambique, Botswana, Lesotho, Swaziland, South Africa, Namibia, Zambia and Zimbabwe. I was covering all health areas, not just the AIDS crisis, and had many pressing projects jostling for my attention.

When I arrived back at the High Commission after that hospital visit, I tried to focus on penning a report requiring a lot of diplomatic tact. How could I improve the working conditions in a dangerous Zambian copper mine, while diplomatically maintaining the UK's trade agreements with the government, as Zambia was one of its major mineral suppliers? Try as I might, I found I couldn't concentrate. My mind kept drifting back to that hospital visit.

I was relieved when I heard a brisk tap at the door, grateful for any distraction. My relief quickly dissipated however, for the pointed face that poked around the door was that of my prickly co-worker, Marianne Roberts.

Marianne was a very tough and experienced colleague who did not suffer fools gladly. She was an economist who had been instructed to keep a close eye on me by our department boss, Alan Coverdale. Alan, an economist himself by trade, worried that I was too passionate and too close to the people that I wanted to serve through our projects. Paradoxically, my personal commitment to the people I was here to help - indeed the very reason I had been given this job in the first place - was seen as my Achilles heel in ODA. Their means to keep me in check was to foist Marianne onto me as a no-nonsense number-cruncher.

Marianne was a bespectacled, slim, precisely spoken, rigorous professional, and possessed of a gimlet eye and a sharp pen. Nominally I was in the lead, being more senior to her in rank, but I knew who the real boss was. Incisive in her criticism, she had the unerring talent of finding the weakest spots in my every proposal. Irritatingly, she was almost always right. In my more objective moments I acknowledged this, although I found her way of viewing the business of helping people through a clinical, economic standpoint very jarring with my own, more compassionate view.

More than anything, I resented her interference in "my projects," as I liked to think of them. I wished she would leave me alone to get on with my job of lifting people out of poverty, unhindered by her pesky budget limitations.

"What can I do for you, Marianne?" I asked, with all the brightness I could muster.

"Mukesh, glad I caught you. I wondered if you'd finished that project memorandum for the sexual health initiative in Angola?" she asked with her usual frosty efficiency. "Alan wants me to look over it before you get too far along."

"Yes, I think it's here somewhere" I replied, leafing through the stacks of papers on my desk. "Let's see now, where could I have put it…"

Marianne, impatient with my messiness, came further into my office to help me locate the misplaced document. I glanced up from the chaos to see her squinting at me from behind her glasses, a look of concern on her face.

"Are you okay, Mukesh?" she asked. "You're very pale. You look worn out. Has the pressure been getting too much lately?"

I hesitated. I wasn't sure what I should say to her. I certainly didn't want her thinking I was cracking under the strain, but she had worked in our office in Lilongwe longer than I had, so maybe she could help. I decided that honesty was the best policy.

"I made a visit to the hospital earlier today," I ventured.

"Ah," she said. "That makes sense. Quite a gargantuan task trying to work out what we can do, isn't it?"

I nodded my silent assent.

"Well then," she continued, in her usual business-like tone, "you could doubtless do with a stiff drink. Come on." With that she turned on her heel and headed out of the office. In the doorway she paused. I must have looked as shocked as I felt, sitting there open-mouthed surrounded by scattered paperwork, because she sighed exasperatedly and repeated.

"Come on Mukesh. It's almost clocking off time anyway, and you look like what you need most right now is a beer and a sympathetic ear. You're clearly not going to be of any use to anyone sitting around pondering things and sulking. Don't forget your jacket. I'll drive."

Still very surprised that my steely colleague was suggesting bunking off work half an hour early to drink beer, and not knowing how to - or even if I should - refuse, I mutely followed, as Marianne marched out of the building. In the carpark she climbed into the driver's seat of a large Toyota Hilux pick-up truck.

Even more bemused by this unusual choice of vehicle I climbed into the passenger's side. Before long we were making our way towards the edge of the Lilongwe city limits. I wondered where she could be taking me. Most of the bars popular with expats were located in the foyers of ritzy hotels close to the city centre, but it turned out that Marianne didn't go in for that kind of thing.

When we reached the fringes of the city, she pulled up outside a local drinking den, locked the truck and we went inside. The bar was little more than a shabby tin hut with dim, smoky lighting, a beaten dirt floor, a few garishly coloured plastic tables and chairs, and a dance floor to one side with raucous Congolese music blaring out of loudspeakers.

We sat down at one of the tables. Marianne gestured to the barman, who she knew by name, calling for two bottles of "*green*". These were locally brewed Carlsberg and had a green label. But unlike any Carlsberg I'd ever tasted. Brewed nearby from the clear waters of Lake Malawi, the *greens* had a unique, crispy flavour.

In Marianne's bar that evening, I would be exposed to a very different type of life. Sugar daddies came to drink with their young girlfriends, students stopped in to have a beer on their way home from the local university, and in the smoky corners all sorts of business deals and illicit trading went on. This was a side of Malawi I hadn't seen before, and I was fascinated.

But after my first few swigs of *green*, and as I was busy wondering how they managed to make Carlsberg taste so different here, I caught Marianne studying me with that same worried expression she'd worn earlier in the office.

"So, you were at the hospital?" she probed. "Those poor people. Was it the first time you'd been?"

"Not the first. I've been back and forth a lot - though it doesn't get any easier. I've been talking to the doctors and nurses about what they really need, where our time and limited resources can be best spent to do the most good, but it's not easy. Observing the suffering is as harrowing as you might expect, but there's a load of bureaucracy too, and many, many egos that have to be handled diplomatically. That balancing act is something of a challenge."

"Vested interests in the city hospitals?" she asked, as if it wasn't any great surprise to her.

"Exactly. What we really need is more healthcare workers to go out and help the poorest people who are far from the city, living in remote settlements and also dying of AIDS, and unable to get any treatment."

"Too true," Marianne agreed. "For every pound you spent on the district hospital, ten times the benefit would come if you spent that pound in primary health care."

For once her fiscal statistics were backing me up, not undermining me and I joked to myself that maybe Marianne was capable of using her mathematical superpowers for good after all.

"Precisely," I confirmed, "but for doctors and the doctor-led admin systems, public healthcare is not sexy. You don't go to medical school and become an expensively trained doctor with huge income potential, and then sit under a mango tree in some fly-swept village tending to people's aches and pains."

"That's our dilemma," Marianne agreed, "because without the cooperation of the district medical officers and doing something for the elite tier of the system, there will be no progress. They'll never put their heart and soul into improving the health of the poorest people far away, without some kind of incentive for themselves first. But do you think even that will be enough to kick-start anything?"

I shrugged. "I'm not sure. We can improve the situation in hospitals - further training programmes, rewarding staff, and taking a more holistic look at improvements for the hospitals as a whole. All that will help. Yet, out in the countryside where people are poorest we're struggling to deliver health under very difficult circumstances."

I knew from long practice that to transform the health of neglected populations, it wasn't simply a question of doing your job, co-operating with officials, or running a health district. You needed motivation. You needed to go the extra mile. Bringing health to the villages had to be a burning mission, one that inspired and fired up those at the top. Motivating those disheartened people had to be our primary goal, but it wasn't going to be easy.

"There must be a better way to bring health care to those far-off people," I mused.

"Well, they already have healthcare of a sort." Marianne suggested.

"They do? Like what?" I asked, wondering if I had overlooked some charity or other bringing aid to the rural population of Malawi.

"Traditional medicine is always there in African culture."

"That's true of every culture in the world really," I ventured.

"Exactly my point. People need healing wherever they are; it's human nature. Treatment for aches and pains. Something to soothe the body, the soul and the spirit. Someone to trust in and make you feel better, even if it's mostly just belief. Malawi is no different."

"I have respect for such healers, of course,' I told her, 'but d'you really think that it's enough for the rural population? To stick to spells and salves and magic potions? They need vaccinations and malaria medication and I don't think witchy mumbo-jumbo works against those."

"You're being a bit reductive, Mukesh," Marianne chided me. "But anyway, that's not what I meant. I meant that if the first port of call for a sick Malawian deep in the bush is the local medicine man - or woman or spiritual healer or witch doctor or whatever - surely that means there is a network already in place. A network that we could piggy back onto? If we could make use of an already existing system, then we could deploy our own resources for greater returns, while still keeping the city doctors on side."

Just when I thought I was safe she would hit me with that economist's jargon again. But as much as I was loath to admit it, she'd made a very good point. In many of these places, local healers would be the first place a sick Malawian would go. I wondered about how to make a visit to understand this kind of healthcare, especially in such a large and sparsely populated country.

At that moment we were interrupted by the arrival of two of Marianne's friends. Unlike the foreign diplomatic community, Marianne chose to spend much of her free time in the company of local Malawians. These two, named Nelson and Prince, were both business students at the local university. They joined our table and we spent the rest of the evening discussing Malawian politics and current affairs over many more bottles of *green*.

But with their help we also learned of a famous medicine man based about four hours' drive from Lilongwe. We discussed a visit, and I agreed that it was only fair that Marianne accompany me. Despite being a penny-pinching pain in my neck, she had technically had the idea to go in the first place, plus she could share the driving.

***

Shortly after setting off in Marianne's truck, the following week, we came to a group of travellers resting by the roadside in the shade of a wide acacia tree. Marianne hit the brakes and we slowed to a jolting halt in front of them. They immediately got up and clustered around the truck - mothers with babies, men lugging heavy possessions, old women carrying bundles on their heads. Marianne gestured for them to climb up onto the back, where they settled themselves down as comfortably as possible on the metal floor of the truck.

Once all were aboard, Marianne resumed our journey without comment, as if this was all perfectly normal.

"Does this happen often?" I asked her when no explanation was forthcoming.

"Oh yes," she replied. "That's the whole reason I got the truck."

I had been wondering why she had chosen such an apparently unorthodox vehicle for a female expat to drive. I didn't know anyone else with a pick-up truck. She explained to me that with transport being at such a premium in these parts, she felt it was her duty to help by giving lifts to whoever was traveling the same way as she was on these lonely roads. As a woman who often travelled alone, she felt secure in her locked truck cab, while travellers could hop on and off the back at will. She was happy to drop her charges along the way, as long as it was in her direction of travel.

I was starting to see Marianne in a whole new light. Despite being prickly in the office, and overly direct at times, deep down she was a kind person with a truly warm heart. She clearly loved this country and its people - preferring to drink in local bars than spending time with the expatriates we worked with. This in itself was unusual, particularly for such a seemingly strait-laced woman, and it threw light onto my own latent prejudice.

I was beginning to develop my own theory of good donor-ship. Yet if I really believed my own rhetoric of raising people out of poverty by treating them as true equals, why was I not joining them for a beer after work? Marianne had no such qualms, and I was starting to really appreciate her for that.

***

The traditional healer was easy enough to find. He was pretty famous in this part of Malawi, and whoever we asked for directions was able to set us back on the right path.

When we arrived at his "hospital" it felt as if we were visiting an army encampment. Stretching over an area at least as big as two football pitches, the complex was fenced with sharpened wooden sticks set around the perimeter to keep out wandering animals. Inside were a number of round thatched *tukuls*. There were several large ones that were the in-patient wards and the biggest one right in the centre was for the out-patients. It was inside this largest one that we found our medicine man.

He sat atop a woven mat on the floor, surrounded by an eclectic collection of strange objects. There were wicker baskets full of roots and berries; roughly hewn wooden spoons; strings of beads; bottles of mysterious coloured liquids; small, neat piles of fresh leaves and gnarled bark; vividly painted gourds; coconuts; small whittled wooden figures; and inlaid bowls of herbs and dried grasses.

At the centre of everything was the healer, his bare chest slung with a dozen necklaces. Small pouches on leather thongs hung amongst the strings of glass beads, shells, and what looked to be a combination of both animal and human teeth. He wore a coat made from the hides of many animals and a head-dress of beads topped with a thick crown of black feathers. Around his waist and each ankle, he wore strings of hundreds of small pieces of metal. These clattered together as he stood to greet us.

"Good afternoon," he welcomed us in a warm voice that resonated powerfully. "My name is Chifundoh. It is a pleasure to have you with us. I will gladly answer any questions you have for me. We are happy to help our western friends understand more about medicine and culture in Malawi."

He held in his hand a whisk of hairs like a horse's tail, which he brushed against us as part of his formal greeting. He was not a particularly tall man, but he was possessed of a weighty presence. It was easy to see why people respected and trusted him as their doctor.

"Thank you so much for taking the time to meet us," I replied. "I know you are a busy man, and clearly have a lot of patients to care for here." I gestured around, acknowledging the impressive size of the hospital complex. "Let's waste no time." With that we sat down together to begin our interview.

"What kinds of illnesses do people commonly come to you with?" I asked

"Oh everything. They come with everything. Everything you could imagine. You will see." He said with a smile.

"And what do you use all these things for?" I enquired, looking at the bizarre assortment of items in front of us.

"Again many things," he said and continued, "this herb is good for joint pain; in old people mostly, for feet, ankles and knees. This root is used to keep someone's blood pressure low. This bark, boiled into a tea, is a remedy for worms in your stomach. It is very bitter but it kills the intestinal worms."

His attitude seemed to be very clinical and his answers were a lot more specific and scientific-sounding than I had imagined.

"What about this?" I asked, eyeing up a jar of grey powder.

"Ah that? "The healer chuckled. "That powder is good if a man is losing his erection during sex."

"Oh right!" I exclaimed, "and these things?" I asked, moving on quickly and indicating some of the ornately carved wooden figures.

"Those? They are representative of different spirits. Everything in the body is controlled by spirits. Good spirits coming into the body can make you strong and healthy but bad spirits can make you sick. If you have a bad spirit visiting inside you it can do you a lot of harm. That's why it's important to know which spirits to invite in and which to shoo away."

I nodded in understanding.

"How do you do that? How do you call down the good spirits to help you and shoo away the bad ones?"

"There are dances and chanting. Many types of ritual. I will be performing one tonight for some of those who are ill, so you will see."

He invited us to sit beside him as different people approached for healing, so we could see what treatments he offered.

The first patient was a teenage girl who had a bad burn on her forearm. Her mother explained in a panicky voice that her daughter had had an accident with their kerosene lamp and the burning oil had caused the injury. Chifundoh took a look at the angry red-raw wound. It was weeping nastily.

"When did this happen? Today?" he questioned the girl.

"Last night" she told him in a small voice.

"An ointment I can blend will help it heal," he told her reassuringly. "If you apply this morning and evening with fresh bandages, and keep it very clean then it may not even leave much of a scar."

Mother and daughter smiled, seeming a little more relieved as they watched the medicine man selecting ingredients from around him. A leaf here, a dried herb there, a jar of powder here. He skilfully crushed them together in a large pestle and mortar. Then he added a few generous drops of a golden liquid poured from the mouth of a gourd and pounded everything together into a thick, speckled paste, pale green in colour. He applied a thick layer to the girl's arm. She winced with the pain but did not pull away. He then wrapped it in a clean bandage.

"This will cool the angry burn and has antiseptic properties to prevent infection." He told us as he spooned the rest of the creamy potion into a clear glass jar and handed it to the girl's mother. "Make sure you change the dressing twice a day."

They thanked him and left. The mother seemed much calmer. He turned to me and explained. "I am descended from a long line of famous healers and many of my herbal cures come from old recipes that have been crafted over many generations. This burn salve is one such formula."

Next came a young man sweating and shivering. He said that he had been suffering from nausea and vomiting. Chifundoh examined him briefly, checking his temperature, and asked a few questions in Chichewa, the local language, before shaking his head and sending the man away.

"What was that about?" I asked him. "Why did you send him away? He is clearly sick. Isn't he?"

"He has all the symptoms of malaria," Chifundoh replied. "This can be cured very easily by western medicine, so I told him he must go to the hospital in the nearest city."

"So you can't treat everything here?" I enquired, glancing a little dubiously around me as I said so.

"Oh no, not everything. There are many things we can treat of course, but when somebody comes with malaria, TB or HIV it is not advisable for me to recommend my practices alone. Something I try might work of course, but it's far better with these diseases to use western medicine. If they come with these, I tell them that they need the white man's magic, and should go to the hospital," he said with a wink.

I was impressed by this. Clearly, Chifundoh understood the limits of his traditional methods and was not about to deny when a patient required western drugs or treatment. I felt a little abashed at the lack of faith I had felt when first coming here. Why shouldn't the two healing practices exist in harmony, rather than denying each other's importance?

Marianne smiled, and I smiled back, acknowledging that she had been right to suggest coming here. A partnership with this form of healing might very well be the way to get primary healthcare to the rural people of the region.

The next visitor was a woman who came complaining of frequent headaches and fatigue. Chifundoh examined her briefly and asked some questions. Then he took up some small items from a wooden bowl, a handful of shells, and an animal tooth of some kind. Crouching up on his heels he threw these things deftly over the wicker mat as if he was playing a game of dice. He analysed where they had fallen for a moment, before collecting half of them up and throwing them again. He asked her some more questions and came to his conclusion.

"The most likely cause is a wicked spirit. You should stay this evening for the dancing ritual. We will scare away this spirit and invite a friendly healthy spirit to come and take its place."

***

That night, as part of his repertoire of magic and healing, was the promised dance. A special ceremony had to be performed which would last all night. The patients who required supernatural intervention as part of their treatment lay or sat around on mats in the vast central *tukul*, and Marianne and I joined them on the floor. There was an air of intense expectation in the room and we were excited.

A steady pulse rang out from large drums stretched with animal hides, beaten by half a dozen men dressed in vibrant robes. The rhythms reverberated around the room, growing more and more varied and intricate in their complexity. The families of the patients joined in with clapping.

Next came a group of dancers dressed in ceremonial garments. They wore feathered head dresses like the one Chifundoh had been sporting earlier, and as they moved to the rhythmic drumming, their bare chests and flowing limbs gleamed in the firelight. They wore belts and anklets strung with dried seeds and pieces of metal that clattered as they whirled and spun through the smoky air, creating a cacophony of sound.

Finally, the medicine man himself appeared. He had changed into a more dramatic feathered crown, which perched high on his dreadlocked hair, and he had thrown off his cloak of animal skins in order to move more freely. As the dancers soared in dramatic lyrical motions he remained static. He stood with his head bowed, his body making almost imperceptible motions attuned to the crescendo of the drums. These small movements grew in intensity until he was stamping his feet aggressively on the earthen floor.

He threw his bowed head back and I saw he was whispering, chanting, speaking in tongues. He was blowing air in and out of his cheeks and his eyes rolled back in his head. The complicated rhythms rang louder and faster, and were joined by whistling and shouting from the healer as he began to jump around.

He approached many of the sick people in turn and evoked different spirits and deities to help them to heal. Many blessings were performed and he combined Christianity in the ritual too - and why not? Surely it's wise to hedge your bets by invoking the white man's god along with the ancient African ones? It could certainly do no harm.

His healing practices seemed as diverse as his curious collection, but I couldn't deny the feeling of magic and rejuvenating power that reverberated along with the music.

Chifundoh approached the woman who had complained of headaches and fatigue and blew smoke from a pipe of herbs around her. He reached out and touched her head, muttering words I could not hear. I watched her expression transform from anxiety to a look of trusting calmness under his healing hand.

After a time, fragrant smoke from the pipe mixed with the clouds of dust thrown up by the dancers meant I could barely see what was going on any longer. Tall dancing figures were silhouetted through the cloudy air, their limbs distorted by the firelight. Then Chifundoh was right next to me, stamping his feet vigorously on the ground and slashing the air with the whisk of black hairs he carried with him always.

I was alarmed by his sudden attention, but only momentarily. As I met his gaze, the atmosphere made my spine tingle and the hairs on the back of my neck stood on end. As he swished and stomped around me, fixing me with the intensity of his fiery glare, I was sure that whatever evil spirits might have been lurking inside me were long gone by now, terrified away by the fierce energy of the medicine man.

This dancing ceremony went on for the whole night. As I lay on my side watching Chifundoh paying attention to each of his patients in turn, I thought about his form of medicinal practice, and what it did for these people. I knew enough about alternative healing by then, through reading and experience, to realise that these systems could not have survived for centuries if there was not some degree of effectiveness in them. A ritualistic healer would go out of business if he didn't bring some degree of comfort to his patients.

Usually, non-serious conditions are self-limiting. You'll get over the symptoms and cure yourself eventually. So, it made sense that the most important thing for these healers to do was to provide a sense of well-being for their community. Amidst the daily misery and grind of life - the struggle for subsistence here was hard enough - maintaining your morale and psychological energy was extremely important.

When your husband was getting drunk at home, children were getting sick, and now you had AIDS and malnutrition rampant across your homeland, the local healer was a source of comfort and counselling for life's many problems - not all of which were of a physical nature.

The strength of Chifundoh was that he understood his countrymen and women. They appreciated the connection between the physical and the metaphysical. That was how these people lived, survived and made sense of the world around them and their own place within it.

I must have fallen asleep there on the mat, dreaming of healing spirits and malevolent demons, because the next thing I remember I was being shaken by Marianne as the first fingers of dawn light began to curl around the door of the *tukul*.

"Mukesh, we fell asleep," Marianne told me, looking bleary eyed herself. "We should get some proper rest before the drive home." We stumbled out to find our own sleeping quarters.

I awoke in the afternoon feeling refreshed and energised. The ceremony last night had clearly worked for me and the effects certainly felt real, even if my scientifically-trained mind told me this was little more than a psychological reaction. Marianne and I went to see Chifundoh one more time to thank him for having us and see if he had any last wisdom to impart before we went away.

"You two look well," he remarked as we approached. He was clearly taking it easy today after the rigours of the night before.

"We feel very well," I told him. "Thank you so much. Not that I felt there was anything particularly wrong with me when I arrived, but I feel great now."

"Ah well, you say that," he began, his face showing that knowing smile, "but healing is a process. In western medicine there is too much of a focus placed on the end destination rather than the healing journey. There is a significant difference between treatment and healing. Treatment is about administering a pill or potion for some condition to cure or eliminate the problem, then you are cured right? You are healthy now?"

Marianne and I nodded and shrugged, not sure what he was getting at.

"Not true!" he shouted delightedly "Healing includes treatment but it is also so much more than that. A person can be cured but they may not be healed. Likewise, you could be healed without being cured because if you come to accept your condition, come to peace with it and live with it, then you are healed of the trauma of having it. I deal with a person's wellness here - the health of their body and mind and soul. That is how I strive to provide true healing."

At hearing those words I understood something my scientific

teachers had not really realised themselves. Healing is a fine art and requires the highest levels of empathy, kindness, and dedication. Faith is such an important part of this and Chifundoh inspired the faith and trust of his patients. In a country like this with very few health resources or modern infrastructure, this faith was worth so much more than conventional medicine would have us believe.

We said our farewells, thanking Chifundoh for all he had taught us, and climbed back into Marianne's truck. Along the road, in between picking up and dropping off hitchhikers, we discussed what we had learned.

The facts were very clear: when someone fell ill, especially in rural areas, their first port of call was a medicine man or woman. These wise people knew centuries' worth of healing techniques, but more importantly they knew their communities and, in turn, were trusted by their people. Therefore, in designing any system we shouldn't focus on replacing them with medically trained doctors, nurses, or midwives, but work together with them to bring more healthcare options and resources to their repertoire. This way they would have the best tools and support available to do their work.

We decided that the way we could best help would be to modernise their education with more up to date medical knowledge. Things like oral rehydration for diarrhoea, immunisations, recognising serious conditions - like the man who came with suspected malaria – so they could be referred to the nearest hospital. AIDS education must be a high priority too, so that the traditional healers, so trusted by their communities, could advise about safer sexual practices and help to slow the epidemic.

I arrived back in Lilongwe feeling reinvigorated and eager for the tasks ahead. It would not be easy, and the road to universal healthcare in Southern Africa was sure to be long and full of pitfalls. Yet understanding the needs of the rural population better meant we were one step closer to delivering healthcare that worked across the whole region, so that nobody was excluded.

I felt changed from this encounter. I had begun to see the value of working in close partnership with local people. Not only using their knowledge to supplement our own understanding as I had done in Cameroon, but to work collaboratively from a place of mutual respect and understanding. With a deeper appreciation for the power of healing, I felt confident we could supplement and enhance the services already on offer by Chifundoh and others like him.

All humans need healing in one form or another, whether that's a salve for a burn, malaria medicine or just the comfort of being heard and understood. With AIDS spreading further and faster than ever before, knowing that the inhabitants of the rural landscape had healers like Chifundoh looking out for their communities gave me confidence that, with the right communication and partnership, we could bring health to even the hardest to reach.

Chapter Five

Now is the time to understand more, so that we may fear less.
Marie Curie

I SPENT MOST OF MY POSTING IN SOUTHERN AFRICA flying around from country to country visiting our various projects. Yet just as with the traditional healer in Malawi, many of the people who needed our help most were in inaccessible destinations that were unreachable by plane.

After all I had learned on the trip to see Chifundoh, I made the decision to do a tour of some of these more remote areas by road. I felt sure we'd learn more at a grassroots level than by meeting with stuffy diplomats and aid administrators in identical-seeming urban hotels.

My boss, Alan Coverdale, was eager for me to do this, but as usual insisted that Marianne accompany me to keep me on the straight and narrow. I feigned annoyance, but secretly I was pleased that Marianne would be joining me.

As she and I had begun to trust each other more, she had introduced me to more of her friends. Some were volunteers from the US Peace Corps, teachers and engineers, but most were local Malawians. Our conversations provided me with a unique sounding board for my ideas, talking with Malawians as friends rather than through the usual – and unavoidably unbalanced – donor-recipient relationship. This unfettered, more human way of communicating was a far better means of doing things than the unequal power structure I'd experienced in Bangladesh and elsewhere.

I had also started to appreciate Marianne's economics viewpoint. Before any project could go ahead, it had to be checked over by an economist like her, to make an estimate of the rate of return. If you planned to invest a million pounds in a health programme, you had to assess how many people would it benefit. What would those benefits be? Would it be possible to predict the wider benefits of healthier populations? For example, healthier children learned better and got better jobs and became more productive citizens, which was an economic benefit.

It was a cold and calculating approach to the business of saving lives, but I had to concede it was a sensible one.

I was starting to understand how development is a fundamentally risky business. You can plan and design as vigorously as you like and write beautifully polished Project Memoranda in elegant English, but if your multi-million-pound castle of dreams is built on shallow foundations it will collapse. That would not only waste millions but also potentially worsen the situation we were trying to improve.

For all these reasons I was happy for Marianne to join me, but there was one other reason I wanted her company. I knew how much Alan Coverdale respected her and how he liked to have her keeping an eye on me. If I could win her over and get her to believe in the importance of the projects I wanted to back, then the purse strings for my work might be loosened. By working together, we could massively expand our impact, or so I hoped.

Previously our projects in Southern Africa totalled only a few million pounds annually. I wanted to take this to hundreds of millions. My goal was to develop the biggest overseas health programme ever seen under British aid. Partly – looking back now with the benefit of hindsight – this was driven by my own vanity, though the needs were truly enormous. The projects I had inherited here were simply scratching the surface. I wanted to go much deeper.

The only way I could do that was with serious financial backing, and my biggest obstacle to that was Marianne, who still had a habit of casting disapproving glances at me from behind her severe-looking glasses. I needed her on-side. After loading Marianne's pick-up truck with a cargo of food and water – and flinging some cushions into the back of the flatbed for the comfort of our passengers – we set off on our odyssey.

The first leg of our Southern Africa road tour took us through Mozambique, whose extremely long and bloody civil war, fuelled by cold war rivalries, had only recently come to an end. Donors like us were helping re-build the country's destroyed highways and bridges. Hundreds of kilometres of road, known as the *Tete Corridor*, had been just re-opened as a short-cut leading directly through the country into Zimbabwe. It took us two days to drive this route.

All along the way we saw the budding fruits of peace. Refugees were making their way home clutching their few possessions. Our truck was kept busy picking up and dropping off these travellers. You could see people clearing mines and replanting crops into fields that had stood untilled for decades.

As the hours passed we came through a town where workmen were busy installing electricity cables. The sight reminded me of a long distant memory from my early childhood.

***

I remembered that evening so clearly. Dusk was beginning to fall over the tiny railway station in Doraha, a provincial town in Punjab,

Northern India. The air was very still and except for the sleepy chirping of insects in the undergrowth, there was not a sound to be heard.

I was about to change all that.

With my chubby jaw set in serious determination I straddled the seat of my shiny red tricycle, poised my foot on the pedal and set my sights on the unsuspecting railway porter who stood unawares at the other end of the platform. I took a deep breath and pushed the entire weight of my four-year-old body down onto the tricycle pedals. It sprang into motion, cogs and wheels squeaking loudly and I went clattering off.

Laughing with glee I came bearing down on the porter until I was almost upon him. At which point he deftly caught me under the armpits, swung me around in a wide arc and sent me hurtling off again in the opposite direction, where another porter waited ready to do the exact same thing.

Doraha was not a busy station and the trains that came thundering through from Delhi to Amritsar seldom stopped there. My grandfather knew when they were scheduled. He would don his smart, starchy uniform with the shiny polished buttons and stand out on the platform with his green flag as they came roaring through, sparks flying all around.

The green flag was taller than I was, and whenever I saw him getting it into position I felt an immense sense of pride that my grandfather controlled the mighty trains. He was the station master and as such had allocated a couple of porters to watch that I didn't go tumbling off the edges of the platform as I rushed about playing trains on my tricycle.

"Choo-Choo!" I called out as I turned around again, breathless from the exertion of pedalling, "Chucha-chucha choo-choo!"

"Babloo? Babloo! Are you still out there? Come in now it's getting dark."

I turned to see my grandmother calling my nickname. She was wearing her usual large white petticoat, standing at the threshold of our little house, which was owned by the railway. This was my grandparents' house, but my mother and I were staying here with them while my father studied abroad.

My grandmother was a spirited woman with a vivid imagination and a quick wit. Though I loved her dearly I knew better than to disobey her. Reluctantly I turned towards her and began trundling slowly back across the platform.

At that moment the sun seemed to rise in the middle of the gathering darkness. It was a very confusing experience for a small boy. I stopped pedalling and stared upwards, open mouthed, gazing at the seemingly miraculous source of light. My eyes fixed on a giant glowing orb atop a pillar close by. What was this night-time light that seemed to appear from nowhere? Was I being visited by one of our Hindu gods?

I turned to my grandmother, my face betraying my confusion and fear. She laughed kind-heartedly, clearly unafraid of whatever spectre was visiting us. My heart lightened a little - if she was laughing we could not be in any danger. Perhaps this was simply one of the benevolent ghosts from her bedtime stories.

"Babloo, don't be silly," she scolded me gently. "It's only one of the new lights installed to illuminate the station, nothing to fear. Goodness isn't it bright?"

This was the first time I had seen electric lighting. My mother and grandfather came out to join me. Then came the railway porters followed by more and more of our neighbours until half the township seemed to be out on the station staring reverently at the gently buzzing miracle.

To my delight, the newly installed lamps became a busy hub each evening. The night's darkness stretched out black and velvety quiet all around, but in the illuminated pool under each of the platform lights there was a hive of activity.

Children came to do their homework; women came to do their sewing; men of all ages gathered together for night time education classes, and moths and insects fluttered around everyone. Previously these kinds of activities would have been conducted at home in the spluttery stink of paraffin lanterns, if at all, but now thanks to the miracle of the station lights, neighbours could congregate and learn together well into the dark evenings.

I didn't know it then, but the station lights planted a seed inside my young mind. It was my first true experience of development, which would go on to become a crucial part of my life's work. When this technology had come to our remote little town, it bought with it the potential for increased self-betterment for all.

Moreover, the enthusiastic, entrepreneurial response of my neighbours taught me a valuable early lesson; that people want progress. Every person on the planet wants to lead a more fulfilled, more accomplished, more comfortable life. Old customs and cultures must be respected, as I had witnessed across Africa, but ultimately, it's a feature universal to humanity that we want to learn, grow and flourish.

***

The seemingly small development of illuminating a tiny patch of the town after dark had made a huge impact on the lives of our community and ever since development work has always felt very personal to me. Thanks to seminal experiences like that, I had always possessed a compassionate outlook towards these types of projects, and I saw similar parallels now in Mozambique.

My road trip companion however possessed a very different outlook. We shared the driving a little, though mostly Marianne insisted on taking the wheel because I had a predilection for taking my eyes off the road and waving my arms about whenever we got into heated argument. But mostly, she just didn't trust me to drive her pride and joy.

This ultimately worked to my advantage, for driving encumbered her own powers of argument. She couldn't debate as well as me when she had to keep her attention on the road. We were always quarrelling. Although we worked well together and were similarly motivated, we would disagree on everything in between. We strove to find the best way of reaching our goals and there was a lot of scope for discussion. Although I found her exasperating at times, in retrospect I was grateful for these arguments, because seeing things from both sides helped me better comprehend the issues we faced.

Driving through the majestic African grasslands with dramatic mountains rising in the distance, we discussed strategies for post-conflict peace-building. Typically, she held the attitude that economic incentives, job creation, good governance and strong rule of law would bring and consolidate peace. I was not so sure.

"In order to overcome people's sense of hurt, it's important to address their historic grievances and the reasons why they started fighting each other in the first place. If peace is to last, we need to look at the root causes of conflict, otherwise reconciliation will not be transmitted down the generations."

"But Mukesh, peace has come to Mozambique. Look around you. People are tired of fighting. Addressing past injustices will just re-open old wounds. The country is tired. The people are tired. What they need now is sound investment to rebuild their infrastructure in a post-war world."

I snorted derisively. "Brushing the conflict over with a layer of economic development will only mean that resentments will fester - and burst out like a volcano later. They might be old wounds, but surely it is better to open them up and address them *now*, rather than leaving them to putrefy indefinitely."

"It's not about that," Marianne insisted. "Economics is everything. If the Portuguese had invested in education and employment for the native people in the first place, the financial collapse would never have happened when they were forced out. If fiscal expansion had come earlier there would have been no need for civil war." (Mozambique was previously a Portuguese colony).

"Are you really suggesting that years of white oppression could have been rectified by more investment?" I countered. "The scars of colonialism cut deep. The vacuum of power and the history of violence left behind have deeply traumatised nations. No wonder there was civil war here. Nation building is not just a matter of increased GDP and elections, but the bringing together of people through the heart as much as the head."

Our arguments became more and more heated and we had not resolved anything by the time we arrived at the Zimbabwe border. At that time Zimbabwe was among Southern Africa's best organised nations and the physical contrast to Mozambique was immediate. Here were well-kept roads, towns with smart houses and lush grassland that stretched to distant horizons under vast blue skies.

Along the road were neat service stations where you could get drinks and snacks while your car was washed and fuelled. We would stop by the road side to drink a cup of tea or a bottle of Coke, always accompanied with glucose biscuits. These biscuits are, in my opinion, one of mankind's greatest and most delicious inventions. They come in little packets and they are very common in developing countries. I remember munching through scores of them greedily as a child.

There is nothing quite like a sweet crumbly biscuit served with a scalding hot cup of tea by the roadside. Little children gathered around us, wanting to have their photos taken. Some of them had never seen a white person before - Marianne, not me. We'd both stick our tongues out, to make them laugh. Sometimes this had the reverse effect of making them cry. Maybe they feared that all they had heard about the "white devils" was coming true!

Whenever we could we would stop to buy big bunches of bananas and stick them in the back of the truck for the people we picked up along the road.

And so we passed the time, bickering and arguing, picking up and dropping off hitchhikers on the long twisting road that led up into the White Hills area of Zimbabwe. Here, nestled in the dramatic, rolling landscape, was the reason for this leg of our trip - a little Quaker hospital that had been quietly working away in this under-developed corner of Africa for at least the last hundred years.

We parked the truck under the shade of some tall pine trees. I jumped down, grateful to stretch my legs after the long drive.

***

Marianne and I approached the main building, an elegant colonial-style establishment with riotous bougainvillea trailing across the red brickwork. We were greeted on the front steps by the medical superintendent missionary, Dr McAlister. An elderly man, he wore frayed trousers and an open shirt under his white smock. A stethoscope hung around his hunched shoulders and his clean-shaven face was full of vitality and graced with a kindly smile.

"Welcome! Welcome!" he said in a soft Scottish accent "So pleased that you could make it. Let me show you around."

We dutifully followed him while he told us more about himself and the hospital. He and his wife were Quakers who had come to work here forty years previously and had never left. As I listened to him nattering away good-naturedly I had no way of knowing that here, in this remote little hospital, I would encounter something that would alter my life completely.

"We're doing very exciting things here, very exciting indeed!" Dr McAlister exclaimed, "Testing some of the latest medical advances where they are really needed the most. Not in the cities where the rich people can afford to look after themselves - and thanks be to God that they can - but out here where poverty and hardship mean that life and death dance together much more intimately. It is hard of course, but all God's creatures need love and care so we do what we can for them without judgement. Only God can judge. Isn't that right?"

Marianne and I nodded away politely, as he gave us a tour of several barrack-like structures.

"These are the wards" Dr McAlister explained as we followed his shuffling, sandal-clad feet. "That's the maternity ward… critical care department… paediatrics…"

These were all doing what looked to my eyes to be excellent work.

"And this?" Dr McAlister said, pausing at the door of one of the buildings, "This is the AIDS ward."

I stepped over the threshold. Inside, I have to confess, I believe I was truly present at a miracle.

Dr McAlister introduced me to a young man who had been admitted several weeks earlier, apparently very, very sick with AIDS and with only a few more days to live. But here he was, his strength and youth returned to him. He was sitting up, able to stand and walk around. By all accounts he would soon be ready to go back to his job and to resume life with his family.

I couldn't believe my eyes.

One side of this cool and shaded ward was lined with beds full of emaciated AIDS patients, their gaunt bodies and hollow-cheeks a sight I recognised all too well from the hospital back in Malawi. Dr McAlister explained that these were the ones who had only recently been admitted. He was optimistic that these skeletal creatures would walk out within six weeks, just like the young man being discharged today.

He explained that the other side of the ward was for those whose treatment was already underway using the first generation of anti-retrovirals. These people appeared to be much recovered. They were still very thin but their waxy complexions had given way to a noticeably healthier glow. Many now had the energy to sit up in bed. A few were even well enough to smile and talk quietly with relieved-looking family members, many of whom wept quiet tears of gratitude and disbelief.

I was so overwhelmed I felt like crying myself.

I had, of course, read about these new anti-retrovirals. But this was the first time that I had realised their effect could be so extraordinary. Religious hospitals like this one were well-funded, thanks to the famous generosity of the Quaker church. That meant they had the means to try these new and expensive drugs right on the very frontier of the AIDS epidemic.

Here were people snatched from the jaws of death, literally rising like Lazarus from the grave. For the first time since my early experiences with this horrific virus, I saw that it was not necessarily a death sentence. The doctor smiled at Marianne and I, both rendered utterly speechless by what we had seen.

"Come along," he cajoled. "Looks like you both need a good meal and a little sit-down, to put it mildly!"

We followed him to a large, well-built table shaded by a sprawling grape vine. We joined him and his wife for lunch – I'm sure it was wonderful, but I can't remember tasting one mouthful, so distracted was I by what I had seen.

The McAlisters did not seem to mind. Mrs. McAlister, a tall, straight-backed lady with sunbaked skin and neatly cut grey hair, shared her husband's mission in life. She was also a doctor, a child specialist, and had been achieving equally miraculous results with antiretrovirals in the little ones who were HIV positive.

Stunned as I was, I couldn't help but feel a pang of envy for the lives of these kind Quakers and their noble vocation. I too had trained as a medical doctor, and I thought perhaps I had made the wrong decision to specialise in public health work after all. I could have come to a place like this instead. This was what could be achieved when the kindness of true humanitarianism was paired with the latest medical technology in order to make a real difference.

I pondered what it would be like to dedicate your life to faithfully working and serving in a little community such as the Drs McAlister were, not just bringing empathy, understanding and hope, but real professionalism and the latest medical advancements.

I had always admired the Quaker way of life. Passing through London on the way to meetings at the Wellcome Trust, I had often passed by Friends House, in Euston. Now here I was seeing the practical expression of their altruistic beliefs. I am not a religious man myself but I have deep respect for those whose spiritual motivations – regardless of which faith they follow – guide them to serve their fellow human beings.

For a moment I allowed myself to imagine returning here one day, to get away from the rat race and to work in this or a similar hospital. I'd often remember this in years to come, musing that maybe I might return to this beautiful oasis of peace and caring, transforming the skeletally sick into people full of hope and vitality once more. Putting smiles back on the faces of the children.

It was Marianne who jolted me back to the reality of the present – as she so often did. "We've had a wonderful time – in the truest sense of the word – but we really must be going if we're to make it to our next destination by nightfall."

I gave a small involuntary groan. I didn't want to leave this place of tranquillity and miracles but Marianne's practical thinking was immutable, as usual. I bid a reluctant goodbye to the kind doctors and their beautiful home, and climbed back into the pick-up truck.

Back on the road, both Marianne and I were unusually quiet. My mind was full of images of those rows upon rows of dying AIDS patients in the corridors of Lilongwe hospital, back in Malawi. All the while here, in this quiet enclave of the Zimbabwe hills, treatment existed that could turn those lives around. I knew exactly what we had to do, but it was going to be more ambitious and more expensive than anything I had ever attempted before.

I glanced at my colleague, her eyes glued to the dusty road ahead.

Would she agree to the massive expenditure necessary to facilitate the grand plan I had in mind? There was only one way to find out.

"Marianne," I said, my throat suddenly dry, "I think we need to design together the largest HIV and AIDS treatment programme that Southern Africa has ever seen. What the McAlisters are doing here with these antiretrovirals must be replicated in health centres and hospitals up and down the region. I don't give a damn about the costs, because sometimes Marianne, the human cost is too damn important to ignore."

I sat back in my seat, steeling myself for another round of fierce arguments, but none came.

"I completely agree," Marianne replied, in her usual crisp manner.

"You… you what?" I asked, dumfounded.

"I completely agree," she repeated. "You're not the only one who witnessed something remarkable back there, Mukesh. We must bring this kind of healing to everyone. Not to do so would be inhuman." She turned to look at me momentarily to gauge my reaction, before continuing, with half a smile. "Sometimes, Mukesh, I feel like you forget that there are more important things in the world than money."

I was amazed. Had the strength of her human compassion vanquished her inner economist?

***

We drove on. Our next destination was Zambia. As we crossed the border from Zimbabwe we treated ourselves to a break at Victoria Falls. We could hardly go past without admiring the magnificent waterfall straddling the border between the two countries. Marianne and I were exhausted from the driving and from the emotional impact of what we'd seen, so this detour was a necessary rest. We had driven thousands of kilometres and I was grateful for this time to regroup and consider my forward strategy.

I took a moment to stand right by the edge of the falls. I was spellbound by the millions of tonnes of water cascading down into the foaming river below. A thick mist of vapour rose up from the broiling water, covering the whole area in an all-enveloping mist. You had to be careful that you didn't misjudge the edge and tumble into the water yourself, as there were no barriers in those days.

In truth I felt elated, and not just by the natural wonder that stretched out before me. AIDS had always been my nemesis. The demon prowling by my side for much of my professional career. I knew there was still a long way to go, but for once it seemed as if this beast was no longer the invincible monster it had always seemed.

This was not a helpless condition. There was lots we could do, and now we could move on to a world where contracting the disease would no longer be a death sentence. I was suddenly glad that I had trained as a medical doctor, for now I could see the value of those hard years of medical learning and public health apprenticeship. Now I was in the position where I could place that experience within the wider political and social context of development. I thought back to the words of our Malawian medicine man, and was reminded again of the value of healing, both of individuals and communities.

Then and there I vowed to renew my purpose: no matter what I did I would bring hope to people with HIV and AIDS. I would strive to bring healing to communities torn apart by the virus. And I would bring hope to those who suffered from other seemingly fatal conditions. I was filled with optimism, for if you could turn HIV from certain death into a chronic but liveable condition - what could we not do with the other scourges of humanity?

***

Zambia is a vast country, and we drove the entire length of it to visit our many projects. The final leg of our journey took us through Luangwa National Park, which was a long day's hard driving. The landscape was stunning, but very different from Zimbabwe's rippling hills. This looked like the Africa I had imagined from watching nature programmes back at boarding school in England. The kind of landscape where golden dry grasslands unrolled across endless plains. I couldn't help but imagine that each patch of tall grass or scrubby bush concealed a pride of lions and every acacia tree was the lookout spot for a hungry leopard.

As we sped across this scrubby brush-land we noticed there were fewer and fewer people and we had long ago run out of hitchhikers to collect. Before long, we realised we hadn't passed another living soul for miles: there was just nobody there.

As the sun set and the day ended so too did the tarmac road. We found ourselves negotiating deep pot holes on an ever-worsening dirt track. The night fell incredibly fast, and shortly we were making our way along in pitch blackness, with only the truck's headlights to pick the way ahead. The occasional tree, looming out of the darkness, became the only distinguishing features, and with no sign of human habitation anywhere I began to feel nervous.

This was a time before portable GPS systems and there was no mobile phone coverage. We had no satellite phones either. Then, to our horror, the road abruptly ended and there were many paths in front of us. We took the one that seemed the most well-travelled, though there wasn't much in it really, and continued to drive in a tense, stony silence.

It wasn't until we passed by a big baobab tree – which looked *identical* to one we had seen before - that we realised we were well and truly lost.

The African night drew in thicker around us as we debated what we should do.

To keep on driving was pointless, for we would only go around in circles and run out of fuel. Having not seen anyone on the road for hours, we weren't sure of the likelihood of coming across help. Reluctantly, we decided there was no other option but to sit tight and wait until morning.

Marianne and I sat in the truck eating our stock of glucose biscuits, finding little to say to each other anymore. The chorus of roosting birds provided a noisy backdrop to our mounting anxiety. We settled down as best we could on the straight-backed seats of the pickup. The noises emanating from the bush seemed ever more ominous, and we kept our ears pricked, our brains alert. Sleep was impossible. To make matters worse it was getting colder.

I don't know who was more frightened, Marianne or I. Inside I was petrified but I gave little outward sign of it. Marianne would only use it against me back at the office, I decided. We kept trying to impress each other with our laissez-faire attitude, competing as to who could seem the most calm and collected.

Still, I was worried. It would do no good at all if, when I had finally got this tight-fisted economist to agree to spending an unprecedented amount of government money to eradicate AIDS in Southern Africa, we were both trampled to death by a herd of rampaging elephants.

"Why didn't you pack any spare fuel?" I ventured.

"Why didn't *you* think to get some?" Marianne countered, and we lapsed into silence once more.

From time to time one of us would venture out in the night, to answer nature's call. I don't think I have ever moved so fast when having a pee. Apart from the chorus of strange noises - I guessed the grunting of wild pigs or the growling of a wild cat - the air was thick with biting insects attracted by the light from the truck cab.

We shut off the lights and I gazed out at the night sky. The Milky Way was stunningly beautiful; the light from millions of stars burning a ribbon-like swathe across the heavens. As I watched a particularly dazzling shooting star carve a fiery trail across the Earth's atmosphere,

I made a silent wish that we would get home safely, and nobody would be bitten by a tsetse fly or eaten by a lion.

It must have been around midnight - we had long run out of biscuits to eat and arguments to have - and were finally beginning to doze off, when we saw a flickering light in the distance. The terrain was incredibly flat so it was difficult to judge how far away it was, but we estimated it was probably several kilometres ahead across the level ground.

Our spirits soared. We turned on the headlights, flashed them up and down and hooted madly, trumpeting our presence out across the shadowy landscape. The light was moving quite fast, but we realised we couldn't go chasing after it because who knew where we would end up? Probably upside down in a ditch or mired in a patch of treacherous wetland.

Our hearts sank as the light kept true to its path, heading resolutely past us. We stopped honking, as it appeared to grow smaller and smaller. We pictured our potential saviour, totally unaware of our plight, disappearing into the distance.

Then somehow the light started to grow larger once again. We realised that it was turning back, our way. We resumed honking and flashing with renewed enthusiasm. The headlights grew larger and larger. The mystery vehicle *was* coming our way.

Ten minutes later a Zambian ranger's vehicle pulled up next to us. Our rescuer, who introduced himself as Cedrick, had been on his way home from a nearby ranger station, when he'd seen our flashing headlights and interpreted it as a make-shift distress signal. I had never felt so grateful to see anyone, since I was plucked off that hilltop in Cameroon by the white-haired missionary all those years earlier.

Far better prepared than we were, he always carried spare fuel with him. We filled up the tank and followed Cedrick's vehicle through the bush and rough terrain. How he found his way through that dark featureless landscape remains a mystery to me, but thanks to him we finally arrived at our intended destination - a tourist lodge in the centre of the game park.

Overjoyed, we chose to celebrate our escape with the local Zambian beer, *Mosi*. We offered one to our rescuer - it was the least we could do after he had saved us from a long and uncomfortable night at best, and at worst death in the jaws of a wild beast - but he declined in order to resume his drive home.

I realised we had added a good two-hours to his journey. I wondered if his family would be missing him. Did he have to undertake the same drive back through the reserve tomorrow morning? I considered whether I would have made the detour to investigate our flashing and honking if I had been in his position, or simply looked the other way, pretended I hadn't noticed and returned home to the comfort of my family.

Marianne and I toasted Cedrick's selflessness with several *Mosi* beers, grateful as always for the kindness of strangers. All our arguing and disgruntlement was forgotten and we drank to our salvation. *Mosi* beer takes its name from the local word for Victoria Falls, and nothing had ever tasted so good.

The following morning we refuelled the car and took the precaution of buying an extra can of petrol, before hitting the road once more. In daylight the terrain looked very different. The sinister landscape appeared calm and pleasant - we couldn't believe how we'd lost our way, for there was a distinctly marked track - but we had clearly got disorientated.

It took one more day's driving to return to Malawi. Then it was straight into the hard graft of transforming the miracle that we'd seen in the Quaker hospital into a tangible, effective programme to battle HIV and AIDS across the whole of our jurisdiction.

Marianne kept her promise, supporting the exponential growth of expenditure on our AIDS project, though we still argued about almost everything else. I had set out on this trip with the objective of winning her over. I had wanted to get her on board with my ambitions, yet I had underestimated her. Marianne was possessed of true depths of human compassion, and though our methods could not have been more different, she had required no persuading when presented with the way to combat the AIDS crisis.

Together we worked to make that a reality.

Chapter Six

The more you know, the more you know you don't know.
Aristotle

AIDS TREATMENT AND PREVENTION WAS MY MAIN FOCUS in Southern Africa but I was still at the beck and call of the British government who could send me anywhere in the world on ODA work. One night as I had just tucked my three young daughters into bed and was reading them a story, the phone rang. It was a call from London requesting that I head to Erzincan as urgently as possible. There had been a devastating earthquake in this remote region of Turkey, and I was needed on the ground immediately. The ending of the girls' story - the happily ever after - would have to wait.

I bundled together a few things and left for Ankara, the Turkish capital, on the next available flight. As the plane sped onwards, I pondered what lay ahead. The powers-that-be in London had grown wary of writing blank cheques for disaster-affected countries. They wanted to get an idea of the real needs of the people on the ground and how they could provide the type of help that would be most useful. That's why they were sending me in, to get an accurate picture of the extent of the damage and advise on what British money could do.

There was no such bod as a humanitarian advisor at that time. This was a brand-new idea. I was flying blind, directly into the maelstrom of the emergency, to assess the situation on the ground.

This was an unusual assignment and I felt intuitively that I was somehow being tested. I sensed that if I was successful - if I could handle the pressure of making life-saving decisions in the midst of an unfolding disaster - then my bosses at ODA had some kind of plan in store for me.

When my flight touched down in Ankara I headed straight to the British Embassy, a huge, grand building where ambassadors from the UK had connected with Turkey since the days of the Ottoman Empire. There I met the Ambassador for a briefing, utilising what scarce information he had to hand.

By all accounts it was a major earthquake, measuring 6.7 on the Richter scale. Many people had been killed and hundreds more displaced when the town of Erzincan was torn apart by a shift along the highly active North Anatolian fault line.

I was introduced to Murat, a local staff member from the Embassy, who would be accompanying me as my Turkish-speaking counterpart. He was a slightly-built man, attentive and alert, and I warmed to him immediately.

The ambassador secured us places on a Turkish Air Force flight heading into the region. Soon we were strapped into a Hercules transport aircraft hurtling across six-hundred kilometres of mountainous terrain. As row upon row of rugged mountain ranges passed beneath us, interrupted very, very occasionally by a string-thin winding road, I began to get a true sense of the problems here. This rugged countryside would take days for aid convoys to traverse, and far longer if any of the roads had been rendered impassable by earthquake damage. If the situation in Erzincan was as bad as we feared, getting supplies in was going to be one hell of a challenge.

No sooner had the Hercules set Murat and I down amid the brooding Turkish mountains, than it was airborne again, powering through the heavens towards its next destination.

The small military airstrip upon which we had been deposited remained mercifully undamaged by the quake, but it possessed no artificial lighting and was dangerous for even the most skilled pilot to attempt take-off or landing. No wonder the Hercules pilot had taken to the skies again so quickly.

I shivered in the darkening air. Turning my face upwards, I saw three other aircraft circling the tiny runway. No doubt these were the first of the aid agencies bringing supplies to the area, but they had no easy way of landing now without guiding lights on the ground.

There we stood, Murat and I, totally alone, dumped in forbidding mountain country, night falling all around us. We had no defined strategy for what to do next. This was the first time a representative from the British government had been deployed to assess needs in the very heart of an unfolding disaster. We had no methodology in place and no previous experience to base our actions on. All we had between us - apart from a small bag each of clothes - was a suitcase full of government money. We were really winging it.

Despite the landing-strip's apparent isolation, we knew that the town of Erzincan lay a few miles away in the rugged country below. We threw on a few more layers as it was bitterly cold and began picking our way carefully through the terrain. We struck lucky: no sooner had we found a road than we saw the gleam of headlights coming our way. We hailed the car, a little green and white Fiat, which mercifully trundled to a halt in front of us.

Murat began a friendly exchange with the driver. Chatting away in Turkish, he convinced the man to let us hire his car and himself for the next few days. We would pay him in cash. Because the city below was in a state of catastrophic chaos, with most houses destroyed and those still standing rendered uninhabitable due to the danger of aftershocks, we would all need to sleep in his car too. The driver agreed to everything, thanks to Murat's persuasive character and the power of dollars.

Deal cut, we bundled into the little car for the journey to the ruined city. I knew we were getting close, not from the usual bright lights you'd expect to see when approaching a city with a population over 90,000, but from the sounds that carried through the night air. As our driver cautiously manoeuvred the Fiat through the ruined streets, using the few landmarks still standing to guide his way, the eerie sounds of wailing and crying reached our ears.

It was dark and cold, but for the occasional pinprick of light from hurricane lamps or torches swinging to and fro, as people searched for their loved one. To make matters worse, a light but freezing rain had begun to fall. Deciding that it was pointless to explore further in the night, we found a quiet corner to park and tried to snatch a few hours' sleep.

Dawn broke to reveal a sea of destruction that the sights and sounds of the previous night had only really hinted at. Where streets had stood were now only precarious piles of rubble that threatened to crash down on top of those who scrabbled frantically, searching for missing family members. Here and there bobbed the red helmets of the first search and rescue teams, as they plumbed the debris to locate those still buried - dead or alive.

Everyone was out in the streets because even those structures that seemed stable were vulnerable to the aftershocks that reverberated through the earth at our feet.

Families separated in the quake searched for their missing loved ones. Lone children wandered about, dazed and dusty. Traumatised people scrambled around, salvaging whatever that they could from what used to be their homes. Men and women clawed at the rubble with their bare hands, despite the danger this posed to themselves and those potentially still alive below.

The first thing I wanted to see was the hospital. Our driver could identify the rough location thanks to its proximity to a mosque, whose minaret somehow still stood tall above the surrounding carnage. Of the hospital however, nothing but rubble remained. From a conversation with locals, Murat deduced that the quake had struck during hospital visiting hours. Scores of doctors, nurses, patients and their attending families had been crushed, as the huge building crumbled and fell around them.

It was catastrophe piled upon catastrophe. Rescue teams with dogs climbed over the piles of debris which had once been a fully-functioning hospital. Occasionally, people would be pulled from the wreckage miraculously unscathed. Dusty and coughing, they were somehow still alive, but mostly it was limp and lifeless corpses that were extracted.

From there, our driver took us to the civil administration centre, an old building that had survived the quake, although thick cracks had appeared in its walls. I quickly learned to tell the difference between vertical cracks, which usually meant the building was structurally sound, and cracks that ran horizontally, which meant the building was unsafe, due to the way the quake had shaken it.

Inside the civil administration centre I found local officials working away at their desks. Murat and I spoke to them and learned that many had been doing just this when the earthquake hit. When the shaking had subsided and the dust began to settle, they had returned to their desks and switched to organising the search and rescue mission and coordinating relief.

Many of them didn't even know whether their own homes had been destroyed or the fate of their own families, but they kept stoically working away to bring what help they could. I was touched by their bravery: many must have lost close family members. Perhaps it was better for them to put off the reality of discovering who of their loved ones had perished, by keeping busy.

The situation was dire. The city was largely cut off by road, as the earthquake had damaged what access existed through the steep terrain. Many streets ended in huge chasms, and our driver had to be careful that we didn't plummet into one as we made our way back out of town to the airstrip. We'd decided to formulate our final assessment of the situation there.

As the little Fiat slowed to a halt beside the runway, we realised how busy it had become here. The only way to bring in relief supplies was by air, so the sky above was thick with planes. Some were trying to bring in valuable search and rescue teams, complete with search dogs and fibreoptic equipment. They were desperately needed on the ground. But to my dismay I realised that most of these planes were unable to land. The airstrip and surrounding area was already clogged with aircraft unloading supplies.

When news had come of the terrible disaster, the humanitarian agencies had been quick to respond. Countries and organisations across the globe had sent what relief items they could. However, without the proper organisation, much of this well-intentioned support was doing little good. Nobody was prioritising what was needed most urgently. Everywhere was turmoil and confusion.

Some harassed looking men and women from the local Red Crescent society were attempting to bring some order. They were yelling and shouting in an attempt to clear some of the huge crates of donated food, clothes, and other non-priority items, so that further planes had space to land.

As the minutes ticked by and vital time was wasted, it became clear to me that the good-natured impulse to help was actually endangering the lives of the victims still further. Every passing minute that the search and rescue specialists were kept in the air, it became less and less likely that those still trapped beneath the rubble would be discovered alive.

Clearly, we needed some kind of dedicated first response disaster coordination to make sure that the right assistance would come in at the right time.

***

A local football field had become an informal camp for displaced people. It was out in the open and so safe from the threat posed by collapsing buildings. The grass had been churned into mud by the influx of people who huddled together, trying to find whatever shelter they could. Some were openly weeping, others stared ahead blankly in an obvious state of trauma. It was still bitterly cold, flurries of snow clung to the hedgerows surrounding the field, but now aid agencies had started to arrive and set up camp.

I saw the logos of many organisations fluttering above the tents. Scanning the field I found the iconic white flag with a red half-moon emblazoned upon it - the symbol for *Türk Kızılayı*, the Turkish Red Crescent Society. I honed in on it as a beacon of dependability amidst the mayhem.

I introduced myself to those inside and asked to borrow their phone to call London. The local phone tower had collapsed so I had no other way to reach the UK. I vowed to travel with my own dedicated satellite phone after that. It seems so obvious now but we had no template for how to go about this kind of fieldwork and were learning on the job.

I called London, ready to deliver a rapid assessment of how the British government could provide the best help possible.

"Hello Mukesh, good to hear from you," came the distant voice at the end of the line. "What do you need there? Search and rescue experts? We have our best and brightest briefed and ready to fly out on your word."

"No need," I replied. "Search and rescue is already well underway, the sky is full of trained professionals trying to land from Switzerland, Austria and Italy. They have the best experience in mountainous areas; no point for us to send any more.

"What these people really require now is shelter. It's bitterly cold and raining. So send tents. They're also in dire need of medical supplies. Many have broken bones from the earthquake. All the infrastructure has been destroyed, as well as clean water and sanitation, so we should send medical packs to help people who get sick. Those are the things we need urgently. Later we'll consider what is necessary for rehabilitation, but that can wait right now. One more thing: coordinate with Turkish air traffic control for a landing slot before flying out."

"Understood Mukesh. Over and out."

***

Now that London was briefed, I took another look at the flags of organisations that flapped damply above the field of tents. In one corner, I spotted a world map and olive wreaths on blue - instantly recognisable as the emblem of the United Nations. I weaved my way through the guy-ropes and tent pegs towards it. I was met not by the hub of order and organisation I had expected, but by one solitary representative looking dirty, brow-beaten and exhausted. I recognised him as Ula Almgren, a lanky Scandinavian who I knew from his work for UNDRO - the UN's disaster relief organisation based out of Geneva.

He stood alone with nowhere even to sit down. All he had apart from his tent was a flip-chart and a few maps.

"Ula!" I called. "You look rather lonely over here, what's going on?"

"Hello Mukesh," he replied. "UNDRO sent me in blind as first response just so we'd have someone on the ground. Not that it's made much difference. I'm here alright but what can I do? I've got no communications, no information collection system, no transport, and no idea when to expect reinforcements. They might be trying to land now, but can't touch down thanks to everyone trying to bring in every kind of irrelevant aid item at the same time."

"Is this level of disorganisation usual in this kind of emergency?" I asked. "This is really my first time on the ground in a disaster zone - unless you count shimmying up palm trees to escape Bangladeshi cyclones as a volunteer when I was eighteen - so it's really all new for me."

"It's a big problem yes," Ula sighed. His work in the UN meant he was well-seasoned in this area. "Particularly in a location like this. An urban landscape by all accounts, with all the problems that come with that - broken gas mains, heavily populated sectors, lots of buildings collapsing close together - but it's also remote and hard to reach, which means bringing in assistance is difficult. Have you been up to the airstrip?"

"I have," I told him. "I have to admit I was shocked by the total lack of organisation."

"It's not improved then?" Ula asked me. I shook my head.

"There has to be a better way," he volunteered.

"There does," I confirmed. "And we need to make it happen. It's too heart-breaking to see the suffering of these people, all the while knowing that help is so close yet out of reach."

There and then Ula and I decided that, once the Erzincan response was over, we had to set up a much better system for the coordination of international disaster assistance. It was heartening to see how the peoples of the world had responded, but the spontaneous help given by countries had to be more efficiently channelled and directed, rather than adding to the madness.

I was reminded of my time in Bangladesh when I had come across a bizarre cache of ski jackets. The country has a tropical climate characterised by high humidity. Yet for some reason - probably its relative closeness to the Himalayas - the refugees there had received a relief delivery containing nothing but ski jackets. The inappropriateness of this aid perplexed me, until I came to realise that the random impulses of kindness - to help those effected by disaster - are all well and good, but they needed proper organisation in order to be useful.

Over the next few days we tried to help to bring order and calm to the Erzincan disaster. We began by identifying the most vulnerable people, like the lost and traumatised children wandering the rubble, and ensured they received care. In the chaos of an emergency like this, it's often easy to overlook those who are in the most danger.

We organised a rota system for the exhausted locals working for the relief effort. The civil administrators, many of whom still hadn't been home, couldn't work effectively after days and nights without rest.

Though I was inspired and humbled by their dedication, I saw that despite their stoicism, they needed space to grieve. They didn't know if their own relatives had survived or not, yet as time went on the chances of finding them alive were slipping away. As hope bled away, we had to make space for people to come together to mourn, both personally and with what was left of their communities.

As I strove to be useful on the ground, all the while I was thinking of systems we could implement that could ensure this kind of work was done faster and more effectively in future.

After about a week in Erzincan, my briefcase was empty of its dollars. I had given them out to the local governor's fund which was being used to buy food - Turkish bread and drinking water - for the camp at the football field. It was time to return to London to feedback to my bosses all that had happened and how I thought the system could be improved.

Back in the ODA's London headquarters, I sensed again that I was being assessed somehow. It seemed like Erzincan had been a test, and now they were trying to get the measure of me and my response to the crisis.

I had a feeling that my bosses at ODA felt the same way that Ula and I did; that the way we delivered disaster relief needed a major overhaul. I had a subconscious inkling that I would be asked to get involved more in humanitarian work in this capacity as the first person on the ground, making priority assessments for the most pressing needs.

Little did I know that the next disaster I would be sent to would take me straight into the heart of darkness, to witness the very worst of man's inhumanity to man, and would change me forever.

Chapter Seven

We must develop and maintain the capacity to forgive. He who is devoid of the power to forgive is devoid of the power to love. There is some good in the worst of us and some evil in the best of us. When we discover this, we are less prone to hate our enemies.
Martin Luther King, Jr.

IN SPRING 1994, WHEN I WAS STILL A HEALTH ADVISER based in Malawi, horror stories had begun to emerge from the small East African country of Rwanda. Britain did not have a presence in the country at the time, as it had historically fallen under the sphere of Belgian colonial control. However, the UK government felt they could not ignore the appalling stories seeping across its borders. My recent experience assessing the needs of disaster victims in Turkey meant I was asked to go in as a first responder to bring back news.

I hitched a ride on an ODA-chartered Ilyushin, a huge leviathan of a Russian aircraft packed to the gunnels with aid supplies. The long and uncomfortable flight took me to a refugee camp on Tanzania's Rwandan border. It sprawled across the landscape, hastily pitched tents creating a patchwork of white and blue against the bright green and ochre-brown of the countryside. As the British volunteers began distributing their relief cargo, I took stock of the situation.

The population of Rwanda are all descended from the same people, the Banyarwanda, but differences between two of the tribes, the Hutus and the Tutsi, were emphasised and exacerbated by the European colonialists. They employed a strategy of "divide and conquer," as they knew that their own meagre forces lacked the manpower to subdue the locals. Their solution was to exacerbate any racial tensions that might exist between the two groups, so they would concentrate on fighting each other instead of uniting against a shared enemy, the colonial invaders.

As an Indian teenager coming to 1970s Britain, I had experienced my fair share of racism. Although I had excelled at my studies, become a champion member of the school fencing team, and even managed to beat one of my meanest bullies one-on-one at a long-distance run, I had felt the pressure to constantly fight for everything, so as to be considered equal to others. I could never just "be" and found it hard to shake my "outsider" status.

I told myself over and over that I was above taking such prejudices seriously. Through all of it I clung to my own identity. I knew I was the equal of any of them. I was too proud to give much significance to the barbs that people threw at me. I kept reassuring myself that in spite of how they acted, I was pretty special to have made it halfway across the planet to the same place as them at the age of sixteen. By repeating this mantra to myself I developed my own form of robustness and resilience.

More than anything else I understood that racism made no sense and was just a method for asserting power over others.

Although my experience of racism cannot be compared to the evils of Rwanda, the initial impetus was the same. Racism is a mechanism for dehumanising your opponent. The belief that you are superior to someone else due to nothing more than the colour of your skin, your parentage or the accident of your birth, somehow gives you the right to subjugate others because they are innately less than you.

The rivalries between the Hutus and the Tutsi originated from this misguided belief in ethnic superiority. There had been violent clashes and bloody feuds between the two groups in the past, thanks to the unequal status each held in the power vacuum after the Belgians granted independence to Rwanda. Yet something told me that whatever was underway now was on a magnitude hitherto unreached by either side.

The refugees in the camp I was visiting were mostly Tutsi and the fear that stalked the place was present on every face. Everywhere there were stories that corroborated what I had heard in London. Hostility was at an all-time high and hordes of armed Hutu militants - known as the *Interahamwe* - had been growing in strength and numbers. Tales were whispered of machete-wielding men riding into Tutsi homes under cover of night and massacring whole families. Everywhere fear buzzed in the air like a swarm of mosquitoes, infecting everyone with a terrible dread.

These stories seemed too brutal to be true. After all, the Hutus and the Tutsi speak the same language, practice the same religion and live side by side with each other in relative harmony. I knew I would have to see for myself if I was to believe these monstrous rumours.

I returned to London to brief my superiors and before long I was back on a plane, this time to Kampala, en route to Rwanda itself. By my side was Peter Troy, the desk officer covering the Rwandan emergency in ODA. He was a quiet, retiring civil servant in his late thirties and this flight was one of his first trips abroad. He seemed noticeably apprehensive about our coming journey. Our plan was to fly into Kampala, the capital of Uganda, and from there to journey overland to Rwanda.

On arrival in Kampala, the British High Commission provided two Land Rovers with Ugandan drivers, one for us and one for our supplies of food, fuel, tents, etc - all of which we needed to bring with us as we had no idea what to expect. The drive to the Rwandan border was executed swiftly. We knew that forces of the Tutsi-led RPF - Rwandan Patriotic Front - headed by Paul Kagame - were advancing through the country, clashing violently with the Hutu militia and taking the fractious country under their control. Our plan was to follow in the wake of their advancing troops until we reached the capital city of Kigali.

Once we had passed through the Ugandan border post into Rwanda, our lonely convoy crept slowly into unknown territory. We were jumpy and tense as the vehicles crawled onwards. We knew the RPF were supposedly ahead of us, forging their way towards the capital, but every shadow and every tree seemed like a hiding place for the *Interahamwe*, crouched with machetes in their hands and malice in their hearts.

After about fifty kilometres we reached a small town occupied by RPF units. Dressed in camouflage combat gear and with khaki caps, the RPF appeared disciplined and orderly. They were a far cry from the hordes of rebel fighters they'd been described as, by their detractors.

Every man stopped what he was doing to watch the approach of our Land Rovers, each with his hand on his rifle. I sensed Peter felt as anxious as I did. We were here as aid workers and, as such, protected under international humanitarian law. But this was a lawless country in the midst of a civil war where every last rule of decency had long since broken down. What was to stop these men from turning on us? After all, we did represent the international community that had let the Rwandan people down so utterly. Our failure to protect them had allowed thousands to be slaughtered.

Despite our misgivings, there was nowhere to go but onwards. We sought out the commander of this unit and explained that we were here to bring assistance from the British government. Mercifully, we were well received.

"We are pleased you are here to help the Rwandan people" he told us. "However, you are expressly forbidden from continuing any further. The road ahead is not yet secure. We cannot guarantee your safety. You must go back to the Ugandan border until we have the area clear and under control."

There was no arguing with him so we had little choice but to turn around. We spent a fitful night in a roadside motel just across the border, but the following morning we were back on the road. We sped through until we reached the town where we'd been turned back the day before. There we found the remnants of the soldiers, though the bulk of them had moved on.

The RPF units were on the move now, advancing at a fast pace towards Kigali. We pushed forwards, inching along in their wake. The terrain became increasingly hilly and forested as the hot afternoon's sun beat down. The atmosphere grew steadily more sinister and once or twice I felt sure I'd seen movement in the shadows beneath the thickly growing trees. Still we pressed on.

Just as the sun sank behind the horizon, the road reached the brow of a hill and we had our first glimpse of the darkened city of Kigali below. Here and there were flickering pinpricks of light - oil lamps and camp fires - but no moon hung in the sky to light our way and all else was darkness. We began to descend the hill with a strong sense of foreboding.

As we entered the city what struck me most was the absolute stillness. There were no RPF on the streets; no road blocks; nothing but the eerie, empty, menacing silence. The whole city was deathly quiet. Not even the birds were singing - and Rwanda is famous for its birds - it was as if even mother nature herself had fled. It struck me this was the kind of absolute hush which descends on a place when horrific atrocities have been committed.

The only sound we heard was the occasional howl of a feral dog. We soon realised why. As the Land Rovers progressed we saw that there were corpses everywhere. Dead bodies littered the pavements, lying crumpled or sprawled where they'd fallen. Packs of feral dogs roamed around, feasting on human flesh. The whole city stank of death. Sweet and sickly and putrefying.

We drove onwards, unable and unwilling to comprehend what we were seeing, until we spotted a group of 'Save The Children Fund' vehicles. We went inside the building they were occupying, explained who we were and asked if we could stay the night. They agreed. We crawled into our sleeping bags and joined a group of around twenty people huddled together. We were all very shaken by what we had seen. We tried to catch some sleep between the nightmares.

The next day Peter and I resumed our harrowing mission. We bore witness to the aftermath of a brutality and butchery that we had never thought human beings might be capable of.

I witnessed dark red smears of blood adorning the walls of the city's Cathedral. I witnessed the promising young minds of Rwandan academics spilled in the corridors of Butare university. I witnessed children, once loved and cherished, abandoned by their families. I witnessed women and girls, some little more than babies, savagely raped by their neighbours. I witnessed the destruction a pack of wild men armed with machetes can wreak on a human body. I witnessed what damage such monstrousness could do to those who had somehow survived.

More disturbing though were the thoughts that I could not drive out of my mind: that the international community had done too little to prevent this abominable tragedy from happening. Though I could not ignore the barbarous depravity of the *Interahamwe*, I was fast learning what wider circumstances had ultimately led to the breakdown of all law, order and human decency in Rwanda.

More and more information was coming to light that implicated the rest of the world - and the UN in particular - for what had unfolded here. The trigger had been one incident: the plane carrying the Rwandan president, Juvénal Habyarimana, had been shot out of the sky by mystery assailants. That was the catalyst for spiralling outbreaks of violence between the Hutu and Tutsi peoples, ones of ever greater savagery and horror.

Canadian General Roméo Dallaire, head of the small UN peacekeeping force in Rwanda, had identified deliveries of weapons headed for the Hutu militia. They were obviously gearing up to escalate the violence. He had requested permission from the UN Secretary General to seize these arms caches and thereby limit the destructive power of the Hutus.

He was denied permission to do so. Worse still, the UN peacekeeping forces had been ordered out of Rwanda as conditions became "unsafe" for them. This left the vulnerable Tutsi, many of whom had come to the UN-controlled areas seeking safety, at the mercy of the Hutu militias.

I knew Dallaire was a military man and as such was bound to comply with the orders of his superiors, but I wondered what I would have done if faced with the same dilemma. Would I have had the courage to go against authority, question the ethics of obeying orders like his and follow my own beliefs instead? If I was ever in the same position I hoped that I would.

Though the experience of all we saw was deeply traumatising, by focusing on whatever task was most pressing at hand, we somehow managed to keep ourselves together. First and foremost, if the British government was truly committed to helping end the anarchy in Rwanda, we needed a base to operate from. A headquarters. Somewhere from which we could establish some form of strategy to help orientate the NGOs and emergency agencies who would be arriving soon, and later to assist the new RPF government in getting the country back on its feet.

Many homes in Kigali seemed deserted, their occupants fled or killed. We selected a large house on a small hill in a residential area with a wide and open garden all around it, so we could keep an eye on what was going on outside. The long grass out front suggested that this place had been empty for some time. We jumped down from the Land Rover and approached the house with caution.

Basic training had taught us to be prepared for boobytraps. We looped a long rope over the door handle, stepped back as far as the length of rope would allow and, holding our collective breath, gingerly pulled the door open. Nothing happened. We carefully made our way inside.

Peter and I decided to camp out together in the main living room, not daring to explore the rest of the house until more of our number arrived. We set up our sleeping bags, camping stove and satellite phone to report back to London. I relayed the bloody details, only to hear a chilled silence at the other end of the line. After a pause, where I assumed my counterpart in the UK was having trouble processing my words, she thanked me for my news and informed us that reinforcements were on the way. A brigade of Royal Marines were headed to Kigali and would shortly be with us.

This house had now become the official British Government HQ in Rwanda. The first mission for the Marines upon their arrival was to ensure it was safe for us to remain, by clearing it of any potential hazards. Peter and I thanked our lucky stars we had not ventured to explore any further. The Marines found hand grenades, with pins removed, balanced on top of the doors left ajar upstairs. Anyone who wandered into those rooms would have been blown apart if the grenades had been disturbed.

More sinister still were the bodies they discovered in the garden. Nothing unusual about this in itself - by now we had become almost entirely desensitised to the decomposing human remains that littered the city - but these bodies had also been boobytrapped, so that anyone disturbing them would be blown to pieces. As the Marines dealt with the booby-traps, Peter and I realised just how close we'd come to death these last few days.

But even here, in the cold heart of this evil, a small flame of human kindness burned resolutely on. Peter and I came across an orphanage run by a group of ageing Indian nuns. We entered into a courtyard where there must have been at least a thousand babies and infants. We had to walk very carefully to avoid treading on them as they were so densely packed together. We learned the sisters had accepted each and every child given into their care by anguished parents trying to escape the cursed city. They had not discriminated, but had welcomed all in need, creating an oasis of humanity amidst the carnage.

They told us how, when the *Interahamwe* had come to kill the children, the nuns had stood firm. Though they were armed with nothing but their faith they had challenged the blood-crazed mob.

"No, you cannot enter," they declared. "For this is the house of God."

The militia retreated, and so the innocent children were saved.

I was astounded by their bravery. These seemingly frail, unarmed women had stood up to this monstrousness, where even the great United Nations and its armed peacekeepers had basically run away.

Evidence of the genocide - and by this time it was clear in my mind that what had occurred here truly constituted genocide - was everywhere we went, but the experience that would torture me most lay outside Kigali, in the countryside, at a place called Ntarama. Peter and I had heard whisperings of what had taken place there. Thousands of Tutsi had been murdered, the Hutu mobs revelling in jubilant celebrations.

Our hearts heavy with the prospect of what we might encounter, we set out through the forest that surrounds Kigali. Though the landscape was verdant green and the birds chirped merrily, the forest still seemed to brood with a wicked presence in every shadow.

The Land Rover slowed as we entered a small clearing in the trees. All was eerily quiet - no birds sang here - and in the air lingered a stench so horrendous that it overpowered my senses, filling my mouth, my head, my brain, and leaching deep inside my body to carve its hideous memory into the very sinews of my being.

My first instinct was to flee; to get as far away as possible from this terrible place that reeked of evil, but my eyes were fixed on the small red brick church that stood in the centre of the clearing and I could not look away.

We were in no doubt what lay inside, but despite my animal repulsion to get far, far away, my feet dragged me forward. It was not a morbid curiosity I felt but a need to see for myself the very worst of what man was capable of doing. Sins this horrible had to be witnessed so they could be understood and fought against. I could not shy away. So I stepped doggedly forward.

As I approached the door of the church, the brightness of the sun, incongruous amidst the horrors, threw the insides of the building into dark shadow. I stood at the threshold, and as my eyes became accustomed to the gloom, I saw shapes moving inside. My stomach lurched with fear: could someone still be alive in there? It was then that I recognised the hulking shapes of feral dogs gnawing at human remains.

The bodies of several hundred people lay in the tiny space. Human viscera splattered the walls and floor. The blood-crazed Hutu mob had surged inside the church with their clubs and machetes, swinging them viciously amongst the huddled people. Skulls had been beaten-in to spill their brains; limbs severed; babies cleaved in two; everywhere bodies hacked and mangled terribly. And everywhere were faces twisted and eyes wide with terror and pain.

I don't know how long I stood there surveying this hellish carnage. It might have been half an hour, more likely it was only a few minutes, but for however long, this abomination would be seared into my memory forever. I would never un-see that vile sight.

We drove back towards Kigali in utter silence. There were no words to express what we had seen. But my brain was racing with questions. How could this have happened? How could this have been *allowed* to happen? The UN peacekeepers had been present in Rwanda, they were aware of the tensions, they knew what was going on. These people - who now lay dismembered on the floor of the church where they had run for sanctuary - should have been protected. Why had they not been? What had happened to the international presence here to allow such sickening violence?

I was pulled back to reality as the Land Rover jolted to a halt. There was a long queue of trucks and cars seemingly held up at a checkpoint, one that hadn't been there when we left that morning. I was in the front passenger seat so I had an unobstructed view of what was going on. The cars in front were being stopped by a band of teenage soldiers. These young men were little more than children really, though they were dressed in full combat fatigues and carrying AK-47s. As they moved down the line of cars they thrust their guns into the open windows, brandishing them at the people inside. One of the young soldiers stepped backwards, staggered slightly and I realised with dismay that they were drunk.

Another boy stumbled over to our car. His face showed him to be little more than fourteen years old, but there was nothing childlike about the way he barked the order to roll down the windows. The driver obeyed and the boy pointed his rifle directly between my eyes. I could smell the alcohol on his breath and see the spittle collected at the corners of his lips, where the first wispy fuzz of hair had begun to sprout.

The driver explained that we were from the British government and returning to our office in Kigali. I was paralysed with fear and had no idea what to do. Should we offer them something? Food? Money? After what felt like eternity, he pulled the gun out of my face and lurched on to the next car. I breathed a deep sigh of relief as my head lolled back against the headrest. But all too soon the boy soldier was back, waving his gun around from person to person. He seemed to be angry with us, but we had no idea what to do to appease him or diffuse the situation.

He was little more than a boy who needed guidance, patience and trust. I was just thinking that I could offer him my father's Swiss-made watch, when I heard another barked order coming from the distance. An officer with epaulettes was approaching. My heart quickened still further. Had we found ourselves on the wrong side of the rebel army, after all? But instead he ordered the boys to clear the road and the traffic passed through unhindered.

Returning to my bed at our makeshift headquarters that night, I was far too wired-up to sleep. The fear I had felt looking down the barrel of a gun wielded by a drunk child-soldier kept the adrenaline surging through my veins. I lay awake and alert as my brain bombarded me with visions of genocide.

I thought back to a day in my early childhood, and remembered how my own family had barely escaped a genocide themselves.

***

During the school holidays in India I would leave the Christian Brothers' School to go home to see my family. Though I enjoyed living with my grandparents, I loved returning to the familiar sights and smells of the family home in Bihar.

One very hot summer evening, my father and I were out on the veranda that ran along our house. I was reading as my little brother

Bitu, about seven years old at this point, was quietly playing with a sleek, back, German-made train set that my father had bought back from his time studying in Europe. My mother was busily preparing dinner. She was pregnant again with a third child, her stomach huge and swollen, though she was still smiling and singing as she made delicious dhal, happy to have all her family together again for the summer.

My father seemed in a pensive mood. He watched Bitu in silence as he pushed the model train across the wooden floor.

"Babloo?" he called my family nickname gently.

"Yes?" I said, looking up from the copy of Somerset Maugham's *Of Human Bondage* that I was engrossed in.

"Have I ever told you of the train ride that brought your grandmother and I from Pakistan to India?"

"No father, I don't think so," I replied.

"Close that book in that case," he said. "I've got a story for you. It's not a pretty story, but it's important."

I closed my book and paid attention as my father recounted his tale. In the kitchen I noticed my mother had stopped singing.

"It was 1947 and India had just succeeded in reclaiming her independence from the British after almost thirty years of nationalist struggle. It should have been a time when the people of our nation came together, but instead we were torn apart. The partition of Hindu India and the new Muslim state of Pakistan meant that, as Hindus from the North-West region, our family had to relocate to India.

"My father went ahead to make preparations. He intended to return to accompany my mother and their children - your uncles and aunts and I - a few weeks later. While he was gone, riots began. In the vacuum caused by the abdication of British power, mob mentality took over and vicious fighting broke out between Hindus and Muslims. The cry went out that any Hindu families who still remained in Pakistan must leave immediately.

"With no time to wait for my father's return, my mother gathered up her ten children plus as many of our possessions as possible and we boarded a train heading south. I must have only been about fourteen at the time but I remember it all so clearly. The intense heat, the crowds of people, and the palpable feeling of panic in the air. We were all squashed tight as more desperate people strained to fit inside, and I hung my head out of the open window, hoping that the breeze from the train's movement would cool me.

"There was none of that though, the train inched forward so slowly

NO STRANGER TO KINDNESS

I thought we were going to bake in the sun. From my position by the window I saw another train coming from the other direction. I was transfixed by the frightened face of the driver staring straight ahead, his eyes seemingly unseeing and wide with fear.

"The next moment I understood why. That train was as tightly packed as this one. But it was filled with corpses. Every single man, woman, and child on board had been slaughtered. Killed where they stood, presumably as unarmed and defenceless as ourselves.

"I wanted to turn away. I wanted to close my eyes against the evil. But I was paralysed with terror and couldn't move as carriage upon carriage of mutilated bodies rolled past. I've never forgotten it.

"At the time I was only a teenager. I had heard about the Nazi camps and the trains that took away the Jewish people never to return, but that had felt like a faraway nightmare, something of the past, something that could never take place again. How wrong I was. Our countrymen were turning on each other. People who had been friends, neighbours, and school-mates, were now subjecting each other to horrific acts of violence.

"When the train we were riding on came into a station it was surrounded by a crowd of men, mad with blood lust, and all clutching weapons - rifles, swords, knives and even farming tools. I didn't know if these were the same murderers who had butchered the people on the other train, or if these were the other side who had seen that train and were now seeking retribution. The only thing I knew for sure was that if they got on board they would most certainly massacre us all.

"To my alarm we slowed to a stop. I felt sure this was the end and said a silent prayer to any god who might be listening to deliver us from this terrible fate. But as the mob surged towards the door one solitary figure came out to meet them.

"He was a young Swiss man from the Red Cross. The Red Cross flag flew at the front of our train and he was their representative on board. It is the Red Cross's mission to ensure the Geneva Conventions are upheld. This means protection for prisoners of war and refugees. There he stood, unarmed yet firm. I expected he would be cut down where he stood, but do you know what this mob of killers did, Babloo? They stepped away, and the train was able to continue.

"I remember thinking that this emblem, this red cross, must be invested with some kind of sacred power. Alone this insignia held back the mob, though they could easily have overpowered this one man and his flag. Time and again this happened along our journey, and time and again this one man, evoking the power of that symbol, stopped these blood-crazed murderers in their tracks.

"And so we were able to cross into India and to safety." He finished.

I stared at my father open mouthed. I had never once inquired into our family history or background. I knew my father had travelled from Pakistan during Partition, but I had no idea of the danger and lasting trauma of the story.

"But why did they want to kill you in the first place?" I asked, dumbfounded.

"Ideology can do funny things to people," he replied, evasively. "Over a million souls were killed in the fighting and it lasted only a few months. Hindus and Muslims who had previously lived side by side turned on each other. We were very lucky to escape with our lives.

"I'm telling you this, Babloo, not to frighten you - although there are things in this world to be feared for sure - but so you understand and you never forget. Not only the violence that men are capable of inflicting on each other, but also the power and bravery of that one man who stood up to save us all. No matter the danger, I hope you will always stand up for what is right."

Maybe it was that conversation - that lesson from my father - that had driven me to a place like Rwanda.

***

When I had first heard of the sinister deeds unfolding within Rwanda, I was concerned, but I had been entirely unprepared for the extent of the savagery. Now, I felt changed forever by it. Despite our family history this was my own first-hand experience of genocide, and I was filled by a certainty that what I had witnessed here could not be for nothing.

Genocide is considered one of the most grievous atrocities prohibited by international law. It goes against the very nature of what it means to be human. To systematically eradicate the existence of a group of people based on their identity is to render them less than human. It reduces living, breathing, laughing, empathising, struggling, thinking, loving people to the status of cattle fated for the abattoir.

The words of my father returned to me that night in Kigali, reminding me that I must stand up for what was right. Though I could not understand what could make people turn on each other in this way, I resolved to dedicate my life to fighting genocide and upholding the principles of humanity.

Questions chased each other through my head. How could this unspeakable evil be combatted? How could it be overcome? How could encountering violence this horrible be turned into something positive for the future? How could hope be returned to this terrible situation? Would the power of human forgiveness be strong enough to heal Rwanda, after all this?

Above all, how could this kind of crime against humanity be prevented from occurring again?

Chapter Eight

You must not lose faith in humanity. Humanity is an ocean; if a few drops of the ocean are dirty, the ocean does not become dirty.
Mahatma Gandhi

THE ATROCITIES WE SAW IN THE CHURCH AT NTARAMA were repeated a thousand-fold in village after village. I travelled up and down the length and breadth of the country. Everywhere was the same. We saw evidence of killing on an industrial scale. It made me wonder about the human capacity to undertake such methodical and absolute evil.

Eventually, Peter and I flew back to the UK to report on all that we'd seen and heard. By now we had a clear grasp of the situation within Rwanda that had led to these mass murders - this genocide. However my sense of justice told me there was more to it than that.

My status as a civil servant meant I had access to all the papers that went back and forth between the Foreign Office in London and British diplomats at the UK Permanent Mission to the United Nations in New York. From looking through those communications it was clear to me that the international community had not done enough to intervene and stop the bloodshed in Rwanda. Indeed, the removal of peace-keeping forces at the crucial moment meant that the *Interahamwe* had been able to advance unchecked.

Douglas Hurd, the British Foreign Secretary, was in negotiations at the UN at the time, and seemed intent on avoiding embroiling the UK in the Rwanda situation. He argued that because the country was not under the UK's sphere of influence, we should avoid being sucked into this malodorous black hole.

There had been little ignorance of the extent of the slaughter or the fact that it was clearly of a genocidal nature, but as there had been virtually no news coverage yet, there had been little pressure from the media or public to act.

I was sickened by this official apathy, in the face of blatant crimes against humanity. Who cared if the British had no historic involvement in the region? Did we not owe it to our fellow human beings to help if we knew - as we had known - what brutality was taking place, and if for no other reason than to prevent a catastrophe like this from ever happening again? Surely we were duty-bound by our shared humanity, if nothing else?

I decided that I needed to return to Rwanda forthwith, so that the British government could not abdicate their responsibility so easily.

***

Reports were coming in of refugees arriving into Zaire (now the Democratic Republic of Congo), on Rwanda's western border. So, Peter and I - joined at the hip by this point - went to investigate.

We jetted into Nairobi, Kenya's capital, from where we chartered a Beechcraft to fly straight to Goma, a city that was once the jewel in the crown of the Belgian Congo's Riviera. In those times, Goma must have been very comfortable, set on the edge of the vast and beautiful Lake Kivu, with many colonial beach villas dotted along the volcanic shoreline.

Now, it looked rundown and depressing. As our tiny plane circled around, decreasing in height, the landscape appeared harsh and inhospitable, formed of large expanses of black volcanic rock, speckled here and there with sparse clumps of foliage. The brooding volcano, Mount Nyiragongo - still ominously active - cast a menacing shadow over the town.

We checked into the one hotel that was still open. It was full to the brim with aid workers and journalists and we had to share a room with a couple of reporters from *The Times*.

The next morning we made contact with the UN representative, Sergio Piazzi. He told us he was going to cross into Rwanda that day. Realising we had no vehicles of our own and not a moment to lose, he offered us a ride.

Peter and I clambered into Sergio's Suzuki and we set off. We were quickly waved through the border which seemed to be open, and took the tarmac road towards Ruhengeri, western Rwanda's principal city. We sped along the first dozen kilometres before coming to a grinding halt. The road was jam-packed with people as far as the eye could see. It seemed as if the whole world was on the move.

Entire families trudged along on foot, the women hauling handcarts and wheelbarrows filled with possessions. Everywhere were bawling children, in danger of being trampled by the multitudes. Old people dragged themselves along on sticks. Men on bicycles weaved as best they could through the tight-knit throng.

The odd vehicle, crowded with refugees, carved its slow progress through the press of bodies, everyone moving in the same direction, like a great human tide. We were the only ones travelling upstream.

After another ten kilometres we began to see light tanks and armoured vehicles topped with canons. These had stressed looking young men clinging atop them, waving their rifles around. We realised that these must be what was left of the defeated Hutu troops. They had been overcome by the RPF forces, and were now being driven out of the country.

Then it struck me; this had to be the mass exodus of Hutus from Rwanda. This frantic crowd were not the victims, but the *perpetrators* of the genocide. As the crowd parted around our Jeep I regarded a man who seemed brow beaten and exhausted, dragging his wife along by the arm. Then I remembered the severed limbs that plagued my dreams. Could this man, now so seemingly hopeless and pitiable, be one of those who, a few days before, had taken the cold blade of a machete to the flesh of a defenceless baby? I looked into the face of a young woman trudging along behind him, with two small children strapped to her bowed back. Could she have sold out her Tutsi neighbours to be abducted and raped by men crazed with bloodlust?

I was struggling to process this complex mixture of anger, pity and revulsion. But wherever my eyes looked there were the génocidaires.

I used my watch to count how many people we saw along the road in two minutes, then multiplied that by two to take into account everyone traipsing through the bush that we couldn't see. We then timed how fast we were moving through the sea of fleeing bodies to calculate how many new refugees the Congolese would soon have on their hands. It seemed that the entire Hutu population was leaving Rwanda. We estimated that there had to be close to a million people moving along that road, which made this a humanitarian disaster of unprecedented scale.

The normal journey to Ruhengeri takes around an hour. This time it took us three. As we finally approached the town, the crowd thinned out until there were only stragglers left. The elderly hobbled resolutely onwards. People with missing limbs crawled desperately through the dust. Abandoned children looked lost and forlorn in the wake of the departed crowd.

We stopped outside the hospital on the main road into Ruhengeri. We recognised it as such by the hospital beds that littered the side of the road – ones that still had their occupants lying on them, injured limbs hoisted into the air. They had been wheeled from the wards by family members, only to be abandoned in the street when they realised the futility of trying to push a hospital bed all the way to Goma.

On the steps of the hospital stood a small boy in dirty shorts and a t-shirt. He looked no more than five years old. He did not cry, but he seemed utterly lost and alone. For me the image of that child was a metaphor for the traumas of Rwanda and the hopelessness I felt deep inside myself. I have often thought back to him, wondering what kind of man he grew into, if indeed he survived at all.

It could very well have been members of his family who had perpetrated the genocide. Committed some of the worst evil I had ever witnessed. Murdered Tutsi children no less innocent than him. It was upon spying that helpless child alone on the hospital steps that I realised how complicated the process of post-conflict peace-building would be for this nation. Delivering punishment, justice, rehabilitation and ultimately healing, when so much blood had been spilt, was going to be the hardest challenge Rwanda would ever face.

Inside, the hospital was deserted. From the hills outside however we could see the glint of cannons and light machine guns. These were the RPF troops closing in on the retreating Hutu militia.

I wanted to push on to see what the situation was like further inside the country. But Peter and Sergio thought it at best unwise - at worst a death wish - to drive our Jeep into the encircling RPF troops. Besides, there were a million people on the move that were about to become the most urgent crisis on the planet. We needed to get word to the outside world before it was too late.

So we turned back towards Goma, joining the exodus of people flooding across the border. Sergio steered the vehicle through the crowd, weaving expertly between the armoured vehicles of the *Interahamwe*. Soldiers on top of these tanks drunkenly brandished their guns. Now that their fates had suffered such a reversal, they seemed particularly angry and unpredictable. Even with the UN flag fluttering on our bonnet, I realised what an easy target we would provide for a renegade Hutu fighter who wanted to take out his anger at becoming the hunted, rather than the hunter.

Now that we were moving with the flow, rather than against it, everyone seemed to want to board our vehicle. People were hammering on the doors, clawing at the windshield and climbing onto the roof, bonnet and bumpers. Others were rocking the vehicle from side to side menacingly. We were in a Jeep with only tarpaulin side and top panels, not even metal skinned. All it would take was for someone to slash the soft canvas and we would be done-for - ripped from the safety of the vehicle and our supposed UN protection.

As figures swarmed around the car, each face a mask of panic and wretchedness, I realised again what they were guilty of. These were the people who had perpetuated the abhorrent acts we had witnessed. Now, faced with the reality of their crimes, they were fleeing from retribution. Having shed the blood of so many Tutsi, they were seeing their own lives destroyed, and were abandoning their homes in order to escape the vengeance of the RPF.

The atmosphere on the road was one of heightened desperation. Somehow, Sergio maintained his cool composure throughout. No matter what we faced, he continued inching the car forward. The crowd grew thicker and angrier as we crawled towards the border and Goma.

After many, many anguished hours we finally crossed back into Zaire. Seconds later, the barrier came crashing down, bisecting the crowd in two. The border was closed and we had only just made it in time. I looked back to see people doggedly climbing over the gate, determined to seek safety outside their home country.

***

The situation in Goma was like a scene from Biblical times. I found out later that this was the fastest movement of people in history since the Partition of India, when my grandmother had fled with my young father on the train from Pakistan, along with millions more. Goma was packed with refugees and everywhere was a state of chaos. It was obvious that a humanitarian crisis of monumental proportions was unfolding, and we were right in the thick of it.

We had to act fast to help prevent catastrophe, but I felt paralysed with doubt. The city was flooded with men, women and children, and it was impossible to distinguish between innocent civilians and criminal génocidaires. I was certain that these people needed aid - and fast - if they were not all going to die of disease, starvation and exposure, but visions of those dismembered bodies piled high in the church in Ntarama kept coming back to haunt me.

Try as I might I could not shake that image. A small but immutable voice in my brain - a voice I am by no means proud of - whispered quietly, but persistently: *Let. Them. Die.*

My mind oscillated between the certainty that we needed to mobilise help, and the memories of all the horrors we had seen in Rwanda. It was Peter who jolted me back to the reality of the task at hand.

"The plane is waiting for us at the airport, Mukesh. What do you want to do?"

Well, I couldn't very well admit to him that half of me wanted to see those refugees - guilty though many of them undoubtedly were - left to fend for themselves in the wake of the emergency. I forced those thoughts down to a deep hollow place buried in my gut, and focussed on preventing what could soon escalate into a disaster as deadly as the genocide that had created it.

The plane we had chartered was empty other than us, so before we had left for our nightmare drive into Rwanda that morning, we had offered a free ride to any journalists who wanted to get out of Goma. Several were assembled when we arrived at the airport.

"You can't come," I told them plainly. "You can't come. You have to go back. An unprecedented crisis is unfolding in Goma. You need to return to cover the story."

We described all that was occurring - the biblical flood of refugees - and convinced them to stay and report on that living hell.

Peter and I boarded the flight alone. I sat in silence. Deep in thought. It was then I felt Peter's eyes on me, and glanced up to meet his gaze.

"I know what you're thinking, Mukesh," he volunteered, "and I'm thinking it too. But we have to help them."

I blinked back at him, unsure what to say in response.

"Let the guilty live long enough to face judgement for their crimes. No more lives should be lost. I've seen enough death. I have no wish to see anymore."

As his words sunk in, I knew he was right. We had the power to help. We had to use it.

***

Without another word we got down to our task: compiling everything we had seen into a report, so that on arrival in London our counterparts in ODA could embark on the deployment of a large-scale relief operation for those refugees.

We had not been scheduled to return to London right away. A small part of me did feel as if I was fleeing from the genocide myself. Did I lack the strength to cope with prolonged exposure to such suffering? Was that the real reason I was returning to the safety of the UK?

I banished such thoughts from my mind. I had seen the British government's apathy towards Rwanda already. I felt I had to get back there myself, to ensure that they acted on this crisis. Without our first-hand accounts, I felt that nobody would believe. It was too big - too inconceivable - to be true.

As soon as our aircraft touched down in Nairobi, I booked us onto the first available flight to London. Only first-class tickets were available via Paris, and while the stewardess offered ice-cold champagne to the well-heeled travellers, I sat in the same clothes I'd been wearing since leaving for Ruhengeri, and frantically scribbled down what we had seen.

We arrived in Paris at 6 am with my hastily hand-written report finished. We caught a direct transfer to London and before long were speeding from Heathrow in a cab to Whitehall. I stumbled into the office of the Minister for Overseas Aid - Lynda Chalker - much to her surprise. We had made it from Goma to our London headquarters in some twelve hours.

To her immense credit, Lynda showed no irritation at my sudden appearance, unkempt and stinking, demanding an immediate meeting. She joined me on the floor, kneeling in the thick carpet, as I pored over a faded map of the area where Western Rwanda met Eastern Zaire.

I described all I had seen, tracing the path of the exodus on the map and explaining the situation in Goma. A million people on the move. No water other than the lake. Terrain of volcanic rock so nowhere to set up camps quickly. The toxic mixture of civilians and soldiers together. Plus the fact that many of these people were responsible for the mass killing of thousands, mere days beforehand.

***

Once I was sure that Lynda and the others understood the gravity of the situation, and our Ministry was galvanised for urgent action, I returned home to Cambridgeshire for a much-needed respite. But back at home in the Fens, rest proved more difficult than expected, as my nights were plagued by dark visions of blood and terror.

More disturbing even than the nightmares of the church filled with bodies, or the *Interahamwe* surrounding our Jeep, was the evidence that the international community had abandoned Rwanda at her time of greatest need. The spilled blood of millions was on our hands. My frantic return to London had convinced my superiors that the situation in Goma could not be ignored, but knowing our government had weaselled out of getting involved in Rwanda in the first place made my blood boil.

Even in the peace of the Fens I couldn't rest. Days later I was back on a plane to Goma, hitching a lift with aid supplies directly from London, including precious water-purification kits. There had been a massive cholera outbreak, just days after the refugees had arrived. Tens of thousands of people had already died.

On my first day back, a man wandered out and collapsed in the road ahead of our vehicle. We slowed to a halt to see what could be done to help. I checked his pulse but it was no use. He was already dead. This happened countless times over the days to come.

The body count here seemed to rival what I'd seen upon arrival in

Kigali. I had never quite understood the term "dying like flies" before now. Men and women were dropping down dead wherever we went and in such quantities that a body collection system had to be set up. A truck drove around all day between the city and the lake collecting up the bodies of those who had curled up by the side of the road and stopped breathing.

Was it just disease, hunger and exhaustion, or was it also the insurmountable trauma from the terrors they had seen - and often times perpetrated - that caused their hearts to cease beating?

***

The superlative aid agency Médecins Sans Frontières had set up a field hospital, which I visited to see what they were doing. A local nurse, Elodie, showed me around.

After visiting those being treated for diseases, and mutilations inflicted by the fighting, she took me to an area reserved for those who were survivors of sexual violence. I looked around at the young women in their teens and twenties, many of whom had children themselves. We walked down the rows of beds that were packed closely together, as Elodie explained quietly that the patients here had been brutalised, and violently raped.

I stopped by a woman nearest to the door. She was tall and slim and could have been no older than twenty. She was dressed in a pale green hospital-issue smock and had her daughter with her, who must have been around three years old.

The nurse saw my interest and volunteered their story in a hushed tone.

"This girl and her child are Tutsi. They arrived before the Hutu exodus you witnessed."

I nodded. I had heard that a stream of Tutsi refugees had been trickling into Goma for weeks now.

"Both of them have been raped. Neither have spoken a word since their arrival."

I was sickened beyond words. "How do you know what happened?" I managed to ask.

"We examined them, and that's how we know." She said simply.

The young woman looked up as we stood talking quietly, but then lowered her eyes again, saying nothing. The child in her arms looked around, sucking her thumb and clinging tightly to her mother. I saw a drip in the child's arm where she was receiving treatment. Antibiotics, I guessed.

Looking at this woman, who was obviously so broken and destroyed by the sickening acts that had been inflicted upon her and her child, I felt a wave of shame. I was ashamed to be a man. Humiliated that my gender could do such things to those who are weaker and less able to defend themselves.

It was plain how utterly traumatised the women in this ward were; many of them might never completely recover. I could not help thinking about my own three daughters. I imagined this being done to them and me being forced to watch, as many of the Tutsi fathers had been, and how I would feel about it.

The only small salve to my shame and my anger was that I could at least do something to help. "What do you need most?" I asked Elodie.

She listed the supplies that were most urgently required and I made sure she would receive everything she requested. I marvelled at her professionalism, for she was not just treating the Tutsi survivors, but many Hutus who were also in this hospital.

I wondered how she could handle this, having seen up close the savageries inflicted on the soft, undefended bodies of women like herself by the Hutu men. How she found the tenderness to care for those complicit in this violence was beyond my comprehension.

***

At this stage Peter and I were the only needs assessors here from the British Government. Everything we demanded was provided by London. Perhaps our leaders were now ashamed for their earlier neglect. We did whatever we could to pour money into the NGOs, Red Cross and UN organisations on the ground, so they could bring the most help to the most people. I felt we were doing good at last - even if rather late.

As well as giving money for the refugee camps, we were now also providing funds inside Rwanda to help set up the new government in Kigali, so they could begin the long journey to recovery.

Peter and I never again talked about what had passed between us on the flight from Goma to Nairobi, but that was the first and only time I ever heard that sinister voice in my head. While working with the refugees we beheld women and children and old people dying needlessly before our eyes - innocents, who were surely not responsible for any of the slaughter.

Even those who had carried out those unimaginable crimes against humanity were now suffering terribly. They deserved to be called to account and we had to think about delivering justice. But for now, our purpose was to bring relief here and secure a new stable government in Rwanda, one that would deliver justice and foster peace.

***

It was some six months after I first set foot in Rwanda that I returned home to the UK for a longer break. I hoped never to return to Rwanda. I was glad for the chance to do some good there to atone for the evil, but now I hoped to put all that terrible darkness and horror behind me. Truth be told, the last few months had taken their toll emotionally and physically. I had lost a lot of weight and my jet-black hair was now peppered with grey. I was also dog-tired.

I felt constantly drained. I put it all down to being always on the move, making assessments, travelling around and catching innumerable and uncomfortable cargo flights. Any semblance of a normal routine was a distant memory and what little sleep I had been able to snatch was fraught with night-terrors. Yet it turned out my fatigue signified something far more serious. Finally forced to get medical attention, a blood test revealed something alarming: my blood sugar was sky high. I had developed diabetes.

I was shocked. I had been sure that I was just exhausted from over-exerting myself. That my body could have been fending off a serious life-threatening condition like diabetes, while also undergoing the ordeal of Rwanda was almost unbelievable, yet it had. As I underwent specialist examination and learnt how to inject myself with insulin, I felt distraught. I would now need to inject myself four times a day, each and every day for the rest of my life.

One question haunted me: how was I going to manage to keep this a secret, so they wouldn't try to stop me from doing my work? If my bosses at ODA found out about this, they might try to stop me from travelling to the world's most dangerous places. I pictured myself desk-bound in a pokey office in Whitehall, forbidden from going on any more overseas trips due to the risk to my health. It was too awful to contemplate.

I made the solemn decision to tell no-one. Better to die from diabetes in the field than to die of boredom chained to a desk in London. After three days of insulin training, I returned to my office and began injecting myself in secret.

I soon realised that my work might take me into challenging situations where getting supplies of insulin might be impossible. I went to see my diabetologist, Dr Jonathan Roland, and explained a little more about my predicament.

"I am often away in war zones and challenging places and I'm worried about my insulin supply. If I was kidnapped by terrorists for example, or obstructed from coming and going, what could I do?"

After a few moments of thought Dr Roland replied. "We can work out a strategy for this. You would need to cut out certain foods - carbs and sugary stuff - to prolong your insulin supply. You should also cut down to one meal a day - that way you'll use less insulin; and be sure to keep fit and active to burn up energy."

"How long would I last without insulin?" I queried.

After another moment's thought he said, "You could probably survive like that for two weeks ... but there would be long-term complications."

"What kind?" I enquired, dreading the answer but needing to know.

"Well, first you'd get organ failure. Typically kidneys and eyes to begin with. Then your legs, fingers and toes would clog up... but if you escaped within a few weeks at least you would survive."

"And what would happen then? If I could not get away?"

"After that, well, you'd die."

I laughed - what else could I do? Shrugging it off, I thanked Dr Roland for his advice. I was grateful to him for giving it to me straight and for not trying to dissuade me from my path.

Later that afternoon as I walked my dog, Megan, through the Cambridgeshire fens, I considered my doctor's words. I felt an odd mixture of emotions. Although I was afraid of finding myself without insulin and of dying slowly from organ failure alone in some far-flung corner of the world, I was more afraid of the prospect of giving up my career, and all the good I still wanted to do. I determined the main priority had to be not to let my diabetes impair my life's purpose.

For all that I had seen and done in Rwanda, I had paid the cost of going grey and diabetic. Yet ultimately I felt it was worth the price. Despite the sleepless nights, I had never felt more absorbed in the challenges of my work or so driven. I also realised that I was good at it. Having done a lot of important work in Rwanda and for the refugees outside, I wanted to do more.

At this time I was a uniquely qualified humanitarian advisor in the British Government: my background in medicine and public health meant that I filled a crucial role and, as such, I was pioneering this kind of action in the field. I felt that I was on an important mission, and I was utterly desperate to continue. I would view my diabetes simply as an inconvenience. Being medically qualified myself, I was sure I could manage my condition in order to do my job, and do it well.

After everything I'd seen over the last few months, I felt more and more interested in how these kinds of atrocities could be prevented in the future. I was sickened by the absence of moral fortitude revealed in the papers that had gone back and forth between New York, London, and other major world capitals. These revealed the international community's double-dealing, self-interest and paralysis.

They revealed an unforgivable lack of concern. For them the killing in Rwanda was little more than an inconvenience and their reaction seemed to be largely a case of: 'how can we get away with doing as little as possible to make it all go away?' This abdication of responsibility was inexcusable.

I'd been granted many incredible gifts to be in the position I was in now. Chance had been kind to me. I wanted to use the privileged position in which I now found myself to continue my work to prevent genocidal atrocities like I had seen in Rwanda, from happening ever again.

Chapter Nine

If the Lord comes and burns - as you say he will - I am not going away;
I am going to stay here and stand the fire.
Sojourner Truth

IN THE AFTERMATH OF THE FALL OF THE SOVIET UNION, the breakup of Yugoslavia brought conflict to Europe once more. For the first time since Nazi Germany's terrible predations, there were whispers of concentration camps and mass executions carried out by Europeans on their neighbours. Villages were being destroyed all over central Bosnia and sinister stories of systematic rape camps were emerging. Refugees were pouring into neighbouring countries and the picturesque Adriatic coast where many Brits were accustomed to taking their summer holidays. The whole thing felt incredibly close to home.

Events escalated rapidly and before long Sarajevo, the beautiful, historic capital of Bosnia and Herzegovina, was under siege by the Army of Republika Srpska, the Bosnian Serb Army. Again, I was asked to go and take a look, assess the situation and see what the UK government could do to help.

The first problem was how to get there. Sarajevo had been besieged for months and reports from inside told of a worsening situation. The whole of former Yugoslavia was incredibly unstable. Everyone was fighting: the Croats were fighting the Serbs, the Serbs were fighting the Bosnians, and within Bosnia the Muslims were fighting the non-Muslims. Ensuring safe passage was going to be very difficult.

I flew from London to Ljubljana, the capital city of Slovenia. Their airport was open, as Slovenia had remained relatively peaceful despite the violence raging all around. From there I took a six-hour taxi ride through the beautiful but war-scarred Balkan countryside to Zagreb, Croatia's capital. Their airport was closed after being bombed by the Serbs.

On arrival in Zagreb I checked into the Intercontinental Hotel, where I planned to base myself for the night, while I worked out the next leg of my travels. It was the weekend and I doubted I'd be able to get into Sarajevo until Monday, so for now I could rest. I flopped onto the bed exhausted from the mammoth journey and flicked on the TV. The face of Douglas Hurd, the foreign secretary, swam into focus. I was just in time to hear the announcement he was making to the world over BBC News.

"We are very concerned about the rapidly deteriorating situation in Sarajevo. We have sent a high-ranking envoy from the British government to assess what exactly is going on there and what help Britain can offer the besieged civilians within the city."

I couldn't believe this. They had gone above my head and sent in someone more superior. Who else had they sent? Why had I not been informed? I rolled my eyes and lay back against the pillow in exasperation.

"Bloody Whitehall bumbledom," I told myself. "I wonder who is the other guy they've sent in?"

Then I jerked bolt upright as realisation hit me: maybe Douglas Hurd had been talking about me! I had never considered myself as being a high-ranking anybody, but maybe the British Government was packaging me as such for the purposes of external spin! The more I considered it, the more it had to be the case. There was no-one else they could have dispatched ahead of me.

"Oh my God!" I thought, leaping out of bed totally naked, and scrambling around for my things. "I'd better get there as fast as I can rather than dilly-dallying in this hotel!"

I made contact with the British Embassy in Zagreb and spoke to the Military Attaché, insisting that I needed to get into Sarajevo without a moment's delay. "Be careful what you wish for," is all I can say in hindsight.

As dawn broke the next morning I found myself strapped into a Royal Air Force C-130 Hercules, airlifting a cargo of military kit into Sarajevo. A small but densely populated and cosmopolitan city, Sarajevo lies in the valley of the Miljacka River and was settled in ancient times. The Dinaric Alps rise majestically all around, resplendent with snow-dusted peaks. But the warring factions had taken up positions in the mountains on every side. Now, the once peaceful valley rang with the sounds of gunfire as the opposing forces shot at each other from hillside to hillside, across the city below.

The airport was located right in the midst of all that and flying through the hail of fire was the only way to get in.

"Don't worry," the military commander in charge said to me, as he handed me a bullet proof vest, "our pilot is one of the best. He's used to landing in war zones and manoeuvring aircraft into spaces you'd never believe. The kind of evasive manoeuvres we need here he could do with his eyes closed."

I nodded, and gulped, wondering what the evasive manoeuvres would entail. It wouldn't be long before I found out. Looking around at the soldiers strapped to the plane's interior, I noticed none of them were putting their bullet proof vests on, but were sitting on them instead.

The man next to me, sensing my confusion, leaned over and yelled into my ear over the roar of the engines: "So your balls don't get blown off, mate."

I nodded in mute acquiescence and sat on my vest too.

After a long approach to the city the aircraft began to climb steeply to get out of range of the cannon fire. Then she let out flares in all directions and seconds later we were plummeting into a tight corkscrew and hurtling towards the ground. We dropped like a stone before pulling up jerkily and screeching to a halt on the runway. I was promptly sick all over myself from the aerial acrobatics.

The door was flung open. I looked up to see the soldiers pulling on their vests and helmets and jumping from the cabin. They ran unprotected across the 200-metre stretch of runway and into a tunnel of sandbags that marked the entrance to the nearby hangar.

I struggled to pull on my bullet-proof vest. It was cumbersome - very, very thick and very, very heavy. Once I'd dragged it on, I pulled the large helmet onto my head and hauled myself to my feet. The dispatchers were yelling "OUT AND RUN" and I did my best to obey. I'm not the most physical person and wearing a big bullet proof vest, and carrying my luggage, it felt more like "out and waddle" than "out and run."

As I stumbled down the aircraft's ramp to make my dash, I glanced up at the wing and realised it was peppered with bullet holes. I felt sure that on departure those holes hadn't been there. Now I could appreciate just why that stomach-churning aeronautic manoeuvre had been so necessary.

Bullets came pinging past me as I floundered across the runway - inexplicably missing me and burying themselves deep in the sandbags on either side, throwing up puffs of grit on impact. I flung myself down the tunnel and into the dugout safety of the airport reception area, where "Movement Coordination" had set up their base.

Shortly, some fellow aid workers and I were shoved into a large white armoured personnel carrier with huge "UN" letters painted in black on the side. The route into Sarajevo took us down a street that those on the ground had dubbed "sniper alley" - a long boulevard lined with high-rise Soviet-style tower blocks. These anonymous looking buildings provided the perfect cover for gunmen who, after installing themselves in one of the abandoned apartments, could proceed to shoot at whatever they wanted with little fear of detection.

From my position in the bowels of the APC, I could hear the periodic "ping, ping, ping" of small-arms fire as bullets ricocheted off the vehicle's armoured skin. The soldier who was accompanying us, a burly man with a thick set jaw and stubbled chin, seemed far too relaxed for someone who was being shot at, which showed just how commonplace this had become in the city. Periodically he would look out of the turret in between the "pings" to observe what was going on.

He'd drop back down with a grin and remark: "Welcome to Sarajevo."

Though I was petrified, I tried my best to appear nonchalant in the face of danger, as if I was seasoned at being dropped into war zones and getting shot at all the time. I was used to being the first on the scene by now, but nothing I'd seen so far had prepared me for this.

Apart from the obvious dangers, I was largely concerned with what I was going to do here. How was I going to find my way around? And more immediately, where was I going to sleep that night?

The APC slowed to a stop. After another glance out of the turret our grinning soldier announced we were safe to get out. I climbed into the pale morning sunlight and blinked up at the building in front of us. It dwarfed everything in the area, a huge cavernous warehouse. I noticed UN peacekeepers stationed at strategic points around the perimeter. This was UN headquarters in Sarajevo. As I went inside, I realised it was home to most of the major aid agencies in the city too.

I introduced myself to a stressed-looking young man named Pàulu, the resident representative from WHO (the World Health Organisation) here. Despite his very obviously frayed nerves, he was friendly and invited me to stay in his office. All foreign relief workers slept in the warehouse overnight, because it was relatively safe... apart from the occasional bullet that would come flying through when the building got caught in the crossfire.

Pàulu explained to me with great sadness that people had actually died in the offices from catching rogue bullets. He told me I could sleep under his desk while I was staying here - an arrangement that suited me perfectly. He chose to sleep on the sofa, but I was happier on the floor as I figured I was further out of the line of fire. After taking stock of the situation as best I could, I settled down to sleep for the night.

***

"Wake up, Babloo! Wake up! Out of bed! Hurry!" my grandmother's voice cut through my dreams, as she grabbed me by the arm and yanked me from my bed. I stumbled groggily after her as she dragged me along in the wake of her rippling petticoats, clutching my pillow and blanket close to me as she half carried me out into the warm spring night.

The air reverberated with the high-pitched wailing of air-raid sirens. The dark street was awash with people all frantically hurrying in the same direction. Figures banged into each other in the darkness and confusion. I was terrified of being separated from my family and trampled under the feet of so many rushing, frightened people.

The air-raid shelter was very close to our house, though there was always the fear that this time we might not make it in time before the bombs began to fall. We had been lucky so far, but I had no idea how long that luck would hold. Fear sharpened my sleepy senses and I quickened my pace to keep up with my grandmother, holding tightly to her hand. Before long we were clambering down into the relative safety of the dugout.

The bunker was little more than a large hole in the ground, totally open to the elements above. Even in my child's mind I remember questioning how much good it would really do if bombs began to fall, or if the military air-base nearby managed to shoot down an enemy bomber right on top of us.

We squeezed in and tried to make ourselves as comfortable as possible. I clung closely to my grandmother, as we all turned our faces towards the heavens, watching the war that raged in the skies above. India was at war with Pakistan and battling warplanes blazed their trails across the dark night sky.

I watched my grandmother's face, illuminated now and then by the light from a far-off explosion. She looked worried and I could see her scanning the crowd for sign of my grandfather. He was the area's air-raid warden so when the sirens went off it was his job to march about, shouting at people to put out their lights and showing lost stragglers the way to the shelters.

I began searching for him too. Then the sky burned vividly, illuminating the whole pit, and I spied a stricken plane screaming down towards us, flames trailing from its underbelly. I shrank back, tighter into my grandmother's embrace, sure that it would crash straight into us and explode in a deafening cacophony of tearing metal and the anguished screams of my friends and neighbours. But it sailed on into the darkness.

A pale, rosy dawn was breaking over the horizon when the sirens finally fell silent and it was safe to emerge, cramped and aching, from the hole in the ground, to reunite ourselves with grandfather. Safe for now, but for how long? Spending a part of my childhood mired in the midst of a violent conflict, I realised then how much I hated war and how keenly I wanted to contribute towards a world wherein children were not kept awake, gripped by terror.

I understood intrinsically that this situation was not right. It was unfair that we were subjugated to those long nights sheltering in the dugout. The fear I saw reflected in my grandparents' eyes was not fair. Civilians - men, women and children - should not fall victims to war.

***

That first night in Sarajevo I reflected upon the unfairness inflicted on the city's population, by a siege that had infiltrated all aspects of their lives. As a child I had been affected by a war that I wanted no part in. I knew what it felt like to be unable to escape the violence and I wanted to help the citizens of Sarajevo caught up in such a brutal siege.

Over the following days, I began to assess who were most at risk within the city. I spoke to as many people as I could, to ascertain what aid was reaching them, what else they needed, and who was likely to be stuck or hiding in remote areas and might be suffering in silence. As I spent more time with these besieged people, travelling around different areas in one or other APC, I got an impression of the character of the population.

I marvelled at their sheer resilience. Even the act of coming to work - as I saw evidenced by the local agency staff - was a huge feat of courage. They traversed the treacherous city streets by foot each morning, as no armoured car could be spared for them. They came spurred with hope for change, in spite of the terrible dangers that threatened to strike them down the moment they stepped outside their front doors.

Not only did they turn up for work, they did it in style. The women had their hair cut fashionably, lips painted with bright shades of lipstick, and wore dresses that reflected the latest trends. The men sported smart suits and ties with faces clean shaven and shoes polished. I understood that they dressed this way in an effort to keep their morale high, even though many lived in the same kinds of tower blocks that I had seen along sniper alley, most of which had no electricity or running water.

Despite my Hindu upbringing where cleanliness is highly prized, I have often been known to skip out on bathing, or to wear the same clothes for days when conditions have been difficult, or the pressures of work too intense. Indeed, this was one of the unavoidable side effects of working in the field - the pungent aroma exuding from the bodies of myself and my peers.

I understood that it was an act of defiance for the local Bosnians to dress so nicely, despite their hellish conditions, to show that their lives would go on as normally as possible. No matter how long the siege might last, their spirits would not be broken. Above all else, they would maintain their dignity.

***

Bringing aid to Sarajevo was particularly challenging as it was not the kind of situation I had ever encountered before. This was not a poor rural population. It was a cosmopolitan city of relatively rich people.

All the disaster relief I had been in charge of administering before had been for poor people who were living in poverty and without much infrastructure. They were used to cooking over open fires and drawing their own water for washing, and they often lived in houses made from daub with thatched roofs, or tented refugee camps.

The metropolitan environment of Sarajevo created all manner of unique challenges. We were used to providing care packages for African or Asian refugees, where we would give them bulgur wheat or corn that they could then cook out in the open on a camp fire. How were these besieged Bosnians going to cook grains on the twentieth floor of a tower block with no electricity, gas, or running water?

The conflict itself was very much urban warfare, using sophisticated planes, tanks and guns within a modern European city. It was clear that we had to find new ways to assist these people. I now understood the importance of working with the beneficiaries of aid, as they knew best how to improve their own lot. I elevated this notion to the next level in Sarajevo and resolved to speak to as many different people as I could to understand their real needs.

I met a local lady named Ajša who was the unofficial leader of a women's support group. Their husbands and sons had all gone off to fight in the war and they had no way of knowing if they were alive or dead. Many of the women were survivors of sexual violence, who had fled burned and pillaged villages in the countryside. Hoping to reach sanctuary in Sarajevo, all that had awaited them inside the city limits was a different form of hell.

This close-knit circle of women had banded together to form a self-help group. They met in a day-centre in the basement of one of the many tower blocks. I went to see them and heard their stories over thick cups of Bosnian coffee. I asked them what they needed from the international community, while the staccato rattle of cannon fire rang out in the distance.

Ajša was a striking looking woman in her late forties with long dark hair and classically fine Balkan features. She, like most of the besieged, was always smartly turned out and never to be seen without her damson-coloured lipstick applied perfectly. She had a no-nonsense attitude and a sharp tongue, but underneath she had an incredible capacity for kindness. I noticed the tenderness she showed, particularly to the younger women in the group and felt they looked up to her as a surrogate mother figure.

"What we really need," she explained, "is a way to keep ourselves clean and fresh."

I blinked in surprise. This had not been what I had been expecting. Certainly, nobody I had encountered before had prioritised cleanliness over other more life-saving options. Sensing my confusion, Ajša elaborated.

"We need toothpaste and toothbrushes - these things ran out long ago. Also deodorant and ways to clean ourselves without running water. But most of all we need sanitary supplies. Tampons and pads." She told me matter-of-factly. "Now when we get our periods we have to tear our precious clothes into rags."

I had never thought about this before, but now that Ajša mentioned it, I saw this was a real necessity. Yet the relief kits we had put together in other places had never contained sanitary items. I wondered why the women in Rwanda hadn't asked for the same? Maybe it was embarrassment? Or maybe they were more used to making do with washing out pieces of cloth to re-use?

Either way it seemed like a very reasonable request. I felt foolish to have overlooked such things. I made a mental note to always ask disaster-effected women if these supplies were needed.

Some of my male colleagues turned out to be highly sceptical of Ajša's request, enquiring whether it was really necessary. The women in Africa had no need of such items, so why did the women in Sarajevo?

"Of course it's necessary," I explained. "Just because this kind of thing is usually hidden from men to preserve our comfort, doesn't mean it isn't a legitimate problem. The stigma around menstruation means it is something women usually keep to themselves, yet that doesn't mean it doesn't present a real challenge in this environment. When women ask for help managing their periods we should believe that it's necessary, the same way we'd believe anyone else when they told us of the problems they faced."

Together with Ajša and the other women we developed a programme of collaboration. We provided them with the supplies they asked for - of sanitary products and other toiletries - and they took charge of disseminating these kits in their own way.

Of course, it was a risky business for anyone to go distributing relief in the city, but for aid workers particularly, as we were unfamiliar with the terrain and didn't know where gunmen might be hiding. Ajša and her women knew where there were others living amidst the sprawl of high rise towers and were eager to bring help to them. In every way they were more courageous than I, for they didn't have access to bullet proof vests or APCs. It might seem foolhardy to an outsider - risking your life to pass out tooth brushes and tampons - but their bravery was about much more than that.

The war had stripped these women of almost all their dignity. By distributing hygiene packs they had a purpose again and could recover a little of what they had lost. Here was a way they could take assertive action, while helping their sisters in the process. So much had been taken from them. They wanted to restore their agency to act and to do good in the world.

This was working in true collaboration. I understood the value of developing alliances with the people who were most in need, and I was starting to appreciate the resources and capacities they themselves brought to the table. Ajša and the others did not wish to be our dependents. They wanted to be treated as our equal partners.

***

Another unlikely partnership in Sarajevo came in the form of a ferocious border control guard who everyone knew as Big Bertha. After my initial terror-stricken flight into the city, on subsequent trips I tried whenever possible to enter Sarajevo by road, catching a lift with any aid convoys that were going in.

On one such visit I was accompanying a delivery of medical supplies. The hospital was running very low on equipment - x-ray machines, defibrillators, surgical kit for the operating theatre - all essential but high-tech stuff. I had taken an inventory of what was needed, returned to the UK to procure the items, had everything loaded onto trucks and headed right back into the maelstrom. The convoy came trundling through the Bosnian mountains and rumbled to a halt at Checkpoint Sierra One, on Mount Igman, just outside Sarajevo.

The Serbian border guards queried what was in the trucks. We explained it was medical equipment for Sarajevo hospital. They scowled at us, cold, bored and full of resentment and barked some instructions across the checkpoint perimeter to attract the attention of a senior soldier, who they engaged in a disgruntled conversation in Serbian.

Moments later the door of the checkpoint building flew open. My heart sank as a large and fearsome woman hefted herself out and approached our truck. I wanted to shrink back into my seat and make myself as invisible as possible, leaving the convoy's driver to face this menacing foe. Instead, I took a deep breath, opened the door of the truck and jumped down onto the gritted tarmac.

"Bertha," I said with my best attempt at smiling, "how good to see you again."

Big Bertha, as she was infamously known, narrowed her piranha eyes at me. I tried to remain as calm and unfazed as possible as her gigantic bulk loomed over me - I felt sure she could crush me to death easily, if she was so inclined.

We had had several altercations in the past, as I had come into Sarajevo via this route before. Being Asian, with dark hair and a beard, no doubt I looked like a Mujahed - a Muslim holy warrior and implacable foe - to Bertha. Yet here I was empowered with authority, with my UK passport and UN ID. She did not like that at all and was forever attempting to play tricks with me, like trying to take my identification card away to "check," even though she knew we were under strict instructions not to give up our ID.

I'd spent many, many frustrated hours hopping from foot to foot to keep warm on this desolate mountain road, while she purposefully delayed my entry to the city for no better reason than she didn't like the look of me. This time she appeared unusually mean-looking. After expressing her distaste for me with a glare, she went to speak to some higher-ranking officers. After some furtive whispers, and several sidelong glances in my direction, they appeared to come to a consensus.

The senior soldier strode over to me, Bertha waddling by his side, clearly delighted to deliver what I was sure was going to be very bad news.

"We also need medical supplies in Pale hospital," Bertha stated.

"You UN people always favour the Bosnians and give nothing to us Serbs. You are supposed to be impartial, but no help comes to Pale."

I considered this for a moment. The Serbians had been, until this point, very defensive about the town of Pale, allowing no international teams inside for fear of compromising the security of this strategically placed outpost, situated just south of Sarajevo. For all I knew the situation in Pale hospital might well be as bad as Bertha claimed, but held at this checkpoint in the swiftly plummeting temperatures, seemed like a weird place and time to discuss the requirements of their hospital twenty miles away.

"We're very happy to come to Pale and assess the sit…" I began, but Bertha cut me off.

"You must split the trucks. Half can go through. But the other half must go to Pale."

Outwardly, I remained a picture of well-meaning cooperation but inside I was seething. What right did these border guards have to make demands on UN relief supplies? Aid - and UN sanctioned aid most of all - is supposed to be sacred in times of war. So they were technically behaving like war criminals. Moreover, did they not know the wretchedness going on inside the nearby city? Had they not seen the flashes of gunfire? Heard the stories of civilian life under siege? Bertha might be monstrous, but surely she was still in possession of a human heart? How could she deny the besieged these life-saving supplies?

I was further outraged at the sheer preposterousness of their request. Even if I was inclined to split the aid, what good would that do? Who could use half an x-ray machine? It would be about as good as sending nothing at all to either Sarajevo or Pale. I swallowed hard and replied as calmly as possible.

"No, we will not split the convoy. These are specialist medical supplies that have been sought explicitly to respond to the needs of the hospital in Sarajevo. I am happy to send aid to Pale too, but your authorities will have to let health professionals inside the town first to assess what is required."

Bertha looked even angrier than ever. When she next opened her mouth, I half expected enraged wasps to come swarming out.

Instead she bellowed, "No access into Pale. You are biased and side with the Muslim Bosnians. We will split the convoy."

"We will *not* split the convoy." I told her quietly but firmly. "That would do no good and help nobody. You cannot split machines in half - sending a few bolts to one place and tubes to another - they must go all together or not at all. Surely you can see that this is a ridiculous request."

Bertha's face reddened still further as she turned to the officer next to her to mutter something in Serbian. He barked a response and she nodded in what looked like vindication.

She turned back to me. "Then you will not pass. The convoy is split and half goes to Pale, or none may go to Sarajevo."

She crossed her arms and set her chin in un-budging obstinance. I realised I had unconsciously taken up the same posture too, chest puffed up defiantly, squaring up to her nose to nose. Self-conscious of my blatant stubbornness, I uncrossed my arms and returned to the driver at the head of the convoy. He looked down at me awaiting instruction.

"We wait." I said simply, and wait we did.

For twenty-four hours we remained on that mountain. I could not idle there forever as I had more urgent things to attend to inside the city, so I went ahead alone leaving instructions that they were not to split the convoy under any circumstances. A day turned into a week, which turned into a month, which turned into a freezing Slavic winter - and still there was no budging on either side. The medical supplies - thousands of tax-payers-pounds-worth, given in good faith - spoiled in the icy temperatures.

I had long given up hope on Bertha and the other Serbs, instead reordering the same supplies for Sarajevo hospital and having them airlifted-in instead. But the trucks remained on the mountainside.

I came under criticism from my WHO friend Pàulu, whose desk I was still sheltering under to sleep each night. "How can you justify letting all those medical supplies rot in the cold? Surely it would be better to give in to the Serbs and send them to Pale in their entirety even - at least then they could be of some good to somebody? Who are they helping abandoned on the road side."

"It's not about the supplies," I began. "Although don't get me wrong, I am loath to leave them spoiling on that mountain as much as you are. But what precedent would it set if I were to give into their demands? Where would it end? First, give in to them and split this convoy of medical aid - which would render it useless by the way - in order to get things moving. What next? When we need to bring in a shipment of food what is to stop Big Bertha refusing us entry unless half is given to the Serbian side too?

"One of the founding principles of humanitarianism is to provide assistance based solely on need. If we were suddenly splitting the relief, helping to feed the Serbian soldiers at the expense of besieged civilians, we would bring the entire system into disrepute.

"We must show that we cannot be obstructed like this. So, in a way the symbol that those trucks stuck on that mountain provide, is even more valuable than the thousands of pounds' worth of cutting-edge medical supplies. It shows that we hold true to the Geneva Conventions and cannot be bullied, bribed or bought."

He saw my point in the end, I think, although the wastefulness definitely struck hard. Here we were living amidst these brave civilians as they got thinner and thinner and greyer and greyer, seeing resources becoming scarcer and scarcer, but I stuck to my guns.

***

Many months later when the war had finally come to an end after so much bloodshed, we were busy setting up on the ground to help with recovery and rehabilitation, moving towards a semblance of normal life again. One of my local staff came scurrying towards me looking somewhat harassed.

"Sorry to bother you Mr Kapila,' he began, 'but there is a Serbian woman here to see you. She says you know each other very well and that she wants to speak with you, and that nobody else will do."

I thought on this for a moment, wracking my brains for who this mystery woman might be. My mind raced through all the beautiful Slavic women I had met over my time in the area and wondered which one of them could be described as knowing me "very well". Nobody sprung to mind. I looked back at the young man's pale face and then the penny dropped.

"This woman," I asked quietly. "Is she tall, plump and imposing with a face like an angry piranha?"

With a quick glance over his shoulder to make sure she hadn't snuck up on him, he breathed a barely-audible response: "That sounds pretty accurate, yes sir."

"In that case I *do* know her *very* well. Send her in."

The confused young man returned to where Bertha was waiting and showed her in to see me. To my surprise she smiled, and held out a piece of paper in her pudgy fist. I looked down at it and then back up at her with astonishment - it was her CV. Since a hard-won peace had finally come to Sarajevo and the borders were open, she was looking for a job.

"I know the place very well, and I know people all over," she announced, with her characteristic bluntness. "I want to work for you."

After I got over my initial shock, I agreed to give her a job as, for want of a better term, a fixer. She really did know her way around, and she was still Big Bertha, with all that gritty authority and the ability to instil dread into the hearts of grown men.

It also felt appropriate somehow. It sent the signal that we were a humanitarian organisation concerned with reconciliation, forgiveness and moving forwards. Here she was, an infamous Bosnian Serb, who had given me much grief but seemingly wanted to turn over a new leaf. What better message for rehabilitation than to give her employment in the new peacetime organisation committed to building a lasting and tolerant future for all sides.

Our partnership ended up being a very beneficial one, and I gradually grew to almost like Bertha.

"Do you remember when you kept me waiting at checkpoints ..." I would tease. We'd laugh and toast each other with throat-burning *slivovitz*, and I'd remind her that she thought I was a Mujahed and we'd laugh some more.

It was important to me when setting up new projects not to come in all guns blazing, thinking I knew best, that my way was the only way, and everything else that had come before was irrelevant. I much preferred assessing what was already in place, taking the good parts and using those to build a strong foundation for what was to come. Using Bertha's skills, in spite of our past history, was a prime example of that.

This lesson stood me in good stead for the next phase of my professional life when much change was coming.

Chapter Ten

Of course we need action, but it should be just action.
Clare Short

A HUSHED SILENCE SETTLED OVER LONDON AS I MADE MY way to work on the bright sunny morning of 2nd May 1997. Maybe everyone was too hungover from celebrating the election results as they had poured in during the night before.

Tony Blair - the young, engaging leader - had succeeded in winning over huge swathes of the traditionally Conservative British public and Labour had come to power in a landslide victory. This promised more left wing, inclusive politics. Though the city was very quiet, the air seemed to vibrate gently with optimism for the possibility of a kinder world ahead, after the long Conservative years.

The ODA's high-rise office had views over Victoria, across Whitehall to Big Ben and Parliament Square. I looked out over London, with all the wealth and power it symbolised, glistening in the morning sunshine. I pondered what changes might be in store for me. Surely this new government with its message of compassion and hope would want to shake up my department, and I prayed I would be allowed to keep doing the good work I had been committed to under the Tories.

Despite the atmosphere of excited expectation at the longed-for end of years of Conservative-led austerity, I felt a small but unwavering anxiety nipping at my heels: I had been working closely with the Conservatives for a long time. Was I too close to the previous regime? There was a good chance that this New Labour government, full of youthful pugnaciousness, would want to sweep away the old and build their own vision for international aid. I felt optimistic for the country as a whole under the new leadership, but I couldn't help but wonder: was my personal position, career and livelihood in jeopardy?

Little could I have guessed, as my colleagues and I wound our way down the stairs to meet our new department leader, how much change was coming.

I was right in suspecting a shakeup. Compassion really was a driving force behind New Labour's attitude to international aid and they were so committed to this, they formed a new dedicated department. Under the Tories I had worked for the Overseas Development Administration, a subdivision of the Foreign and Commonwealth Office. While we dealt with relief for poor countries we were still answerable to the politicians above us who were enacting British foreign policy.

In essence: foreign aid was seen by the Conservatives as just another tool to improve British relations around the world and convince other countries to toe their line. Who we helped and when was, first and foremost, calculated around how we could best serve British interests.

New Labour freed us from those shackles, by transforming ODA into its own government ministry, the Department for International Development, known as DFID - with a seat in the cabinet and the same status as any other ministry. No longer would the basic human impulse to improve the lives of others be tied to narrow national interest.

The news of this transformation came from the woman who was to be our first Secretary of State. She was tall, her hair cut into a short, simple bob, and she had an undeniable air of outspoken defiance about her.

That morning she delivered her first address to our new, barely-nascent department of state. As she spoke, her bright, penetrating eyes moved from each face to the next, looking us over and sizing us up. I felt like a school-boy again who had been told to pull his socks up and sharpen his act, or there would be severe consequences.

But her open, friendly smile and no-nonsense manner underlined all I had heard about her - that she was the kind of person who would get things done. As Clare Short finished her introduction, I was convinced that here was somebody who could really implement change.

A shakeup under her promised the chance for doing real, important work in the developing world and I prayed that my previous time under the Conservatives wouldn't count against me. I badly wanted to be a part of this trailblazing Labour government initiative.

I needn't have worried. Clare made the pragmatic decision not to do away with everything that had come before. Instead she chose to refine the old Conservative elements that were working well and build upon the existing system. She was not however afraid of making changes.

She had little respect and even less time for the "old boys" network that had infested our work under the previous government. She urged us to concentrate on big issues and empowered us in our own work.

During the earlier Conservative years, it was very normal for the minister in charge to get a phone call from the head of one of the large agencies – such as Oxfam or Save The Children - calling for a friendly chat, with the aim of wrangling a few million pounds in government assistance for some project they were working on. Because they all knew each other, the requests were agreed, and we civil servants were expected to write out the cheques without question.

These big, powerful agencies felt like they didn't have to go through the proper channels to secure funding because they knew the right people. When Clare got in, they had a nasty wakeup call.

"I deal with policy," she told them, in her typically frank manner. "I have nothing to do with the money. If you want to discuss money you should speak to my staff." With that she did away with the decades-long system of grace and favour. I thought this showed great ethics and integrity.

Not everybody felt as favourably as I did though, and it wasn't long before my boss, Andy Bearpark, made the decision to leave. I think he was too entrenched in the old ways to bend in the winds of change. I became acting head of our team for the interim, until the right person could be found to take Andy's place.

It was a time of huge upheaval. Many members of the new government had only ever served in the shadow cabinet and never led a department of state. Everyone was busy doing what was necessary to get New Labour off the ground, all under the resentful gaze of a recently-unseated Conservative opposition.

One of Clare Short's first moves was to commission a White Paper on Development. This meant creating a radical blueprint for the new government's vision and intentions for this area. Effectively this would be our bible for future decisions regarding international relief and development.

In this busy environment where everyone was frantically trying to adjust, Clare Short came to me and asked: "Mukesh, will you write the parts on emergency aid?" My heart leapt. Here was my chance to influence official policy and make real change. I agreed immediately.

There were two sentences about development in the Labour Party manifesto. It was left up to us to fill in the blanks and turn those into a White Paper that dealt with the government's official line on how it handled international aid, relations with poor countries and global relief in all its forms.

I realised then how a country is run: politicians provide the big bold visions, broad headlines and sweeping statements, but the blood and guts of what actually gets done is left to civil servants like us. It was hugely exciting and I felt more than ready to step up to the plate. I had plenty of arrogance in 1997: at forty-two years old I was very confident in my abilities.

I felt like my sacred mission was to take all I had learned in Rwanda and elsewhere and to distil it to inform this epoch-altering shift. Now was my chance to steer the course of development in a real and profoundly powerful way. To make the world a better place working from the very heart of the new British government was a once-in-a-lifetime opportunity.

I stayed up late each night, frantically writing and rewriting. I needed to capture the sense of possibility and fervent excitement of that very special moment, as well as delivering a proclamation that would stand the test of time. To my amazement and delight my composition was accepted practically verbatim into the White Paper. I wondered then if I should have been more radical, but ultimately I had got all I wanted.

I had advocated that conflict prevention should be prioritised to reduce poverty, because often the poorest people on the planet are those effected by war. I'd made it clear that it was our responsibility to tackle the root causes of violent conflict in order to bring about lasting change and peace. We would commit to multilateralism via supporting the UN and Red Cross and Red Crescent systems, NGOs and partner governments. We would also work to curb the trade in weaponry as the means for waging wars and thus promote a more peaceful world.

I revelled in this new sense of mission and responsibility. It seemed that I was now viewed as one of the well-respected decision makers. It was in this capacity that I could do the most good. Clare Short had an inspiring leadership style, whereby she motivated her team with a freshness of vision and trust. We in turn responded to this with an improved work ethic, dedication to our jobs, and loyalty.

I was the Acting Head of the Emergency Aid Department, but I was keen to take on the role in a more permanent way. But there was one more obstacle to overcome.

***

The British Government is made up of thousands of civil servants who handle the day to day running of the country. The very highest tier are the Senior Civil Servants. These are the people who make decisions that affect the whole nation, plus they are permitted access to the top-secret information that the country holds. This is a huge responsibility in itself and it is vitally important that such sensitive intelligence does not fall into the wrong hands.

The promotion I sought meant I would join this elite rank, but before

I was cleared I had to undergo vetting through a most stringent security check. I knew it was an incredibly intrusive process and that no area of my life would be left unexamined no matter how personal, but other than that I knew little else.

It was the only thing left in my way. Would I pass the test? Or would some skeleton from my past come rising up to thwart me?

I was informed that one of these vetters would be visiting me at home. They needed to see how I lived, they said. On the appointed afternoon, a small, fat man in a camel coloured rain coat and matching hat turned up at my door. His face was so generic looking he seemed practically featureless, and dressed as he was, he resembled exactly the image of a cartoon spy. I would have laughed out loud at this cliché, if I hadn't felt so nervous about the coming investigation.

"Mukesh Kapila?" he asked me as he stood on the doorstep. I nodded assent and stepped aside to let him in. I was half surprised he didn't pull out a little reporter's notebook to start jotting down clues. We sat awkwardly at the kitchen table as he glanced around my family home.

"Born in India, yes?" he began. "Where else have you travelled to?"

I swallowed the lump in my throat as I answered him. His manner of questioning made me feel like a criminal, even though I was almost positive I had nothing to feel guilty for. The questions kept coming thick and fast.

"Have you ever had any homosexual relationships?"

"Have you had any extramarital affairs?"

"Have you spent any time or had any contact with anyone in Russia?"

"North Korea?"

"China?"

"What sexual relations have you had with people from outside the UK?"

"Have your parents ever been involved in terrorism?"

"Are you a Fascist?"

"A Marxist?"

"A Communist?"

Most of the questions seemed probing yet quite predictable: "Do you have any financial problems we should know about?"

"Have you ever taken illegal drugs?"

"How often do you access pornography?"

But then he asked me something that seemed to come totally out of left field: "Do you have any radios?"

"Sorry, what?" I answered, in confusion.

"Any radios? Or any amateur radio hobbies?"

"No... well there's the radio over there on the window sill that my kids use to listen to the charts sometimes... and I like to catch *Woman's Hour* whenever I can..."

He went over and inspected it. He returned seemingly satisfied. By way of clarification he gave a slight shrug and said, "We need to know you're not a ham radio enthusiast who could broadcast classified information to the Russians."

I answered everything totally honestly. If I fibbed about anything and they caught me in the lie it would all be over. They had to know I would be trustworthy, but they also needed to know all my past secrets in case I ever *was* captured by the North Koreans and tortured or blackmailed. I had to confess to all my dirty secrets, so they could weigh up if there was anything so compromising they felt it could be used against me. Was there anything I would want to keep hushed up so much that I would betray my country in order to protect myself or my family?

After several gruelling hours he seemed satisfied. I got the impression that he already knew the answers to almost all of the questions, but needed to know if I would answer them honestly. I guessed that my answers were probably satisfactory as I hadn't lied at all. In fact, compared to the potential intrigue implicit in his questioning, I felt I had led quite a boring life, when I thought of all the debauchery I could have been up to.

"We will need full access to your bank account," he told me, "and a list of friends and relatives who can corroborate your story."

Then he looked at me with those suspicious eyes again and said finally, "Is there anything else you feel like you should tell me?"

I had been afraid of this. I had wracked my brains over the days before trying to think of the worst thing I had done. Something that might compromise me or make me unfit to do this job. I had only come up with one thing. Only one act of rebellion. I took a deep breath and the words tumbled out in a rush.

"Once, when I was an undergrad at Oxford, I threw a stone at Richard Nixon. It was the early seventies and he was there on an official visit. Myself and a bunch of other students, well, we stoned his limousine as it passed in the street. I was part of a big crowd of people. They all threw stones and I did it too. I did it because he was a nasty man and I was against the Vietnam war... and also because everyone else was doing it." I finished sheepishly, looking down at my shoes.

When I felt brave enough to meet his gaze again I thought I saw a faint smirk playing on his nondescript features. What did that mean? Was he smiling in victory at having caught me out? Or was my confession so vanilla compared to some of the tales he had heard in his time that he found it rather amusing? He left me in suspense a few moments more, before smiling in a good-natured way and waving his hands dismissively.

"Everyone has secrets like that," he assured me. "I mean, if you're not going to protest and throw stones at the age of nineteen when are you going to do it?"

I nodded in agreement and let out a long sigh of relief. I hadn't realised it, but I had been holding my breath. After he left it took a further four more months to get my clearance. Concerned friends kept calling me up saying that strange people had been asking all sorts of personal questions about me. I told them not to worry and to please cooperate. Eventually I got my top-level security clearance and became the official head of my own department within DFID.

The first thing I did was to rename us from Emergency Aid Department - which sounded like a fire brigade - to Conflict and Humanitarian Affairs Department, or CHAD for short.

Once the name was changed, I embarked on a huge reorganisation that would bring my original staff of fifteen and budget of fifty-million pounds per annum, to a team of one-hundred and an annual budget of four-hundred-million pounds by the time I left DFID.

I was overjoyed. I could surround myself with an elite team of talented, hardworking, dedicated individuals; I could act on my own deep-rooted beliefs about how best to bring help to those most in need; and I enjoyed the encouragement of a sympathetic boss in Clare Short, who I knew supported my efforts.

***

This leadership reform put me in mind of my university experience: Oxford University had felt like an enlightened sanctuary, after the challenges of boarding school. It brought out the mischievous side in me, that had been sadly absent during my school days at Wellington College. In Oxford I felt relaxed and could really be myself.

I made many friends while at university. There were still the elite rich kids from the highest strata of British society to grapple with, but most were too preoccupied with their boisterous behaviour trashing restaurants, chasing girls, and so on, to pay attention to me. There were also more people like myself who had come from less lofty beginnings and bootstrapped their way into Oxford on their own merit. It was with these people that I bonded.

Together with my buddies, Steve Pull and Chris Waddington, we would buy a loaf of bread to share between the three of us. We quickly found ways to make our money go further, so we could spend more of it on ale in The Welsh Pony, our favourite drinking hole. We discovered that if you went out just before the shops closed, you could buy one rasher of bacon and one egg cheaply so we would have that for breakfast to mop up the alcohol from the night before.

My accommodation was one of several small identical rooms in the front quadrangle at St Peter's College, in the centre of Oxford. It truly felt like the illustrious heart of learning that I had longed for. Everything was made from deep solid oak, rich old stone and worn red brickwork, weathered by the passage of time and the buzz of thousands of smart and eager minds.

Though our studies were rigorous, we found a lot of time for fun. One night upon returning home from the pub we discovered one of our friends had drunk too much and slunk home early, but had failed to make it all the way. Instead, he had curled up to sleep on the lawn in the middle of our courtyard. It was a warm spring night but still we could not leave him like this - what kind of friends were we?

We fished his keys out of his pocket and unlocked his bedroom, yet he looked so peaceful sleeping. We did not want to risk waking him. Instead - and with the true ingenuity and out-of-the-box thinking that sets Oxford students apart - we transported all the furniture from his room down to the lawn, where we set it up in an identical formation, so he would feel at home when he awoke. With one swift and gentle motion we scooped him into his bed in its new position under the stars and left him there for a comfortable night's sleep. It was worth the effort just to see the expression on his face when he awoke under the sky next morning.

Though my new companions were a lot of fun, they meant more than that to me. I felt happy to be finally surrounded by like-minded people who accepted me for myself, without expecting me to compromise my own beliefs. Although we studied different subjects, I understood that our core convictions were the same. I trusted these friends and felt that we were working together to fulfil our potential and to do some good in the world.

This was how I felt about the changes under Labour. In the elite boys' club of the Conservative Government of that time, my liberal views had been tolerated but never celebrated. I toed the line and didn't ask too many questions regarding the morality of how we engaged with international development. The victory for Labour felt like finding trustworthy allies, all working towards the same purpose.

***

The White Paper published in those first months went on to become the foundation for our core belief system and our modus operandi. My part of it was christened *The New Humanitarianism* and, with Clare Short at the helm, we radically transformed the way Britain approached international relief. She had spent long years in opposition studying, criticising, reading and thinking critically about the whole business of humanitarianism and our responsibilities as a donor government. We spent long hours discussing our vision, rethinking and reshaping how help was given to crisis-affected populations in their hour of greatest need.

"We need to take a comprehensive approach to aid and tackle the causes of problems," she told me one afternoon, as we travelled together between meetings. "Everything. Poverty. Violent conflict. Natural disasters. We must look at the root causes in order to prevent devastating crises from occurring in the first place, rather than mopping them up afterwards. What do you think?"

This was a totally radical departure from the way we had operated before. "I couldn't agree more," I stammered, excited by her radical vision. "Before, it was always dealt with in more of a cause and effect scenario. Relief would deal only with the symptoms of disaster."

"So if a famine desolated Ethiopia, Britain sent food. Civil war broke out in a troubled country, Britain provided tents for refugees? That kind of thing?" She asked.

"Exactly"

"And how did that work? You've seen it on the ground Mukesh, haven't you?"

"I have. My past experiences in the field have taught me that this is not the way that you save the most lives. The search and rescue teams that were sent after the earthquake in Erzincan pulled many lost souls from the rubble, but better, shock-proof architecture implemented in the city before the quake took hold would have saved hundreds more.

"The volunteers in the refugee camps in Goma worked valiantly to rehabilitate those whose lives were torn apart by brutal genocide, but some thoughtful conflict prevention between the Hutus and Tutsi might have meant they could have settled their differences without such horrific bloodshed. If we could look at the underlying causes of these problems and put in place measures to help people in the first place, then more lives could be saved.

"Take the cyclones in Bangladesh: they come every year, and surely there must be some way to prepare for them ahead of time rather than simply sending food and water to patch them up afterwards."

Clare smiled. "But surely this would diminish the impact of our publicity stunts: Britain praised as the benevolent giver of aid. If disasters could be prevented before they even happened then who would the *Blue Peter Appeal* (a popular children's TV programme) collect all their used stamps for?"

Although the previous government hadn't solely been concerned with making the UK look good internationally, they saw poverty reduction in other countries as a way for us to make money at home too. There was a condition written into our aid contracts decreeing that the money we gave was to be spent on British goods. Under the previous Tory leadership, it was estimated that for every one pound we gave in assistance, three pounds came back to our economy.

Clare Short abolished all that. She argued that a prosperous, self-reliant, safe world was more in our interests than short term gains from hawking British goods and services.

"Surely this is not the reason we should help? To make money for ourselves? To profiteer off the bad luck and suffering of others? We give in good faith to assist the beneficiaries in whatever way will bring most help and regardless of what we get in return."

Working from this viewpoint we abolished all the previous pomp and ceremony. We no longer celebrated our generosity by putting the British flag on crates of relief. No more plastering welfare packages with slogans like: "A gift to you from the kind-hearted people of Great Britain." I remembered seeing such similar nonsense on bags of rice during my childhood in India, and it had grated back then.

Instead, we focussed on ways in which we could make people in crisis feel more motivated. We wanted to help without turning the recipient into a victim or a passive recipient of our charity. I watched the ideas that Ajša's women's group had pioneered in Sarajevo being rolled out as national policy. It felt wonderful.

"Imagine for a moment, Mukesh," Clare remarked, in one of our meetings, "that you are down and out. What little you had has been taken away by a disaster or burnt up in a war, right? You are starving. Cold. Hungry. Desperate. Without hope. You lost your whole dignity as a father. As a mother. As a citizen. Then along we come and dole out charity. We make people feel indebted to us. We shred their dignity *even* further. Like supplicants. Like beggars. We need to be treating entitlement to aid as a basic human right, rather than a capricious favour that people of lucky, rich, privileged nations are granting."

I nodded my agreement. I felt so lucky to be part of this honourable change for the better. In essence *The New Humanitarianism* was really about a shift in the philosophy of giving. It was about preserving or restoring dignity above all else. No longer concerned with the naked promotion of UK self-interest, it exemplified a much kinder and more selfless commitment to poor people around the world.

I thought back over my own role as a donor and how my personal ethos had progressed over the years. I was no longer the Lord of Poverty, presiding over the life and death of others. My experiences had, I hoped, made me wiser and more humble. I was privileged to be part of a DFID that was transforming the UK's relations with poor countries. Tackling not just the symptoms of poverty and deprivation but addressing underlying causes. This was the evolution I had been waiting for.

Clare Short was a public personality with the strongest moral compass I had ever encountered. She brought a deep knowledge of course, but what I admired most were her instincts, which were to do the right thing by the people that mattered and her courage to stand true to her beliefs when everyone around would be clamouring and criticising.

Our humanitarian assistance team at DFID quickly gained a reputation as one of the best in the world. Leading this team was truly the most fulfilling time of my life. It was so exciting to be part of an enterprise united under one common objective. To do good. To bring hope. To lift people out of crisis and disaster. To reduce their poverty and vulnerability simply because it was the right thing to do.

Nothing else mattered.

Chapter Eleven

I want to stay as close to the edge as I can without going over. Out on the edge you see all kinds of things you can't see from the centre.
Kurt Vonnegut

THE *NEW HUMANITARIANISM* FELT LIKE A CULMINATION OF all I'd learned. This pinnacle of achievement, or so I saw it at the time, made me ponder what had first awakened my own humanitarian instinct.

My parents had wanted me to be a doctor, but that was not my own heartfelt desire. I had just wanted to please them and improve myself through education. I found a way to do both by squeezing my way into Oxford University to study medicine, but with a year's deferral.

I had a year to kill before I could take my place at that apex of academic excellence. I hadn't been home to India for almost two years. I felt a longing to see my family again. I had managed to secure funding to study at Oxford, and I had spent the last few years attending one of Britain's most prestigious private schools for free, so I figured that there must be a way I could get someone else to finance my trip home.

Luckily, I found an NGO, the *International Voluntary Service*, which sends keen young people abroad to do useful work all over the world. They gave me an attachment as a volunteer with its counterpart, *Service Civil International*, in Bangladesh. This meant I could go to Bangladesh for a four-month posting, and hop across the border to see my parents in Bihar before travelling back to Oxford in time for the start of term the following autumn.

This felt like the perfect way to reconnect with my family, before the long years of medical training began, and hopefully I could do some good work along the way. The journey to the island of Moudubi from the Bangladeshi capital, Dhaka, was an adventure in itself. It consisted of two days of travel on every type of boat I could conceive of, through this vast river delta terrain.

Bangladesh had won its independence from Pakistan in 1971 but not without huge human cost. I had read much about the country and its problems before I left England. I learned how the Pakistani military had undertaken ruthless attrition against the Bengalis of the area, systematically burning villages, raping women, and killing indiscriminately and without mercy. After nine short months it was estimated that three million were dead, with a further thirty-million displaced from their homes.

As my journey meandered deeper into the country's backwaters I saw evidence of the war all around. Bridges and roads had been completely destroyed by bombing, so the only way to travel was by boat. Everywhere I looked the waterways heaved with life.

I had been a little nervous about how I was going to find my way to Moudubi, as it required changing boats three times, but I needn't have worried. Everywhere I went it was clear to people that I was an outsider. Everyone helped me find my way.

The Bangladeshis were smiling and kindly, but very thin. It was clear that the after-effects of the war, plus the ravages of cyclones that beset the country every year, had taken a heavy toll.

From Dhaka I took a steamer to Barisal, then a smaller launch to Patuakhali, and then an even smaller wooden punt with an outboard motor down-river almost to the point where the brackish water merged into the Bay of Bengal. The boats made many, many stops along the way letting people on and off, carrying all manner of strange cargoes.

We wound down the tributaries, in and out of little jetties and pulled up at innumerable riverbank landings. Here and there traders selling groundnuts would pull up beside our boat. They would serve piping hot tea, cooked aboard their own small crafts on portable stoves.

The whole river teamed with life and at times it seemed like there was no limit to the amount of people who could clamber aboard. Our own boat must have had upwards of fifty people on it at one point, perched on the gunwales with arms and legs swinging freely over the muddy water below. There were times when the vessel sat so low in the water from the weight of people I was concerned we might sink. I needn't have worried. These boatmen knew what they were doing.

I sat back, munching away on my groundnuts, content to take in the view. Unlike the boat, my spirits felt incredibly buoyant. I had come from next to nothing in India to school in the UK, and won myself a place to study medicine at Oxford. Now here I was on an exciting adventure discovering a brand-new country. The world was here to be explored, just waiting for Mukesh to make his mark on it. What would I do next?

We meandered further and further out towards the sea. Here the tides ebbed upstream from the ocean and the islands of land were spread far more sparsely between green-brown expenses of briny water. The people thinned out, and the boat stopped less often, until there were only a few passengers left on board. I knew Moudubi was the second-to-last stop, and when the boat butted up against the makeshift jetty - just a few planks reinforcing the muddy fringes of the island - the skipper smiled at me and gestured that this was the place.

I thanked him as I got to my feet, scattering a cloud of ground nut shells from my clothing, and clumsily climbed off the boat. My legs were stiff from sitting still so long and I stretched them on the wooden boards. One of the boatmen passed up my suitcase before they continued their journey downstream.

***

My job here was to teach English, administer first-aid and bring health to the hard-to-reach. I was not a doctor, not even a medical student yet, but I had purchased a basic kit in Dhaka and I was full of enough teenage bumptiousness and childish naiveté that I believed I could do some good for the island.

The Moudubi headman had come to meet me, flanked by a group of his teenage sons. I quickly learned that in a crowded country like this you never did anything by yourself. He smiled at me in welcome, gold tooth glinting, and placed my suitcase on his head to carry it for me.

Then he glanced down expectantly at my shoes. I looked at them too. Then at the muddy ground ahead of me. Then down again at the feet of my welcoming party - all bare and caked in dirt to well above the ankle. Well, I thought, I may as well get stuck in - in for a penny, in for a pound as they say in England. I rolled up my trouser legs, removed my leather shoes and socks and tentatively plunged my toes into the sticky mud.

I remained this way for four months, sloshing about between the green paddy fields, the blue ocean, banana trees, palm trees, mangroves and mud. I would walk for miles and miles, traversing the numerous little streams that crisscrossed the island, to visit my patients at their paddy farms and fishing villages.

The island's little school became my home. I set up my makeshift office in one corner of the classroom and, by day, I would either help the head teacher, do some basic English tutoring, tend to the maladies of anyone who came by, or else go and call on my patients in their homes.

The inhabitants of Moudubi were incredibly friendly, warm and curious. I learned much about community hospitality from them. Here they lived so closely with nature that the margins between life and death were incredibly thin. They were very poor and often hungry.

Yet, at every meal time, one family or another would deliver me delicious food with rice, dhal and curry, or fish, separated into different sections in a tiffin carrier. It was always good and piping hot. Meal times were an exciting surprise and I always looked forward to prying the lid from the steaming pot to discover what lay within. I was amazed by their kindness. I knew they were very poor and were obviously making sacrifices to feed me in some style.

After my initial encounter with the head of the island he invited me to his house - built on stilts - for dinner. I learned that he was a very shy man. In time he grew to trust me and even consulted me on the ailments of one of his daughters-in-law, a young woman named Farzana. This was a big accomplishment for me, as it was very unusual to be permitted to examine a female patient.

She was not much older than myself and had already produced three children. She complained of pains and aches everywhere and from feeling tired all the time. This general malaise was a common affliction on Moudubi, doubtless down to the hard physical labour that both the men and women performed in the paddy fields, combined with the limitations of their diet.

Almost everyone was malnourished to some degree, particularly the women. Their diets were good on paper - they had fish, coconut, rice, fruit and vegetables but, in this South Asian culture, the women would prepare the food for the men to eat first and then have whatever was leftover for themselves. This, combined with the strains on the body due to repeated child birth, meant that the health of the women was most precarious.

As far as I could judge, Farzana had nothing specifically wrong with her other than the psychological stresses of living in the huge extended family that consisted of this patriarchal headman, his domineering wife and five sons, three of whom were also married with children. I prescribed her my standard treatment of multi-vitamins and iron tablets - she was bound to be anaemic - and suggested she take some rest away from the family from time to time. This was the answer I gave to most of my patients - vitamins and rest.

After my day's work was over, I would climb onto the school roof to watch the magnificent sunset, followed by the star-rise over the sea. Once it was dark, I would crawl into my makeshift bed under the teacher's desk in the classroom below, to read by the light of my hurricane lamp. Along with some medical manuals, I had brought with me the thickest books I could find - Charles Dickens, Tolstoy's *Anna Karenina* and a couple of *James Bond* paperbacks. There I would sleep until I was awakened by the sound of people bathing under the nearby pump in the morning.

The school was very important. It was the centre for education, my makeshift clinic, and the location of the water pump. Its high status as the only concrete structure on the island meant that it was also the cyclone shelter. Cyclones can sometimes reach utterly devastating winds of one-hundred-and-thirty miles-per-hour, but storms this bad were unusual. Mostly they were an unpleasant yet manageable part of island life.

When the weather front would come in - characterised by accelerated winds and rising sea levels - everyone within distance would make for the school to take shelter. If the water levels rose higher than usual you would climb onto the school roof and hope that they would not overspill the two-storey building. If however you were away from the school when a cyclone hit you would need to seek safety elsewhere.

***

This is exactly what happened to me one afternoon, when I was out on one of my many walks across the island. A cyclone - mercifully not a very bad one - struck and there was no way to get back to the concrete stability of the school building. I was instructed by some of the locals in the correct way to scramble up a palm tree and hang on there for dear life.

It had to be a palm tree, they explained, because they are incredibly well-designed for surviving this environment. Their trunks will bend and flex in the high winds and gushing waves, but they are strong and supple enough not to break.

Despite the grand sporting traditions of Wellington College - the British boarding school from whence I had just come - I was still not strong and the trunk of the tree was smooth and slippery, slick from the lashing rainwater. Yet I was amazed at how fast I could climb with the fear of the storm propelling me upwards. As an honoured guest, I was ushered up the palm tree first, and supported by those below me. They wanted to look after me and could tell I was not the world's most natural tree-climber.

There I clung, at the top of this swaying, bending tree, in seventy miles per hour winds, for six long hours. By hour three my panic had subsided somewhat and I had time to reflect. Only a few short months ago, I had been studying the latest scientific theories from the comfort of a warm, oak-clad classroom tucked away in a quiet fold of the Berkshire countryside. I could not have imagined then that the following summer I'd find myself clinging to a palm tree, so close to the seething storm water below that I could have reached out and touched it with my outstretched hand.

It occurred to me then that Wellington was still there, of course. Those sumptuous classrooms would be empty now, ready to welcome a fresh crop of haughty, spoilt young boys come September. That such wealth and privilege existed in the same world as the abject poverty I saw here seemed unbelievable to me. Progress steamed ahead elsewhere, while even the most basic development by-passed far-off places like this.

The people here were clever. The children I taught in school learned easily and were, I suspected, far more eager for knowledge than many of my peers had been at boarding school. I wondered what these island children would be capable of doing, if only they were given the same chances as I had been.

They were incredibly well adapted to their environment. They were very savvy and knew how to survive - not just with local knowhow like this palm tree trick, but with the cohesion of a community that took care of all its members, especially in such a marginalised society.

Thank god they extended this magnanimous spirit to care about a clueless visitor like me, or I'd have been drowned by the storm. In my teenage immaturity I had thought I was the one coming to help them, but here it was me that depended so totally on them.

Moudubi was my first experience of *humanitarianism* - not just through my own volunteering on the island, but also from the kindness the people showed me in return. It really changed me. Before I came, I had been concerned mostly with improving my own standing through pursuing education at elite British institutions. Now, all that had changed. My experience living as part of this society who had so little yet gave so much, transformed my purpose. I now wanted to use my huge luck and small talents to improve the lives of others across the world.

When my companions in the tree judged it safe to descend again, it was really difficult to unclench myself as I had been holding on so tight. I had lacerations all over my arms and stomach from the sharp palm fronds and my muscles screamed from the effort of holding on.

I had clung to the tree for what seemed like hours, but now that I no longer had extreme fear to drive me on, climbing down proved very, very difficult. The tree trunk was wet and salty and I fell the last few feet into the waiting arms of my new friends.

This was the first of several cyclones I spent stuck at the top of a palm tree, oscillating back and forth in high winds over rushing water. Weeks into my time on Moudubi, I thought nothing of shinning up a palm tree to wait out the worst of the storms. Living there was certainly precarious, and although people walked perilously close to the edge each day, it was a way of life that I admired and enjoyed.

I had been on Moudubi for three months, tending my patients for their aches and pains, hook-worm, vitamin deficiencies, and anaemia. Everything was going well. I had settled into island life, had long ago switched my western clothes for a light *lungi* - a loose wrap - and my feet were hardened to walking barefoot in the mud.

My favourite spot on the island was the one and only café. A rough, wooden building standing on stilts, it was strategically located alongside the main pathway that ran from the jetty to the school - Moudubi's answer to a major highway. This was also where the island's mail was delivered. It was a true hub of the community and people were always stopping-by.

I would sit at one of the benches, my back resting against the wooden wall, and order hot, strong *chai* - spiced tea - from Munim, the café owner. He would squat in the middle of the room on a slightly raised platform, surrounded by his pots and pans, tending to his constantly burning *chula* - an open cooking fire.

He would also make *chewra*, fluffed up roasted rice. This could be eaten with a pinch of salt or a touch of rough cane sugar, known as *gur*. He also had, much to my delight, my old favourite - glucose biscuits. I had missed these during my time in England and devoured them with relish. Munim would keep them in a large glass jar to preserve their crispness in the moist climate, and I was grateful for that. There are few things more horrible than soggy biscuits.

Munim was a rather shy, middle-aged man. He was very unlike your typical gossipy café owner, but as the weeks passed - and often the café was empty apart from the two of us - we became friendly. Other than the schoolteacher, nobody on the island spoke much English. So my Bangla had rapidly improved. Between this, some broken English and a touch of universal sign language thrown into the mix, we were able to hold quite in-depth discussions.

***

The biggest problem for Munim was the lack of basic services on the island, a problem I was about to encounter for myself with tragic results. I was in the café one afternoon sipping tea from one of Munim's transparent Pyrex mugs and reading my favourite book at the time, David Werner's *Where There Is No Doctor,* when a distraught-looking boy came sprinting into the café to grab me by the arm.

Startled, I set down my tea and dropped my book. "What is it?" I asked him, in Bangla. "What's wrong?"

"Come quickly Mukesh *bhai* (brother). It's my sister. We need you," he gasped, breathlessly. I dashed after him, pausing only to retrieve my makeshift doctor's bag from under the bench. Together, we splashed through the mud and water to his home. There, in a small house surrounded by a crowd of concerned onlookers, lay a young girl in a pitiful state. She couldn't have been any older than sixteen but her limited diet had stunted her development, so her body resembled that of a much younger child.

She was heavily pregnant, drenched in sweat and writhing in the agonies of labour. I was informed that she had been this way for twenty-four hours and the local midwife had not been able to deliver the baby. In their desperation they had called on me to see if I could help. They had great respect for me that I felt was quite un-deserved. If the midwife had had no luck, then what use was I going to be? A teenage boy with vitamin pills and a head full of books, but no practical experience?

I had never done anything remotely like this before. I examined her, but had no experience to work out which way the baby lay and if the midwife had not been able to deliver it, what hope did I have? Still, I did my best to look doctorly. "Look, we have to get her to hospital upriver, as this is very serious," I announced.

We set about organising the construction of a makeshift stretcher to transport her to the jetty. I sent Saif and some of the other boys to find someone to ready the fastest motor-launch around, to facilitate the evacuation, a gruelling six-hour slug upstream against the prevailing tide. Then began the task of transporting this poor girl across the island. Her village was close to Moudubi's centre and an hour's walk from the coast across the paddy fields.

A cyclone had hit two days before and the water levels were still high. In conditions like this, walking from village to village was an expedition in itself. Deep gullies and trenches that separated the paddy fields filled up with gushing water and were only passable by bamboo-rod bridges that you clung onto with your toes.

Having to manoeuvre a stretcher over these with a woman in obstructed labour took incredible effort and skill. Luckily the men and women of Moudubi had been living this way their whole lives, so there was nobody better equipped to deal with this challenge.

The girl was not very heavy, even nine months pregnant. I think the real problem was that the baby was just too big for her undernourished body to cope with. She screamed and writhed in pain as the stretcher bearers continued doggedly on, until we arrived at the jetty. Saif was there, hopping from foot to foot, and behind him bobbed the motor boat, puffing smoke, ready to whisk her away.

I began directing the stretcher-bearers on how to get her aboard, but before we could manage it, her small writhing body fell suddenly limp. The expression of pain vanished from her face and her countenance became suddenly blank.

She was gone.

We could not save her.

I could not save her.

The local people were very philosophical about the whole thing. Even little Saif's expression hardened resolutely, as the realities of life in Moudubi hit home. But I was heartbroken and shocked.

I lamented my own lack of knowledge and felt guilty that I had been unable to save her. I had come here thinking I was invincible, that I could do anything I put my mind to, but I learned the hardest way that sometimes, despite all your best efforts, there is literally nothing you can do.

I felt so hopeless, helpless and angry at myself, plus I was furious at the circumstances that had allowed this to take place. The unfairness of it all overwhelmed me. Why had she been married so young? She was just a child really. Why were there no medical services on the island? Why were there no proper doctors or clinics? Why didn't these people act earlier? She should have been moved hours before. These questions chased each other around my head for weeks.

Speaking to the locals in Munim's café, I learnt that on Moudubi, this was just what happened. Here you were born and you died and that was that. In a country that was so poor and underdeveloped, maternal and infant mortality was a tragic fact of life, but I found it much harder to accept.

***

My journey to Moudubi had awakened something inside me. I had seen the incredible kindness of the people. I had felt the heartbreak of my failure to save the young girl in labour. My eyes had been opened to a way of life - and death - that I had known nothing about. I would never be the same again. I felt much, much older than when I'd arrived on the island.

When my time came to leave Moudubi, a large part of me didn't want to go. This trip was only supposed to be a stopgap. A means to an end to facilitate my journey home to India, but instead it had altered something inside me. I felt that I had found my true calling. I knew what I wanted to do with my life. I wanted to do good in places like Moudubi.

However, I also knew that in order to achieve this I had to return to my studies in the west, so that I could learn how to do good in a useful and meaningful way. Once I was a qualified medical doctor I was sure I would not feel so helpless when faced with similar situations.

Resolutely, I opened my suitcase to retrieve my western clothes and leave my barefoot life behind me. I pulled on my trousers, but they were too big for me now that I had swapped bread and butter pudding for coconut curry. I searched for my leather belt only to find it completely covered with green fungus. My shoes were rotted away too from the humidity, so I returned home in flipflops.

I bade farewell to all my good friends on Moudubi. Practically the whole island had come to wave me off, and there were hugs and tears all around - most of them from me. I clambered onto the little boat and waved goodbye, as we put-putted upriver and back to my 'real' life.

From then on Moudubi haunted me. When you live for six months on a diet of coarse rice and prawns it is a hard thing to forget. It was really a culture shock going to my parents in India, let alone on to Oxford. When I arrived home my mother was horrified. I had returned from an elite school in England looking like an emaciated tramp, my trousers hanging off my skinny hips by a length of string.

The whole time I was home she was busy in the kitchen, feeding me up on delicious home-cooked meals. By the time I returned to the UK I was back to my old self again. On the outside at least. But the memories of Moudubi hadn't left me, and I was still resolved to lead a life where I could be useful to people who lived in poverty on the edge of the world, their lives hanging in the balance, constantly under threat of floods, famine and the other vagaries of fate.

More than anything, I felt I would never get over the grief of losing Saif's sister. In a way I never have. I felt abject heartache and regret at the circumstances that led to her death. Ever since that lamentable day I have fought my hardest for women to get access to healthcare and to end violence against women, for that's what this was in my opinion. Violence against women comes in myriad forms and this young girl's death in childbirth was certainly one of them, because she should never have been married so young.

Bringing about change to combat such ill would become one of my life's great missions.

Chapter Twelve

*I would like to be remembered as a person who wanted to be free…
so other people would be also free.*
Rosa Parks

MY LOCAL GUIDE, DRIVER, AND ALL-AROUND FIXER, Kunal, glanced at me in the rear-view mirror as he steered the car through the thronging backstreets of Calcutta (now called Kolkata).

"We're almost there Sir," he said. "Though I have to tell you, if all you wanted was a nice girl I could have arranged one for you back in your hotel. There was really no reason for us to drive all this way."

I rolled my eyes good-humouredly at him. Though I was growing tired of his jokes - there had been many on this very long drive - it was a very particular red-light district that I was interested in, and for a very different set of reasons than Kunal implied.

The Sonagachi area of Kolkata is South Asia's largest and most infamous prostitution district. The name translates literally as "golden village," but the only gold being made there lines the pockets of the pimps and smugglers as they profiteer off the trade in human flesh.

Sweet, ripening, virginal, peach-like girls - that was how they described their victims, some as young as twelve, when they sold them into sexual slavery to the highest bidder. The fresher and juicier the fruit, the better the price, so they claimed.

I was on an official visit to India to review some British aid projects, and realised I had just enough time to squeeze in a trip to this infamous place. Women's health remained very important to me, so I wanted to see for myself the conditions in which these women and girls lived, how we might help them and how we might eventually bring about a stop to this most evil business, where sexual violence and exploitation ran riot.

Kunal parked the car and we clambered out into the furnace-like heat. Life at its most noisy, dirty, precarious, squalid and energetic oozed from every garishly-painted brick and rusted pipe. Here, where the standards of living were so terribly low, life clung on doggedly. The air seemed to hum and vibrate with it.

We entered Sonagachi. I knew where we were even without Kunal's explanation, for there were women everywhere. Women of all ages, sitting on steps, leaning against walls and doorways, chatting together, brushing each other's hair, or breast-feeding young children.

My first impression was that of glimpsing a girls' sleepover. I had three daughters back at home in Cambridgeshire and was accustomed to the house being full of young girls, gossiping about friends, consoling each other over first heartbreaks, conducting makeovers and trying out different fashion trends.

Here in Sonagachi, as with my teenage daughters, I sensed a real bond of female support and friendship. Some of these girls looked terribly young, but there were much older women too - who had presumably worked in the brothels since they themselves were young girls.

I was overwhelmed by how colourful they all were. I didn't know quite what I had been expecting, really. India is famous for its colour and Kolkata is one of the four largest cities in the country, so of course it was going to be colourful. For some reason I had expected the grizzly realities these women lived through to have sucked the joy and vibrancy from them, leaving them despondent and pallid, like the survivors of sexual violence I had met in Rwanda.

Not so here. These women had brightly painted makeup, and often styled their hair uncovered, flowing loose, long and dark down their backs. They wore vivid saris, *salwar kameez*, and western-style dresses too. They ornamented themselves with elaborate hair decorations and cheap garish jewellery.

Many had lightened their skin with white makeup - as paleness is considered desirable in India - and their faces shone almost blue against the warm tones around them. They reminded me of the paintings of Hindu goddesses I had seen growing up as a child in Bihar.

In spite of all my prior knowledge, I was surprised to see women who looked like this in the country of my birth. Female modesty is usually prized in India, and although it isn't strictly enforced, I was used to seeing most women covered up in public. To see an Indian girl with her hair cascading around bare shoulders, suggested an incredible level of intimacy that I was unprepared for.

Perhaps I had spent too long in the west, but these women appeared more liberated than most in India, although I knew that in reality the opposite was true. Any personal liberty they seemed to have was a by-product of a life where they were treated as little more than sexual slaves.

They talked and laughed conspiratorially, until they noticed us men wandering around. At once their demeanours transformed. They "turned on" their charms and made eyes at us, attempting to project the right level of sexiness and mystery to lure us into their rooms and out of our clothes, and our money out of our wallets.

We walked on. Kunal strode confidently between the rows of colourful brick-built buildings. Indicating the district in front of us he announced, "All these are whorehouses. As far as you can see."

The buildings closest to the road didn't seem so bad, but as we wound our way deeper into the maze of alleyways the brothels became increasingly ramshackle. Dwellings built from a combination of rusty panels of corrugated metal, woven grass-fibre, sheet plastic and planks of wood, all patched together to form shelters. Each had curtains of hessian sacking or thinning cloth hanging at the doors. Most were tied open, so I could catch a glimpse of the makeshift rooms inside. Some were drawn closed for privacy, though often they were so threadbare I could discern human shapes moving within.

***

After my postgraduate degree, I'd taken my first job at the Health Education Authority in London, and nobody could have predicted then how AIDS would explode into the worldwide crisis it did. It became the nemesis I would have to contend with again and again throughout my life.

Back then we understood little about it. We knew that it had been discovered first in Africa. We also saw that it seemed to target those at society's fringes - promiscuous people, gay men, drug addicts and sex workers. The days of Margaret Thatcher's reign were rife with intolerance and contempt for those marginalised groups, so there was a huge stigma attached to the disease.

I had encountered similar attitudes in Southern Africa, but thanks to the Drs McAllister and their ilk - the missionary doctors who had run the Zimbabwe hospital - we were fighting AIDS with new drugs and treatment.

Here in Calcutta, I once again saw the tell-tale signs of AIDS. I felt naturally predisposed to notice these now, after so many years spent in close proximity to the virus: extreme weight loss, swollen necks, ulcerations on the mouth, rashes on the skin. I wondered how rampant it was here, and how many of those seemingly radiant, smiling women were already infected.

One girl stood by herself at a doorway. She wore a yellow western-style strappy dress that was fraying at the hem. A grubby-looking toddler played in the dust at her feet. I assumed this was her own daughter, though she looked to be no more than fifteen years old herself. She smiled at me and I smiled back, in what I hoped was a non-threatening manner, and approached her for a conversation.

At my approach she shooed the small child out into the street and I heard her whisper "Oh, uncle is here. Uncle is coming. You need to go and play outside for a while." The little one looked distraught and clung to her mother's bare legs. As she continued to coerce her out of the door, I could see it was desperately hard for the young woman to ignore the baby's pleas for closeness.

"Oh no, no," I told her, waving my hands, palms towards her, to try to convey the innocence of my intention. "Just a conversation. I just want to talk to you; the baby can stay."

She frowned at me with distrust in her eyes. I guess this must be a weird request to get from a man, particularly an Indian man in his forties dressed in western clothes, speaking with her in patchy Hindi - for it always takes me a little while to readjust to my mother tongue, after so long surrounded by English speakers. I must have seemed suspicious.

"What do you want?" she asked, with caution in her voice.

"I just want to ask you some questions," I told her, with what I hoped was a friendly smile.

With this her eyes glanced past me to look into another shadowy doorway across the small dirt street. With the slight movement of her head I noticed the blue blush of a bruise under the pale makeup on her left temple and around her eye. I turned to see where she was looking and saw the shadow of a man watching our interaction with interest from across the dirty pathway. I had not noticed him before.

She looked back at me, fear visible in her features and whispered pleadingly, "No trouble, no trouble."

The man in the doorway seemed to have made up his mind, and began to approach me threateningly but Kunal, ever vigilant, intercepted him with a charming smile and disarming words.

"Hello my brother, how are you?" He slipped his arm around the man's shoulder and made as if to introduce him to me like they were old friends. "This is my friend Mukesh," he went on. "It's his first time, and he is ignorant of our customs here, and clearly so impressed by your beautiful girls he forgot his manners."

Seemingly appeased by Kunal's fast-thinking, this small, mean-looking man smiled a lewd grin and said that, of course, we were welcome to any of his girls that took our fancy.

"Oh, but I wish that we had time," Kunal charmed. "Unfortunately we have to leave, but next time my brother, next time for sure. We really must be going now, isn't that so Mukesh?"

"Uh, yes?" I ventured. "Yes we must."

I glanced back to the girl with the black-eye, but already she had scooped up her infant daughter and retreated inside her room. Kunal steered me back through the mean streets, one hand firmly on my shoulder should I try to cause any more trouble with the locals.

I hoped that by trying to speak to this girl I would not bring retribution down on her from her pimp. I hoped we would be able to do something to help her, and to make sure her little daughter was saved from the same sad destiny in a few years' time. A group of women waved us goodbye, asking us to "come again soon" with cackles of wicked laugher and salacious glints in their eyes, like a flock of coquettish parrots.

After some chastisement from Kunal about knowing when, where and to whom to ask questions without getting us beaten up, he settled into silence for the drive back to my hotel and I was left with only my thoughts for company.

On the hot, dusty drive I reflected on all I had seen. There was clearly a true bond of solidarity here among the women, but the men obviously ran the show. Hustlers and pimps were ever-present, and they were clearly none too happy with nosey do-gooders like me snooping around.

But the question remained - how was I going to find out what these women needed if I was unable to talk with them? Despite the power of the female sisterhood they offered one and other they were clearly in dire trouble.

There were children having children who would grow up in the brothels and, no doubt, soon find themselves subjected to the worst kind of physical and sexual abuse. There was also the ever-present threat of AIDS that stalked those rickety streets. The questions of how to make them safer and how to best solve these problems whirled around in my head.

***

I returned to London and spoke to my boss about my discoveries. It was agreed that I should return to talk to those women, but as we were very busy in the department, it could only be a short trip. I got back to work, thinking of everything I wanted to ask them and how best to do so. Why did they do the work they did? How did they get there? What were their plans? How could we help? What did they need?

Returning to my office I asked a junior staff member to send a cable to the British High Commission in Calcutta, to ask them to arrange for a group of sex workers from Sonagachi to come and see me for a meeting. If Kunal thought it was unsafe to speak to them in their own environment, I would ask them to come to me instead.

The official channel for the Foreign Office in London to communicate with Embassies and High Commissions across the globe is by diplomatic cable. These go through a secure system. Any government department communicating abroad uses the same cables, which have different levels of security clearance - Top Secret, Secret, Confidential, Restricted - and by convention, there is a standard contact list that is cold copied into these cables, for purposes of wider coordination.

The cable I had requested my staffer to send went out, and I realised with a mixture of dismay, embarrassment and amusement that he had sent the following:

DR KAPILA VISITING CALCUTTA OVERNIGHT FROM LONDON STOP PLEASE ARRANGE MEET AND GREET AT AIRPORT AND ACCOMMODATION AT THE OBEROI STOP HE WOULD LIKE 10-15 SEX WORKERS FROM SONAGACHI IN HIS ROOM THAT EVENING DASH PLEASE ORGANISE STOP

This was sent to all the major embassies and government departments on the South Asia cables distribution list. The staff member who sent it was a little inexperienced. I hoped that there was no harm done, as everyone was surely aware that if you really wanted to solicit sex workers you didn't do it via diplomatic cable! It kept our office laughing for weeks.

At the very least the cable did its job, for when I returned to Calcutta a group of twelve women came to see me at the Oberoi Grand, the smartest hotel in the city. I met them in the luxe lobby with its inlaid floors of green patterned marble and crystal chandeliers tinkling gently overhead. I did my best to make them feel comfortable and at ease. I offered them dinner and I thought it was only right to pay them for their time, although claiming expenses for the entertainment of twelve sex workers did little to quell the office giggling back in London.

Again, I admired the effort they had made with their appearance. In addition to their bright clothes they had varnished nails, wore powder and lipstick and dramatic kohl around their eyes. They each possessed an aura of gravitas and composure and I soon forgot the incongruity of seeing them in this hotel. Before long, they seemed to blend perfectly with the majesty of the place - until I remembered the corrugated iron hovels they had left behind.

Their choice of profession did not shock or embarrass me. When combatting AIDS in the 1980s I had spent a lot of time speaking with sex workers in the UK. They taught me a great deal, least of all about my own prejudices. After much agonising I still struggle with the ethics of selling sex. Ultimately, I long for a world where people are not valued as sexual objects but as equal humans. In such a world prostitution as we know it now would not exist. Unfortunately, that reality is still a long way off.

Until this kind of enlightened outcome is reached, we have to do more to make sex work safer. I could not do much to render prostitution obsolete, but I could focus on tackling the exploitation of vulnerable people who often get caught in its web. The sex workers I met in London were truly remarkable women. Like many who inhabit the "underclass," I discovered they were often very intelligent. Much like the storm-wracked islanders of Moudubi, you had to be smart or you wouldn't survive for long.

Essentially, they were clever professionals running their profitable business like any other. A lot of them even had husbands and kids at home. Some had been forced into the game by circumstances beyond their control, but none of them were anything less than dignified human beings. They had made - or been compelled to make - certain choices and were managing them as best as they could.

It was in their interests as businesswomen to remain healthy, and they wanted improved safety for themselves and their sisters, as sex was often attended by violence. They were courageous women and we were not interested in trying to force them to stop what they could not. Instead we provided them with a service where they could get testing for sexually transmitted infections, condoms and advice to keep safe and healthy.

The sex workers in Calcutta were similar in some ways. They too were highly intelligent women who were, by and large, making the best of a difficult situation. They too wanted education and resources to make the business of selling sex safer. They too wanted safety and protection for themselves and their families. But for the majority, the only families they had were the women they surrounded themselves with, and the children sired by their pimps, traffickers or nameless, faceless clients.

One woman named Ambi, who was twenty-two, and had been

working in Sonagachi for nine years, told me a story typical for girls in the golden village. She had a lovely round face with prominent cheekbones and a wide smile. She wore a golden *bindi* on her forehead, a small golden stud in her nose, deep red lipstick and a vibrant orange sari. In a soft, high voice, that was remarkably calm and measured given the traumas of her story, she recounted her own experience of human trafficking.

"I am not from India," she began. "I am from Nepal. We are mostly Nepalese, the girls in Sonagachi. They bring us here from our home country because our skin is naturally paler than Indian girls and that is what is considered to be most beautiful to the men in this culture.

"One day, just after my twelfth birthday, men came to my village to barter with the families. My parents were poor and they were promised a lot of money to let me go with these men. I didn't want to go, but they said I was to be a child minder in the big city and that I would be helping to support our family, so really I had little choice but to agree.

"I have given it much thought over many sleepless nights and I think that honestly in their heart of hearts my parents never really believed that story. I have heard from other girls that they take only the prettiest. The prettier the girl, the more money they make. Why would it matter how pretty you were if you were only going to be looking after children? They must have known the truth, at least on some level.

"The smugglers transported us over the border very easily, myself and some other girls, and brought us to Calcutta where we were shown to the brothel owners and inspected like a crop of apples. I was still unaware of what was going on, but I suspected, even in my child's mind, that I had been lied to and something was terribly wrong. The traffickers seemed to be showing us off, like prized pigs. 'Juicy young virgins' they called us; 'Succulent flesh, just ripe to pluck.' For a terrifying moment I was worried they were going to eat me! But the reality of what they were planning wasn't really much better.

"The man who bought me from the smugglers, Sparsh was his name, did not have his way with me then but instead wanted to wait to sell my virginity to the customer willing to pay the most for it. Virgins are a rare thing in Sonagachi as you can imagine, and many men will pay top rupee for one.

"He took me to the brothel, not a bad one all things considered. I suppose I am one of the lucky ones. He showed me my small room where I would be living and sharing with two other girls. That night I huddled up against the wall in a tiny ball, shaking and alone, quivering with fear, my small body wracked with sobs. I flinched when I felt a warm hand on my shoulder. But then a woman's voice, low and sweet spoke gently to me.

"'Shush child, there-there, I know you're afraid. But there is comfort here for you, and kindness. Not everyone here wants to hurt you - although I am not going to lie to you, there are many who do.'

"I lifted my head and squirmed into a sitting position. Back pressed defensively against the wall and knees still clutched tight to my chest. But I turned my tear-stained face upwards to meet the gaze of that soft and kindly voice.

"I remember how her appearance startled me then. Her face looked exactly like one of the ceremonial-style puppets the women in my village made to sell to tourists. She had painted it such rich colours, and she wore her hair uncovered and only had a small shift dress.

"My mother warned my sisters and I against the perils of being an 'immodest' woman, a concept I was still too young to really understand, though I knew that makeup and shift dresses definitely signalled that this woman embodied everything my mother had feared. Still, she was smiling and her words were tender, and I was in dire need of a friend at this moment.

"'My name is Zoya,' she told me. 'What is your name?' I blinked dumbly at her.

"'You do have a name, don't you? Little mouse?' she asked, patiently. I heard a small giggle from behind her then and glanced to see that we were not alone in the room. About six or seven other young women, ranging from Zoya's age - about twenty - to some girls even younger than me. They had all crept in while I had been crying and were watching me with interest and pity.

"'I'm... I'm Ambi' I whispered, barely audibly in the hushed room.

"'Welcome, Ambi,' she said warmly. 'There will be time for the rest of the introductions later, but be assured all the girls are eager to meet you. We're a family here, aren't we girls? And we take care of each other.' There was a mumble of general agreement from the assembly.

"'But first there is something very important I have to explain to you. I am going to tell you what is going to happen next. It's going to be scary and I'm so sorry that I have to have this conversation with you, but it is very, very important that you listen to me and you understand everything that I say.'

"Zoya then went on to explain that a man would come and he would force himself onto me. That it would be horrible and it would hurt but that I must try not to cry and I must not fight back, that was the best chance I had to prevent him from getting violent.

"I cried and cried. I couldn't believe it was true. But the next day everything she said came to pass. It was terrible, but I was glad I knew what to expect or I would have been even more traumatised.

"After that Zoya and the other girls taught me the ways of life in Sonagachi. We would have up to twenty clients a day, for which Sparsh would be paid around five hundred rupees and we would get only one hundred each day. I learned that Zoya was Sparsh's favourite and she acted as a kind of bridge between him and the rest of the girls. I knew the truth that she hated Sparsh, but she did what she had to do to make the best possible life for herself, and she encouraged me to do the same. There are not many girls who get to stay permanently in Sonagachi, and because I had Zoya to teach me how I should behave, to make myself valuable to Sparsh, I was fortunate to become one of these. The story is very different for many girls."

"Why?" I asked her "What happens to these others?"

Another of the women, Mansi, answered this. She wore a deep cerise sari and her long chestnut hair hung in a sleek plait down her back, and a thin golden chain was suspended between her nose and ear.

"Most Nepali girls are not so lucky," she said. "Most of them are taken from their families as Ambi described and are sent first to Calcutta, where they are used by the men who come to Sonagachi. Often the sex tourists come from all over the world and have lots of money to spend on these young girls. There is always a demand for "fresh" girls, so when the smugglers bring the "fresh meat" as they call it, the girls who have already been used are taken on to smaller cities where they are pimped out again to less sophisticated groups of men. From there they are taken to smaller and smaller cities, getting more and more abused until, well, nobody knows what becomes of them in the end."

I was appalled at these stories of young girls sold into sexual slavery.

"What can we do to help? What can I do to help? What would you like to help your situation?"

"You have heard of the infamous Black Hole of Calcutta?" Mansi continued. "The prison where Indians kept prisoners of war? It was greatly feared, because once you went in you would never see the light of day again? Human trafficking is the real black hole of Calcutta, because there is no way for us to get out. There is no hope of a life of freedom for us.

"Even if we were to escape somehow, there is no normal life for a reformed prostitute. The country is so sexist that no man would ever marry us. No man could look past the life we have led and see us for the people we are underneath the makeup and clothes. What chance do we have on our own? It is too late for us to stop. This is it for us now. But we would like to see the situation in Nepal changed, so that in future the women who sell their bodies in Sonagachi do so out of choice rather than exploitation."

"How would you suggest we do that?" I asked. I knew they would have thought much about this over the long years in the brothel.

"The only way to stop the problem in the long-term, is to bring development and gender equality to Nepal," Ambi stated. "It is a very poor and un-equal country. This is the root cause of all our problems."

"In Nepal it is the custom for the family of the bride to pay a wedding dowry," Mansi went on "Girls must be married off and the dowry must be large in order to obtain a good match. If a family has lots of girls it is expensive for them. Families can be ruined in some cases. So rather than ruining the family financially, they ruin their girls instead."

"If we could make women equal to men, or more equal," Ambi interjected, "there would be no need for dowries and families could stop selling their girls into the sex trade."

"We think the best way to do this is education," Mansi continued. "Education for girls and boys the same, so that everyone can work and get a good job and earn money for themselves. Plus education for everyone in Nepal about places like Sonagachi and what becomes of girls who go there. If everyone in Nepal knew about what is taking place, then the pressure from society would stop families from doing it. Many people are ignorant as to where the girls go, but Nepal is not a cruel country. The people would protect their young and vulnerable if they knew the truth."

"Absolutely," I agreed. "That makes perfect sense. I will do what I can to implement your ideas, and to try to stop what has happened to you from happening to others in the future. We can also devise a programme to educate Indians and Nepalese alike about sex work and promote nationwide efforts for gender equality. Hopefully this will help to break the stigma in the long run.

"But for those for whom you say it is already too late - what can I do to help you? In the short term? What do you need?"

"We are worried about diseases," one woman volunteered. "Some of the girls get very sick, very thin, and then they die... We hear rumours as to why this occurs - AIDS - but nobody knows for sure what the cause of this is. It seems to be all different things."

"The best way to combat AIDS," I told her, "is to provide information about safe sex and how to avoid catching the virus. We can also provide condoms to protect against HIV and different sexually transmitted diseases. We have lots of experience in this field, so this is definitely something we can help you with. What else?"

"The babies and the young children," said another woman, wearing a jade green sari. "When the clients come, we have to turn them into the street or send them to friends to look after, this is not always very safe for them. A crèche - somewhere for them to be safe while we work - would be a big comfort."

"And education," Ambi interjected, fixing me with a stare. "I want education for my daughters that I did not have, so that they can have a better life and not fall prey to the same fate."

I promised I would do all I could to fulfil their requests.

When dinner and talking were done I thanked these courageous, enterprising women for their time, reimbursed them financially of course, and retired to my room. I felt disturbed by Ambi's story, appalled by how widespread this horrendous problem seemed, yet I was impressed by the grace and intelligence she and the others had exemplified.

In spite of the abuses they had endured, their first thoughts for help were not for themselves, but for other girls in Nepal. Above all they wanted long term solutions to bring about lasting change, eventually bringing the sexual exploitation they had suffered to an end.

It was a similar desire to my own. I hoped that eventually, if we could reach a state of equality where women were truly viewed as equal to men, there would be no more sexual exploitation. Until that time however, I was committed to helping the women here any way I could.

On my return to London I devised a programme that would provide childcare and sex education in Sonagachi, with longer term preventative measures to stop the problem of human trafficking in Nepal. We combined humanitarianism and development in one scheme, to combat the long-term causes of the sex trade.

My time in Sonagachi had showed me the very worst of gender violence and inequality, yet I still hoped for a more egalitarian world where women were viewed the same as men. I felt that fairness and freedom between all genders and races is the ultimate goal. Until that goal can be reached, I vowed to continue to champion women's health in both the hardest to reach places in the world, and the marginalised spaces in our own society.

Chapter Thirteen

We are what our thoughts have made us; so take care about what you think. Words are secondary. Thoughts live; they travel far.
Swami Vivekananda

I TOOK A REFRESHING SIP OF MY SECOND GIN AND TONIC and looked out of the airplane window at the sparkling stars. I checked my watch and pondered that we must now be half way between London and New York.

In my frequent trips to America, I liked to catch this 6 pm British Airways flight, as it would arrive into New York City at 9 pm local time, providing the opportunity to catch a few hours' sleep before jet lag would inevitably awaken me at 4 am. I had already done a day's work at DFID in London and had another one starting early at UN headquarters in Manhattan.

I stretched out my legs and considered maybe catching an inflight movie before dozing off, when a call went out on the intercom.

"Is there a doctor on board?" the voice of the stewardess rang out through the speaker.

I was technically a qualified medical doctor, but with over three hundred other passengers I figured there was bound to be an actively-practicing MD on board. A few minutes later another call went out. I ignored this too. "What use could I be as I have been sitting in offices way too long?" I told my conscience.

Then the call rang out again, and I detected a note of panic in the flight-attendant's voice. "We urgently need a doctor."

The Hippocratic values that I had imbibed a long ago came back to me then, and I got to my feet and introduced myself. "I am a doctor," I said to the harassed-looking flight attendant.

"Come quickly," she replied and moved at surprising speed down the cabin in her smart high heels. Now I was on my feet, I felt a little tipsy from the gin but I followed the trademark blue hat with its silver swoosh bobbing along in front of me.

Then my eyes fell on a pregnant woman lying on the floor between first and business class. The sight was enough to sober me up instantly: she was covered in more blood than I had seen for a long time. Despite my medical training, I have always hated the sight of blood but now was not the time for squeamishness.

I got to my knees to check her vital signs. I couldn't feel her pulse. It was so weak from the torrents of blood she had lost. I quickly ascertained that she was bleeding from her vagina. Something must be horribly wrong with the pregnancy. She was very big, I would guess thirty-eight weeks, and I presumed ready to deliver very soon. She was drifting in and out of consciousness. She would not last much longer if I failed to stop the bleeding and neither would her unborn child.

I examined her abdomen and noted that the baby was lying transversely. I worked out she had a placenta praevia. This is where the placenta grows too low, obstructing the baby's way to the birth canal. Then any trauma, like turbulence on a plane, could cause the placenta to start bleeding uncontrollably.

If we had been on the ground, a bleeding placenta praevia was an emergency often requiring a helicopter evacuation, as the patient could bleed to death in a very short time. Standard teaching is that anyone at risk from this should be admitted to hospital at around thirty-four weeks. They would remain under observation, as bleeding can occur at any time in the final stage of the pregnancy and cause dire complications.

"We have to land the plane immediately or this woman is going to die," I told the flight attendant.

"I will inform the pilot," she replied, maintaining the calm-in-a-crisis manner that her training had prepared her for.

I returned to the semi-conscious patient wondering what I could do for her until the pilot was able to land. I tried to give her a drip but her veins were too collapsed. The drastic drop in her blood pressure meant I couldn't insert the needle. This was getting desperate.

"We are almost exactly between London and New York but the pilot can divert the plane to Gander in Canada and save an hour if you think that will help her?" The stewardess updated me.

"An hour could make all the difference," I told her. Yet even with the diversion we still had three hours flying time remaining. If I didn't act soon she would never make it.

Then I did something that I had only read about in text books. I called for the flight attendant to put pillows under the patient's pelvis and we tilted her head down. I balled my hand into a fist, took a deep breath and said a silent prayer to whatever gods might be listening. With that I plunged my fist into her vagina and pressed down hard with my other forearm onto her abdomen to compress the uterus.

I had read in medical school that this manoeuvre forms an internal bandage between the pressure from my hand and her abdomen. This should theoretically stop the bleeding. Much to my amazement, she started getting pinker and opened her eyes. I checked her life signs again and could feel a definite but very weak pulse.

My eyes met the gaze of the stewardess.

"This should quench the blood flow until we can land and get her into an ambulance," I told her.

So there I sat, sandwiched between business-class and first-class in a huge pool of coagulating blood with my fist in a stranger's vagina. I couldn't move because I didn't know what would happen if I did and I couldn't risk re-starting the bleeding.

Thank god it had worked, I thought to myself, or I would probably be arrested on arrival in New York for pretending to be a doctor, contributing to the poor woman's eventual death from blood loss.

***

I had a lot of time to take in the details of the scene during those three hours I spent kneeling by her side. She was a very well-dressed woman, in a fashionable outfit, all dolled up to go to the US. Maybe she had a husband waiting for her, excited for the arrival of his wife and their unborn child.

She was pretty. The makeup, artfully applied to her lips and eyes, stood out vibrantly against the ghostly pallor of her skin. Her long, painted fingernails were a vibrant crimson that competed with the redness of the pooling blood, drying on her skin and matting together her fashionably cut dark brown hair.

I guessed she must have been about twenty-eight years old. So much life ahead of her, I thought, or at least I hoped. I wondered then what had led her to take such a monumental risk in flying so late in her pregnancy. I found out later that she was Syrian and had wanted her baby to be born on US soil so badly that she had bribed her doctor to fake a certificate that proclaimed she was safe to travel. She must have known the risks involved, yet she had decided to make that choice anyway. Why?

I took her to be a wealthy, well-educated woman. At that time, Syria was not the war-torn country that it became later. Yet an American passport could open doors for her child to a better life. Maybe this is the kind of sacrifice that only a mother could make and understand.

Or maybe we had more in common than I realised. Was I too not a migrant? I had moved to the UK seeking education and a better life. Nobody forced me. I was not fleeing cyclones like the displaced Bangladeshis, nor violent retribution like the Hutus in Goma, nor ethnic massacres like my own father in Pakistan.

My family weren't poor or under threat, but we had the same wish that every other human has, the desire to improve our lot if we could. I considered my own mother, sending her eldest boy half-way across the world at the tender age of sixteen. That couldn't have been easy, and part of her must have longed to keep me safe and close by. Yet my parents encouraged me to go so that I might live a better life than they themselves had.

I didn't know this woman's personal situation but I had the impression that she, like me, wasn't running from anything.

The huge jet came screaming into Gander airport for emergency landing. As soon as we were stationary, the steps came up alongside so the medical crew could come aboard. The red lights of the assembled ambulances blinked through the windows of the plane and the air rang with sirens. Yet the first person who walked on board was a tidy-looking official from the immigration department.

He took one look at me and the woman lying in what looked like a scene from a horror movie and asked: "Has she got a visa for Canada?"

I have never been so angry or used such bad language as I did then. "What the f...? This woman is dying! Why do you think we are diverting this whole jumbo jet?"

He was rapidly overrun by the medical staff as they hastened to my patient's aid. They put a drip into her, now that her blood flow had improved slightly, which meant that I could carefully extract my cramped and aching hand.

They eased her onto a stretcher and rushed her to a waiting ambulance. That was the last I saw of her. I believe she lived and I hoped her baby could have been saved too, though I had really only been focussing on saving her life. As I sat there, still covered with blood, attempting to massage some life back into my aching fingers, I hoped that the baby survived to be born on Canadian soil. That would really piss off that immigration officer and make the woman's risk worthwhile.

The inevitable paperwork and refuelling kept us on the ground for several hours before resuming our journey to New York. I passed through customs and passport control unhindered despite being covered in blood and clutching a huge magnum of champagne - a gift from British Airways to say thank you, which I did not really want.

The stewardess had asked me to send the airline a bill for my dry-cleaning - but there was no way I was going to do that. Everything was soaked with blood, even down to my underwear. When I finally got to my hotel room in the middle of the night I took two showers and then dumped all the clothes I had been wearing into a New York City trashcan. They would have been enough evidence to start a murder enquiry if anyone had ever found them.

This experience really brought home to me how much we as humans are willing to sacrifice for the betterment of our own lives and the lives of our children. Movement and migration are not something to be controlled in my mind. Why should people fleeing hardship not be taken in somewhere else? Why, if we are lucky enough to be born into a prosperous and peaceful country should we resent other people from wanting to come and experience the same?

I reflected on my own migration. Just like this Syrian mother, I was not fleeing from poverty or unfairness or discrimination. I was only in search of a better life for myself with more opportunities and potential for progress.

More than anything I felt grateful for the medical education which, thanks to England, I was fortunate enough to have received. Without it, that woman would have surely died tragically on that plane, chasing her dreams of a better life for her child.

Chapter Fourteen

The King is the boat and the common people the water; the water can carry the boat, but it can also capsize and sink the boat".
Confucius

EVERY SIX MONTHS THE EUROPEAN UNION IS HEADED BY a different member state. In 1998 it was the turn of the United Kingdom to take over the leadership role. This meant that the new Blair government got to steer the EU's political agenda and chair all discussions.

It fell to me as the UK representative, to chair the Humanitarian Aid Committee of the European Union. This was hugely important as, at that time, the presidency only came to each country once every seven years. As our government was still very new in office we wanted to flex our muscles and do something truly memorable. The pressure was on to think of something interesting we could do in the humanitarian sphere with Britain at the helm.

I proposed a mission to North Korea. There were reports of famine inside the country, but sending food aid to this dictatorship was a highly contentious subject among many world powers. It was a thorny issue rife with vested interests and, as such, it was often pushed under the carpet. With the legitimacy of the whole European Union behind me, I wanted to bring North Korea to the forefront of the world's attention.

North Korea was famously hostile to outsiders and, as such, I feared for the hungry citizens inside its closed borders. Hopefully the authority of the EU would be enough to convince the country's leaders to open discussions about how best to save its people from starvation.

Korea had been under Japanese control until the American atomic bombs were dropped at the end of the Second World War. With Japan in mourning her assets were split between the war's victors. The North of Korea fell under Soviet influence and the South of the country came under US authority.

In the post-war power vacuum, a former Korean guerrilla fighter, Kim Il-sung, rose to leadership of the northern country. Full of ruthless ambition, he consolidated all power under him by executing any political opposition until he was the unchallenged supreme leader of a ruthless military dictatorship. Kim Il-sung created a cult of personality around himself and held a god-like status for his people.

On his death in 1994, his son Kim Jong-il, took over as leader. He governed using the pseudo-communist ideology, known as *Juche,* which claimed that true socialism could only be achieved if a country was strong and self-reliant. It prized North Korea's independence above anything else. That meant restricted trade with outside nations. However, as the country did not have a good agricultural system, food was often short. A combination of recurrent floods and droughts meant that the country was now at crisis point. Reports from inside told of people reduced to eating grass and leaves to survive.

In spite of the importance *Juche* placed on self-sufficiency, North Korea was now in receipt of huge amounts of food aid in order to keep its people alive. It was this humanitarian crisis that required the attention of my delegation from the EU.

The World Food Programme was running a major relief operation but the North Koreans were proving to be very difficult partners. While they were taking delivery of WFP food into their central warehouses, they would not allow any foreign access to monitor how it was being distributed to the hungry people.

There were suspicions that the relief was being diverted to feed the bloated ranks of the military, who must also be suffering from the food shortages. I wasn't too disturbed by that, as I could understand how important it was to keep a million soldiers calm by feeding them. Otherwise they might grow hostile with hunger and go on the rampage, but our primary concern was to make sure that ordinary families were getting something to eat.

I was also aware that there were conflicting political agendas at work behind the scenes. I knew that the US, UK and other western powers were in intense discussions with Kim Jong-il's government about their nuclear programme. There was irrefutable evidence to suggest that Kim Jong-il's regime was trying to acquire nuclear weapons. If that happened it could cause major instability - or worse - in North East Asia, particularly as North Korea was technically still at war with their US-affiliated neighbour, South Korea.

I had good reason to think that the US was using the delivery of food aid as a stick to beat the North Koreans. As long as the Western powers were satisfied with Kim Jong-il's cooperation, the relief kept coming, but if the regime were seen to be uncooperative it would be withheld until their shrinking bellies made them more amenable to the will of the USA.

I felt deeply conflicted by this. I had visited Hiroshima and seen the memorial site at ground zero where the H-bomb had fallen; witnessed the acres of mangled devastation where a thriving city used to be; read the first-hand accounts from the survivors who told how they had watched their relatives evaporate in front of their eyes; and learned how even today, generations down the line, descendants of the *Hibakusha* - those effected by the bombs - are still at higher risk of cancer than anyone else.

I did not want to see the potential for such annihilation in the hands of a ruthless and impetuous dictator like Kim Jong-il. I agreed that all steps should be taken to stop North Korea acquiring nuclear capabilities, but I considered it to be an unethical violation of humanitarian values to link food aid to the objective of nuclear decommissioning.

I protested to Catherine Bertini, the executive director of WFP and herself an American, as to why they were allowing themselves to be manipulated by the US government, even if the Americans were their biggest donors. Of course, she denied this. She said that the real problem was their inability to monitor food aid shipments inside the closed country, meaning they could not assure their donors that food was going into the right hungry mouths.

This was the political backdrop to my intended trip and the reason I wanted to use the UK's moment of high-profile status to pioneer discussions on this controversial subject.

There was no North Korean embassy in Britain at the time, but the North Korea delegation to the International Maritime Organisation, which is based in London, acted as a quasi-embassy. I reached out to them and arranged lunch with a couple of diplomats. They passed my request for an EU mission back to Pyongyang.

The message came back that the government there would welcome a delegation headed by me. I was amazed that they had agreed. At this point their border controls were still incredibly tight. Nobody was allowed in and all that came out were shady rumours of a regime ruled by a power-crazed dictator who struck fear into the hearts of the people and was ready to arrest, imprison and execute citizens on his whim.

I suspected that they were allowing us to come not just because they wanted the humanitarian aid that we offered but, above all else, they sought some type of political engagement. Kim Jong-il desperately yearned for a diplomatic relationship with the west. This might be their first step away from their pariah status and towards recognition as a legitimate country to be taken seriously by other world powers.

The curious thing was that there had been very few EU donors interested in providing aid to North Korea, but when I announced that the Presidency of the EU would lead a mission there, all fifteen member states wanted to be part of it. Our visit represented a rare opportunity to access one of the most mysterious places on the planet, one that nobody, it seemed, wanted to miss.

We were a team of about thirty-five, two delegates from each member state plus the staff from the European Commission. Everyone came together for the first time in Beijing, where we met to discuss the coordination of our historic trip before actually setting foot onto North Korean soil.

The British Embassy in Beijing had, somewhat bizarrely, booked a working dinner in the elegant French hotel, Le Meridien. It felt surreal and more than a little uncomfortable to be discussing our hopes to alleviate the hunger of thousands, while sipping fine French wines and enjoying Le Meridien's haute-cuisine, all against the backdrop of the hustle and bustle of China's premier city.

As we got to know each other it became clear that only some of the EU emissaries were professional aid experts. The rest seemed to be security or intelligence specialists or diplomats. This was a bit naughty, as ours was strictly a humanitarian mission, but there was little I could do about it now.

As the leader of the delegation I presided over the dinner discussions. The conversations only added to my sense of surrealism. As I tucked into my *foie gras* and washed it down with a heavy Bordeaux, I was assailed with a barrage of unsolicited advice from all directions.

"It is imperative that we take a tough line in Pyongyang and use the trip to send a message to the regime that it needs to demilitarise and get off the backs of its citizens," one security-type barked, between swigs of Muscadet.

"We should do no such thing," a French diplomat retorted, setting down her salad fork to make her own point. "Instead we should try to build confidence and trust with the North Koreans so we can work better together in the future."

"I agree," asserted another voice. "Mutual suspicions have been the norm over the previous few years, with very little contact with the Kim Jong-il's government, and that is not the basis for good diplomacy."

Susan, a Dutch colleague of mine, put down her water glass in turn to present the humanitarian viewpoint. "It is not our job to be concerned with security or political issues," she announced, "but to do our assessment of the people's needs and agree a strategy with the North Koreans to facilitate help. We shouldn't do anything that would compromise that central objective, which is, after all, the raison d'être of the mission."

"No, no, no!" piped up another advocate for the international security community, and so the arguments went back and forth over the crisp white linen table cloths and elaborate silverware.

As the wine flowed and the disagreements got more heated, I felt myself buffeted by a deluge of conflicting opinions. Already jet-lagged by the long flight from Europe, I longed to retire to my hotel room. I tried to hear all points of view, distracted though I was by the sweet creaminess of the excellent crème brûlée. I was happy the meal was almost over, when one of the Beijing-based EU diplomats volunteered: "There is one more thing to consider - protocol."

"Protocol regarding what?" I asked, suddenly very interested, as I knew he was the one team member who had been inside North Korea before.

"The normal protocol for high level delegations. After arrival it is customary to lay a wreath at The Grand Monument - the huge bronze statue of Kim Il-sung on Mansu Hill in Pyongyang."

"But we haven't got a wreath," I pointed out. Was I about to derail our ground-breaking operation because I hadn't got the memo about floral arrangements?

The diplomat smiled at me. "Don't look so alarmed, Mukesh, the regime will provide the wreath. That is not the part that concerns me."

"What concerns you then?" I asked, trying to pretend I hadn't been scheming whether my expenses budget could stretch to getting a Beijing florist shop to open up in the middle of the night.

"After you lay the wreath to the founder of DPRK you will be expected to bow in respect, and retreat without turning your back on the statue. My concern is: should you bow? Or not?"

The diners, who had been uncharacteristically hushed as this diplomat posed his question, suddenly exploded in an outpouring of conflicting opinions, everyone talking over each other at once. A heated discussion ensued.

"To not bow would be seen as sacrilege!"

"Bowing to the image of this ruthless dictator with the whole weight of the European Union behind you, would be seen as a clear message acknowledging the legitimacy of this abhorrent regime!"

"The whole world will be watching!"

"Bowing will send a statement to the repressed North Koreans that the outside world supports the leadership that is abusing them!"

"Not complying with the full protocol by bowing will hardly be a positive start to a highly sensitive mission!"

"The Americans are already unhappy with our mission. They think we are undercutting their position. To bow might jeopardise the US-UK special relationship."

"We are not likely to achieve our objectives if we started off by insulting the ruler."

"Bowing is imperative!"

"You must not bow!"

The arguments went back and forth without any clear consensus and by the time the coffees were served I had a splitting headache.

"Ok thanks for all the advice; I will think about it and let you know what I decide to do." I shut down the conversation. Many of the team members seemed unsatisfied with this, but there was not much more they could say about it.

***

We were up early to catch our flight, a two-hour journey on a Boeing-737. It was nearly deserted except for our team. I must have been unusually quiet because my Dutch colleague, Susan, looked at me with concern in her eyes.

"Anything the matter, Mukesh?" she asked.

"Hmm?" I answered absent-mindedly. "Oh no, Susan, everything is fine." I lied. In truth, I was still wrestling with the problem of whether or not I was going to bow to the statue.

Would I bow and please the North Koreans to facilitate a good start for the important discussions that would follow? Doing so would surely send political signals back to western capitals that would not be appreciated by the hardliners. What would it say to the wider humanitarian world if I was seen to be courting a regime that perpetuated such abhorrent human rights abuses?

***

By the time the plane had taxied to a stop at the edge of an immensely long red carpet I still had no answer to the dilemma. As the plane doors opened, our ears were assailed by the deafening sounds of a large military band. Emerging into the bright daylight of Pyongyang's international airport, I had the unnerving sensation that I had wandered onto the set of a Hollywood B-Movie and been mistaken for the starring role.

At the foot of the airplane steps stretched the red carpet, lined on either side by rows and rows of soldiers, all dressed in the dark green and red regalia of the Korean People's Army. As I disembarked from the plane and descended the steps, the platoon seemed to move as one as they stood to attention and presented arms. The band continued their rendition of a stirring martial tune as I self-consciously led my team down the carpet.

All this surreal, dramatic splendour proved to be too much for some members of our delegation. I had to turn around and give them a glare to stop them from sniggering at the level of pomp. I could understand why they were laughing - the whole thing really was ridiculous - but it would be unforgivably disrespectful if the first thing we were seen to be doing on our arrival was laughing at the over-the-top grandeur of our welcome.

Our hosts, by contrast, appeared very serious: suited and booted in their green uniforms trimmed with red braids, heads topped in military caps with the five-pointed red star of North Korea emblazoned on the fronts, they stood ramrod straight and unflinching, conveying an air of complete inscrutability.

There was no question that for Kim Jong-il's government this was a very important moment. They had made it into something that was going to be political, whether we wanted it or not.

My walk down the carpet felt like it went on forever. When I finally reached the end, I was met by the country's foreign minister. A stolid, square figure also in military uniform, he shook my hand and muttered, "Welcome to the Democratic People's Republic of Korea".

Before I could reply I was ushered into a huge black Russian-made limousine with tinted glass windows and the North Korea and EU flags flying on the bonnet. He got in next to me as the rest of my team were herded into a fleet of identical cars. The extensive cavalcade took off surrounded by military motorcycle outriders. Flashing lights and sirens squealed as we tore out of the airport.

There was no traffic on the road as our path was cleared by the motorcycle escort, so the limousines progressed along the pristine streets at speed. My foreign minister colleague was smiling a lot, but otherwise didn't say anything - perhaps his English wasn't so good. His behaviour seemed automated, almost puppet-like. Just a few minutes later we screamed to a stop. A flunky opened the door and we stepped out. The Grand Monument at Mansu Hill is made up of a whole complex of buildings, set around the colossal gold statue of Kim Il-sung, and it was into one of these that I was ushered to await the rest of my party.

NO STRANGER TO KINDNESS

It consisted of a luxuriously-appointed reception room, complete with glittering chandeliers, deeply cushioned carpets, elegant French style chairs, and exotic floral arrangements. Coffee was served while we waited for the fleet of limousines to catch up with us. With all the drama of our grand arrival, the question of bowing to the statue had been temporarily banished from my mind. But when I saw Susan I suddenly remembered the conundrum, and in that instant I had a brainwave.

"Susan," I spoke to her in a conspiratorial whisper, "we need some gender balance on the team. This is one area that the North Koreans are providing a good example to the rest of the world and it's only fitting that our party do the same. In this spirit I am now electing you as my deputy." I whispered my instructions to her, and she listened and agreed somewhat reluctantly to what I wanted her to do.

Shortly, I found myself at the threshold of another red carpet, this time flanked by two soldiers carrying a giant wreath much taller than I was, and with Susan by my side. This red carpet made the previous one look like a hearthside rug. It seemed truly never-ending. The giant twenty-two metre statue of the country's founder looked almost small all the way at the other end, a good two- or three-hundred metres in the distance. We began our march along the lonely red path, Kim Il-sung's statue looming ever larger with each step.

During this long walk my thoughts wandered back to boarding school in England, where I had read a sonnet by Percy Bysshe Shelley that warned against the arrogance of kings. It described the discovery of the disembodied feet of a golden statue named Ozymandious, a great yet forgotten ruler. Ozymandious had this huge golden edifice constructed in his own image. The statue, along with every memory of the man himself, has disappeared into the sand. Underneath the feet was discovered a plaque that declared: "Look on my works ye mighty and despair". Yet nothing beside it and the feet remain.

I wondered if this statue too might come to the same fate. Would the golden Kim Il-sung become another Ozymandias, toppled and all but forgotten by the empire he had ruled over with an unrelenting iron fist? With my mind busy pondering the hubris of mankind, I was surprised to notice that we had reached the foot of the statue.

The soldiers halted. I laid my hand on the wreath as they held either side and we stepped forward to lay it against the foot of the plinth. I stepped back as the soldiers saluted. Just behind me my newly elected deputy, Susan, gave a stiff bow from her waist while I stood ramrod straight.

We reversed our steps, carefully, so as not to show our backs to the statue as that would denote disrespect. When we were a safe distance away, we turned around and walked back to our waiting colleagues. I was too worried that I might stumble and ruin the majesty of the occasion while the whole world was watching - our visit was being covered live on global TV - to wonder much if our solution to the bowing issue would satisfy our hosts, let alone my fractious delegation.

When we re-joined our team it seemed that everyone was satisfied. The Koreans were pleased, because Susan's bow meant that honour and dignity had been preserved. Yet because I had not bowed, as the official leader of the mission, hopefully western sensitivities had also been mollified.

***

From the monument we rode on in our cavalcade to the Koryo Hotel, a forty-three storey, twin-towered edifice built in the mid-eighties, as homage to the ostentatiousness of that decade. A footbridge linked the two towers together at the thirty-fifth floor, and each was topped with a revolving restaurant. It had been designed to show off the glory of the ruling regime. All international guests stayed here and it was to be our home for the next week.

We entered through an extravagant marble lobby, its walls decorated with jewels and precious metals, and were shown to our respective rooms. As the team leader I was allocated a luxurious corner suite with impressive views of the city of Pyongyang. I flopped into the large bed gratefully. After the excitement of the day I had decided to get an early night.

I flicked on the bedside light but the bulb flashed and went out. I swore out-loud. "Damn, no light," and resigned myself to reading under the main ceiling light instead.

Minutes later there was a gentle tap at the door. It was a man from room service bringing a new lightbulb. I let him in to change it, but it wasn't until he had left that I realised I hadn't actually called anyone to fix the blown bulb. How had he known it was broken?

I took another look around my room with a more critical eye. There was a large mirror opposite my bed and the wall behind seemed unusually thick. There was a lift shaft on the other side, but I figured that there was also enough space to conceal a small room behind the mirror. I was very likely under surveillance, but under the circumstances I guessed that was to be expected. I climbed into bed, whispered "thank you for the lightbulb," before blowing a kiss to my

new friend behind the mirror.
***

The next morning after breakfast I was greeted by a small, slightly built man with a broad, easy smile, who introduced himself as Hwan, my foreign ministry interpreter. He would be my right-hand man for the entirety of our visit, and I quickly learned that he was not just my interpreter and guide, but also my minder and informant, reporting all back to his bosses. As with the two-way mirror, I was not really surprised and wished him no ill will.

As I was chairing the visit I had one of the sleek Russian limousines at my disposal, which Hwan and I would travel in. The rest of the team would follow behind in a bus. The founder of the current regime, Kim Il-sung was known as The Supreme Leader and his son, who was now in power, Kim Jong-il, was known as The Great Leader, so inevitably my delegation nicknamed me The Cheer Leader - which showed what they thought of me lording it about in my limousine!

Though our guides were trying their hardest to show us only the best, most thriving elements of North Korean life and culture, there was no way of hiding that the nation was in dire trouble. As we travelled up and down the country, we were able to piece together a clearer picture of what was going on. In Pyongyang's industrial area there were many, many factories, but hardly any smoke rose from the innumerable chimney stacks. It seemed there was little manufacturing going on.

We visited a hospital that appeared to be modern and reasonably well equipped, but the staff there informed us that there were severe drugs shortages which often prevented them from providing proper treatment. The children in the paediatric ward were pinched and gaunt, obviously suffering from malnutrition.

In the fields we could see men in military uniform helping the civilian farmers plant paddy rice. We pieced together the facts: soldiers from the huge Korean People's Army had been conscripted to boost food production, but they appeared to be doing everything by hand or using primitive horse-drawn tractors. There was no mechanised agricultural equipment anywhere to be seen.

For every acre we saw being sown many more stood fallow. This land had been seized decades before for collective agriculture. But the government had run out of money for inputs - seeds and fertiliser - after frequent droughts, floods and blights had caused havoc with the crops.

On either side of the road we saw small, neat, well-kept houses.

Though they were surrounded by barren fields, a curious riot of green sprung forth around each. I sat up straight to get a closer look from behind the tinted glass of the limousine. Each house seemed to be hemmed-in by a small oasis of crops.

"What's going on here, Hwan?" I asked my guide. "Why are the gardens of these houses flourishing while the fields around are bare?"

"Recently, the Great Leader has generously encouraged the people to grow their own food for home use. These are the households' personal gardens where they can grow vegetables and herbs for their families, or to sell at small markets. *Juche* encourages personal self-sufficiency as well as for the country, where each individual can be the master of his destiny and together we can make the nation strong."

I had heard enough of Hwan's nationalistic speeches by now to be able to read between the lines. What this really meant was that the people were famished and the government had no way to feed them with the failing collective agriculture system, so were letting people grow their own food, despite this going against the regime's founding ideology of communal ownership of the means of production.

I was pleased that the regime had conceded that the people could not eat their ideology, and had relented in order to help them survive. I hungered to know more about what was really going on and how these people survived. But with Hwan keeping me on such a short leash it was very difficult to know what was scripted and what was not.

"What an excellent and enlightened idea of the Great Leader" I replied. "I should very much like to see how it is working in practice. Stop the car, please."

"What?" Hwan exclaimed, caught off guard, "No Sir - we aren't scheduled to stop here. Are you feeling unwell?"

"I'm perfectly well thank you, Hwan, but would very much like to see this inspired new enterprise in action. Stop the car, please."

Hwan looked visibly panicked but could hardly ignore a direct - and seemingly entirely reasonable - request of this nature. He barked some instructions in Korean and slowly the limo pulled over, stopping outside a small, well-kept house surrounded by a patch of green garden. I could see vines of cucumbers, not yet ripe, trained over a neat homemade trellis either side of the door.

The bus with the rest of the group inside came to a halt behind us and our local entourage began a heated discussion in Korean.

"What's going on? Did you break down?" asked Albert, one of the German delegates, a security specialist who seemed wary of the unscheduled stop.

"Not at all. I merely asked to stop to speak to the person who lives in this house."

"Ah I see - no wonder they look so spooked," he replied, nodding his head in the direction of Hwan and the other government minders. "Not keen on going off-script, are they, and who can blame them really?"

Eventually a couple of the Korean minders approached the house and knocked at the door. The woman who answered looked frightened but, after a short exchange, the fear in her face softened. Hwan approached me.

"You may come inside now. This lady is honoured to have you as a guest in her home."

I looked at Albert. "Would you like to accompany me?" I asked, as it was clear that not all of our party would be able to fit inside this humble dwelling. He agreed and we were warmly welcomed by Eun-mi, the lady of the house, a slightly built woman in her fifties with a long face and pronounced cheekbones. I wondered how much of her protruding bone-structure was genetic and how much was caused by hunger.

Eun-mi lived in a simple, single-storey home dominated by a large picture of the Great Leader. Albert and I sat awkwardly at the basic kitchen table, with all the government minders crowded around the edges of the room, their presence reminding Eun-mi that they were watching and would pass judgement on whatever she chose to say to these important foreign dignitaries.

She moved slowly around the kitchen, serving us green tea in small porcelain cups. Though her smile was warm and genuine there was something about her movements, slow and deliberate, that gave off an aura of heaviness. Like almost all the citizens we met, there was a quiet desperation and deep-set tiredness about her. I could not imagine anything in her life feeling light or carefree.

She offered snacks which did appear to be made from leaves with a few grains of rice in between. They certainly tasted like leaves, with a sharp, metallic flavour, and I came to the conclusion that these stories of civilians forced to eat grass and bark might indeed be true. I felt moved by her generosity; although this was all she had to eat, she still shared it freely with us.

We asked her about her life and Hwan translated her responses.

"Life here is hard, we have had many droughts and floods and the crops have not done as well as we would have hoped, but we are managing." She looked at out glowering minders again, before continuing. "The new auspicious policy of the Great Leader generously allowing us to grow our own food and to trade in community markets is really helping us to survive."

"How is food usually distributed to people like you?" I asked.

"Rice is provided monthly and how much is dependent on the size of the family. We also get vegetables, eggs, oil, soy sauce." She glanced at the minders again, before adding hurriedly, "we are very lucky to have such magnanimity and love from our esteemed leaders."

I thanked her very much for her honesty and hospitality and wished her luck with her cucumber harvest, before getting to my feet to leave. Normally, in my role as a powerful donor with the British Government, I would have asked her what it was she needed and endeavoured to provide that kind of aid. Here, however, I knew I had little sway over any relief allocation and even if I was able to provide what she asked, there was no way to know that the totalitarian government would ever allow it to reach her.

The last thing I wanted was to get her hopes up for international salvation that may never come. I was in a sombre, pensive mood as I walked back to where the rest of the team waited expectantly.

***

That night, staring out of my high-rise hotel room, I found myself mesmerised by one of the Pyongyang traffic police women. Dressed in a smart blue uniform and standing on a raised circular platform at the intersection of the junction below, she was turning from side to side directing the busy traffic with dramatic arm signals and an orange-and- white baton. The electricity supply in the city often suffered outages and these traffic women were a more reliable alternative to electric traffic lights.

Watching her from above she looked like a puppet performing an elegant dance, moved by the sway of an invisible hand. As I surveyed the scene, I reflected on what we'd seen that day. It seemed to me that Eun-mi and the others I had met lived like unwilling marionettes, with no control over their own destinies, each of their actions determined by the invisible hand of The Great Leader. Their lives were buffeted about by his whims, an invisible force, never seen but always present.

Now I had seen the situation for myself, I was convinced that the severe sanctions placed on North Korea over nuclear decommissioning were immoral. They were hurting the people far more than the regime. Such a selfish, repressive leadership was not going to have its policies influenced through the imposition of sanctions. All that did was to impoverish the people further and cause hunger and illness.

The elites of the country were not going hungry, that was clear, as they continued to live a rarefied existence of luxury, entirely separate from the harsh conditions faced by the ordinary civilians.

If I needed further proof of this it came the following day. I had wanted to speak to more of the locals, perhaps those living in the city, to be certain how their lives were impacted by food shortages, but Hwan informed me that today we would be playing golf. I was frustrated by this news, but felt it was best not to push my luck further after the impromptu stop to meet with Eun-mi yesterday, so I begrudgingly conceded to golfing.

***

We made our way to a beautiful hilltop resort. It was a luxurious country club that had apparently been built for Japanese tourists… who had never come. My team and our Korean minders ate copiously of fragrant rice, tangy *kimchi*, pillowy steamed buns, and salty *jeotgal*, but I couldn't forget the unpleasant aftertaste of Eun-mi's bitter leaves.

After the feasting I was invited to try my hand at golf. I had never played before but there was a Korean golf professional in attendance and after some brief instruction from him, I took to the pristinely-kept eighteen-hole course.

Korean golf instructors must be the very best in the world because to my amazement I was soon getting my ball straight into the holes. Even when it appeared to have sailed off in entirely the wrong direction, somehow when we reached the hole it always seemed to have come to land exactly where it was supposed to. I was astonished by the regime's ability to turn a non-player like me into a near-champion.

I knew they were trying to flatter me, and I found it all rather amusing, until I thought about the sinister way the government could extend its influence even into the holes of a golf course. Where else did it reach, employing coercion and violence? If the government thought it important to go to such trouble to manipulate the outcome of a round of golf, who knew where else its tentacles of power could infiltrate.

We returned to the hotel early and I invited Albert to take a walk around the grounds with me. Hwan and the other minders had left us alone, sure that were safely incarcerated inside the beautifully manicured grounds of the Koryo, and although I feared that every blade of grass was wired, I hoped we could talk a little more freely out there. I was keen to hear more of his thoughts about the experience of meeting Eun-mi.

As we strolled about the garden, making a show of admiring the vibrant red *Kimjongilia* - a kind of begonia - and orchid-like *Kimilsungia*, we passed near to the hotel entrance. There was nobody around and all our minders had gone home early. So, without a word to each other we slipped out of the gate. Nobody stopped us, so we thought we would take an early evening stroll and try to uncover what Pyongyang was really like. We chose a street at random and began exploring.

The results were depressing. Dilapidated cement buildings stood grey and featureless. Everywhere, the oppressive feeling of hardship spread through the air like the smell of rising damp. The streets had many, many storefronts boarded up or standing empty, and those that were open didn't appear to have much in them at all. There were a few people out walking the streets in old, tired clothes and worn out shoes. They didn't seem to want anything to do with each other, least of all the two foreigners who were wandering about unsupervised. They hurried past with their eyes averted, reminding me that we were in a strictly controlled police state.

We found ourselves in the nearby railway station, a huge building constructed with pillars in the classic style of socialist civil architecture. The vast cavernous hall was very clean, almost sterile. But it was jam-packed with people sitting on the floor, resting or napping, or simply just waiting for their trains. The men and women had that same hungry, pinched look that was becoming all too familiar. The few children we saw were playing quietly, not running-about.

Everyone seemed very repressed and brow beaten. They carried themselves with the same slow heaviness that I had noticed Eun-mi bear like a yoke around her neck. From time to time there was the blare of a message on the loud speakers. This was clearly a perfectly ordinary scene of North Koreans finishing work for the day. For me and Albert, ensconced in our deluxe hotel, whisked about in limousines, or stepping on red carpets and playing fixed golf games, it was a sobering glimpse into ordinary life in North Korea.

We found our way back to the hotel, but the following morning Hwan seemed rather agitated at the news that we had wandered off without our escort. All that day he seemed distracted and quieter than normal.

The following morning I decided it was time for a team de-briefing, where we would share our impressions and discuss our conclusions. I made my way to the luxurious lobby where I expected Hwan to be waiting for me, as he had been every morning. But today he was not there. Instead there was another interpreter.

"Hwan is not able to make it today," she said simply. "My name is Hyo-rin and I will be taking over from him."

"Oh, OK," I said. I was a little surprised, but I didn't think much more about it, as I went into our team meeting in the ballroom.

As we began our discussions I noticed a thin black wire running down the legs of the huge table, on which stood a typically ostentatious floral arrangement. Curious to discover what this wire might signify, I climbed on to the table to get to the very centre, ignoring the consternation of my colleagues. There it was: a microphone camouflaged in the middle of the flowers.

No doubt the regime was following our conversations with rapt attention. Despite the protests of some of my peers I left the mic where it was. I had grown used to being monitored, going to bed each evening under the watchful eye of my anonymous friend behind the two-way mirror.

It seemed to me that this was no bad thing. As the discussion progressed and different points of view were expressed between the hardliners and the humanitarians, I thought it overall beneficial for our hosts to listen in. This way they could learn about the debates that we were having and the dilemmas that we faced, so that they could understand the nuances of the issues from our differing perspectives.

From there we moved onto our formal, above-board discussions with the North Korean regime. We managed to convince them that we would be recommending to the EU to increase food assistance to the country, but this would be on the condition that the WFP, through whom the food would be channelled, would be allowed to monitor right up to the extended delivery points. These were the smaller warehouses dotted across the country.

That would allow the WFP better access, without disrupting the appearance of self-sufficiency, a supposed founding principle of *Juche*. This new level of access also meant that the USA couldn't persevere with linking nuclear disarmament to aid provision. They would have to find new ways to keep Kim Jung-il in check, ones that did not result in denying food to the long-suffering civilians.

All that I had seen had convinced me that the government was not withholding food from its civilians on purpose, even if some of the foreign relief was being diverted to its armed forces. In fact, I was impressed by the public administration system of the North Koreans.

It seemed more efficient if the food aid could go through the government's own channels, rather than set up a parallel system just for foreign-supplied items.

***

Upon our return from North Korea, the EU listened with interest to our findings, accepted our decisions and implemented the increased food aid provision via the WFP. Overall, the mission was a resounding success.

Yet there was one element that tarnished what would have been an entirely successful trip. Once back in London I heard some disturbing news via my German colleague, Albert. He had received some alarming intel from within North Korea that Hwan, our interpreter, had been put on trial and executed by the government. His crime? Allowing two foreign diplomats to wander unsupervised around the streets of Pyongyang.

I couldn't believe it. As the shock subsided, I began to realise the harm that our off-piste excursion had caused. It had cost a man his life. For all the compromises and progress we had achieved with the North Koreans, I was reminded that this was still a brutal police-state that could kill at any time.

There was a post script to the visit, at least for the UK and for me personally. In 2000 Britain opened its first Embassy in Pyongyang and the North Koreans also opened a counterpart Embassy in London. Before this there was very little communication between the two countries. I like to think that our expedition paved the way.

Building further on our commitments, we implemented an English language training programme in Pyongyang. Despite continued tensions with Kim Jong-il, the British government authorised this on the principle that anything that boosted the ability to improve communications with other countries must be a good thing. We were committed to opening dialogue with such nations, as no progress can be made without talking. Plus for me personally it felt important to invest in the country's capacity in the English language, to honour the memory of my interpreter and guide, Hwan, who had lost his life so needlessly.

His death reminded me not to underestimate a government that has no regard for the sanctity of life of its citizens and holds power through fear. Unfortunately, this would not be the last time that I found myself embroiled with a power-crazed government that had broken its social contract of basic respect for its people.

Chapter Fifteen

I don't want to be remembered as the girl who was shot. I want to be remembered as the girl who stood up.
Malala Yousafzai

NORTH KOREA WASN'T THE ONLY TOTALITARIAN REGIME I had to deal with during my DFID years. My remit included what are commonly referred to as the "pariah states." That meant that in addition to North Korea I had responsibility for Iran, Iraq, Afghanistan and Myanmar as well as numerous other countries in protracted conflict.

These were unstable places ravaged by wars, dictatorial governments, corruption and poverty. Dealing with them was notoriously challenging, yet we had to be able to communicate with their governments in order to bring aid to civilians who were innocent victims. Yet this often meant carefully manipulating the egos of their leaders and engaging in negotiations with truly wicked men. Indeed, it often felt as if we were dining with the devil in order to get help to those who needed it most.

Time and again I was faced with the ethical conundrum: was it right to cooperate with evil in order to do good? I had always decided it was, as long as we could bring some salvation to suffering people. In short, the ends justified the means. But never was this tested so much as the time I spent in Taliban-ruled Afghanistan.

After the success of my North Korea mission, I took further advantage of Britain's temporary presidency of the EU. Now that the whole world was looking on, and I had the EU working together, I wanted to advance negotiations on behalf of the people of Afghanistan. This meant tackling the world's most difficult issue at the time; the rise of the Taliban. And what better way, I thought, to use my new-found EU leverage?

Various warring Mujahideen factions had clamoured for control of Afghanistan, in the vacuum of power left by the fall of the Soviet-backed communist government in 1992. Rival militant groups were able to thrive thanks to financial backing from foreign nations vying for power in the region.

Afghanistan is famed for its warrior-like populace. It has famously never been successfully occupied by an outside power. The British invaded in 1842 to protect their assets in Imperial India, but were thrown out. The Soviets had tried to advance their aggressive occupation of Asia, but had been driven out of this rugged, mountainous country by the indefatigable Afghan spirit.

The population is made up of diverse cultural groups descended from fractious tribes, so the idea of one sovereign nation-state is alien to many. Perhaps that was why it had taken so long for one group to finally triumph and lead a central government. That group was known as the Taliban. "Talib" means "student" and the Taliban began as a political movement originating from the *madrassas* - religious schools set up in neighbouring Pakistan. Their revolutionary philosophy was developed by extremist teachers who prized strict Sharia law, preached a rhetoric of Islamic purity and manipulated Muslim doctrine to support their ruthless imposition of totalitarian authority.

On gaining control of Kabul, the Taliban had established a new form of hardline governance, epitomised by their Ministry of Virtue and Vice, passing all manner of new laws. These included the prohibition of music, art, and many other forms of self-expression.

Men were instructed to grow their beards to a certain length. Women had to cover themselves from head to toe. There was even an edict that women were not to make a noise when they walked in their sandals, in case the faintest clickety-clack of feminine steps inflamed the lustful passion of a man.

The curious thing was that I had seen groups of Taliban in Islamabad, Pakistan's capital city, easily identifiable by their long flowing beards, sitting around in cafes and the lobbies of smart hotels with their eyes glued to television sets. I took a special interest in this, for I knew that television was banned under their laws in Afghanistan. I learned that their favourite TV programme was *Bay Watch,* where Western women famously run around in slow motion, clad only in scanty swimsuits - a very different dress-code from that imposed on their women at home.

Hypocrisy flourished under the Taliban. I theorised that they were all sexually repressed - they needed sex education rather than anything else - but there were a lot more urgently pressing issues, before any long-term educational development like that could be implemented.

Afghanistan was one of the most problematic regions in the world at that time. As such I endeavoured to lead a high-level EU mission right to the heart of it all. Just as we had with North Korea, a team of colleagues from several EU countries would fly into the Taliban's stronghold of Kandahar, Afghanistan's second largest city towards the south of the country.

We did just that, and set up base in the local UN guesthouse, commandeering their large dining room as our makeshift headquarters. That done, I wasted no time in requesting a meeting with the Taliban. There were two main issues on our agenda. Firstly, we needed to negotiate access for the UN and NGOs to travel around the country and deliver aid. The Taliban had denied access to everyone and the people were in desperate need, thanks to the ravages of decades of war.

Secondly, we were here to advocate for the rights of the women in the country. We wanted to negotiate more personal freedom for them and, in particular, access to healthcare. The regime was strict on everyone, but the women were suffering most under the puritanical controls inflicted upon them by the all-male government.

The Kandahar *Shura* - ruling council - were anxious to meet with us. Like the North Koreans, they were eager for any kind of international diplomatic engagement, as they were not considered a legitimate government by any world powers save Pakistan and some Gulf states. Our request for a meeting was agreed to, but on one condition: they only wanted to see the men in our party and refused to meet with the three women.

Susan, my deputy from the North Korea trip, suggested we agree to the Taliban's request. "This is an important meeting," she argued. "We can't jeopardise that. You men go ahead and we will stay behind. You can brief us on everything on your return. If you take good notes, I'm sure it will feel as if we were really there."

Some of the men in the party agreed. They conceded that the gender balance of our group was not as important as the pressing topics we had to discuss. They argued that a little thing like sexual equality should not be allowed to get in the way of our bigger purpose here.

I demurred. "Absolutely not," I announced resolutely - almost angrily. "I shall decline their offer to meet on the grounds that their terms are unacceptable. They must meet with the delegation as a whole or not at all."

The others looked shocked. Decline their offer? But this meeting was the very reason we had come all this way.

"Imagine if the word got out that a high-level EU mission jettisons its women and goes to speak with the Taliban man-to-man?" I continued. "Apart from being morally abhorrent, it also suggests that we support this regime's unrelenting oppression of women. It would be almost a green light to them that subjugating and excluding women is okay as far as we are concerned.

"One of the main points on our agenda is to advocate for the rights of women. Who better to advise on women's needs than women themselves? It certainly beats European men discussing these issues with a bunch of chauvinistic Taliban leaders. Does that sound like an informed viewpoint to you? It would be wholly wrong to ignore the female point of view on this."

My male colleagues looked sheepish and said nothing.

"But nobody has ever met with the Taliban at this high a level before," Susan objected. "You are meeting with the second and third in command of the whole movement. Surely there must be something we can do to make the conference go ahead?"

I looked around from face to face, searching for a solution to this problem. Across from me sat one of my French colleagues with his elbow propped on the table, head resting in one hand. With his other hand he filled himself a small glass of mint tea from a silver pot. The tea was long since cold and I guessed he was probably only pouring it to distract himself from the apparent derailing of our mission.

I was struck by a sudden brainwave.

"How about we bow to their sensitivities," I said, my eyes still on the Frenchman and his long-stewed tea, "but instead of going to meet them, we invite them here for tea. This is a UN building where international rules apply, so this saves face all around. They can meet with the women in the group without going against their own laws, and we can talk with them without having to jeopardise our core values."

A local UN fixer was sent as an envoy to negotiate terms for the meeting. I hoped the Taliban would agree, otherwise I would be forced to cancel our whole mission out of principle.

"They will come," the fixer told us, "but we have to be sensitive with the women, as they are not at all happy about that."

"Of course," I replied, delighted that our talks could go ahead.

We worked out a seating plan around the large wooden table in the guesthouse's dining room. I would sit on one side in the middle, surrounded by the male members of the team. The women of the group, Susan and two others, were to sit at the end of the table furthest from the Taliban. It was far from a perfect arrangement, but a workable compromise.

In keeping with the values of their culture, the women would also be wearing long robes, shawls and scarves to cover their entire bodies, leaving only their faces and hands visible.

The Afghan delegation arrived; a group of swarthy, bearded men, including many bodyguards, a protocol officer and four high-level Taliban representatives. They each carried AK-47 rifles, even the political dignitaries, as they seemed to wear these like a badge of honour. I reminded myself that they were all ex-fighters, and very tough men indeed.

The guards took up positions strategically around the room, and the high ranking Taliban seated themselves across from us. They sat up ramrod straight, eyes front, never wavering from myself and my male colleagues, and totally ignoring the women at the end of the table.

Not an ideal situation, I told myself, *but at least they're here and we can talk, that's the main thing.*

Out loud I said: "My esteemed guests, welcome. Thank you very much for taking the time to meet with us. Firstly, I would like to acknowledge on behalf of the European Union that you have bought peace to Afghanistan for the first time in many, many years."

Not a total lie, my inner monologue conceded. They *had* bought peace - just a pity it was a peace enforced by a tyrannical reign of oppression and fear.

"We want to specifically commend you on your anti-drugs work," I continued. "The opium poppy trade has come to a virtual standstill."

Their protocol officer provided translation to those Taliban whose English was not good. They returned a form of gruff appreciation of my sentiments. I took this as a good sign and continued.

"We want to assure you that while the battles fought to bring stability to Afghanistan have been fractious and divisive, we here in this room have little interest in these matters. It is the Afghan people we are concerned about. Know that we will endeavour to provide aid for them no matter what, regardless of politics."

The discussions went on for about forty-five minutes. It seemed that they were amenable to the idea of allowing UN access. They were more evasive, though not openly hostile, when we tried to address the medical issues facing women in the country.

Fresh green tea was served, and we ate sweet almonds, plump raisins, and sticky dates. I couldn't believe how well things were going. When the meeting was over, the Taliban pushed back their chairs, collected their weapons and filed out of the room's low doorway. Only the protocol officer stayed behind, catching my eye.

"How do you think it went?" I asked him, excited to hear his opinion. "I felt it all went rather well?"

"They feel very insulted," he replied solemnly. "The Taliban envoys are very upset. You have greatly insulted them."

"Why? What have we done?" I asked. "I thought it was a good meeting?"

"One of your women was naked," he replied, his voice dripping with disdain.

"What?" I demanded, dumbfounded.

"The tall one on the left-hand side. She was naked."

"What are you talking about?" I asked again, in disbelief.

"We are very upset that you made us sit before naked women," he persisted.

At this point we all confessed our confusion and indignation. Luckily the translator did not hear me remark sarcastically, under my breath: "Where? I want to see the naked woman too!"

We finally managed to get him to explain. It turned out that Susan had been resting her arm on the table. She is a tall woman, even by Dutch standards. When she had borrowed modesty robes in Islamabad there were none that were really quite long enough. During the meeting, as she had been writing notes, her wrist and watch had become visible. This shameless flash of female flesh was what had caused the Taliban such upset.

"I am very sorry," I said, struggling to maintain my professional composure. "It was not at all intentional. We apologise if we have offended anyone, and while this is admittedly a little hard for us to understand, we will ensure we take note for the future."

He seemed satisfied and followed his contingent out of the building. Once he was gone I rounded on Susan in mock fury.

"Susan! What is the meaning of this? You do realise that you derailed our entire operation by going naked! How could you?"

She looked utterly bewildered and spluttered words to her defence, before she saw me smiling. The whole room rocked with laughter, as Susan was good-naturedly teased by everyone. We all referred to her as "Naked Susan" for the remainder of the trip.

The meeting had gone well, all things considered. The affront Susan had provoked had not caused any lasting offence. However, while we tried to see the funny side of this, the Taliban's absurd treatment of the women delegates in this meeting was indicative of a far more sinister attitude that permeated every area of life under their rule.

***

The severity of this gender inequality was thrown into sharp relief the following day, on a visit to Kabul's only women's hospital that stood at the southern edge of the city.

The hospital took its name from the tenth-century Afghan princess Rabia Balkhi. She was a young woman who had fallen in love with a charming local boy of low birth. Her father, the King, had intended her to marry a rich nobleman and, on discovering that her heart belonged to another, had gaoled his daughter in the hope that this would make her reconsider. The tragic young princess wrote poetry about her unrequited love on her cell walls in her own blood, and died in captivity due to the cruelty of her father.

The name, so intertwined with the historic patriarchal control of women, turned out to be prophetic, for the hospital had come to a total standstill since the Taliban's triumph, exemplifying the very worst of their institutionalised misogyny.

Under the new extremist laws, women were not allowed to be treated by male doctors, no matter how ill or injured. In addition to this, women were not allowed to work outside of the home, and this included as doctors or nurses. The result was a Kafkaesque situation where women could not work as doctors, yet male doctors were forbidden from treating any female patients - so effectively it was illegal for women to receive medical care.

The new rules had made it impossible for Rabia Balkhi hospital to operate. We managed to take a look inside the hospital. It seemed to be reasonably modern and well equipped, but entirely deserted. Yet the needs of the women here were considerable. I have had a deep-seated personal commitment to women's health, ever since that seminal moment when I failed to save the life of that pregnant young girl on Moudubi island.

Seeing the way these women were denied healthcare, even though the means to treat them were readily available, made me incredibly angry. Thinking of Rabia in her cell, deprived of life by the man who was supposed to take care of her, made me realise how far Afghanistan had regressed. This country was no better to its women now than it had been in the tenth century.

So began a long and fierce battle for the reopening of Rabia Balkhi. It was too much to hope that the Taliban would reverse their strict laws to allow the many qualified female Afghan doctors to treat the women of their community. Instead, we had to compromise again, suggesting that Rabia Balkhi reopen with an all-female staff of foreign volunteers. That way no laws would be technically broken - no Afghan women were working outside of the home; no male doctors were treating female patients - so face could be saved, while women got the medical treatment they needed.

Negotiating this with the Taliban was a major personal challenge. Denying healthcare to half their population based on gender was tantamount to a death sentence for many women. In my mind they were tyrants, bullies and tormentors, so having to adhere to their ludicrous, sexist doctrine when devising our aid schemes was a bitter pill for me to have to swallow.

Even bending to their insane laws, we could not convince the government on our own. I turned to the World Health Organisation to put pressure on the Taliban to allow foreign aid workers and supplies into Rabia Balkhi. I thought WHO would be an obvious champion of this scheme, as it concerned a true matter of life and death, but it turned out to be more complicated than I could have ever imagined.

The Afghanistan office of WHO was run by a Libyan-British man names Jahd. He turned out to be a conservative Muslim who blocked our progress at every turn. Without WHO it was impossible to move ahead. I was furious. I pointed out that women's health is a basic human right. Even the Taliban could not deny that women are human. WHO should rightly be leading on this issue. Jahd continued to obstruct my efforts, but I would not back down.

I arranged for a conference at WHO's regional office in Cairo, specifically to address the crisis of women's health in Afghanistan and Rabia Balkhi Hospital in particular. There I confronted Jahd over the issue and we met head to head in a blazing row. Finally he conceded, and with WHO's backing we won access to get our health workers into the hospital.

It pained me that this had presented such a struggle. I had expected to encounter misogyny running riot under the Taliban reign, but I was not prepared to encounter such patriarchal values at the heart of the WHO country office, which appeared to be too feckless to stand up to the Taliban's subjugation of women.

At least now the women of Afghanistan had one hospital open to them. It was far from ideal, but it was better than nothing, and in this deeply traumatised country we had to celebrate each and every small victory. They were so few and far between.

***

Afghanistan's ancient capital city, Kabul, had always held a unique appeal for me. I had read about this famous place in countless novels and history books. It has an impressive reputation for being unconquerable, or at least un-holdable, by any invading armies. It belonged to a fiercely quarrelsome people who were not afraid to fight for their independence.

NO STRANGER TO KINDNESS

Though I knew it had been heavily bombed, I couldn't shake the picture I had in my imagination of a beautiful settlement of time-worn buildings perched, high in the mountains, blessed with fresh air and open sky. I imagined fruit trees, heavy with dates and apricots, lining wide sandy roads.

I was heartbroken when I saw Kabul in reality. Large tracts of the old city had been reduced to rubble. All that history, all that civilisation - simply pulverised. In many areas there was just the odd wall standing like a fractured shard of a now-shattered culture. The vicious civil war had decimated most of the vibrant heritage of this country, but the Taliban wasted no time in hammering the final nail into the coffin.

Two immense statues known as the Bamiyan Buddhas once towered over the Bamiyan Valley to the north west of Kabul. Carved directly into hollows of the sandstone rock-face one-and-a-half millennia ago, they stood around fifty metres high. They were both an architectural marvel and a testament to the history of this once prosperous and rich culture.

I was back in my office in London when I heard the terrible news. The Taliban had dynamited the ancient statues. They claimed their actions were retaliatory, protesting at foreign aid donated to preserve the ancient statues, while the common people suffered through famine. They had destroyed the Buddhas - idolatrous effigies to a heretic religion, as the Taliban's fanatics saw it - to teach the west a lesson about prioritising chunks of carved stone over starving people.

The destruction of shared cultural symbols is one of the tactics used by génocidaires, when they are trying to systematically eradicate a societal group from the face of the earth. Without sounding callous about it, while people can be replaced by a new generation, the obliteration of our shared, common heritage like the Bamiyan Buddhas is final.

The choice to destroy those unique monuments was yet another way to enforce the Taliban will over a downtrodden population. By felling those 'heretic idols' that harkened back to a peaceful past, the Taliban did away with another potential obstacle to the extremist doctrine they were using to strangle personal freedom in the country.

***

I returned to Afghanistan many times during the Taliban era. I would fly into Pakistan and then catch a UN flight direct to Kabul. I always dreaded my arrival, for there stood atop a roundabout on the way into the city a sinister gibbet. There, more often than not, there would be bodies hanging. 'Criminals' who had displeased the government. Sometimes the swaying bodies wore garlands made from banknotes, or had banknotes stuffed into their mouths - presumably signalling that the victims had been corrupt.

My instinct was to look away. To avert my eyes. To hide my face and block out this gruesome sight. Yet I forced myself to look. I couldn't be ignorant to the reality of the Taliban. They were brutal and evil and I must not forget that. I needed to know and understand my enemy; otherwise how could I manipulate him into letting me help the people who suffered? I forced myself to look upon every aspect of their cruelty, so I could remember who I was dealing with.

Kabul at this time was dangerous and incredibly unpleasant, even for an international like myself. Between witnessing the brutality of this totalitarian regime and dodging unexploded landmines in the streets, the small international community was having a demoralising time of it. The ban on alcohol, television and most other forms of entertainment meant that there was little respite from the grizzly realities of life under the Taliban.

As I was spending an increasing amount of time there, the Foreign Office had asked if I would look in on the British embassy in Kabul, and encouraged me to stay there if I wanted to, rather than at the UN guesthouse, which I normally frequented. When Kabul had fallen to the Taliban, all the foreign embassies and the diplomatic missions left the country, so the British Embassy was unoccupied, except for the resident staff of Gurkha guards.

The British Embassy in Kabul is a fantastic building up on a hill in the Wazir Akbar Khan district, a grand, high-walled relic from colonial times when the British representative in Kabul came under the British India Office. So links to Afghanistan were controlled from Delhi, not from London. That explained the curious presence of the gurkhas, who had always protected the building. The role of embassy guard was passed down from father to son, and had been for many generations.

There was daily radio contact between these Embassy guards and the British High Commission in Islamabad, and I was told they had been warned I was coming. Even so I felt a little uneasy approaching the large and imposing hardwood gate set in the high, white stone wall. I knocked loudly. Nothing happened. Perhaps they were not expecting me after all.

My heart sank. I had heard stories of the fierce bravery and quick-thinking of the gurkha regiment and I was curious to meet them in person. One story goes that after the Partition of India the assets held by the British in the region were divided up between India and Pakistan. The main British embassy in Kabul, a priceless architectural jewel, was handed over to Pakistan. The British kept the coach house as their new embassy, which was a palatial residence in itself.

Some years later, an Afghan mob had come to burn down the British embassy. They banged on the gate, the very gate that I was now loitering outside, and the gurkhas had come to the door. "No, no, no, this is not the British Embassy,' they told the mob. "That is it. That big building up on the hill." They pointed out the much grander residence that had been given to Pakistan. The mob burnt down the Pakistan Embassy and the loyal and quick-thinking Gurkhas had saved the British Embassy.

I knocked again. Still nothing happened. I waited a while more and was just about to give up when a little door within the gate opened a crack. I explained who I was and the man inside let me into the flagstone courtyard within. It then became apparent why it had taken so long to answer the door. The Gurkhas had delayed as they hurriedly donned their uniforms ready for a formal inspection. As I clambered through the small doorway the last of them sprang to attention.

I took in the surreal sight. Each man was garbed in fifty-year-old ceremonial-looking uniforms of forest green, topped with the gurkha's signature wide-brimmed khaki hats. They lined up for inspection, backs straight, chests thrust out proudly. I was not sure how to react - I had never inspected an army guard before - but I muddled through as best I could, walking slowly up and down the line, nodding in approval, hands clasped behind my back like I had seen generals doing in films. They seemed to be satisfied with this and told me to make myself at home and enjoy exploring the place.

I thanked them heartily and proceeded to reconnoitre the grand old building. Everything was immaculate and felt suspended in time. There were crisp linen sheets on the large oak bed in the Ambassador's bedroom, where a painting of Queen Victoria gazed sternly down from the wall. The bathroom had beautiful Victorian brass taps to fill the huge, enamel bathtub. I took one look at the place and decided that yes please I would very much like to take up the offer to stay here during my trips to Afghanistan.

I continued exploring and discovered the cellar was still stocked with old scotch whisky, fine wines, champagnes and of course bottles upon bottles of the old British-Indian favourite: gin. I reckoned that with the prevailing politics at that time and the well-entrenched

Taliban, there was no way that the British embassy would be reopened any time soon.

It's really a great pity to leave all this stuff sitting around ... I thought to myself, fingering a dusty bottle of vintage Tanqueray. *What a waste...*

At that moment I made the decision to throw a party. I invited all the people I knew from the aid agencies and the UN to join me for an evening. There were not that many internationals in Kabul at the time due to the instability and danger, but maybe twenty or thirty turned up.

Gurkhas are almost as famed for their hospitality as they are for their warrior spirit, and the cooks and caretakers excelled themselves. I think they relished having something to do, other than the mundane job of guarding the empty embassy. Thanks to them we dined on wonderful mutton curry, succulent kebabs, fluffy *pilau* rice - and other mouth-watering dishes from their Nepalese homeland. Each course was washed down with the fine wines and whisky from the cellars.

That night was a fantastic morale booster. Alcohol was of course forbidden under the Taliban, but safe behind the walls of the Embassy, on British soil with the Union Jack fluttering above and our squad of gurkha guards to protect us, we could really let off steam.

Because of the night-time curfew imposed by the Taliban, obviously this had to be a sleep-over, so the festivities continued deep into the night. We didn't quite demolish everything in the cellar, but we definitely made a good dent into the gin supplies, and a great time was had by all.

When I finally dragged myself up to bed in the Ambassador's chamber with its cool linen sheets and soft feather pillows, I smiled contentedly at the painting of Queen Victoria on the wall. I almost thought that she looked amused.

Years later when the embassy finally reopened an audit was called. The inspectors were mystified as to what had happened to the extensive cellar stock that had been left behind and had mysteriously disappeared. I had to confess that the alcohol store had been liberated during Taliban times as a mark of resistance against the despotic regime. There was some grumbling among bureaucrats, but nothing could be done about it then.

Small acts of defiance were so important during this time. I felt like our very presence in the country was a form of resistance. Humanitarian workers like myself had been there throughout the civil war and we were not about to abandon the people now. By providing aid, education and clearing away landmines and explosives, we were not only expressing our solidarity with the Afghan people, but we were also defying the authorities.

"Fine," our actions were saying. "You go. Kill. Pillage. Torture. Do whatever you're doing. We are never going to leave these people."

***

It gets bitterly cold in Kabul at night, as the city sits so high in the mountains and shelter is hard to find. Many of the displaced took refuge in huge warehouses. Never intended to be habitable, these were constructed of metal and concrete, sometimes without glass in the windows, some built without windows at all. Now they were lined with rows and rows of beds. If you were lucky enough to have a bed then this was where you slept; otherwise you slept on the concrete floor, wrapped up as well as you could against the cold. I'm sure numerous people froze to death.

Many of the Afghans who lived here had lost their entire families in the fighting. They fled to Kabul for some semblance of protection, only to be further persecuted. It was particularly difficult for the women who called these warehouses home. Under Taliban law, women weren't allowed to go out on their own without a male relative, yet many of them didn't have any male relatives left, for they had fled or been killed.

We supported the World Food Programme to establish community bakeries, one in every neighbourhood. WFP provided the flour and the locals baked it into *Nân-i Afğânī* - large, flat breads.

One day I went to visit one of these bakeries. I was very impressed. It was all very systematically organised. Every civilian had a ration card. They queued up, presented their ticket and were allocated their pieces of bread according to the size of the family.

The delicious smell of those baking loaves, pulled piping hot from the ovens, wafted on the air and was enough to make my mouth water. I was a well-fed international diplomat, so heaven knows what it stirred in the minds of the hungry civilians. It was a wonder there were no bread riots.

I was admiring their efficiency and trying to ignore the embarrassing rumbling in my belly when I heard a disturbance. I pushed past the queue of waiting people to see what was going on. I was met with a sickening sight.

I saw two very young Talib soldiers, dressed in white, carrying their trademark AK-47 rifles. They were too young to even grow the signature long beards synonymous with their authority, yet they were beating a woman who must have been in her fifties with the butts of their guns. She had made the mistake of coming alone to collect her bread ration, without any male relative. Now the Talib patrollers were lashing out at her viciously. I could hear her pleading with them between the heavy blows, and asked my interpreter to translate what she was saying.

"She is explaining," he told me, "that she has no male relatives left. Her children have been killed too. How would she get bread if she did not come alone? She would die if she didn't get it."

The young men heard her but kept hitting her relentlessly. She had been using her arms to shield her head from the worst of the attack, but when she realised they would not listen to reason it was evident that she could take no more.

She roared a scream of impassioned rage that said more than any words could. After everything she had seen, all she had lost, the worst she had endured, to go through all that and then be treated with such disrespect by these gangly, upstart youths. This insult to her person in the face of everything else was too much to bear.

In one swift movement she ripped her hijab off her head, revealing her tresses of grey-white hair. She grabbed one of these boys by the front of his tunic and screamed into his face.

"What are you! Is this how you treat your grandmother?" Then she started beating these kid-solders furiously with her fists.

The crowd watched open-mouthed with shock. I was enthralled by this brazen act of defiance. I think the Talib boys were the most shocked of all, as they clearly didn't expect such ferociousness from a grey-haired woman. They tuned on their heels and fled down the road while this brave lady screamed at their backs.

"What kind of men are you? Beating up your sisters, your mothers! You are an insult to Islam! Shame on you!"

She snatched up her discarded hijab, marched straight to the front of the queue, took her bread ration and stomped off home, emanating furious rebellion with every step she took.

I was stunned by this act of personal resistance. It was born out of sheer desperation but showed real courage in the face of danger, exemplifying the power of humanity to struggle against injustice. What she had said was true: those boys were bullies, blindly implementing the will of the authorities and enjoying the power to hurt the most vulnerable fellow humans. She did not lie down and take it. She fought back. It reminded me that everywhere, even under such severe repression, ordinary people are striving for their rights, for justice and for personal freedom.

I felt for her. I wanted to talk to her more about her hopes for Afghanistan, but she left at such speed I didn't get a chance. Perhaps that was for the best. She would be a target now. I hoped those boys would be too embarrassed to repeat the story of fleeing from the wrath of an old woman, so she would not meet with further retribution for her act of defiance.

***

However, I soon learned that there was nothing the Taliban loved more than retribution. I witnessed the worst instance of this in the main football stadium. I had heard that a young woman had been accused of adultery and was to be publicly executed. I had vowed to know my enemy and not to turn a blind eye to the unspeakable cruelty that befell ordinary people. I resigned myself to go and bear witness to this monstrous event.

This young woman was to be killed because she had slept with a man who was not her husband. Nothing was to happen to the man, but she was hauled out in front of the raised spectator seating and roughly trussed up to a wooden stake erected for the purpose. All around a crowd of people bayed for her blood.

A wolfish-looking Taliban stepped out in front of her and gave an impassioned speech. I could not understand the words but as I watched his eyes flashing vitriol, white globules of foam forming at the edges of his mouth, I understood the underlying sentiment. He whipped the onlookers into a twisted religious fervour. Each booming condemnation he uttered was met with a roaring from the crowd, as their pulses raced faster and faster with barbarous desire.

It was Friday and the congregation had come after prayers - men, women and children - like some kind of sick family excursion. A fun afternoon out with the kids to watch the brutal murder of an adulteress.

The preacher reached a crescendo before taking up a stone from the ground and stepping back from the bound woman. Her head was bowed, face invisible under the shawl that covered her, but I could see her whole body was tensed for the first impact.

I watched aghast. I felt as if the world had decelerated and I was seeing everything in slow motion. The priest cast the first stone in a well-practiced arc. It made contact with the woman's soft vulnerable body. She seemed to buckle under the first impact but, within moments, a rain of stones from the assembled people pounded her undefended flesh.

I tried to still my doctor's mind, as I imagined what damage those rocks were doing to her unprotected body. How much of a pummelling her organs would need to receive before they gave up on their wretched labour of keeping her alive. How much pain and mutilation she would have to endure before it ended her tragic life.

Mercifully, after the first few stones, her head listed awkwardly to one side and I assumed she must have lost consciousness. Maybe she was dead already. The crowd kept on and on pelting her lifeless body until the blue robes she wore were stained deep red with her blood. I knew it had taken a matter of moments, but it had felt like a lifetime. In a way it had been: those few moments had taken her life.

I bolted from my vantage point and stumbled towards my waiting car. I clutched the edge of the dented Range Rover and vomited violently into the gutter. I wiped my mouth with the back of my hand as I crawled into the vehicle. My driver took me back to the safety of the Embassy, the taste of vomit mingling with the bitterness of all I had seen.

Of all the state-sanctioned depravity I witnessed under the Taliban, this act was the most emblematic of their evil. They showed a callous disregard for the sanctity of human life, ancient cultural heritage and the basic rights of their citizens. The gender violence here was particularly abhorrent, as it violated all I personally believed: the strong should not prey on the weak, but protect them; the privileged and wealthy should use their power to alleviate the pain of others and lift them out of suffering, not subjugate them further.

I hoped my own conduct reflected these sentiments, using my position of authority to help those in need, though lately I wasn't so sure. I still believed in doing good by any means, and by cooperating with the Taliban we had brought at least some relief to the Afghans. Yet spending this much time in close proximity to evil had altered me. I had dined with the devil and I had paid the price.

In North Korea at least the government hid their oppressive actions behind a veneer of legitimacy. Even in Goma our efforts to help were in response to a huge life-threatening emergency. But never before had I encountered such openly-endorsed subjugation and abuse of power as I saw by the Taliban in Afghanistan. I reminded myself of the humanitarian principles: humanity, neutrality, impartiality, but it's challenging to remain neutral and impartial against a regime where the humanity of the people is so utterly abused.

Throughout this fraught, traumatic time it was the ordinary people that I kept my focus on. No matter the ethics of cooperating with their tyrannical rulers, we were bringing hope to them in some small way.

The personal struggle of individuals against adversity kept me buoyant. I knew that in the end their resistance was stronger than injustice.

Humanity will persist and ultimately prevail, no matter the wickedness it encounters.

Chapter Sixteen

We may encounter many defeats but we must not be defeated.
Maya Angelou

AS MY YEARS AT DFID FLEW BY, SOME UNCOMFORTABLE challenges surfaced. I became much busier as CHAD grew into a huge department. We ran an elite esprit-de-corps that was known for delivering tangible, effective results in times of crisis. We had lives to save and I had little time for stroking egos. I demanded the very best from my team because, from everything I had seen in the field, I knew that bringing help to those in trouble was of paramount importance.

My bosses in the UK government, right up to the Prime Minister, appreciated the results we brought as that reflected well on them. But they also thought that I would benefit from some coaching, to soften my harder edges and sculpt me into more of a typically-cultivated Senior Civil Servant of Whitehall. They hired me a life-coach, a thoughtful Irish woman named Annabel, who had thick brown hair and glasses and a friendly air of professional composure. She would come and have tea with me once a week and listen to my woes as well as my thoughts, feelings, hopes, and dreams.

The arrangement was that after four months of listening, she would analyse all she'd learned about me. Then she'd present me with a report telling me how she felt I could improve. In truth, I enjoyed these sessions immensely. They gave me a little bit of time and space to talk to someone in a confidential and trusted manner. Someone who was outside the formal office environment I was so deeply embroiled in, during my long hours at work. It felt like the kind of indulgent "me time" I usually failed to prioritise.

It was at one of these meetings, over our usual cup of tea and a plate of digestive biscuits in my office in Westminster, that she asked me more about my leadership ethos. "So I hear that you have quite a formidable reputation around here, Mukesh?"

I smiled into my mug of tea. "One thing I understand well is that the most important asset I have is my people," I told Annabel. "It's not the size of my budget or the authority that goes with my position or the clout that I wield internationally. Nothing would be possible without the hundred-and-fifty percent being given by my team. I'm a stickler for standards, but that goes both ways."

"How does it go both ways?" Annabel asked.

"I know how much I require from them. In this business of crisis management when you are asking people to go beyond their duty, well - it's not a normal nine-to-five job, is it? Sometimes we're sending people into dangerous areas to work under extremely tough and uncomfortable conditions. I know that first hand. I was in Rwanda when the blood was still wet on the walls. I'm not some stuffy, officious boss who has never seen action.

"I know what I'm sending them into, and if I'm delivering them into the lion's den - and I want to get the very best from my people - well then, that means being one hundred percent dedicated and loyal to them no matter what. I might be tough on them, but in turn I will always support them. They know they have my backing even if they make mistakes or when the chips are down. That's what I think is important."

I sipped my tea and thought more about the style I had fostered within my team. "With CHAD I really feel like we've created a culture of mutual solidarity and a true sense of purpose. People are inspired to work here because our work is worthwhile. We strive to make a difference to the lives of the world's most vulnerable."

"It's interesting how you speak about your staff," Annabel remarked. "I've heard you have an unusual attitude towards hiring people. Can you tell me about that?"

"My staff? Unusual?" I smiled. "Well, I guess maybe when you put it that way…"

I pictured the team I'd surrounded myself with. I had become known as the person who employed waifs and strays, people who were considered misfits in other parts of the organisation, either because they were too independently-minded, or "unmanageable," or had clashed with their bosses elsewhere.

These people would often seek me out and ask for a job. I trusted my own sense of judgement, so if I thought they were a good person, I would usually make a concerted effort to bring them into the fold. I was almost always right in this, as I had built an astute, committed, trusted team that I could rely on completely.

One example in particular sprang to mind. A very determined young woman had come and sat at my desk, introducing herself as Sarah Beeching, and told me in a very matter of fact way that she was going to work for me.

"Really?" I said in response. "I didn't know that I had any

vacancies."

"I know, but anyway, you will think of something and you will create one."

"Will I? Why should I?" I asked.

She proceeded to make many excellent points as to why I should hire her. She joined my team a week later and went on to become one of my section heads. I had a knack for spotting talent and budding potential.

When the Kosovo war broke out, I was asked by the government to gear up the humanitarian response side. This meant I needed more staff - and fast. As Kosovo was a pressing issue, I was given permission to poach whomever I wanted from other departments.

On my way to the canteen to get a sandwich I saw this young man, Matt Baugh, sitting in a corner desk working in an adjoining office. Something about him caught my attention. He looked intelligent and smart, but he definitely appeared bored, like he wasn't being fully utilised. We had a small chat and I learned he was a "fast streamer" - someone earmarked for fast promotion within the civil service because they are considered special in some way. I immediately decided that I would like him to come over and head my new Kosovo unit.

"When can you join?" I asked, and didn't wait for an answer. "Make it after lunch, say at 2 pm today." I figured it was an early test of his capabilities if, within that interim hour or so, he could figure out his release from his current responsibilities.

At 2 pm he reported for duty to my office and made an extremely competent and valuable addition to my team. Years later he became the first UK Ambassador to Somalia, after many years without British diplomatic representation there, and then went on to head the central African department in the Foreign Office.

"I guess I have gained a reputation for taking risks on people," I told Annabel. "But my theory is that anyone who *consciously* wants to work with me must be a very special person."

Annabel laughed at this, but I set her straight, continuing: "Honestly, I am not being flippant. I know I have a reputation." I smiled at her.

"I am known as a hard-driving, impatient, sometimes blunt, and I don't suffer fools gladly. I have definitely created plenty of jealousies inside DFID and outside - and don't misunderstand me - I have never sought to be universally popular either.

"In working for me, people are taking a gamble. If someone wants to join me, they run the risk that they will be seen as "in my camp" and that is not necessarily going to be good for their future careers. Therefore, if someone has the boldness to want to work with me, then I generally do my damnedest to make that a reality. If they know all about me - know all that is going to come along with working for me - and they still want to be part of it - well, that's what I look for in my staff."

"That's really the premier thing you seek?" she asked.

"Yes. It really is. Some people make friendships and alliances with powerful people, and sacrifice those not useful to them on the way. I do the opposite. I gather people who are disempowered or fallen on bad times, but otherwise worthy. I pick them up and give them chances and protect them along the way.

"I'm sure you're well versed in my personal history? Remember that someone read the aerogramme from a 16-year-old schoolboy from Bihar and gave me a chance; someone in Oxford - irritated by me beyond belief probably - read my letters and said: "Okay, you can come to Oxford if you're good enough." I have been given my fair share of chances, so I would like to repay the karmic favour, so to speak."

Now that I thought about it, my own application to Oxford was not unlike Sarah Beeching's job interview method.

***

British A-Levels are not recognised in India, so at the age of eighteen, after leaving my British boarding school, I had little choice but to remain in the UK to continue my education. I applied to many great institutions but only one got back to me - Oxford - offering me the opportunity to take the entrance exam.

Well that was okay, I thought, because really I couldn't picture myself going anywhere but Oxford. It was the best in the world. I had come this far, hadn't I? Against all the odds? Why not Oxford? I sat the preliminary entrance exam, which went quite well, and I was invited for interview.

I arrived on a beautiful day that felt full of possibility. The illustrious university town felt so old, cultivated and steeped in history. Every shop and every pub claimed to be the favourite spot of some famous writer or philosopher and I felt fortunate to be walking beneath the dreaming spires. Before my visit it had all seemed like a pipe dream, but now I saw it for myself and realised how badly I wanted it, and with that I began to feel terribly anxious.

When my name was called for interview I was a bag of nerves. Visions of returning to my grandparents in Chandigarh kept interrupting my thoughts. When I left the interview, I feared I had not presented myself with my usual eloquence.

I had not done very well as it turned out. Within a few days I received a letter from the university saying they couldn't offer me a place, but would put me on the waiting list. I knew that the wait list for medicine was incredibly long, so this was effectively a "no." I had failed.

I knew there was no way I could accept this. It just wasn't possible. There was absolutely no way I could endure two years of Wellington College's freezing dormitories, and rise to the top of my class, just to simply pack my bags and return to India to pick up school where I left off. It was unacceptable.

I took up my pen and began the first of many, many letters written back and forth between myself and the Chancellor of Oxford, the former British Prime Minister, Harold Macmillan. I wrote from my heart, pleading my case and explaining that I simply must come to Oxford - nothing else would do - and included a potted history of my story so far.

I waited in earnest for his reply, which duly arrived, handwritten, saying:

"Dear Mr Kapila, you are a very interesting young man, but you know we have many demands for places and I hope you'll be successful elsewhere..."

Unacceptable. I fired off another letter:

"Dear Mr Macmillan, thanks for replying; I'm sorry to bother you, but in my circumstances it is essential to come to Oxford, to not do so would be a tragedy..."

He wrote back once more to say

"Sorry there is no place for you, however I'm forwarding your letter to Sir Alec Cairncross, the Master of St Peter's College..."

"Aha!" I thought, and wrote a new letter:

"Dear Sir Alec, please consider me..."

He initially replied with *"No"*, but as I was in this far, I was not going to give up now. I wrote again insisting that I could not accept '*no*'. His answer came back:

"Dear Mr Kapila, you are a very persistent young man and we will give you a place if you succeed in getting three A-grades and 2 S-level grade 1s in your exams..."

This reply in effect also meant '*no*' as those grades would require absolutely perfect scores but at least I had a conditional offer. They had given me that most British of all offers: a sporting chance. That was all I needed.

I began studying harder than I have ever studied in my life. I barely left the library, only to wolf down helpings of my favourite bread and butter pudding - which passed as brain-food at Wellington - before returning again to my books. In spite of all the odds I got those grades in my exams and secured my place at Oxford. I had refused to take '*no*' for an answer.

I was fortunate that I had been given the opportunity I had. I now wanted to offer similarly determined people their chance, as long as their principles were in line with my own.

I gulped some more tea before continuing to Annabel: "I also feel that in this world of humanitarianism it's a very difficult line to tread between finding people who are committed to the cause and those who are just greedy to advance themselves. Today it's all about *careers*," I said, emphasising the word with an exaggerated flourish of my hands. "People are ambitious. They want to rise up the ranks. I feel that to make a career out of the misery of others... well, I feel uncomfortable with that.

"Humanitarianism is not a job, it is a vocation. Therefore, the management aspects of that have to be addressed in that style. In my opinion, there is little space for self-serving bureaucracy. It is about common cause, mutually inspired collaboration, and an uncompromising resolve to advance the agenda."

Annabel made a note of something as she nibbled on a biscuit. After a moment's thought she remarked: "You say "uncompromising resolve to advance the agenda" - you really are a diplomat aren't you? Even here with me in a totally confidential environment, your language choice is still so even-handed and un-emotional.

"I can only assume that the "agenda" you speak of refers to the wish to overcome the unspeakable horrors and tragedies that you've witnessed during your work in the field? We've touched briefly on this in previous sessions; the death of the young girl in Moudubi that you could not prevent; the death of the interpreter in Korea that you blame yourself for; seeing the stoning of the young woman in Afghanistan; everything you went through in the Rwandan genocide; not to mention the countless instances of sexual violence you've encountered over your time working towards your "agenda," as you put it. Do you not think that the trauma of encountering such things is taking its toll?" Annabel suggested.

"With respect, I do not," I countered. "Undeniably, all these events have affected me. I have no doubt about that at all. I carry the weight of all that inside my heart. I feel heavy with all I have seen. With guilt for the people I could not save. But after Rwanda, I resolved that if I was in charge I would do my damnedest to make sure that these kinds of atrocities would not happen on my patch.

"Now that I do have a patch of my own, a large and dedicated team working under me who have the capacity and potential to make a real difference, I am going to push them as hard as necessary to get the job done. It is not that I don't care for them - I do care more than I can say - but we have a responsibility first to the poorest, most desperate people on the planet. It is because of all that I have seen that I understand how very important this job is. If my resolve to get the very best from my resources - human and otherwise - contributes to my unpopularity with some, then that is really the least of my worries."

"Why do you think you are driven this way?" she queried, after some more thoughtful scribbling.

***

As I considered this, the memory of a long-forgotten winter's night in Cambridgeshire came to mind. The headlights on my car struggled to illuminate the winding, foggy road ahead of me. It was around midnight and a freezing mist had crept over the Fens, to envelop my little Renault Five in its icy clutches. I finally made it around the last treacherous bend driving at a snail's pace. I pulled into the driveway, turned off the engine and gratefully entered my house. I climbed the stairs, and without undressing, flopped on the bed exhausted.

I closed my eyes and immediately fell into a heavy sleep. Moments later, or so it seemed, I was woken by the piercing bleep of my pager. I glanced at the time. It was three in the morning. I groaned but swung my feet out of bed. I was on-call and as such it was my duty to answer that pager. I was in my year of general practice training under the tutelage of an amazing primary care physician, Dr Piers Recordon, who was teaching me so much about "compassionate professionalism" when caring for our patients. This also involved being on-call at night for home visits in case of an emergency.

I answered the phone to a young woman telling me she was going to kill herself. Cambridge is a university town and suicide is not uncommon among young people away from home for the first time, finding themselves alone and dealing with the pressures of life at an incredibly competitive institution. I left the warmth of my bed to climb back into the freezing car and drive to this woman's address, a student *digs* in the centre of Cambridge.

When she answered the door, I saw that she was not a lot younger than I was, a postgrad student, tearful and crying. She explained to me that her boyfriend had left her and this was the source of her distress. I made her a cup of tea, held her hand, and sat by her bedside. We talked for two hours until the sky outside lightened to a weak, rosy dawn. I remained with her until she seemed calm and I was confident she was not going to harm herself. Then I clambered back into the Renault, returned to my bed, until I was woken again by my alarm at 8 am to go to work and run a normal day's clinic.

This was the turning point. Until that morning part of me had still been toying with the idea of becoming a general medical practitioner. I could have my own local surgery, live in a manor house in a beautiful Cambridgeshire village, become a pillar of local society, earn a lot of money and be very pleased with myself. That night sitting awake at this woman's bedside made me realise that that was not the destiny for me. It was not that I felt no sympathy for her - I truly did. I couldn't help but feel real concern for someone suffering like this. She was in a bad way and clearly hurting.

Yet I couldn't help but wonder, was this what I had left India for? Done all I had done - for this? Had I endured boarding school? Studied at Oxford? Trained through six long years of medical college? Left my family half way across the world? All to be making cups of tea for women in crisis over their uncaring boyfriends? It wasn't that I was unkind - on the contrary I felt deeply for her - but this was not what I wanted for my own future. I was hardly saving the world in wealthy Cambridgeshire.

Part of me hated myself for thinking that way. I feared I had become callous and had lost the ability to care. The truth was I was bored. Bored of seeing the same patients with the same problems day in and day out, all with the same symptoms and psycho-somatic issues. Was I really going to spend the rest of my life dealing with the neuroses of the well-off British elite?

I recounted this story to Annabel.

She took off her glasses, looked at me and asked: "What do you think that young man on call in Cambridge would think of you now?"

"I think he'd be proud," I replied. "I didn't want to be a wealthy doctor, not because I didn't care, but because I wanted to make a real difference in the world. Now I do try to make that difference, and to people who really need it."

Annabel smiled, scribbled further notes and steered me back to the here and now. "You mentioned before that you do not feel you're universally popular? Why do you say that? If that is true, then why?"

"Oh, many reasons!" I laughed. "Too many to list."

"Try," she suggested, simply.

"Well there is obviously the so-called belligerency as you mentioned… But the thing I feel you must understand is that I myself am so busy, juggling all these difficult balls all over the place, travelling continually, supervising this huge team and massive budget. I am somewhat impatient and intolerant by nature, so when I see unreasonable obstacles in my path I tend to find a way around them. I guess that is unusual behaviour for a senior government official."

"When you aren't afraid in extreme circumstances, maybe to ride a little rough-shod over people who get in the way of accomplishing a task quickly, you might make some enemies, but what's the alternative?

"We are dealing with emergencies, disasters, crises, life and death situations. Undoubtedly this means flexibly interpreting rules and regulations, or skating very close to the boundaries the establishment will allow. In a high-pressure situation, often with thousands of lives at risk, it's the rules that have to be adapted, rather than the other way around. I'd rather ruffle some feathers or leave some noses out of joint, if it means getting aid to the places it's needed."

"So you think that the rules are made for other people, not for you?"

"Rules are tools to help us get the job done, that's all."

"But not everyone sees them that way?"

"No, I know that."

"Do you think your special treatment has allowed you to flaunt rules sometimes, and therefore contributed to the unpopularity you mentioned"

I smiled again. Annabel was very insightful. She had no doubt been briefed about me, but she was always careful not to extrapolate beyond what I had already mentioned myself. She led the conversation while letting me think that it all came from me.

***

I really did have special treatment within DFID. As the head of CHAD, I was permitted liberties that other people would never receive. Usually, these consisted of licence to take huge and risky decisions by myself, and spending lots of money.

Sometimes I amazed myself at what I managed to get away with. One year, I overspent my budget by almost ten million pounds. We were allotted an amount of money for the year, but it was very difficult to manage as disasters are unpredictable by their very nature. New conflicts would break out, unexpected hurricanes would strike, so it was a tricky act to ensure that all we spent was balanced at the end of the year.

Once I got it wrong. I overspent. I thought I was going to get my walking papers, but all that happened was I got a swift slap on the wrist, and the following year they allocated me ten million pounds extra, in case I went over-budget again.

CHAD felt like the darling of DFID. We were certainly a favourite of Clare Short and the politicians at the top. The New Labour government was strongly interventionist, and the UK's appetite for helping with disasters and conflicts globally had really increased. We were one of the wealthiest countries on earth, using our status to shine a light into the world's worst places and bring hope. The country was in an altruistic mood, and so were the leadership.

"New Labour have a very magnanimous attitude towards our operations," I told Annabel. "They are passionate about doing good in the world and as such are pushing us to do more work and reach more places. It is our prerogative never to say "no" - we have a can-do culture here and a strong reputation for quality and accountability.

"The way I see it, the more we've done - and done well - the more we have been asked to do. If that makes us unpopular, then it's the price I'm willing to pay. It's not like our exponential growth has been down to corporate greed, or a bloated bureaucracy - it's for bringing salvation to people who have often lost everything. We have a moral obligation as humanitarians to help those less fortunate. We might step on some toes - but only because we are doing what we know is right."

"There have been rumblings in the wider government though, haven't there?" Annabel probed. "There has been fallout from some of DFID's attitudes regarding Britain's interests?"

"Well, we've had a very radical agenda, and that required confronting hugely vested interests here in the UK. We're not too well liked by the establishment in Britain at the moment."

"Why is that?" Annabel asked.

"Well, without mincing words, we have been turning the world order upside down. You know that old system of fusty institutions and gentlemen's agreements? The old boys' clubs, and all those quiet understandings that made the members of the upper echelons very rich? They're suddenly being called out and held up to the same standards as everyone else.

"I think it's only right and proper, but it has meant that Clare Short particularly, and myself too as her hatchet man, have become a little infamous, and there are some very powerful people who would like to see us out on our ears."

"How have you done this?"

"By asking questions mostly. By asking the questions that usually go unasked."

"Questions like what?"

"Oh like...why are we sending aid to this country at the same time as selling weapons to their enemies to kill them?" We've been uncovering the ugly truth about British arms trading, which brings in a huge amount of money to the UK, yet not many know about it. There are a lot of establishment figures whose family members are heavy shareholders in weapons manufacturing, but naturally they keep this very quiet."

Annabel sipped her tea thoughtfully before remarking: "You don't seem to have much respect for institutional hierarchy?"

I chuckled at this. She had got the read on me, there was no denying it. I thought I may as well speak plainly. "I have no respect for authority when it is not earned. Or when it is not helpful. To be honest I don't do well in boxes. I am not an institutions man - yet, ironically, I always find myself working for these big organisations. They seem to seek me out.

"I've gone from an elite private school to the most famous of universities, then straight into the British Government - yet I fundamentally disagree with the structural ways that these establishments work, because they let hierarchy cloud the reality of the best way to operate.

"I understand this must be perplexing and infuriating for many institutions - they must really struggle with what to do with me. I am very lucky to have been given such free rein to grow CHAD; to become such a force within the humanitarian world." I added. It was true.

Annabel assessed her notes for a second. "It seems to me Mukesh, that you are the sort of person that every organisation would want to join them. But then, once they have you on board, they would also be very happy to let you go again."

I laughed out loud. She was right, though I had never considered it that way before. I was the kind of person that anyone would love to have, but would also be glad to say goodbye to. Was that a fault with the institution? Or a fault with me? Or simply an unfortunate incompatibility? Was this something I should be working on changing? Or let it be?

"You are your own greatest strength," Annabel went on. "Your dedication to the cause, out-of-the-box-thinking, willingness to bend the rules to get results - but of course those traits also happen to be your biggest weakness. They mean that those who do adhere to the traditional *modus operandi* often begin to foster a disgruntled resentment against you."

"So, what do you advise I should do? Try and play by the rules more?"

"No, I don't think so," Annabel mused. "If you were to start playing by the rules rather than playing to your strengths, you would not be so effective. What I would suggest for now is to stop using your red pen to write feedback, as it has become somewhat symbolic to your team. Use green."

"OK, I will do that." I picked up my red marker pen and threw it into the wastepaper basket. "I shall do exactly as you advise. Any more tips?"

"Not really," she said honestly. "I think that if you stopped being yourself it would be a loss, both to the organisation, yourself and those you are trying your upmost to help. They'll just have to find a way to accommodate you, until the voices of dissent get too loud to ignore. And then you will have to go. It is the price you must expect to pay."

Annabel helped me by giving me this insight - and I am eternally grateful to her for her profound assessment of my strengths and weaknesses. Maybe I was not suited to belong in institutions at all? Certainly, she was correct in intimating that the end of my time at DFID was drawing near, and perhaps she was right to suggest I jump before I was pushed.

***

I knew my days were numbered. In the civil service you have to periodically rotate departments, to avoid anyone become too stuck in their ways and to allow for fresh eyes and progress. This usually means a switch around every three years. I had already been running CHAD for five years and, as Annabel had pointed out, I had been given unprecedented liberties to expand my operations. I had taken my inch and well and truly run miles with it, but we were fast becoming the victims of our own success.

Under my leadership I had increased our budget tenfold, and had more than tripled my staff. We were literally growing out of our parent department of DFID, requiring larger office space. I felt that Clare Short and the higher level were trying to accommodate me and my giant cuckoo baby that was becoming a little too big and boisterous, but others were running out of patience.

So there arose the problem of what they were going do with me? The way they saw it, I could not be allowed to continue running riot and flaunting regulations, as CHAD grew exponentially. But I didn't want to do anything else, even if they could find something for me.

The writing was on the wall. For the establishment I was getting to be an undeniable pain in the neck. I was admired by many, but resented by others. I worried that my superiors would listen to the dissenting voices and move me from my beloved CHAD to head some other department, say, "facility management" - cleaning and catering, building repair, and suchlike. That would be a death sentence for me.

Then came an event that would shake not only the UK government, but the very fabric of The Free World. There was suddenly an urgent need for me elsewhere.

Chapter Seventeen

Grab the broom of anger and drive off the beast of fear.
Zora Neale Hurston

THE 9ᵀᴴ OF SEPTEMBER 2001 BEGAN LIKE ANY NORMAL Tuesday. I was sitting in my office with my management team. The television was behind me, muted in the background. We usually had it playing, tuned to one of the twenty-four-hour news channels to keep abreast of current affairs.

As I addressed the team I noticed that my normally attentive colleagues were getting fidgety. I looked up from my notes and saw they were all transfixed on the TV behind me, like toddlers sat in front of a cartoon, paying no attention to my presentation at all. I wrapped my knuckles on the table and asked them to return to the task at hand.

Sarah, one of my staff, glanced at me briefly, before pointing to the TV. "So sorry Mukesh, but you'd better take a look."

I rounded on the television to see 9/11 unfolding on the screen. We stared open mouthed at images of the World Trade Center smoking, a giant hole torn from the side of one of the towers. As we watched aghast, wondering what could possibly have happened, another aircraft collided with the second tower live on TV. More news came flooding in thick and fast.

Of course, our meeting was suspended. We gathered around the TV watching the minute-by-minute updates. As more and more information came in, it became obvious that this was not, as we had hoped, a tragic air-traffic control malfunction, but a viciously premeditated attack on the western world. It was evident that this was a monumental day. As I watched, I had a premonition that my own life would be profoundly turned upside down by these horrific events.

Over the following days I was busy with meetings in Whitehall, as the government machinery swung into action. The terrorist group Al-Qaeda, who were based in my pariah-state jurisdiction of Afghanistan, claimed responsibility for the attack. Now we were trying to figure out how the USA would respond and what it meant for Britain and everyone else on the planet.

Within weeks, the US and allies - including the UK - were bombing Afghanistan. Now I was even more certain that the world would never be the same again. I thought of all the Afghan civilians I'd encountered during my many trips to that suffering land. The Afghans had already endured the long civil war, then puritanical Taliban rule, and now they were enduring an unrelenting air attack from the most powerful countries on earth.

As the furious air-war over Afghanistan intensified, hundreds of thousands were displaced in all directions. Some sought sanctuary in neighbouring Pakistan or Iran, while others found shelter internally in the country's caves, mountains and wherever they felt safe. My job was to see what we could do for the casualties. That included redoubling our assistance to refugee camps in neighbouring countries, as well as trying to get essential supplies across the border.

We organised air drops of high-density energy biscuits on top of displaced civilian populations, but flying over the country was incredibly dangerous in the midst of out-and-out war. I knew from my previous visits just how harsh and inhospitable the Afghan terrain is at the best of times, let alone now that all the normal road routes were blocked. People were dying in their droves from hunger and exposure. The situation was truly desolate.

Serious planning went into organising a convoy of donkeys that could cross over the mountains by the goat tracks that ran into the country. Our problem was that there were not enough donkeys available and each couldn't carry much relief really, as it also had to transport its own food supply, for there was little fodder to graze on the journey. Despite its clear limitations we persevered with this donkey plan, such was our desperation.

For us it was important to finish the war as soon as possible and then move in fast to pick up the pieces. This was the best humanitarian outcome we could hope for: a swift end to the fighting, so we could reach the displaced civilians before cold and starvation finished them off. Luckily, I had a lot of experience with Afghanistan and so was invited to many planning meetings at the Cabinet Office, where I fervently argued the benefits of this outcome.

To our relief the war did not last long. The Taliban were routed and the Northern Alliance installed as the new government in Kabul, with Hamid Karzai as president. I felt elated. The Taliban were gone. The cruel tyranny of their reign was over. This was the point our real work began. Now, with the whole world's focus on Afghanistan, it was imperative that the international community ensured that a representative government of the people replaced the oppressive Taliban regime. Many Afghans would not have known peace in their lifetime, growing up forever under the threat of an unstable country. I wanted to make lasting peace a reality for them.

Kofi Annan, the UN Secretary General, visited London for official talks on these matters, and part of his programme was to call upon Clare Short. We met around the big table in her office, Clare and Kofi sat across from each other. I was off to one corner, surrounded by other senior officials and Annan's own UN staff. The discussion touched upon a broad range of issues and many voices were heard in the conversation.

Suddenly and to my complete surprise, Kofi Annan looked directly at me, before turning to say, "Clare, we would like to borrow Mukesh from you for the UN, to help us out in Afghanistan."

I was startled and sat up straight. All eyes in the room were on me. Some looked on in polite interest, some in good-natured encouragement, but none looked more surprised than Clare. She regained her composure much faster than I, and before I could stammer any response she said.

"Well if you think this will help, I am happy to go along, if Mukesh also wants to?" With that the deal was done.

***

I found out later that this was actually the idea of Lakhdar Brahimi, a long-serving Algerian UN diplomat, who Kofi Annan had appointed as his special representative for Afghanistan. Brahimi and I knew each other well. I had supported him in relation to the *Brahimi Report*, which was a seminal review of the way the UN conducted its peace keeping operations. I had facilitated several consultations on this review around the world, and so we had spent a lot of time together.

Brahimi had argued that he needed the assistance of someone from a donor background; someone who knew how the humanitarian system worked; was well connected; and knew the political and historical sensitivities of the region. He had thought of me and sought my secondment from DFID as his special advisor.

I was flattered to be asked, but felt somewhat ambivalent. I had a well-established job in a senior position with influence and resources at the heart of the British government. In addition, I had a family and a comfortable settled life. Heading back into Afghanistan, fresh from conflict, was a step into an uncertain future. Still, I *had* had a premonition that 9/11 would change my life - I just didn't anticipate quite how quickly that would happen.

I agreed to go. I was speedily uprooted and found myself in Kabul in 2002. Brahimi was forging his new administration and I mucked in on all sorts of jobs as UNAMA - the United Nations Assistance Mission in Afghanistan - became established.

I was never without a team of four highly-trained security guards, for I was a British national and there were specific threats against Britons. They worked in shifts, so I was protected 24/7. They would stand watch outside my door at night and do advanced reconnaissance missions of any unfamiliar meeting place in order to determine if it was safe to attend. The downside was that nobody wanted to invite me to meetings or social events, because my attendant security was so disruptive. Yet we managed the best we could.

My main duty was trying to raise resources to fund the newly established government. It was important to understand Afghanistan's priorities for rehabilitation and reconstruction, so we worked very closely with members of the new leadership, Hamid Karzai, Ashraf Ghani and Abdullah Abdullah, the founding members of the new 'National Unity Government' to create our shared vision.

We prioritised food security, de-mining, health, security sector reform and education, as well as facilitating the return of refugees and internally displaced people so they could begin to rebuild their lives in a Taliban-free Afghanistan. There was a lot of hope and optimism that this would be the longed-for turning point for this suffering nation.

My personal priority was to bring healthcare. So much health knowledge had been lost under the Taliban. Under the new government, women had access to healthcare once more, but under the Taliban the country's general health status had regressed massively. I wanted to bring the country up to speed again because, if this was overlooked, the consequences would be dire.

***

This I knew first-hand, from my own family tragedy.

My school days in Chandigarh had whirled by in a happy blur of lessons, books and delicious meals of curry and dhal with my grandparents. But one day when I was around fourteen I returned home from school to find my grandfather collapsed in a chair, a crumpled telegram clutched in his shaking hand. In my experience telegrams meant only one of two things: a birthday or bad news, and I was pretty sure this was nobody's birthday. I took up the paper he was holding and nervously read its contents. My baby brother - little Bunty, as we called him - who was only ten months old, had died.

I sank into a chair beside my grandfather, shocked and disbelieving. How could this be true? The telegram was brief and gave few details.

I learned later that Bunty had got diarrhoea, just childish diarrhoea like babies get anywhere in the world and nobody thought too much about it. But rather than giving him lots of fluids to keep him hydrated, my parents had restricted his drinking to stop him vomiting, and within days he was dead.

It was decided that there was no point in sending me to Bihar for the funeral. It was so far away I would never make it in time, so the following day I was back in the Irish Brothers School. But I was withdrawn and distracted. My face was red and swollen from a sleepless night's sobbing. My classmates noticed something was wrong, and when class was over Brother Drew, my favourite teacher, invited me to have tea with him in the school house.

I normally loved these visits. Reverend Brother Drew was in the habit of giving extra tuition on Saturdays around his sturdy wooden dining table, but today I sat listless and despondent. We were silent for a while as he busied himself with the kettle, the steam mingling with the white smoke from the cigarette he seemed to smoke continuously. Finally, he laid two cups of steaming, sweet tea on the table, sat opposite me, and offered me a sugared biscuit from a large tin. I shook my head.

Brother Drew's gnarled and wrinkly brow furrowed further with concern. He knew things must be really serious if I was refusing biscuits.

"The school received a note from your grandparents this morning, Mukesh," he said in a gentle tone. "I am so sorry to hear about your brother. What was his name?"

"Bunty," I replied quietly. "Everyone called him Bunty."

"Bunty, I see," Drew repeated. "Do you mind if I ask what happened, Mukesh?"

In a small sad voice, quite unlike my own, I relayed the story of Bunty's sickness. When I was done Father Drew sighed heavily and shook his head.

"Such unfairness. Such cruel unfairness. I am so sorry."

He sat back in his chair, hands clasped around his steaming tea cup, surveying me gravely. "It is your aspiration to be a doctor, isn't it, Mukesh?"

"Yes, sir. I mean, I guess so, sir." The truth was that the medical aspirations I harboured were more my family's than my own. Every Indian parent wanted their child to be a doctor, lawyer, or engineer. Law seemed far too boring to me and I was hopelessly unpractical, so medicine seemed like the least bad option.

Brother Drew was quiet for a moment, his cigarette burning low between his leathery fingers. I drank my tea and eyed him over the rim of the teacup. This silence made me nervous, as for all his kindly words he was still an imposing character.

Sighing again he broke his reverie and set his eyes on me. "Mukesh, I am sorry for this, but I feel I must say it plainly: your brother died of ignorance. That is the hard truth of it. Where I grew up in Ireland it was known throughout the country, even in the poorest and most isolated places, that it is imperative to treat infant sickness with rehydration. Ireland was not a rich country - we too suffered grave injustices at the hand of the British Empire - yet this grasp of rudimentary child health is known everywhere. I ask, how can it not be the same in India?"

I was confused at his words. My parents were well educated - an engineer and a teacher - yet this lifesaving knowledge had been unknown to them. I realised that Drew was right. I could see the deep sadness in his face and at that moment I felt I understood him. He had dedicated his life to the education of boys like me, so that we might go out and do good in the world and correct some of the unfairness so prevalent in our country, and further afield.

"I love India," he continued. "Yet I can't see why the wealth of knowledge that exists in the rest of the world cannot be as prevalent here."

"Yes, sir," I replied shyly. I didn't know quite what to say to a teacher speaking so plainly.

At that Brother Drew smiled warmly and I sensed the lecture was over. "I think medicine would suit you very well," he concluded. "You're a clever boy with a kind heart, and if you continue to apply yourself, you will go far. Now have a biscuit."

I smiled gratefully, reaching for the proffered tin and, as the biscuit sweetened my taste buds, I began to feel a little better.

I didn't know it then, but that afternoon at Brother Drew's table galvanised something inside me. I felt determined to use this first-rate education I'd had the good fortune to receive to go out and right some of the injustices I had experienced. Now, so many years later in Afghanistan, I wanted to continue that mission and make sure basic healthcare and education were prioritised.

***

As well as pushing my own agenda, I had to lobby powerful British interests too. The "special relationship" fostered between Tony Blair and George W Bush meant that Britain was complicit in the ramped-up American-driven focus on the so-called "War on Drugs". A big part of establishing the new Afghan government was tied up with trying to eliminate opium production, an export which had re-emerged under the Taliban in later years.

Though I supported the British and US interest in ridding our streets of narcotics, I held out little hope that anything would change. I felt that the socio-economic situation in Britain was more to blame for the drug use there. Poor people had had a very, very hard time of it during the many years of austerity. They had seen previously booming industries fall by the wayside, their hopes, dreams and futures evaporating before their eyes.

I believed that this was a reason that the drugs crisis was such a problem. Even if it were possible to stop opiate production, disenfranchised people would just find some other way to alleviate their depression, at least temporarily. My public health background taught me that looking at the broader systemic issues would be the key to help these people stop turning to drugs to manage their misery.

I also felt it was somewhat futile to implement crop-substitution programmes. The powers that be wanted us to inspire the Afghans to grow potatoes and onions, instead of poppy. I knew this was hopeless from my previous work in Bolivia, where I had seen the coca plantations from which cocaine comes. Foreign powers were trying to convince the poor, local, subsistence farmers to swap their lucrative coca crop to grow vegetables instead.

Apart from the fact that they wouldn't make as much money that way, they were also under pressure from cartels and criminal networks who target poor people and coerce them into drugs production. There is never going to be the same incentive to grow other legal crops. Nobody is going to threaten your family if you want to stop growing turnips.

The real problems lay with those who marketed the drugs, pushed them, trafficked them. Those people got rich by exploiting farmers on one end and addicts on the other. They were the ones who should be targeted to combat the drug problem. The Americans couldn't seem to see this. They wanted to use their air force to fire-bomb the poppy fields in southern Afghanistan and destroy the crops. No crops - no problem.

This is exactly what they had done in Colombia when opium production was rampant there. In desperation - and with an armed conflict raging on the ground - the US, who were sympathetic to the authoritarian regime in Colombia, had bombed the fields. This might have obliterated heroin manufacture for that year, but in doing so, it created a crisis for the farmers. How would they feed their families, with their means of production destroyed? Such punitive action also alienated people, turning them against the government and fuelling the fire of the rebels.

The American military commanders seemed to have no ability to think or care about the longer-term consequences. How many enemies would you make if you suddenly came to bomb their fields and their livelihoods, leaving the people destitute and angry? Of course, it was a similar situation in an already unstable country like Afghanistan.

Nevertheless, we felt obliged to try to work the anti-drugs rhetoric into the fabric of the new Afghan government. I hoped this would serve as an added incentive, when I tried to convince foreign donors to invest money into helping set up the new regime. I embarked on a tour of donor capitals across Europe and the Gulf, seeking to drum up money and support for our work in Afghanistan. Thanks to my time at the UK Government, I was well connected, happily received, and listened to attentively at senior level in donor countries.

Now that I was no longer affiliated with DFID I feared the gravitas I held from working as part of the British Government would be lost. Yet this was not the case. Those I met trusted I knew what I was doing and knew my background and experience. I learned that people believe in people more than they do in institutions. My word was my bond.

***

It put me in mind of a time, when I was still with DFID, a few years back, visiting Honduras in the aftermath of Hurricane Mitch, when I learned the power that comes with personal integrity.

Strong winds gusted the handful of tattered palm trees that still stood tall above the vast expanse of mud and destruction. These few bare and wind-torn trunks were all that remained of what had once been a huge banana plantation. I watched the leaves, shredded to ribbons, slick, blackened and sodden, flap soggily against the backdrop of a forbidding grey sky.

"Bananas are Honduras's premier export crop," my guide, James, a representative from the American charity CARE explained, as he drove me through the shattered landscape in a rugged 4x4. "Or should I say they *were* the premier crop. Not any longer, as you can see."

CARE is a well-known international disaster relief agency. Very often they were first on the scene as a disaster unfolded and were now courting donors like me, discussing the extent of the devastation, explaining the needs of the most vulnerable and trying to secure the vital funds to deliver relief. I had flown in on the first available flight, a bumpy ride as the tail winds of the hurricane were blustering around, and was busy touring the devastation.

It was worse than I had ever imagined. Hurricane Mitch did not rip through the country, cutting a tear of rampant destruction and then moving on. Instead, the storm meandered lazily across the landscape, taking its time to dump more and more rainfall onto the people as they clung to higher ground.

The slow-moving nature of Mitch is what made that particular hurricane - which was not the biggest, nor the most powerful - into the deadliest the area had seen in living memory. The storm dropped a deluge of rain onto Central America, and we learned that there were upwards of 7,000 fatalities in Honduras alone.

Millions of litres of rainfall had pounded the fertile earth, pulverising the ground and transforming it from solid, dependable farmland into treacherous viscous torrents. The fast-flowing mud assaulted the country like an invading army, uprooting trees, drowning settlements, seizing animals and people alike to be dragged away in its surging torrent.

It was difficult to tell quite how monumental the death toll would be, but from the scores of bloated bodies we saw rising to the surface of the mud, there was no denying its severity. The few structures still standing were crowded with survivors. The little shelters were woefully inadequate and I saw whole families huddled tight together, shivering in their sodden clothes. The children and elderly suffered most, for they lacked the strength to hold on in the deluge.

As I watched, it began to drizzle again.

"The rains have been falling intermittently since Mitch passed on, and more rain is expected," James told me gravely. "People are forced to sleep outside under the elements. There are tens of thousands out in the open and at risk of dying. Everything is sodden so they can't even keep themselves warm with a fire, cook food or heat water. The water supplies are compromised, so without the ability to boil water, disease outbreaks are inevitable."

James slowed our mud-caked 4x4 to a halt outside a small roadside café that by some miracle remained relatively intact. We ordered lunch - a simple yet warming vegetable stew - and after wiping the grease from my lips onto the paper napkin, I asked James directly.

"So, what do you need?" He seemed relieved by the bluntness of my question, tired of dilly-dallying around the issue.

"We need shelter. Tents and materials to put a roof over people's heads, and it's bloody urgent - we need it, like, yesterday. We're not talking just a few tents - we have to import enough to shelter thousands."

"Can you do it?" I asked him straight. "If you have the money, can you get the people what they need?"

"Yeah, absolutely," he confirmed. "We've got stocks close by in Miami. We just require the cash to get the ball rolling."

I sat back against the plastic chair and looked out of the window at the downpour. The funds James was requesting were no small amount. Normally to initiate a project like this there are a lot of rules to follow: committees have to approve the proposed use of the money; you have to do a project document; all the paperwork must be in order. Once the donor has transferred the money, the guidelines ask for large sum items, like the materials needed for an operation like this, to be put for competitive tender to make sure they were getting the best deal on the market. These precautions are all in place to make sure that the system is fair and immune to corruption, but the whole process takes weeks, time we clearly didn't have.

I thought of the people sat in sodden clothes, shivering under the glowering sky. There simply wasn't enough time for all that, if they were going to survive.

***

Sitting there with James in Honduras in the middle of a hurricane-sacked landscape, my mind flipped back to the first time I had represented the UK at an international meeting. It was the Humanitarian Aid Committee of the European Commission - a very important forum. Custom dictated that the meeting would be conducted in two languages, English and French. Everyone had to speak English or French - except the French had to speak in English and the British had to speak in French - so that everyone had an even playing field.

My French is patchy at best but I had written out the speech in English and asked my deputy at the time, Roger Clarke, to translate it. When my turn came to speak I got to my feet and painfully worked my way through it, totally massacring the language. I could feel the palpable embarrassment of my colleagues, wincing at my terrible pronunciation. I don't even know if anyone understood what I was saying. Mercifully the session ended and we went off to a sumptuous lunch, as was customary in Brussels.

As I sipped an aperitif, trying to forget the awkwardness of my presentation, my French counterpart approached me and introduced himself. He was an elegant Parisian in a finely cut suit. He welcomed me to my first time on the Committee and asked me where I was born.

"In India," I replied. At that time there weren't many non-white faces representing any European country - so I thought maybe I was a bit unusual and that was the reason for his question.

At my answer, a twinkle came into his eye. "*Voilà!*" he exclaimed. "Then your mother tongue is not English - so please in future you can speak in English." He put special emphasis on the "please". We both laughed and I spoke in English from that time on. No rules were broken and nobody seemed to mind - particularly not the French.

I learned a lesson from that suave Parisian diplomat, who had been in this game for a very long time, that rules are meant only to guide us. They are the platform from which we can work but they are not meant to imprison us. Where there is a will there is a way around the rules, if it makes common sense to bypass them.

With that lesson in my mind, I took a pen from my pocket, picked up my soiled napkin from the table, and wrote out there and then:

"*I pledge to pay the sum of one million pounds sterling to CARE for shelter relief items for Honduras in the wake of Hurricane Mitch,*" signing my name "*Mukesh Kapila, Head of Conflict and Humanitarian Affairs, Department for International Development, UK Government.*"

That was good enough for James. He and I rushed back to his office, which was powered by a temperamental old generator, and he faxed this napkin to CARE headquarters. It was good enough for the administrators back in the USA, and without waiting for the paperwork from DFID they used their own funds to kick-start the expenditure. We had the relief supplies shuttling in and shelters going up within days. I have no doubt that the urgency with which we had acted saved countless lives.

I met up with James years later and he reminded me of this story. "I have that napkin framed in the head office at CARE. We use it as a case study to teach new recruits."

"I always did want to ask you," I ventured. "What made you and the CARE officials agree to it? Surely it was very risky to advance all that spending on something so unorthodox. What if the British Government had turned around and said, "no - sorry but you can't have the money." Governments are tricky after all, with lots of protocol to follow, which we had clearly broken... What then?"

"I wasn't worried," James said. "I wasn't trusting the British government, was I? I was trusting *you*. I knew your reputation in the industry: your methods might be a little maverick but you are true to your word. If I had the oath of Mukesh Kapila, that was good enough for me."

***

As it turned out, my word was good enough for a lot of other people too. As I travelled the globe to advocate for Afghanistan on behalf of the United Nations, I used my connections with governments as well as my personal credibility to extract vast resources for Afghanistan's recovery after the nightmare Taliban years. Of course, I also played on the sense of guilt that world leaders had for their earlier neglect as well as a lot of general public sympathy for the bombed, abused, and displaced Afghan people. I argued that the historic post-Taliban opportunity would be lost without the right kind of developmental assistance to set the country up to succeed as a properly-functioning unified state, instil good governance, and draw up a new social contract between the central government and the citizens of different ethnic groups.

Afghanistan is home to many diverse peoples. The Pashtun majority; the Tajiks; the Mongolian-looking Hazara; the Turcik Uzbeks; the semi-nomadic Aimak and Turkmen; the Kurdish Baloch; the Aryan-looking Nuristani; and more besides. Each was tired of the constant fighting and ready to build peace after the years of war.

They had watched governments come and go. The concept of one united Afghanistan seemed unnatural for a country that was such an ethnic melting pot, but if there was ever a time for unification, it was now. The mood within the country and in the international community was one of hope. The moment felt full of potential to forge a new, peaceful, free, inclusive nation.

That's why I made such a concerted effort to raise cash. I set up a financial tracking service for Afghanistan so we could monitor the money coming in, including private donors and NGOs, to introduce a sense of transparency, and try to match the government's recovery plans with incoming funds. I used all my years of experience to help in any way I could.

After several months of slogging from country to country, negotiating on behalf of the hopeful new leadership of Afghanistan, I had helped to raise some two-and-a-half-billion dollars. I prayed that this would be spent wisely, to stabilise the notoriously fractious country. Everything seemed to be on track at the time of my departure, when my six-month secondment to the UN came to an end. I had only been brought in to raise money. How it was to be spent was up to the new government.

Time would reveal that all our well-meaning hopes came to nought. Precious little of the money went where it was needed due to corruption and mismanagement. I learned a bitter lesson - that peace grows from the bottom up and cannot be imposed from the top down, even if you have the best of intentions and the whole world behind you with billions at your disposal.

Though I had not been able to achieve the progress I'd wanted for Afghanistan, the experience benefitted my own personal development greatly. I became aware of how much I had grown since I'd first joined the British government. Now, so many years later, my personal authority and experience in the field meant that I was a trusted player on the international stage. It felt good to stretch my legs again and test my skills in unfamiliar territories.

I was ready for new challenges.

Chapter Eighteen

Where, after all, do universal human rights begin? In small places, close to home - so close and so small that they cannot be seen on any maps of the world. ... Unless these rights have meaning there, they have little meaning anywhere. Without concerned citizen action to uphold them close to home, we shall look in vain for progress in the larger world.
Eleanor Roosevelt

WHEN MY TIME IN AFGHANISTAN CAME TO A CLOSE, I WAS anxious about what to do next. Though I would have liked to remain, staying on in Kabul was not an option as I had been seconded only to generate funding for the new government. The money had been raised, thanks to the generosity of the wider world and so my purpose there was over.

Although I was supposed to return to DFID, I didn't feel I could. Living right in the thick of things in Kabul had opened my eyes to the challenges there and I was determined to throw myself into some new struggle. I realised that I had outgrown my position at DFID, maybe longer ago that I liked to admit. Returning would be a backward step somehow.

My next chapter opened when I got an unexpected call from Sérgio Vieira de Mello, the UN High Commissioner for Human Rights. "Mukesh, I would like you to join my office as my special advisor," he announced, over the phone.

Sérgio was a dedicated, highly intelligent Brazilian who I had known for years. I had first appreciated his unique talents when he was employed in the office of an old antagonist of mine, Mrs Sadako Ogata, the UN High Commissioner for Refugees. He had been diligently working away under her reign for many years and I admired the way he undertook his tasks despite her troubled leadership. I knew that his humanitarian motivations were honourable, unlike the self-serving attitudes of others in UNHCR at that time.

Ever since witnessing the chaotic response to the Erzincan earthquake, I had felt that there needed to be a more efficient system to manage international disaster relief. I campaigned for the creation of an overarching agency that would coordinate all the different

NGOs, governments, and aid agencies in times of emergency. This would ensure that resources went quickly to where they would do the most good, and where they would not feed the chaos.

In 1998, thanks in part to my persistent agitation from London alongside similar-minded colleagues in other key capitals, the UN Secretariat's humanitarian machinery was restructured, leading to the creation of the United Nations Office for the Coordination of Humanitarian Affairs (OCHA) whose purpose it was to do just that.

OCHA was created to organise the combined resources of the different aid organisations, to respond appropriately to crises around the world. It would oversee the deployment of relief, ensuring it came in the most efficient way to bring about hope and help, both at the time of the emergency and afterwards. This new, powerful agency would have a lot to handle, and I wanted to see someone in charge who had proven and sincere credentials.

It was then that I'd remembered Mrs Ogata's senior staff member, Sérgio. He had an excellent track record as someone who wasn't afraid to get his hands dirty and was known for high-achievement under pressure. He seemed to fit the bill nicely and I did everything in my power to ensure he was considered for the job. With some lobbying backed by the British Government, he was appointed as the new Under Secretary General for Humanitarian Affairs and the UN Emergency Relief Co-Ordinator, which made him the world's top humanitarian official.

Our paths had crossed many times since then, including in East Timor and Kosovo where, in my donor capacity within DFID, I had supported his efforts via opening the purse-strings of the British Government. He had since been asked by Kofi Annan to become the High Commissioner for Human Rights in Geneva. Now, in my hour of need for a new challenge, it seemed that he had remembered how I had championed him, hence the call asking me to join his team as a special advisor.

"To do what, Sérgio?" I asked him.

"I want to commission a review, Mukesh, of OHCHR field offices," he told me in his typically friendly but assertive tone. OHCHR was the Office of the United Nations High Commissioner for Human Rights. "I need someone with a practical understanding of field operations who is not afraid to be honest and frank about our failings - and I thought to myself, who could do that better than you?"

"Thank you Sérgio, but you do realise my background isn't technically within human rights…" I warned him, because it was true, this was not an area that I knew much about.

"Oh, nonsense Mukesh. Everything you do is human rights," he asserted and I pictured him on the other end of the phone dismissively waving his hand. "What's important is that you and I share a common practical, field-orientated background. OHCHR is too scholastic, everyone has grand convoluted theoretical ideas about human rights, but nobody actually knows how to put them into action successfully to improve human lives."

I smiled. I thought I knew what Sérgio was talking about. I was aware that OHCHR did not have a great reputation. It was primarily based in Geneva with a somewhat academic perspective. Although it had done good work over the decades on generating human rights principles and norms, it was not the hard-hitting hands-on agency that Sérgio longed for.

"What I ask is for you to have a long hard look at the way OHCHR's field operations work, to see how they could be transformed into a much more proactive force for confronting human wrongs and promoting human rights. My vision is to make OHCHR much more country- and ground-orientated, rather than all this sitting about in an ivory tower, eating Swiss chocolate, contemplating theories of free speech while looking out over the tranquil waters of *Lac Léman*."

I chuckled at his obvious distain for the luxuries the aid community enjoyed in one of the richest cities on earth, while trying to bring around hope and change for the poorest of the world's citizens.

"The offices are in the Palais Wilson, aren't they?" I asked with a smile. "I hear it's very beautiful there… and I do like chocolate…"

"So you'll come? Brilliant, Mukesh. Bloody brilliant. Can't wait to have you on the team." And he hung up.

***

So I moved from Kabul to Geneva and took possession of a well-positioned corner office. As promised I had a lake view and easy access to the finest bars and restaurants the city had to offer. It couldn't have been further from the carnage and confusion of Kabul, and despite my thorough enjoyment of the finery of the situation, I was determined not to forget. I planned to inject some of the reality of life in Afghanistan into the lofty detachment of OHCHR.

I devoted myself to my new task. I relished the challenge of being personally commissioned by the High Commissioner for Human Rights to critically evaluate what they did in some of the most difficult locations in the world, all with the view to improving their conduct and delivery. What could be more rewarding? I only had four months to complete my report and I had a huge amount to cover.

I studied all the resolutions and reports of the UN general assembly on human rights, since the adoption of the Universal Declaration of Human Rights in 1948. I poured over files from other countries and personally interviewed Sérgio's senior staff. Considering my own prior experience as a donor, I spoke to the governments who funded the office to hear their opinions, as well as the thoughts of other departments within the UN. I extensively quizzed the so-called 'special mechanisms' - the expert rapporteurs and advisors for torture, disappearances, human trafficking, violence against women, xenophobia, and myriad other human cruelties - who held important roles within the global human rights system.

It was the most extensive investigation I could do and I had free access to any information that I wanted. NGOs were consulted, advocacy groups were interviewed, as well as the governments who sat on the Human Rights Committee. It was a very, very busy time for me and a huge contrast to my previous work.

I learned that OHCHR had many committed, true-hearted professionals, with specific focus on different critical issues. They had committees on economic, social and cultural rights; elimination of discrimination; migrant workers; on the rights of the child and many other functions. These were many of the issues that I had been trying to tackle in DFID, where I had wanted to see the most high-risk groups represented and supported.

When Clare Short and I had dreamed up *The New Humanitarianism* all those years before, we didn't know - well I at least didn't know, Clare might have - that the topics we were focussing on all came under the umbrella of human rights.

As I learned more, I realised that Sérgio had been right - everything I did really *was* human rights - I just hadn't recognised that until now. As I became increasingly entangled in the struggle for fairness in this world - ever encouraged by Sérgio Vieira de Mello - I got more and more enthused, committed and passionate about it. I even contemplated that working in human rights was a logical next step, after my public health and humanitarian careers.

It was an intense time of travel and enquiry. As my report was to focus on field work, I embarked on a round-the-world trip. I visited OHCHR's projects across four continents to learn what I could from talking to both victims and survivors, as well as their protectors, before making my way back to Geneva.

***

Sérgio's own grand office was close to mine. Once I returned, I made my way straight there. I was eager to talk over everything I had encountered on my trips. At the sound of my entry, Sérgio rose to his feet from behind his large desk and greeted me warmly.

"Ah, the weary traveller has returned! Mukesh! It's good to see you."

"It's good to see you too, Sérgio," I exclaimed, and it really was. Sérgio was a delightful man with wit and charm and an extraordinary sharp emotional intelligence that, along with his life-long experience of the UN system, made him highly effective in navigating its Byzantine corridors. I knew I had a lot to learn from him. To enjoy the confidence of the developing world, the EU, Russia and China, and the USA, as Sérgio did, was an extraordinary feat that I had not seen anyone achieve so well before or since.

He was also intensely loyal - though highly critical - of the system to which he belonged. It was this matter he was keen to discuss with me, now that I was back from my travels.

"There will be time tonight to talk over all you've seen. But first," he said with a wicked grin, "whisky."

Sérgio poured us both generous glasses of a fine, pale, Scottish malt and we moved outside to the balcony. The sun was fast disappearing behind the mountains that encompassed the city. Its last rays cast a warm, orange glow onto the elegant lakeside buildings. Their rooftops glittered in the twilight, punctuated by large neon signs, ostentatiously spelling out the names of the famous Swiss watch companies and grand hotel chains that pervade Geneva.

I was grateful to take the load off my tired legs, as I had come straight from the airport. I sank into a chair, picked up my whisky, clinked it against Sérgio's outstretched glass, and took a hearty swig. A heavy sigh left my lips as I felt the pleasant burn of the fiery liquid spreading down my throat. I had been all across the world and was pleased to be back. My mind was buzzing with all I had encountered. Luckily Sérgio was as keen to hear what I had seen as I was to talk about it.

"I feel like I've observed so many inter-twining factors, my brain is totally fried," I began.

"The night is young!" Sérgio exclaimed, settling back into his chair.

"The interesting thing," I said tentatively, "is that the more people I met where OHCHR has field offices, the more their experiences seemed to galvanise the theoretical ideas I had been learning about human rights."

"Aha!" Sérgio laughed, his smile flashing. "I did hear that you had been swatting up on theory like a nerdy kid before exams. You must've read every report we've ever published by now, I'd say?"

"True - although I've been more like a lazy student who spent too much time drinking beer and chasing girls all term, who is now cramming to save his own neck. I told you my human rights knowledge was a little patchy at best.

"But as I was saying, all the people I met and stories I heard served to deepen my knowledge of the theory. That's what I think OHCHR is missing. This whole office is sclerotic with staff who are reluctant to leave their comfortable Geneva life to grapple with the tough and often bloody realities of actual human rights in the field. Yet if they were to go and see for themselves it would only enhance their comprehension and strengthen their commitment to the philosophy."

"That's interesting. It's something I've often pondered," Sérgio responded. "Though let's not get into the solutions you want me to implement so early in the evening. I don't want to think about my own responsibilities yet. First I want to hear these stories that improved your understanding?"

"Where to start..." I thought, collecting my memories of the last few weeks. I'd travelled to OHCHR field offices as far apart as Burundi, Cambodia, Guatemala and Lebanon. It was difficult to remember it all, but I picked the first story that came to me and began.

"In Guatemala the staff at the local office arranged for me to meet with one of the civil rights activists who was challenging the local government - a woman named Nina who must have been in her sixties, her dark hair almost entirely grey, her russet coloured face crossed with many age lines.

"Nina exemplified a unique form of resistance. She refused to give up looking for her disappeared son. He had been targeted as a troublesome element by the government and subsequently vanished without trace. Guatemala - as you know - was wracked with civil war for many years and is still pretty turbulent right now. These kinds of disappearances, tortures and killings were rampant for a time as an oppressive government fought to assert control over a disenchanted populace.

"Most people whose family members were 'disappeared' knew that there was no chance they would ever find out what had befallen them, let alone receive justice in their name. By contrast, Nina was determined to persevere until she had the answers she was looking for.

"She told me how she went to the government building every day.

There she could be seen standing with a photograph of her son on a placard demanding answers. It was very touching to see, as if by displaying his picture, she was refusing to let him disappear wholly."

"A tender sentiment," Sérgio interjected, "but she must have known that under a government like that, the hope of finding her son again, or even finding out for sure what befell him, was next to impossible?"

"I'm sure in the core of her heart she probably did," I conceded, "but really it's not about that. Now her actions have gone beyond her own individual search for justice. 'It is not just about me and my son anymore,' she told me. 'I make a stand for all mothers and sons. All who have been disappeared and are in danger of being forgotten. I will remember. I will not let *them* forget us' - and with this she gestured to the government building."

"I think that of course we must stand up for the things we want to change, but for activism to work, we also need to safeguard the progress we have made, defend that work too, lest it be taken away."

"It's about the ongoing struggle," Sérgio agreed.

"Exactly. People act like struggle is something we should avoid. We shouldn't toil for things. We shouldn't strain. To be contented, human beings should aim for simple care-free lives. I'm sure in an ideal world that would be the case, but I think coming to terms with living with struggle - at least until all the wrongs are righted - it's the way things have to be in order to make progress.

"The actions of this Guatemalan woman were not just about coping with her own personal grief at her son's disappearance. Not emotional comfort alone. Not even individual justice. Nina's continued actions are important because they are about discovering meaning in the struggle. While all human rights are an individual personal battle, our actions only have real meaning when they also benefit a wider group."

"I think you've been searching for too much meaning in that glass of whisky," Sérgio joked, reaching for my empty tumbler. "I'll fill you up. It's the least I can do for The Great Struggle."

I laughed. I knew Sérgio was only teasing me and with good reason.

"Sorry Sérgio. You know I do have the tendency to descend into long, meandering monologues if I'm not careful."

"Oh, I know that Mukesh, old friend," he replied, "and I am happy to listen, but not without a full glass to take the edge off. What else did you see? Tell me more of your adventures on the front lines."

"Well, to continue on the theme of personal struggle of individuals…" I mused, "let me take you now to Burundi. Visiting Burundi I saw a very different situation. This country is still in the midst of bloody conflict with many people internally displaced and lots of fresh murders and disappearances, implemented by the predatory military government, as well as other fringe groups. Yet the individual crusade on the part of humanity lives on.

"The OHCHR office there - which we must talk more about, remind me Sérgio - introduced me to a human rights defender called Emmanuel. Now Emmanuel has dedicated his life, each and every day, to safeguarding a local politician. He provides protection by physically accompanying this man everywhere he goes. This politician has been championing improved civil rights for civilians and as such he's been constantly under fire from the ruling government. They're threatening him with death or imprisonment all the time.

"The fear was that he would be arrested and disappeared into the depths of some dark prison from which he would never emerge and that would be the end of him, as it has been for so many. So Emmanuel has been acting as this man's literal human rights guard, by accompanying him absolutely everywhere he has to go, even sleeping in the same house, so that if anything untoward happened to him it could be witnessed, recorded and documented, even if it could not be prevented.

"Imagine that. Imagine waking up every day and dedicating your life, unpaid, to protecting someone whose politics you believe in. Forgoing everything else and putting yourself in harm's way in order to preserve the brave ideology epitomised in that man. So from Emmanuel I learned that for human rights to flourish personal courage is required. Real people putting themselves in harm's way. It's not just some abstract academic exposition of theoretical norms and standards in legal journals and political declarations. It's real and it's brave and it involves people standing up for themselves and for each other."

"This is exactly why I brought you on, Mukesh," said Sérgio excitedly. "This is what I want my staff to understand. None of the items mentioned in that most poetic of documents - *The Universal Declaration of Human Rights* - has ever been achieved without sacrifice. Without someone somewhere struggling for it, and others joining in until it became a local and then a national right and then a right for everyone everywhere."

"Precisely," I agreed. "What's notable is that not a single human right has ever been won without striving for it, and sometimes through violent struggle."

Sérgio looked at me questioningly. "We're not going to get into the debate about necessary conflict are we? You know how problematic I find your views on this."

"It's very challenging for me too, and I am in no way decided on this," I said. Sérgio and I had spent, I don't know how many hours, discussing whether or not conflicts - and specifically violent conflicts - were ever necessary. Going around and around in circles and inevitably coming up short every time.

"But consider for example my next tale," I went on, "my journey to Cambodia. Looking at the bones of the slain of the genocide there and talking with both the perpetrators and those whose families were victims. It throws up a lot of questions about morality."

Sérgio's expression towards me changed, this time to one of concern. "Of course. Are you alright, Mukesh? That must have been very hard for you to see, given your experiences in Rwanda."

"I'm fine," I told him. In all honesty I *was* fine, but seeing evidence of killing on the same scale as I had seen in Rwanda really had triggered some unpleasant memories. "It was unpleasant opening up old wounds, but I chose to focus on post-genocide rehabilitation in Cambodia and what can be learned from that."

"And what did you take away from that? How are the OHCHR staff doing there in terms of aiding long-term regeneration after the genocide?"

During my stay, the local OHCHR office had arranged for me to speak to both the survivors and the perpetrators of those heinous crimes against humanity. I debated with the local government, civil society groups and some other institutions over the trade-off between justice and accountability. We discussed the need to heal, unite a traumatised population and ultimately move on to rebuild Cambodia.

"They're doing a very good job in my opinion," I told Sérgio. "Your country office is focussing on the creation of new human rights protection institutions. They are stimulating national legislation to promote and safeguard the liberty of everyone. They are also committed to creating curricula in schools and colleges so that Cambodians may learn from their recent past."

"And you think that's working?" Sergio asked. "The nation is coming to grips with the horrors of its own history and mending those wrongs through shared education? Perpetrators and survivors forging a joint future? Forgive me for playing devil's advocate, but this does not sit well with your notion of "necessary violent conflict" in the face of genocide, which has been your belief until now?"

I pondered this for a while, playing for time with a sip of whisky. In all honesty I had no straight answer for Sérgio. I felt then, as I do now, irrevocably torn over the question of armed responses to oppose genocide. I blamed the UN's failure to hit fast and hard with decisive action in Rwanda - an armed peace-enforcing force to stop the spiralling violence of the Interahamwe could at least have reduced the scale of the atrocities - but the situation in Cambodia was very different.

"I'm not sure that they're the same thing, Rwanda and Cambodia... Of course there is no universal answer, but each society has to find its own way forward in the context of its own suffering and renewal."

"Spoken like a true diplomat," Sérgio replied with an arched eyebrow.

"In my view, armed resistance is necessary to oppose injustice and unfairness when no other way will work. In the quest for the advancement of human rights, history shows us - as you yourself said - that no progress has ever been won without a fight.

"Are all conflicts bad? To oppose injustice and unfairness? When being nice is not sufficient? Looking at the bones of the Cambodian genocide, I understood that conflict was not just necessary but justified when confronting this most evil form of oppression."

"So what do we take from that, moving forward?" Sérgio probed. "We must learn from the mistakes of Cambodia and Rwanda so as to make *'never again'* a reality. What can we learn to apply to places that are still beset with civil wars, corrupt governments and institutionalised racism, and are at high risk of genocide?"

"Well, for a start, we need to better support our teams that are working in such unstable countries," I volunteered. "Take Burundi for example. Sister to Rwanda with much of the same colonial history. Western invaders ruled by keeping the local people divided against one another. Deep divisions created on ethnic lines. Huge history of animosity between different sides. Many people internally and internationally displaced due to fighting. If there is anywhere that is a potential risk of genocidal violence, it is there."

"But when I visited I found that the OHCHR office was demoralised, underfunded and poorly led. The true consequence of this is that there is a huge vacuum in which civilians suffer and the worst human rights abuses occur in larger numbers. People are killed. Tortured. Raped. Disappeared. I really think that if OHCHR is to have a real purpose and to make a difference, it is in places like Burundi. But we are failing."

"How can we make that difference? What is the solution, in your opinion?"

"One of the main problems that I've identified is this big chasm between the headquarters in Geneva and field offices. We have astute, intelligent staff in Geneva whose inspired thinking could really help alleviate problems in these high-risk spots. Yet there is no incentive for them to come. There's no structure in place to provide them with job security if they do so.

"The best people in Geneva don't want to go to the field. They don't want to move to places where they could really do some good. Not from laziness or fear of dangerous regions - many of them got into humanitarian work, as we both did, because of the wish to do the most good wherever that might be. No, the reason that they don't come is because there is no system by which they could rotate between the field offices and headquarters, without losing their permanent posts and all the privileges and lucrative benefits of that.

"Now I ask you, why would you leave your prominent job with all its perks in pleasant Geneva to live in Bujumbura? Why would you leave your secure income and your family behind, losing your excellent health insurance and school fees for your children, while you soldier on in Bujumbura with no assurance of being able to return to your job at HQ after a two or three-year tour of duty in the field?"

"I see your point, Mukesh. That is really fascinating. We should make it possible to transition easily between Geneva and the country offices, and implement an incentivised system for doing so. In fact, we should instigate reform whereby it is impossible to get promoted in Geneva without having done some field work, really getting your hands dirty."

"Even better," I agreed.

"That would also weed out some of those "career humanitarians" who are advancing their own wealth and status through the business of human suffering."

"Yes!" I chuckled. "I bet you'd see some very, very fast department transfers if some of these high-minded pencil-pushers suddenly found themselves faced with a year of field work in Guatemala City."

"That would really shake things up, wouldn't it?" Sérgio laughed. We clinked our glasses together in a toast to our new plan to transform the department from a scholastic policy factory into a hard-hitting task-force, one that would place some of the world's most qualified minds into areas where they were most urgently needed to transform dire situations on the ground.

***

My spell with OHCHR gifted me a structured and a systematic way of understanding what before then was an incoherent set of values. I had learned about the legal base, the ethical foundations, the historical roots, the cultural traditions, the social forces and above all the politics of human rights in theory and practice. But I had also seen that these theories were nothing if they were not actively implemented.

With Sérgio's mentoring, I had learned that the fight for human rights was a permanent struggle. It wasn't something that was achieved, once and forever. It had to be guarded, renewed, and strived for, every day, everywhere, in many, many different ways, because any victory was at best temporary. There were enough evil, power-hungry forces in the world that were more than willing and capable of pushing back.

I was deeply moved and inspired by the stories I had heard from ordinary people. Not the cautious academics in Geneva, but the brave heroes like Nina and Emmanuel. They had suffered and fought back in circumstances that would have crushed many others. From these encounters I realised that if one was determined to engage in this kind of mission, it was tantamount to making a lifelong commitment. It was more than just a job in an organisation. It became the central driver of one's identity, what one stood for and what one was prepared to sacrifice to remain true to one's vision.

What became known as the *Kapila Report* was duly incorporated into a lengthy submission to the UN General Assembly that unanimously adopted a resolution to re-orient OHCHR. This took a lot of political lobbying.

What I had taken as a job and a chance to reconnect with an old ally had transformed into an experience that changed my whole understanding of humanitarianism and development. I resolved that whatever I undertook in the future would be done through my newly acquired human rights perspective. I had new eyes now and I felt better equipped than ever to go out into the world and implement change.

***

What I didn't realise was just how soon I would have to put these grand notions into practice, or how far these new formed beliefs would be tested to the limits of what they, and indeed I, could endure.

The next few months would throw up my greatest personal struggle for human rights and ultimately my life's most daunting challenge: Sudan.

Chapter Nineteen

I learned that courage was not the absence of fear, but the triumph over it. The brave man is not he who does not feel afraid, but he who conquers that fear.
Nelson Mandela

SADLY, SÉRGIO AND I COULD NOT STAY AROUND TO SEE the grand overhaul we had envisaged for OHCHR come to full fruition although many of my recommendations were put into effect over following months. He was reassigned to Iraq as Special Representative of the UN Secretary-General.

"Come with me to Iraq, Mukesh" Sérgio asked me. "Be my special advisor there - I could really use your practical mind."

"I am tempted," I told him. "Iraq would certainly be a new challenge - though I do believe they still have a price on my head there after all that business with the Kurds..." During my DFID days I'd ferried aid and assistance to the Kurds, and Saddam Hussein had actually put a price on my head as a result of a very public disagreement I'd had with him over chemical weapons abuses against minorities.

"Nonsense," Sérgio dismissed, with a wave of his hand "You have to come. You're not looking at the bigger picture here, Mukesh. The important question is not whether you would be killed as a traitorous political criminal, but who would I argue with, if you do not come? It would be beyond selfish of you to stay away."

I laughed but then a sense of seriousness settled over me. Now was the time I would have to reveal to Sérgio that I truly would be leaving him, in order to become head of my own UN mission, and it seemed so final. I knew that he would be happy for me, but I had learned and laughed so much with him it felt sad to say goodbye. I seriously considered accompanying him to Iraq instead. It would certainly open up a whole world of fresh challenges, yet in my heart I knew it was time to move on.

"You'll have to find someone else who likes whisky as much as I do," I told Sergio. "I've been approached by the powers that be to become the UN Resident and Humanitarian Coordinator in Sudan. I'll be the head of my own UN mission. It's been a tricky decision to make and I have weighed up all the..."

But my speech was cut off by a huge bear hug from Sérgio. "That's fantastic news, Mukesh! Of course, you must go for it. Head your own UN mission? That's fantastic! I am beyond pleased for you."

"We should probably have a whisky to celebrate?" I joked, but I was touched by Sérgio's delight for what I thought of then as my good fortune.

In all honesty I was thrilled to be heading back into the field. My human rights world-tour had thrown the relative inertia of my life in Geneva into sharp relief. I vowed that I was too young for corner offices and desk jobs and chocolate - not to mention too diabetic - and relished the chance to do some work on the ground in one of the most tumultuous places on earth.

The detailed account of this time in my life is published in my first memoir, *Against a Tide of Evil*. I have no desire to go over old ground. Yet it was the most monumental experience of my life so far and I should not gloss over it.

***

I arrived in Sudan on 1st April 2003, in the hope of preparing the country for impending peace. After decades of conflict, both sides were tired of fighting and it seemed as if the planned peace agreement being negotiated in Naivasha would be signed within mere months.

The independent nation of Sudan and I are about the same age, born within a few months of each other when the country gained freedom from its Anglo-Egyptian rulers on 1st January 1956. It had been ravaged by a civil war, almost since then due to the seemingly insoluble grievances between the largely Christian and animist, black African south and the predominantly Arab Muslim north.

Like the Belgians in Rwanda and Burundi, the British had implemented a policy of divide-and-rule in Sudan, encouraging suspicion between the citizens. When the British relinquished power they effectively handed over leadership to the Arab Muslim north. They governed from the northern city of Khartoum and held most of the country's wealth on very unequal terms. Combined with a history of ethnic mistrust between the two groups, conflict was inevitable, and the resulting civil war lasted decades.

I had not been in Sudan for long when reports of bloody skirmishes began emerging from its western periphery of Darfur - a vast region the size of Spain. Darfur's terrain varies from fertile arable pasture to sparse forests, from featureless desert to rocky mountainous terrain, and fresh challenges blow in with the wet and dry seasons. The indigenous people knew how to make a living amidst such precarious conditions, and there were many ancient villages of black Africans living in the area.

Historically not all was harmonious however. Nomadic Arab farmers would bring their herds into fertile areas of Darfur when the season changed and grazing became sparse. This caused occasional clashes, as elsewhere in the country, between the black Sudanese and the Arab Sudanese.

When the first whispers of trouble in Darfur reached my ears, most of my team at our UN base in Khartoum put it down to a seasonal escalation of the age-old problem. Nothing out of the ordinary. Soon however, we heard reports of increasing numbers of refugees fleeing conflict between the government of Sudan and a group of black African rebels calling themselves the SLM - Sudan Liberation Movement.

I learned from the charismatic leader of the southern rebel forces, Dr John Garang, that - as with his rebellion in the south of the country - the SLM were fighting against mistreatment by the central government.

"Khartoum treats black Africans all across the country like second class citizens," he told me. "There is no development for us, no investment and it's unfair. I think the Darfuris are reacting to that, as indeed we are right across Sudan. In Darfur, nomadic Arab tribes began stealing the grazing from the original black population. They think they can take whatever they want but the time has come for us to stand up for ourselves. We are motivated by the need for liberation from Khartoum's oppression."

That was how it started. Rebel groups fighting back against injustice. Struggling against an oppressive regime. Ordinary people striving for the protection of their human rights. It ended with the first genocide of the twenty-first century, and whether I like it or not, Darfur became my defining moment. The question I faced was either to stand up and do the right thing or to be complicit in mass murder. I have thought long and hard about what made me blow the whistle on Darfur, to stand up to the UN and to face-off against the Khartoum regime. I think that, as in Afghanistan and Honduras, my word is my bond. Without personal integrity what do I have?

I had reached a place by 2003 where I was professionally and personally well-respected. This meant people trusted me to do the right thing. I could not betray that faith. When so many people put their trust in me I had a moral responsibility to do the right thing by them. For me there was no other option.

With this in mind, I remember very clearly the actions of two brave women that I encountered during my time in Sudan. They put their faith in me to help their people, and with total disregard for their own safety. More than anyone, it is for these two women that I spoke up. The first of these I met on my initial trip to Darfur, but before I introduce her I need to set the scene a little and provide some background to the situation on the ground at the time.

At that point, the regime in Khartoum had taken an increasingly hostile attitude towards the conflict in Darfur. Their rhetoric was overtly fascist; Nazi-like. I met with one senior presidential advisor who actually used the term '*final solution*' to describe the tactics they planned to employ against civilians. All around, high ranking members of the regime were demanding that the government forces, "crush the cockroaches without compromise."

I could hardly believe what I was hearing. After my experiences of ethnic violence in Rwanda, I knew what people were capable of doing when ideologies like these were thrown around. My mandate in the country was purely humanitarian. I did not have the jurisdiction to act politically, but just as I had wanted the UN to intervene in Rwanda, and just as I knew that the struggle for human rights was a personal one, I felt compelled to act.

I wrote to my superiors in New York, but encountered nothing except silent dismissal for my concerns. In order to intervene, I knew that the UN would require more evidence than the troubling rumours I'd reported. They would need first-hand accounts of what was occurring on the ground. I decided that I would go and see for myself.

As with most of my fieldwork in Sudan, this trip to Darfur was heavily controlled by the Khartoum regime. Their means of control was the *Mukhabarat*, a shady and vicious secret police force who hid behind the mask of the civilian government. Under the guise of 'preserving my safety' they rarely allowed me to meet or talk with anyone, and those I did speak to were too afraid to tell me the truth about who was oppressing them, for fear of retribution.

This trip to Darfur was similarly frustrating. Government officials and those acting in their interests delayed us with formalities and apparent pleasantries. This meant that I had very little time for what I had come there to see: exactly how Khartoum had planned to execute their '*final solution*'.

I did manage to get a brief look inside one of the main hospitals. Thanks to my medical training, I was able to recognise that all was not well. There were a disproportionate number of patients admitted for the treatment of gunshot wounds, and none of them seemed to be military personnel. There were also large numbers of children in the hospital, many of whom had also been wounded by gunfire, but when I asked where their parents were, the harassed-looking doctor, glancing first at my government minders and then at me, asserted that the children had been found wandering the bush and nobody knew where their parents could be.

Despite his caginess I had extracted the answers I wanted - everything pointed towards armed attacks on civilians. After more government-orchestrated diversions, I was finally taken to visit a camp for internally displaced persons (IDPs). This was where those fleeing the conflict had ended up. In this camp, just outside Nyala, survivors confirmed my worst fears.

Though the dangers in speaking to me were very evident - the Sudanese government's goons lurked intimidatingly at my side - survivors of the violence were burning to talk. Hurt and anger were written plainly on their faces. I figured those who were willing to suffer the threat of further violence just to have their story heard must have something important to say.

It was evident that the speakers had lost almost everything. In some cases, their terrible stories were all they had left. Their recollections were undeniably similar. All pointed to the systemic, organised destruction of the lives, homes and livelihoods of innocent civilians. Though the IDP camp was full of villagers who had fled there from every corner of Darfur, all yearning to reveal to me their own particular nightmare, they all pretty much amounted to the same terrifying sequence of events that had happened again and again.

"Arab raiders on horseback attacked the village before anyone was awake…"

"They carried flaming torches and set fire to the roofs of our homes with the families still inside…"

"We ran into the bush for our lives but they chased us on their horses, cutting people down…"

"Men, women, children, old people, they didn't care who…"

"There was no time to look back…"

"I lost my family…"

"We hid in the bush…"

"I saw my whole town destroyed - every home and grain-store burned fiercely into the night…"

"I felt powerless to do anything but hide…"

"They threw the bodies of our fallen friends and family into the well to poison the water…"

"There was no way to fight back…"

"They captured young women and girls and dragged them off into the bush…"

"We heard hideous sounds…"

"I don't know who is alive or where my family are, if they still live at all…"

My blood ran cold as I listened to these chilling accounts. This kind of racially motivated scorched-earth policy, where villages were being systematically destroyed - food stores burned, wells poisoned - was all too familiar. So too were the sickening accounts of the weaponisation of rape. These all pointed to one ethnic group trying to methodically destroy another. I didn't want to admit the horrible suspicion that was becoming harder and harder to deny - was I in the midst of an unfolding genocide? Was the government of Sudan committing genocide against its own people here in Darfur?

I looked sideways at the faces of the government officials who had accompanied me from Khartoum. Their expressions remained unmoved and resolute, as if we were talking about some minor inconvenience. If these stories were true, then the blood of the murdered fathers, mothers, brothers, sisters and children of these displaced men and women was on their hands.

I felt disgusted to stand so close to men who could listen, expressionless, to these heart-wrenching accounts, knowing all the while that they themselves were tacitly responsible. But I kept my composure - it would do no good to let them know that I suspected their complicity in this immeasurable evil. After some questions about the humanitarian needs of the displaced - food, water, sanitation - I asked a final question, feigning a good-natured curiosity.

"Who was responsible for these attacks? For what happened to you?"

The atmosphere seemed to buzz with an under-current of electricity. The assembled crowd, who moments before had been so eager to speak to me, seemed suddenly reluctant and wary. After a pause one man with a look of defiance burning in his eyes began to tell me who was blameworthy. But one of the government minders I was with barked out something aggressively in Arabic, and the speaker's expression fell. He finished lamely that he didn't know who had sent the Arab riders into his homeland to destroy everything he had cherished and held dear.

I did not blame him at all for losing the courage to speak. It very probably would have cost him his life. These survivors had been through immeasurable hardship, his life may very well have been the only thing he had left of value and I was not going to ask him to risk it for me.

The next Darfuri I spoke to, however, showed a bravery that I have rarely encountered before or since. Maybe she had lost so much she felt her own life and safety was a small price to pay for the defence of her people. Maybe she felt that there was no point in having a life if you were not going to use it to strive for justice. Whatever her motivation, I couldn't be more grateful for her bravery, or more regretful that I could not do more to protect her.

When the conversation got too hot at the IDP camp my government minders rushed me back to central Nyala, where I was informed that we were to hear from the community elders at a meeting organised by the governor. Assembled inside their equivalent of the town hall sat around seventy people, mostly Arab Sudanese and almost entirely men. My heart sank. As the first of the elders began to speak, discussing crop failures and recent local skirmishes, my disappointment was confirmed: this was all a piece of Khartoum-directed theatre. We would learn nothing helpful here at all.

As the men droned on, taking as long as possible to reach their point, I scanned the crowd despondently, searching for anyone who might have something of meaning to add to the proceedings.

I noticed a tall slim woman rise to her feet at the back of the room. Her glossy skin shone out with a dark luminance against the sea of Arab faces. She was very obviously black African. I knew instantly the strength of character it must have taken for her to infiltrate a space like this that was so hostile to her very presence. I wanted to learn what burning message had led her to risk coming here.

"Let's hear from the young woman at the back," I called out, cutting off some pontificating old man mid-sentence.

Mercifully, the governor was nowhere to be seen. Maybe he was as bored as I was by the sham meeting and had stepped outside for some respite, but it meant nobody had the jurisdiction over me to intervene. The woman was allowed to speak.

She stood up straighter, her colourful robe, dark features and commanding presence making her impossible to ignore. She fixed her eyes on mine and, in a level and purposeful voice, she began to relate her story.

"The people in this room are talking about food shortages, skirmishes for land and crop failures, but this is not what happened to my village, my family and I. Raiders invaded our home in the middle of the night. They ordered everyone out of their houses and set fire to the thatches. They beat us with sticks and lashed us with whips. They called us 'black dogs,' *'abeed'* and *'zurka'* - slaves and rats - and chased us away into the darkness. We ran. We hid in the bush until morning. When the sun came up, we ventured back to what had once been our home. Everything was burnt, looted, destroyed. We could not stay so we came here, to Nyala. Worst of all is that some of the young women and girls are missing. It is feared that they were stolen by the raiders."

The crowd who had at first been silent, erupted into loud aggressive shouting now.

"Sit down and be quiet!" yelled one.

"Shut up!" barked another.

A chorus of "Lies! Lies!" broke out from all corners of the room.

"Let her finish her story," I demanded. "This is an open meeting. We are here to listen to all sides. Please carry on."

Seemingly unperturbed by the vitriol spewing at her, the woman continued speaking, though I noticed that her voice now shook a little.

"We have searched for these missing women but we have been unable to find them. Some are very young, only children, little girls. We fear for what is happening to them wherever they have been taken. We want help to find them. Help from the authorities."

The men around her were on their feet now. The interpreter had stopped translating as the whole room was in uproar, brandishing fists and shaking sticks, but there was no mistaking the threat in their voices. The woman sat down, her immense courage steamrollered by the boiling mob of angry masculinity. The meeting was declared over.

The image of this lone woman surrounded on all sides by such rage was all too familiar. Disturbing memories of the stoning I had witnessed in Afghanistan years earlier rose to the surface of my mind, usurping all other thoughts. I barely registered the government goons at my elbow as they frogmarched my colleagues and myself into a waiting vehicle.

The last I saw of this heroic woman was her bowed head surrounded by thickset men in sunglasses - unmistakably the *Mukhabarat*. Within seconds we were hustled away in a cloud of dust. I felt frozen by the resurgence of that memory from Kabul, and the disbelief that something similar could be happening again, here in Sudan, and under my watch.

I regained my senses all at once in the back of the car. "Wait," I called out to the driver. "We have to go back. Turn around. That woman risked her safety to bring us that information. She is in danger and we have done nothing to help her. Turn the car around."

But nobody paid me any attention. The driver either couldn't hear or more likely was ignoring my pleas, far more concerned for his own safety should he obey my wishes and face the vengeance of the *Mukhabarat* himself.

I was distraught. This brave woman had risked her own safety to bring the plight of her people to the attention of the UN. To my attention. She had acted exactly how my human rights experience had taught me as imperative for individuals to act - taking a huge personal risk to protect rights that were being abused - and what had I done to help her? Nothing.

I had been frozen into inaction during the moments that would have counted. I could have taken decisive action. Refused to leave until I knew she would be safe. Taken her with us even. Or at least made some parting comment that the UN would be watching if anyone laid a finger on this woman. Instead I had done nothing.

***

As we flew back to Khartoum, the rugged landscape of the country I had grown to love flitting by beneath me, I was resolute. The story I had heard today could not be ignored. I had failed to protect the brave woman who had risked everything to speak on behalf of the people of her village - many merely girls, who at this moment were probably enduring a living nightmare at the hands of the raiders. I could not fail them too. I must do everything I could to save the Darfuri people.

On my return to Khartoum I called meetings with all the UN agencies and other international players. To my disgust barely anyone wanted to know or to help. This silence from the UN over Darfur endured, while the genocide raged on unchecked. Reports came in thick and fast - none more terrible than the testimony of the second incredible woman I want to mention here, a Darfuri teacher named Aisha. Her's was a story of extraordinary pain and bravery.

I was sitting in my Khartoum office when I became distracted from the report I was writing, by a noisy argument breaking out in the reception outside. I heard the banging of doors and shouting in Arabic before my assistant, Mona, came rushing into my office.

"Sorry for the intrusion, Mukesh, but there is a very irate woman here who is insisting she speaks to you. The guards have tried to get her to leave but she just won't go."

"Then send her in," I told Mona. "Of course she can speak to me if she wants."

Mona returned moments later accompanied by a tall, slender woman with ink-black skin and a blue scarf wrapped over her head and shoulders.

"She says she is from Darfur," Mona relayed to me. "She has travelled a very long way. She says she is from a village in North Darfur near Tawila."

At the mention of Tawila my blood ran cold. One of my key persons on the ground, Daniel Christensen, had recently sent me a report describing his eye witness account of an attack on a Darfuri town called Tawila, led by the infamous *Janjaweed* leader, Musa Hilal. Daniel had seen the Sudanese military inflict the worst kind of cruelty upon the civilians. If this woman had come from there I dreaded to hear what she might have to tell me.

I came out from behind my desk, and indicated an armchair. "Please sit down. You've come such a long way. Please rest."

Instead the woman sank to the floor and sat cross-legged on my office carpet.

"She feels she will dirty your beautiful chair," Mona explained to me. So I joined her on the floor and sent for some tea and plenty of digestive biscuits.

"What's her name?" I questioned Mona.

"Aisha," she replied.

"Aisha," I began, "please tell me what it is you've travelled so far to say."

Though it was traumatic for Mona, she translated Aisha's story for me into English.

"My family had gone in to Tawila to buy some things" she began. "It was market day and so the town was busy. Then hundreds of men descended on us. Men with guns. Some were in uniforms, some in blue and white robes. They came in Land Cruisers and on horses. They rounded everyone up. They took all the women and girls into the centre of the market square…"

My blood ran cold. I knew from Daniel's reports what she was about to describe. There had been accounts of brutal and systematic gang rape. Arab raiders violating women and girls while their husbands and fathers were forced to stand by, unable to help.

This is a vile tactic of génocidaires. Women are targeted as the reproducers of their people. Not only was rape a brutal act of violence and dehumanisation but also a systematic attempt to dilute the bloodline of the group under attack. These *Janjaweed* invaders spoke of impregnating their victims with 'fine Arab babies'.

"After it was done the raiders looted the market, loaded the young women and boys into their vehicles and set fire to everything" Aisha went on. "I couldn't find my family anywhere. My husband, my father, my two young sons. Even when I returned to my village I could find nobody left from my family. I didn't know what to do. I gathered a few things and travelled by truck to Khartoum. To the UN. To find you."

I felt deeply shaken. It was one thing reading reports of the atrocities, but quite another hearing such traumatic first-hand testimony from a survivor. I tried to hide my own distress and focussed instead on what we could do for her here and now. She had travelled over a thousand kilometres, battled her way through the high walls and tight security of my UN office, all to come and find me.

"It took unimaginable strength to come all this way after everything you've been through. What made you come?" I asked.

"I came because I had nowhere else to go. Nobody else would help us. The police? The government? They are all in on it. We can't turn to them. They are the ones committing these crimes. I have seen that the United Nations have people on the ground in Darfur. They are trying to help us and they are powerful. This is why I came to you."

I nodded. "Thank you for coming. We will do our best to help. I want to take down your testimony officially, with a proper translator, if you can bear to retell the story again?"

"I can." She replied simply. "I can come back tomorrow? I have relatives in the city I can stay with tonight. I'll come back tomorrow morning."

The greatest regret of my life is that I let her go. At the time, after her ordeal, I thought she should go to the comfort of her family. I should have insisted she stayed right there and then, and take asylum in my office, for her own safety. I never saw Aisha again. I can only guess what became of her at the hands of the *Mukhabarat* once she left the sanctuary of my UN office.

Though we never had a chance to record it officially, her testimony ignited and fuelled the rage that had been growing inside me. I could not allow this kind of crime to continue. My UN bosses in New York might be content to turn a blind eye, but I was not. I had to do something. If the power and reputation of the UN meant Aisha was willing to travel so far to ask me for help, then we could not abandon her people now. She had found me. Sought me out. I must act.

***

There was one more event that galvanised me to take action, during that fraught time in Sudan. It was not an atrocity as abhorrent as Aisha had experienced. Instead, it was a personal tragedy that for me carried a different kind of sadness. I had been packing my bag for a flight to London when a call came in on my mobile. I sank onto my bed as my head of security relayed the heart-breaking news.

There had been a bombing in Baghdad by Al-Qaeda.

Sérgio Vieira de Mello had been killed.

I don't remember hanging up the phone. I don't remember turning on the radio to listen to the news. I don't remember any of my actions in the aftermath of hearing this news. I was totally shocked at losing the man who had taught me so much. It was not only my own sorrow, but the grief I felt on behalf of the whole world, who had lost a shining humanitarian and a spirit that burned with such bright intensity. It was impossible to believe that his light had been extinguished and I would never again experience the sunny warmth of his company.

While I sat there on the edge of my bed, trying to come to terms with this news, another gut-wrenching realisation came over me. If I had decided differently, making the choice to accompany Sérgio to Iraq rather than taking up my post here in Sudan, then I too would very likely be lying lifeless in the rubble of that bombing.

Losing Sérgio was senseless and wrong, yet I had survived while he had perished. I had come to Sudan for a reason, and I would not let all that Sérgio had taught me go ignored while crimes against humanity were being committed in Darfur. I remembered all the discussions we'd had over the proper way for individuals to conduct themselves in order to maintain human rights principles. The responsibility each of us held to struggle, to defend one another, to do the right thing.

My friend's death strengthened my resolve. I would act as Sérgio would have wanted me to - fighting for what is right, no matter how difficult. UN headquarters were choosing to ignore Darfur, demanding I stop causing waves and stick to my humanitarian remit. The dozens of hastily typed reports I had sent to New York were left unanswered. They already knew the worst of what was happening, yet had chosen not to act. The situation in Darfur could not get any worse; if they hadn't taken action against the génocidaires already, I concluded that they were never going to.

It was also clear that the government of Sudan were not going to cease the killing any time soon. They'd used the phrase '*final solution*' and I had no doubt this was entirely what they sought. I thought of Aisha, who had risked everything to come to me for help. She had endured so much to stand up for her people. Now I had to stand up for her. Her memory strengthened my resolve. I knew now, with surprising clarity, exactly what I had to do.

***

I had no other option. I had to blow the whistle on the whole thing. The leaders of the world knew the severity and the scale of the atrocities. Repeatedly, I had alerted them to the very worst. They had decided to do nothing. I resolved to take the truth to the world's people, in the hope that they also would not turn a blind eye to the slaughter.

I knew this would be the end of my once bright and promising career within the UN. They could never forgive such a transgression; publicly calling them out on their inaction in the face of unfolding genocide. The thought of this saddened me, yet the organisation had failed me. Failed to listen to me, to support me and act in the right way. Far worse than this they had failed the Sudanese who were under attack. I had no other option.

I arranged to speak to the people of the world via the BBC's Radio 4 early morning *Today* programme. I did not inform them ahead of time what it was about exactly. I didn't even prepare a script or any notes on what I wanted to say. But I promised them an earth-shattering scoop.

The decisive moment came. I was counted in - "three, two, one" - by the small team stationed at the BBC World Service's Kenyan recording studio, to where I'd travelled expressly for this purpose. "Dr Mukesh Kapila coming in live from Nairobi…"

I spoke from the heart, a broken heart, heavy with the knowledge it held. I spoke of the killings and destruction I had witnessed. I told of the Sudanese government's complicity in the slaughter and I related how the UN had failed to intervene.

I outlined what I wanted to see happen next, that there should be an investigation at the highest possible level and that peacekeepers should be sent into Darfur to safeguard the remaining civilians, and that the president of Sudan should go before the International Criminal Court to stand trial for the cold-blooded murders he had orchestrated. Once my BBC radio interview was done, I took dozens of calls and did scores of other interviews with the foremost media outlets around the world.

The people of the world responded, as I had hoped they would, with fierce outrage and an outpouring of compassion. I truly believe that the humanitarian spirit exists within every human heart, and never had this felt truer than when I broke the silence over Darfur. There had been a media blackout regarding these atrocities up until now, but once the public knew the reality of what was unfolding, there was uproar.

The BBC was just the beginning. As the story broke, it was picked up by more and more news stations. I spoke to everyone I could. After completing a whirlwind of press conferences and interviews, I returned to my office in Khartoum. Despite the obvious danger I faced, I was still the chief of the United Nations there and I would not slink away quietly, under the cover of the media storm.

As the world's press blew the crisis in Darfur wide open, the newspapers in Khartoum took a very different tact. Everywhere vitriolic headlines screamed in Arabic about my lies, cowardice and treachery. Some even called for my head.

Between the international media outrage over Darfur and the Sudanese press bellowing *jihad* against me, there was one institution whose silent message I heard louder than any other: the UN. The UN had said exactly nothing. They had issued a statement that the situation in Darfur was grave and that they were looking into it. I had heard from friends on the inside that the New York headquarters was in turmoil, trying to deal with what they had dubbed my 'feral' actions, but to me they remained sternly taciturn.

This felt disquieting and ominous. I had no idea of what would become of me now. As the political temperature heated up in Khartoum, and the UN remained an impenetrable edifice of silence, I debated what to do.

It was far better to jump before I was pushed - or worse. So I made the decision to step down from my position, before I could be ousted by the UN. Or by the *Mukhabarat* and its proxies, with the mounting death threats against me. In any case, with the irretrievable breakdown of my relationship as the UN Head in Sudan with my host government, I was sure that the overall United Nations mission would be neutralised if I stayed on in Khartoum. Whatever my disappointment with the feebleness of my UN bosses, I believed in its noble mission that was bigger than any individual.

So, having alerted the world on Darfur, it was obvious that my usefulness was done, and my days numbered. I left Sudan exactly a year after my arrival there as the UN's man on the ground. Instead of the peace and prosperity building that I had been hoping to preside over when I had agreed to come, I had, instead, witnessed the new Millennium's first genocide unfolding *on my watch*.

As my plane powered up and away from Sudanese territory, I wondered if I would ever again set foot in that country. I wondered too whether my whistleblowing would make any difference. Had my actions been enough, or too little, too late?

Chapter Twenty

The true measure of a man is not his intelligence or how high he rises in this freak establishment. No, the true measure of a man is this: how quickly can he respond to the needs of others and how much of himself he can give.
Philip K. Dick

TO SOME, THE ACTIONS I TOOK TO BLOW THE WHISTLE ON Darfur might be considered a success. Never before had the combined authority of the world, as represented by the mighty United Nations, been forced to perform such a rapid U-turn on its policy. It went from taking absolutely no action on Darfur, to installing peace-keepers on the ground; to flooding the area with relief workers and delivering aid to the victims. The Security Council also instigated a formal enquiry into what happened that may hopefully lead to the perpetrators standing trial for crimes against humanity, war crimes and genocide, at the International Criminal Court in The Hague.

For myself, however, I felt an overwhelming regret over that whole gruesome period. Our actions had come too late to halt the suffering of the people of Darfur. On them, the worst imaginable horrors had already been inflicted; their families murdered, their culture obliterated, their homes and livelihoods razed to the ground.

What's more, they had not seen justice done. The perpetrators of the crimes committed against them remained in power. Despite the efforts of the peace-keepers and aid agencies they were still unable to return to their villages, as Darfur remained painfully insecure thanks largely to Khartoum's continued support of the *Janjaweed* militias.

By day, I was tormented by guilt at having allowed all this suffering to happen on my patch. By night, I was plagued by ghostly apparitions of all I had witnessed and been unable to prevent. Sure, I had played my part. Blown the whistle. Turned the eyes of the world on Darfur. I had acted in accordance with my beliefs and upheld my principle that one person acting alone really can make a difference. Yet I had paid the price for my actions, both in terms of my mental wellbeing and my once-promising professional future. I had no idea what I would do next.

Technically I was still in the employ of DFID, as I had only been on secondment to the UN. I found out later that there had been intense discussion between the British government and the top players at the UN about what they were to do with me now.

Unbeknownst to me, my old friends at DFID fought my corner, arguing that I could not simply be thrown to the wolves. If the UN wanted to jettison me, they would have to clarify exactly what wrongdoing I had committed, bring the proper charges against me and adhere to their standard personnel process.

DFID forced the UN to acknowledge that I had not done anything against the rules. On the contrary, I had in fact served faithfully the charter of the United Nations. If they did charge me with any wrong doing, it would only serve to put their own misconduct under a microscope. I was certain they did not want the world's attention turned upon their shameful negligence over Darfur.

***

The to-ing and fro-ing about what exactly to do with Mukesh caught the attention of David Nabarro, the man who had originally been responsible for recruiting me into ODA, and who was now head of the Health Action in Crises department at the World Health Organisation, in Geneva. We had worked well together on a whole range of health development programmes, before diverging down different paths. David recognised this and, encouraged by London, was well-disposed to help me.

At this point I had no idea what I would do. Despite DFID's loyal defence of me, I did not want to return to work there, as I felt it would be a step backwards. Other than that, I was utterly rudderless.

So when I received the surprise phone call from David Nabarro, offering me a place with him at WHO, I accepted without a moment's hesitation. I expressed my heartfelt gratitude right there and then, for his call was truly a lifeline. It came when I least expected it, hadn't asked for it, and when all doors had seemingly shut on me.

A brand-new position was created for me at WHO, taking into account my background and expertise. I was appointed as Senior Advisor for HIV and Emergencies, and my new post was at senior director level, thus retaining my status and even increasing my salary.

WHO is still part of the UN system, so this appeased my champions in DFID. I think it also represented an easy option for the UN itself. They were afraid that if I was cast out, they would be unable to keep any control over what I might do or say. Far safer to keep me close, and still inside the UN system as it were.

Gagged with even more money, I accepted the job. Truth was, I didn't really care much about it at the time. I was still in shock from Darfur and devastated by my experiences there. My human resources officer in WHO understood this. She said that I should take things slowly, spend time readjusting to Geneva, and that I was under no pressure as there was no hurry whatsoever to deliver any tangible results.

***

So there I sat. In my big empty office in WHO. With no work to do.

In reality I was totally numb. My senses seemed blunted, as if I was bundled-up in cotton wool. I felt very small within myself, like a turtle retracted far inside its shell, experiencing everything that happened to me as if from a great distance. I went through the motions of coming into work in the morning and pushing around the few bits of paper that landed on my desk. I would attend the meetings I was asked to, but rarely paid attention, as my mind would inevitably drift back to the violence of Darfur.

One afternoon as I sat at my empty desk, bookshelves standing bare behind me, blank walls featureless and unadorned, I heard a brisk tap at the door. I had been reliving some tortured image from Sudan, but the freckled face that peaked around the doorframe jolted me back to the present.

"May I come in?" she asked, and before I had time to reply she had installed herself in front of my desk. She was a tall woman in her forties with an unruly head of curly auburn hair, long fingernails, and a disconcertingly frank stare, which she now fixed upon me.

"Linda Clemensson," she introduced herself. "I heard that you had just arrived at WHO and I would like to work as your assistant."

I blinked. "I, I'm very flattered..." I stammered, "but..."

"Great!" She cut me off. "I can start immediately."

And that was that.

I found out later that she had been working elsewhere in WHO and had suffered some disagreement with her boss. It seemed that news of my recruitment style from my DFID days had preceded me. Linda saw my arrival as a fortuitous opportunity, though it turned out to be far more auspicious for me.

She proved to be a fantastic asset and an invaluable ally. She was a skilled linguist, experienced administrator and I discovered quickly that she was also a talented networker. She was an incredible font of information on the internal workings of WHO, with its vast and complex structures and Byzantine internal politics.

In an institution like this - governed as it was by hierarchy -

scheming, plotting and double-crossing ran rife. Having Linda at my side proved indispensable. She was my first-mate helping me to stay afloat on the high-seas teaming with institutionalised sharks. But more than anything else, she proved an incredibly kind person and a true friend to me when I needed one most.

She took me in hand, organising everything I had felt too lacklustre to take any interest in, and this included my personal welfare. She would order in hot food for lunch - Thai soup one day, noodles the next - insisting that I eat well, rather than simply having cold sandwiches at my desk each lunchtime.

She began to invite me home after work and I got to know her husband, Martin, who worked in ILO - International Labour Organisation - another specialised organisation of the UN system - and their two delightful little girls, aged four and eight, to whom I became "Uncle Mukesh". Poor Linda must have considered me to be somewhat of a third adopted child, as she would serve us all fish-fingers for dinner followed by jelly and ice-cream. Sometimes she would bring the girls to work with her and they would sit at my big desk with their crayons and draw unflattering portraits of me while I worked at my computer.

Linda could see that I was shell-shocked from Darfur and not taking proper care of myself. She was worried, especially about me returning to my empty house each night after work, and she hoped the normalcy of being around her family might help bring me back to my former self. It felt reassuring to be enveloped into their warm, funny, welcoming home. I found myself gradually re-humanising thanks to their kindness.

***

I was reluctant to admit that I was suffering from post-traumatic stress disorder, but thanks to the patience of my colleagues and friends, I slowly started to take more of an interest in my new life. I reconnected with a friend I had made during my time at DFID, a young man named Mukul Bhola who now worked for UNDP. Mukul was a lot of fun. His rapier wit and mischievous attitude reawakened the rumbustious side of my personality that I thought had perished for good.

We would often spend our evenings exploring Geneva's nightlife. As well as being the epicentre of the humanitarian community - site of the famous Geneva Conventions and the original home of the Red Cross - the city has an air of cultivated opulence. Its streets are lined with luxury goods stores and advertisements for jewel-studded watches - all designed to tempt the most elite clientele. The nightlife also reflects this with plenty of swanky bars and clubs with strict admissions policies.

After drinking beer one evening until last-orders in one of our favourite bars in the *Paquis*, Mukul and I found ourselves with a night full of potential adventure stretching ahead of us but nowhere to go. The only places still open were the fanciest of clubs. As we wandered merrily down one of Geneva's picturesque streets, he hatched a plan.

Mukul went on ahead of me to confront the doorman of one of these ritzy places, while I hung back, out of sight. A group of women, all dressed up in gowns and high-heels, clustered around the entrance and looked like they were hoping to get inside too.

"My friend!" Mukul addressed the surly looking man on the door. "There is a very important man on his way here. He is an Arab Sheikh who wants to bring his harem out for a night in your club. He is an incredibly wealthy client of mine. I wanted to forewarn you he will require the best VIP treatment."

On cue I strolled up, looking vaguely unimpressed by the finery around me, and surrounded by this group of women we had never met before but who quickly got into the act. I am Indian, not Arab, but my general brownness and the fact that I was flanked on all sides by a group of beautiful women, despite being rotund and middle-aged, must have been enough to corroborate Mukul's story.

The doorman waved us all inside, our new 'friends' thanked us for getting them into one of the classiest clubs in Geneva and disappeared to find their own entertainment, leaving Mukul and I to continue our evening of carousing.

But despite all these distractions, I could not shake my depression. I went through the motions of working and friendships like Linda and Mukul lifted my spirits temporarily. But most of the time I still felt numb. I constantly carried with me the crushing weight of my failure. In Sudan, I had failed in the most fundamental of tasks with the most tragic consequences for millions of people. I had failed to prevent genocide.

If I could have curled up under a stone or disappeared into a hole in the ground, I would have been relieved to do so. I think in some ways I did exactly that, inwardly anyway, despite my friends' valiant efforts to pull me out. I also felt let down. I went to Sudan full of confidence and trust in the system I was part of, but ultimately I'd been cut adrift by it, even though my conduct was morally right.

My high-flying career as head of my own UN mission had come

crashing down around me. I now felt I was banished to WHO. I was grateful for the job of course but, although it felt like a life belt thrown to me, it also felt like exile. In my mind I had been earmarked for a UN political career, that's what I had been preparing for and striving towards. Now I was back working in healthcare, the same field I had started out in as a graduate.

Though I was still not yet fifty years old, the future - the long future I still had left to me - felt empty. Here I was with my status and salary maintained in a big office in beautiful Geneva, and the world going about its business. I couldn't believe that my life could go on, but it did. The days and weeks passed, mindlessly pushing paper, attending boring meetings and engaging in equally asinine leisure pursuits in the bars and clubs of Geneva. These provided temporary relief from the endless, nagging regret that was always with me.

I had lost purpose, lost direction, lost focus. I had even lost touch with my family, living isolated in Geneva. There seemed no purpose to live for. I felt bleak and depressed. So much so that the thoughts of suicide, which had flitted across my mind since leaving Darfur, became more of a permanent feature as I lay alone in bed at night.

As an insulin-dependent diabetic I had the means to end my life easily. I consulted the expert medical journals in the WHO library to figure out the insulin dose that would be necessary to ensure that it would kill me, rather than leave me in a vegetative coma. The thought of ending the unendurable pain of my failure felt increasingly attractive. All it would take was to inject a massive overdose one evening, and with a bit of luck, I would never wake up. With this in mind I began stockpiling insulin.

***

Lonely in Geneva, consumed by my guilt and absorbed in my own trauma, I had grown distant from my family. When the Christmas holidays came around it felt surreal to be back at our cheerful Cambridgeshire village home. I barely noticed the fairy lights twinkling on the tree, logs roasting on the fire, or the concerned expressions on my family's faces as they did their best to tempt me out of my depression with glasses of port and home-baked mince pies.

I was so engulfed in my own misery I knew I was not being much of a father to my girls, yet they were tolerant and understanding. I had gone to bed early on Christmas day after stuffing myself with all my festive favourites, though these seemed to have lost all flavour.

The next morning I was startled awake by the trilling of my telephone. The call delivered news of a natural disaster so catastrophic that it would leave 250,000 dead, thousands of miles of coastline irreparably altered, vibrate the very planet on its axis, and even jolt me out of my own melancholy.

My colleague from WHO, Rob Holden, who had also been my right-hand man in Darfur, instructed me in the clear yet urgent tone of a paramedic arriving on the scene of an accident. "Put on the TV, Mukesh. There has been a massive earthquake and a Tsunami near Aceh in Indonesia. Get yourself on the first flight back to Geneva."

I stumbled from my bed and into the living room. I flicked on the TV set. I lowered myself onto the carpet, still strewn with paper hats and scraps of wrapping from the day before, to watch bleary eyed as the reports came streaming in.

Indonesia, Thailand, Maldives, India, Sri Lanka, Myanmar, Madagascar and even the Somalian coast had all been affected. The earthquake, emanating from a point where the Burma and Indian tectonic plates collide, measured a gargantuan 9.3 on the Richter scale. As the epicentre lay under the Indian Ocean, it triggered a succession of tsunamis that devastated the countries all around.

My eyes were glued to the screen as I forced myself to my feet, pulled on some clothes and scrambled to say goodbye to my family. I checked my jacket pocket for my passport and was on the next available flight to Geneva.

***

I met the rest of the WHO Emergency Team, all looking just as dishevelled as myself, back in the operations room at headquarters. We poured over aerial photographs of the Tsunami-impact zone. The perimeter of the coastline was unrecognisable. I had to double check that we were in fact looking at images of Aceh, or what was left of it.

Thanks to the world's most technologically advanced satellite imaging, we could see that the town of Aceh had disappeared under a sea of mud. Thousands had perished there and in neighbouring areas, and the effects of the quake had been felt as far away as the other side of the Indian Ocean.

I was the only person without a real job at WHO, but who had enough significant disaster relief experience to coordinate the agency's world-wide response. I was instructed to travel immediately to New Delhi where the WHO headquarters for that region is based.

For now at least, my time for stagnating in misery behind a desk in Geneva was over. WHO needed me to step up to the plate and prove my credentials. More than that, the millions of survivors whose lives had been torn apart by that crashing wave needed rescue, shelter, water, sanitation, food, and healthcare. Thousands had been killed already and we were in danger of losing thousands more if we did not act fast. There wasn't a moment to lose.

In New Delhi I spent a few days helping SEARO - Southeast Asia Regional Office of WHO - in setting up its emergency operations centre. I wasted no time in organising the secondment of specialised WHO staff from across the globe. We would need logisticians, public health specialists, epidemiologists and medical professionals if we had any hope of choreographing a response large enough to deliver aid to the worst-affected countries.

Though time was of the essence, this part of the process was painfully slow. I learned here more than ever that WHO was hugely bureaucratic and rife with vested interests. The senior staff at the regional office did not appreciate someone from the Geneva HQ showing up and stealing the wind from their sails. This was horribly frustrating.

After finally laying the foundations of the regional emergency response system, I flew on from Delhi to Bangkok. This would be the site of my Special Tsunami Field Office. From here our team of specialists would oversee daily operations closer to the action.

The people of the world responded to the disaster with unparalleled generosity. Never before had so much money been raised so fast. The selfless impulse of everyday people to give to their fellow men and women in need is incredible. I believe that such altruism is the most admirable quality that humans possess, and never before had I seen it mobilised on such a massive scale.

Despite the availability of funds my task of coordinating Tsunami relief proved challenging. The greatest barrier to achieving fast and effective deployment was the administrative protocol of WHO's emergency response mechanism itself. One huge obstacle was the deep mistrust felt between the global headquarters in Geneva, the regional field office in New Delhi and the individual country offices. Dealing with these tensions consumed a lot of energy, to the detriment of the effectiveness and timeliness of our response.

In addition to this there was continual tension within the organisation as to how much action we should be taking. Was WHO purely an overarching, standard-setting, norm-creating institution? Or did it have a hands-on operational role in helping countries to manage this crisis? Certainly the former had largely been true in the past, but times were changing.

Now we lived in an increasingly globalised, interconnected world, where diseases knew no boundaries and health crises spread quickly across huge areas and populations. It was time for WHO's traditional role to evolve into something more relevant for the modern era. Luckily my superior, David Nabarro, was able to skilfully navigate these tensions in order to protect and support us working in the field.

***

Once my team in Bangkok was working well I decided to move on to the U-Tapao Royal Thai Air Base, a few hours to the southeast of the city. U-Tapao is a large and strategic military facility, and would become the command centre for the multinational response rapidly taking shape around us. The armed forces of many different countries - from Japan to Singapore, Thailand to Australia, India to America - lent their military assets to what was shaping up to be a massive search, rescue and relief operation.

Naval vessels began amassing along the Gulf of Siam and U-Tapao itself was crowded with aircraft. Everyone wanted to do their part to help, but nobody was quite sure what that meant. We had to ensure the seamless coordination of military and civilian operations. I had widespread relief-coordination experience to facilitate this, but would they listen to me? In a world so structured around inflexible hierarchies, would these military men agree to take their orders from someone like myself - an aid worker with no military experience? I had to convince them. I had no choice if we were to save the lives of the stranded, the wounded, and those who had lost so much already.

My first stop before U-Tapao was to visit one of the enterprising tailors of Bangkok. I hastily invested in a couple of very smart suits that I felt would inspire respect from military men. I had packed hurriedly and was not appropriately prepared for a role instilling confidence in the military.

Once I was sharply suited and booted, I headed straight on to U-Tapao. As I pulled up at the air base and looked out at the hangers, offices and portacabins, all laid out with precision and orderliness, I felt "butterfly wings" beating against my ribcage. I had to impose my will as the UN's representative - and fast - if I was going to have any hope of commanding the respect necessary to get help to the disaster victims. Technically I was WHO, but the UN had granted me the honorary rank of a two-star general to act as their envoy to the military contingent.

Luckily my new title and fresh suit did much of the talking for me. I was accepted into the top levels of U-Tapao decision-making without any challenge to my legitimacy. My main task was to decide on the priorities. In the confusion and chaos, with so much going on and so many different actors clamouring to be heard, it was important that we brought organisation and order as fast as possible.

The Americans offered some of their key naval assets that had been en route from Honolulu to relieve their fleet in the Gulf. They had been on a port call in Hong Kong when the Tsunami hit and were asked to divert to Aceh to help. The flotilla was led by the *USS Abraham Lincoln*, a vast 100,000-ton aircraft carrier known affectionately as Abe, and accompanied by a state-of-the-art hospital ship, an oil tanker and several other high-tech vessels.

I dispatched Rob Holden to Abe's on-board air-coordination centre. He would be my right-hand person in the field. Rob, who had called me with the initial news of the Tsunami, was both a former nurse and a former navy man who had worked alongside me, first at DFID, and then in Sudan. I could think of no better person for the job.

Of course, my first instinct was to do what I had always done before - go into the field myself, right into the thick of things to assess the problem from the ground. This time however it made much more sense for me to stay back in command at U-Tapao, where I could use my rank and status to handle the military leadership. I was forced to admit that my role was changing. Had the time finally come for me to give up my hands-on approach for the security of a desk job?

With Rob reporting back to me several times daily from his post on board the good ship Abe, and the commanders of the fleet looking to me for their next move, we devised a strategy to make the most of these unique resources.

The coastline of Indonesia is shallow at the best of times. Now it was unrecognisable thanks to the Tsunami. This meant that deep ocean vessels like Abe and her entourage could not approach the shoreline themselves, but luckily for us they did have a fleet of helicopters on board.

We devised a plan whereby the US navy would sail systematically down the coast, beginning with the area that had suffered the worst damage. Here they would wait while the helicopters departed from the carrier to fly at low altitude over the unrecognisable landscape. They would assess the lie of the land, record the destruction, and locate the survivors. Whether they were marooned on an outcrop of rock, clinging to a tussock of vegetation, or just sitting on a high spot in the endless mud, the low-flying helicopters could spot them.

If it was unsafe for them to land nearby they would drop food parcels and fresh water supplies to the stranded, and alert more specialised search and rescue teams of their location. If the pilots could manoeuvre their craft to land, they would dispatch their on-board medical teams to administer whatever treatment the survivors needed. If anyone was seriously ill or injured they would be airlifted back to the hospital ship.

Once an area had been swept by helicopter, the terrain and population recorded, and medical aid administered to any survivors, the pilots would return to the ship. They would refuel while Abe crept on along the coastline a few kilometres further, where they would repeat the whole process over again.

By this method Rob and the Americans combined triage and location mapping to systematically piece together a picture of what was going on down on the ground. This would prove instrumental in the rescue missions that followed. Any distinguishable landmarks had been obliterated, so the coordinates of the survivors' locations that we provided were all the rescuers had to orientate themselves against the featureless mud-scape.

When I had left Geneva I thought I would be staying only a few weeks in Southeast Asia. As my position in the relief and recovery effort became clearer, I realised I would be remaining far longer. I had been there so long that I was in danger of running out of insulin. Fake drugs are a huge problem in the developing world, so I could not risk stocking up locally. Luckily, Linda had a key to my apartment in Geneva and I requested she stop by before flying out to join me.

I paused as I asked her to collect my insulin - hoping she wouldn't question why I had so much - and realised how my outlook had transformed since the Tsunami hit. I had a huge stockpile of insulin at home in readiness for the day I would commit my suicide. Now there was no more thought of that. I marvelled for a second at the turn-around I had made. I no longer wanted to die. In fact, I wanted to stay alive so badly that I was concerned for the quality of my medicine.

I could not die. What a ridiculous and self-indulgent thought now that there was so much to do. Too much still to accomplish. To rebuild. To bring hope to so many desperate people.

Once my insulin stocks were replenished, I abdicated my throne in U-Tapao to go and see for myself what the situation was like on the ground.

***

A Japanese air force Hercules C130 was providing an airbridge between U-Tapao and the partially destroyed airstrip in Aceh. The next morning, I boarded this flight and headed into the centre of the disaster zone. The monotonous drone of the aircraft's engine was interrupted only occasionally by announcements in Japanese. Other than that, the flight seemed quite unremarkable. When we landed some hours later I gathered up my things to disembark, eager to see the city of Aceh for myself.

To my surprise it didn't look too bad. There were some buildings standing beside the airfield and it wasn't muddy at all. I began to inwardly congratulate the disaster relief teams, thinking the extraordinary generosity of the world's public must have really done wonders for the destroyed city, until I realised that we were not actually in Aceh. We were back in U-Tapao. The landing conditions had proved too treacherous after recent adverse weather and we had turned around mid-flight. I can't understand Japanese so I hadn't realised.

The following day we tried again, and this time we did reach Aceh. There was no way I could mistake it for anywhere else. What had once been homes, gardens, streets, schools, shops and markets were now a mangled mass of detritus. Plant matter was mashed around the dislodged roofs of long-gone buildings. Rubble, planks of wood, and smashed furniture lay all bunched up together. All the buildings had been razed to the ground and here and there an upturned car or stranded boat punctuated the expanse of stinking, muddy trash.

The only landmark that had survived the disaster relatively unscathed was the imposing Masjid Raya Baiturrahman Mosque. It shone out as a beacon standing tall above the ruination. People claimed it was a miracle. That Allah had protected it. Maybe this was true, but the open-sided architecture that had allowed the force of the wave to pass through it, rather than crashing into it, may have helped in its preservation too.

All was covered in thick grey mud. There was no way of avoiding it. As I dismounted the Hercules and said *arigatou* to my Japanese companions, I resorted to tucking up the trouser legs of my smart new Bangkok suit and wading barefoot through the sludge. It was the only way.

***

As I became acquainted with the situation on the ground I was struck by the bravery and open-heartedness of the Indonesian people. Here, as in Erzincan, I learned that many of our local team had lost family members. One woman had no idea where her husband or children were. Yet she reported for work and toiled from dawn until dusk to bring help to others; struggling through the mud, carrying supplies and setting up tents wherever we could put up shelter.

I really valued the contribution of these local health workers. There had been a huge influx of international medical teams from different countries, all wanting to be seen to be doing the best job in front of the TV cameras and squabbling over who got to use what in the hospital. Yet many of them were nervous to venture out of the city into the unexplored vastness of the real devastation to tackle whatever desperate medical conditions lay there.

Meanwhile, local doctors and nurses came wading through the mud and debris to report for service. Though bruised and battered themselves, they were utterly dedicated to their people's needs. We partnered with them to restore public health services and to bring primary healthcare to the displaced survivors. These Indonesian professionals really brought home the importance of localisation when implementing relief missions. Utilising the skills and willingness of local people to bring about regeneration was crucial.

***

I hoped that the international teams would learn from the locals, as I had learned so many years earlier on Moudubi in Bangladesh. Though I was only eighteen at that time, the experience had really stayed with me. I had gone to the developing world with the idea of helping the Moudubi islanders, but had certainly come away with more than I gave. The experience had made me much wiser.

After Moudubi, I had resigned myself to continuing with developing my medical career at Oxford, but I could not completely ignore the pull at my heartstrings to do something meaningful and worthwhile for others, particularly the friends I had made in Bangladesh. I kept wondering how people were doing? Who had had a baby? Who was getting married to whom? Imagining how their lives were progressing, balanced between the harshness of nature and the strength of their community.

I could not forget them, so I had started a small charity of my own. I founded a student group called "Friends of Moudubi" to raise money to help development there. To start an organisation you had to have a committee - so I roped in my drinking buddies, Steve Pull and Chris Waddington, and together we started fund raising.

All the Oxford colleges have a Junior Common Room, or JCR, which organise social events for the college, provide communal space for letting off steam and create a general hub of collegiate activity. Each JCR is allocated a yearly charity budget to donate to good causes of the students' choice.

I wanted some of that money for Friends of Moudubi, yet there was one obstacle in my way. In order to convince the JCR committee, I, along with other would-be do-gooders, had to present a ten-minute pitch to the whole Junior Common Room on why they should give the money to bird conservation, or care for the elderly or, as in my case, my Friends of Moudubi. The committee would then vote for the cause they liked best or deemed the most worthy.

I was more than a little nervous. It may seem hard to believe now, but then I was terrified of public speaking. Steve, Chris and I retired to our usual refuge, *The Welsh Pony,* to work on our pitch and settle our nerves. After two or three pints we decided we were ready, just in time to present at the common room meeting.

When my time came to speak I got to my feet - a little unsteadily - and presented our pitch. I don't remember what I said but everyone just laughed and laughed and laughed. I have no idea why, I didn't' think I was that funny, and we were certainly dealing with the very real challenges of eradicating poverty in Bangladesh. This was serious business.

Whatever I said seemed to work, because we came top and were allocated one hundred pounds worth of funding. This was a lot of money in the 1970s. We used it to provide enough basic drugs for a thousand people for the entire year, but that was just the start. We did sponsored fasts, sponsored walks, sponsored runs, sponsored discos - anything we could think of sponsoring. All the money went to Moudubi for whatever little projects they needed: school books, medicines, tools and seeds.

In true Mukesh fashion this was not enough for me. The famous charity OXFAM are based in Oxford and I asked for an appointment to meet Brian Walker, its radical director, on behalf of Friends of Moudubi. If I had learned anything from my experience getting my place at college it was that, if you don't ask, the answer is always 'no'. To my great surprise I was granted an appointment, pleaded my case and was inexplicably awarded seven hundred and fifty pounds from the director's own fund. That was a real fortune for our purpose.

I was over the moon, and so were Steve and Chris. With these endowments we organised our programme for Moudubi's support on a bigger scale. We took on scholarships for children to go to school and college to improve their education. This had been my first foray into organised humanitarianism.

My personal highlight was that we were able to pay for a trained midwife to go and live on Moudubi. Though I would never forget the girl who had died writhing in agony on that makeshift stretcher by the jetty, I felt like the work we were doing now would somewhat atone for my failure to save her. We were striving to ensure that her death was not in vain, for it had motivated us to bring about lasting change to save others.

***

Women's health was also a priority in post-Tsunami Aceh. When meeting the survivors, it became clear to me that there were far more men than women. Evidently when the monster wave had approached, the mothers had begun searching for their children. Encumbered by their long traditional garb and the weight of their little ones, many of them hadn't stood a change as they tried to flee the torrent. Many, many women perished.

A large number of the men, by comparison, were out fishing when the wave hit and had no knowledge of the destruction until they returned home that evening to a coastline they no longer recognised. The men who were on land were often strong enough to flee to safety - to run faster, to climb higher, to hold on tighter when the powerful waters washed over them. These reasons combined to leave a surviving population with far more men than women.

There was a strange tragic consequence to this that became obvious during the recovery period. Many of the surviving men, having lost their own families, wanted to start new ones, marry again and have children. The surviving women, now perhaps left widowed, or too young to get married in the first place, were under huge pressure to wed themselves off to these men. UNFPA, the UN women's agency, did a magnificent job protecting unwilling women from being forced into marriages with men often three times their age.

In some ways it was clear that the Tsunami had been a life-transforming event for a whole generation. The surviving women and girls didn't want to get married or remarried. They wanted to go to school or college to learn the kinds of skills that would make them self-sufficient. Then later, if they wanted to, they could marry not out of necessity but out of choice.

Working together with the NGOs on the ground the local people were rebuilding houses, starting new businesses, reimagining their society in a more enlightened, egalitarian manifestation than before.

The survivors had all lost at least one family member or loved one and though their grief ran deep, most were determined to rebuild their ruined community in a fairer and more progressive way. For one thing it had brought an end to the longstanding insurgency in the area. There had been a lengthy and merciless civil war going on between the Indonesian regime in Jakarta and the Achinese, who wanted independence from the rest of Indonesia. A large chunk of the rebel fighters, plus the civilian populations who supported them, had been wiped out. Those who remained were in no mood to resume the conflict.

With so many dead, even those who had fought so viciously for one side or the other, could not envisage a future where the people of Indonesia were not united going forward.

With a stab of pain in my heart I thought back to Sudan. Could the genocide in Darfur have had the same effect as this natural disaster? Could peace be found for Sudan? With so much blood spilled, the entire population of a vast region displaced and unable to return home, could the Sudanese ever hope to find common ground like the Indonesians? No, I concluded, as I looked about me at the desolation. It was terrible to behold, but it was nobody's fault. This was a 'natural disaster'. In Sudan the regime had perpetrated the killing, bringing about very deliberate bloodshed and destruction. I doubted peace would ever be reached in the same way.

***

With WHO fully staffed and geared up across Southeast Asia and the regeneration programme well underway, I boarded a flight back to Geneva. Four months had passed since I had flown out in the aftermath of the worst natural disaster of my lifetime. I disembarked at Geneva's small, well-polished airport feeling exhausted, yet curiously energised.

The Tsunami experience had revealed to me the very best and very worst of WHO. The best was the professional dedication and incredible expertise of skilled individuals who grappled with the organisation's rule-bound encumbrances. The worst were the petty jealousies and turf battles between senior managers, which severely compromised our abilities.

I considered this to be an outrage and, as in Sudan, I felt that I had a moral responsibility that exceeded any bureaucratic loyalties. I was angry that personal squabbles had jeopardised the brave and fast-thinking actions of staff in the field and I was not afraid to make this clear. I was not looking for a long WHO career. I had no interest in working my way up the ranks. I would try to do what was right during my time there, even if this meant breaking eggs, cracking heads and making myself unpopular in certain circles.

I felt like a changed man. I had taken my directorship at WHO as a lifeboat when I was drowning, yet it had allowed me to be re-born. I would always be grateful to WHO for that, however frustrating it was to work in its vast self-preserving bureaucracy of that time.

Through bringing assistance to those on the front lines of the Tsunami disaster, I had also brought healing to myself. For at least a few months, I had not given much thought to my own personal trauma over Darfur. I still resolved to never forget Sudan - and assured myself that I would return to this when the time was ripe - but for now I would try to lead a useful life again.

Chapter Twenty-One

Let us realise the arc of the moral universe is long, but it bends toward justice.
Theodore Parker

IN SPITE OF THE STIFLING BUREAUCRACY, I STAYED ON AT WHO. During this time I did my best to overhaul the system from within. My frontline crisis experiences had changed me. I couldn't abide the petty red-tape and cumbersome etiquette of the institution. I was more determined now and unafraid to cause waves.

I knew I was under sufferance at WHO. My Darfur whistleblowing had made me an embarrassment to the international system. My 'insolent' behaviour was only tolerated thanks to the forbearance of old associates like David Nabarro, who I sensed might be beginning to regret taking me on.

Though they had made space for me in the institution, I was forbidden from talking about Darfur. This was not written into my contract, but neither was it unspoken. The understanding was that when I was rescued with this job, I could have nothing more to do with Sudan.

Although the whole world now knew the depths of the crisis in Darfur - the outflowing of millions of refugees and the eruptions of disease could hardly go unnoticed - WHO did not want to get involved. This was the "see-no-evil" policy the organisation operated under, in those days.

I was increasingly disappointed that WHO were so completely swayed by political pressure and would not speak out against governments - even those led by criminals like Omar al-Bashir, the Sudanese President and architect of the Darfur atrocities - for fear of causing offence. They fled from anything that could be considered controversial.

Instead, WHO subscribed to the principle that its job was to ingratiate itself with governments, advise on technical matters, and avoid fundamental questions over the factors affecting the life-chances of the most vulnerable and marginalised populations. The words "human rights" were banned from any documents produced by WHO, so fearful were they of criticising those in power.

Darfur was still too much of a political hot potato for WHO. But seeing the urgent needs there and being unable to act proved heartbreaking for me. I have always felt deeply uncomfortable conspiring with corrupt governments at any level, particularly since working with the Taliban in Afghanistan, and then the execrable regime in Khartoum. I struggled to understand how WHO could be so seemingly comfortable turning a blind eye to such evil.

I consoled myself with the notion that, although WHO was spineless, they had at least welcomed a highly-controversial whistleblower like me into the fold. Or so they had me believe.

One afternoon I was summoned to meet with WHO's Legal Counsel. The organisation's top lawyer slid an envelope across the desk towards me. As I looked through it, my initial curiosity transmuted into angry disbelief. The letter concerned many, many months of correspondence between WHO, the UN, and the International Criminal Court. The ICC it turned out, had been trying to get me to give evidence in the case against Omar al-Bashir, the President of Sudan, who was charged with committing crimes against humanity in Darfur.

Totally unbeknownst to me, the UN and WHO had been engaged in a protracted struggle with the ICC to prevent me from testifying in front of the Prosecutor. Naturally, the ICC had sought the permission of my employing agency - the UN and WHO - for me to give evidence, and had been blocked at every turn. The UN said they couldn't ask me to appear as I was now an official of WHO and so no longer employed by them, while WHO had argued that my previous job was nothing to do with them, so they could not ask me to appear either. It was semantics and double-speak, and I had been left totally unaware.

Significantly due to my whistleblowing, there had been a UN Security Council resolution passed requiring all countries and international entities to cooperate with the ICC over Bashir's indictment. Incredibly, the agencies I worked for were clearly in breach of this requirement. Even worse, I learned that the UN Secretariat in New York had refused to release documents from my period in office, or any of the reports I had authored warning about the Darfur atrocities.

I guessed that the ICC's lawyers must have won in the end. Otherwise, I wouldn't be here. Conversely, if WHO's Legal Counsel had been successful, I would probably have never known about any of this.

I was outraged. Enraged. How could they have attempted to obstruct the course of justice like this, and especially when they knew what inhuman wrongs had been committed? What's more, how could they have tried to prevent me from giving evidence, when they knew that I was a direct witness to what had happened, and had even chosen to sacrifice my UN career over it? This felt like a deeper level of betrayal, both of myself and of the hundreds of thousands of murdered Darfuris.

I was burning with a cold fury, as the WHO lawyers obliged me sign a long, complicated document which stipulated that if I promised not to bring WHO into disrepute, I was permitted to go and testify at The Hague.

How dare they! How dare the UN behave in such a double-dealing, duplicitous and deeply unethical manner. It should have been axiomatic that I would give testimony, for there were few better placed to do so than the former Head of the United Nations in Sudan. The survivors could better speak to the horrors they had endured, of course, but who knew better than me about the machinations of those in power in Khartoum who had authored and then executed their '*final solution*'?

***

I spent two weeks with the ICC prosecution team in The Hague, returning twice to report on every aspect of my time in Sudan. The questioning was so detailed, at times I felt like I myself was on trial, contained as I was in a small, featureless interview room for days on end with lawyers taking down every word. But I understood why. If my testimony was to carry weight, every minutiae had to be checked and crosschecked and checked again. This meant going over those traumatic events time and again, and from all angles.

Re-living those stories over and over, forced to recall everything meticulously, was incredibly painful. I had to dig deep into memories that I had quite clearly been repressing. Once again, I was filled with remorse, wishing I could have done more at the time to prevent or stop the genocide.

One memory of that time that I forced myself to face was excruciatingly hard: daily, the situation was worsening in Darfur. More displaced people swarmed into refugee camps in neighbouring countries, and horrific first-hand accounts of the atrocities were filtering out.

Using funds I had secured from generous donor countries, I did my best to ensure there was a revitalised UN presence on the ground in Darfur. I had hoped that by flooding the area with international personnel, the government of Sudan would be forced to halt their campaign of slaughter. For a while it seemed to be working, but Khartoum was not out of tricks just yet.

I began receiving worrying reports from my security chief that the Darfur city of El Geneina was about to suffer a major attack. If this was true, it meant that many of my staff and affiliated aid workers were at risk. My mind raced from the UN workers killed by the *Interahamwe* in Rwanda, to Sérgio murdered by Al Qaeda in Iraq. My primary obligation was to protect my staff, but if we were to evacuate them, then who would be our eyes and ears on the ground? Who knew what would happen if we removed the very people whose presence was providing protection for the people of Darfur?

I agonised over that decision. I avoided evacuation for as long as possible, but when my security chief threatened to report me to New York for refusing to take his concerns seriously, I had no choice but to listen to him. It was either that or face losing my position in Sudan, and I would be able to help the Darfuris even less then. Reports of armed confrontations around El Geneina became ever more concrete, and I was forced to give the order to pull out all our staff from the region.

The Khartoum regime reacted with apparent anger. They claimed that by withdrawing the UN contingent it appeared as if we didn't believe the government was strong enough to ensure their safety. Seemingly incensed by my actions, they argued that if I feared for the welfare of my UN staff around El Geneina, then I must withdraw my personnel from all of Darfur. Access would only be reinstated when the government would guarantee the safety of my people, and I could accept such reassurances.

I realised at once what a terrible mistake we had made. The Khartoum regime had played my security team like fools, feeding them false information, and we had fallen for their tricks, hook, line and sinker. I was forced to remove all my UN staff from across Darfur, the very last thing in the world I would ever have wished to do. In the vacuum so created, the *Janjaweed* militias, supported by Khartoum, wreaked the very worst of their atrocities, secure in the knowledge that they were safe from international scrutiny.

Allowing myself into being tricked to remove all my staff from Darfur was one of my greatest regrets, for when we were eventually able to return to the area it was far too late. We had been denied access to Darfur for eight long weeks. During this time, the regime had used our absence to intensify their genocidal campaign to unimaginable proportions. By the time they allowed us in again, their "*final solution"* was as good as done. As our humanitarian staff fanned out across the region, the stories that came back proved to be more horrible than we could have ever imagined.

Whole swathes of the countryside were simply devoid of their native black African peoples. All their villages had been decimated - torched to the ground - while the neighbouring Arab settlements were left untouched. The *Janjaweed* militia had struck not from horseback - their normal form of transport - but from Toyota Land Cruisers provided by the government. Their savage attacks had been supplemented by crude petrol bombs and cannon fire, delivered from high-flying Khartoum regime aircraft.

Wells and irrigation systems had been dynamited or poisoned by dead bodies, the corpses of the slain thrown down to bloat and rot in the water. Livestock had been stolen or senselessly slaughtered. Women and even young girls had been publicly raped in front of their families, by the *Janjaweed* raiders crying: "I will give you an Arab baby who will steal this land from you." Children and babies had been torn from their parents' arms and thrown onto the flaming huts, where they burned to death, their piercing screams rending the desert night.

These were the memories that haunted my mind during those weeks testifying at The Hague. While it was a traumatic experience for me it was also cathartic in a way. At least now my version of events was being officially recorded. I knew the chances of Bashir being brought to trial were incredibly slim, yet I remain optimistic that perhaps, one day, he and the others in his high circle indicted for the genocide will be held accountable. When that day comes I hope my witness record will help to bring proper justice.

I felt comforted too that my testimony was now preserved. It could be used in evidence at any time, no matter what might happen to me. Since leaving Sudan I had received numerous death threats. No matter how many times I changed my phone number the sinister phone calls kept coming. Now I knew that no matter what might befall me at the behest of Bashir and his ilk, my testimony would survive.

Another consequence of this sudden licence to speak, even in the strict confidentiality of the ICC, was that now I hungered to talk publicly on the subject. It was as if a taboo had been broken. In spite of their best attempts, the UN and the WHO had failed to keep me totally silent and now I burned to speak out.

I was approached to do some interviews for the BBC. They were investigating the truth of what took place in Darfur. I told them that I was not allowed to comment due to my contract with WHO, or not unless the UN Secretariat agreed to let me do so. The BBC contacted the UN and threw down the gauntlet: they were going to run the story anyway, revealing how a key witness to the Darfur genocide, the UN Chief in Sudan at the time, was forbidden from speaking *by the UN itself*. They calculated that this charge would be feared more by the UN than anything I might say.

They were right. The UN granted me leave to speak to the BBC. During that interview I strongly condemned the Khartoum regime and the UN's response to the genocide. This generated a lot of interest. I was invited to appear on the BBC's flagship programme *Hard Talk* for an exclusive, one-on-one, unedited interview. I was grilled by one of their star journalists, Zeinab Badawi, herself of Arab Sudanese origin. This interview was one of the most difficult interrogations I ever faced, on par with the ICC's questioning.

Bizarrely, the UN had sent me a briefing note, attempting to guide me on what to say. It was laughable. I thought by now the UN would know who they were dealing with and that they couldn't censor me. Yet when I re-watched the interview, I feared that I had held back. For all my bravado, all my burning desire to reveal the truth about Sudan, I feared I had pulled my punches when it came to condemning the international community.

Perhaps a small part of me still hoped that one day I would be welcomed back to the UN family. Despite all I knew of their failings, perhaps I didn't want to burn those bridges totally.

***

My outspokenness - however much my punches had been pulled - still burned bridges. Seen as somewhat of a maverick within WHO, my candidness on the BBC had further worn the patience of those at the helm of the organisation. Luckily, I was still protected by the Director General, Dr Lee Jong-wook. Dr. Lee was a genuine advocate for health. He was a true adventurer and a man of action in the health world. His work on leprosy in his native Korea, his rolling out of tuberculosis vaccination across the world, and his ambitious targets for HIV reduction had led me to admire him.

Likewise, Dr Lee had come to respect my preference for action over etiquette, and I think he appreciated my ability to cut through the red tape that left so many in WHO paralysed. Dr Lee was also amazingly tolerant of my unusual working practices and kept me going.

One morning, I was in the queue at the café in the WHO foyer and turned around to see Dr Lee just behind me. "Hello," he said, "How is it going? What are you up to?" Spontaneously, I blurted out, "Nothing.

Just packing - I leave at the end of this month."

He seemed genuinely startled. "What? I did not know! No, you are not leaving. Come and see me." And thus began the second chapter of my life at WHO as I was catapulted up to the Director General's personal office as his adviser for audits and evaluations - looking particularly at the performance aspects of WHO's vast network of "collaborating centres" around the world.

At that time there was a scam going on whereby many institutions around the world had somehow got themselves recognised, over a long period of time, as designated collaborating centres of WHO. This brought them prestige and it was ostensibly for cutting-edge research and training in specific areas. But many did nothing except to misuse the WHO logo to raise funds for their own routine purposes. There were scores of such centres and my job was to review each of them and renew or repeal their status. Of course that did not endear me either to the internal WHO departments who were part of the scam, or to the many renowned bodies worldwide who were not renewed as designated WHO centres of excellence, due to the tough new criteria I put in place.

Then, on 22nd May 2006, Dr Lee died suddenly and unexpectedly of a subdural hematoma. He had been a compassionate visionary and I realised this was also the death knell for my own position within WHO. My friends and defenders were gone and I knew I would not last long without them. I had made too many powerful enemies.

***

While I mourned the loss of Dr Lee, I felt little regret at the thought of leaving WHO. Why had they been so determined to keep me quiet over Darfur? It showed a shocking lack of moral fortitude, when such an institution chose to sweep evidence of crimes against humanity under the carpet, just to guard their own self-interest. A part of me couldn't believe I had stayed in this job for so long. It was testimony to how traumatised and disturbed I was after Sudan, that I had remained part of an organisation that were so opposed to my core values.

I was determined to leave: the question was, what to do next with my life?

The option of returning to DFID was long gone. I was grateful to the British Government for their support of me since I had left DFID many years earlier, but I had little desire to ever return to those offices in Westminster.

Rescue came, as it had so many times before, in the form of a serendipitous phone call, taken in my WHO office surrounded by half-packed boxes. I had resigned my post at WHO, and a mystery benefactor had heard and was calling with an offer.

It was Markku Niskala, Secretary General of the biggest of all humanitarian organisations: The International Federation of Red Cross and Red Crescent Societies.

Chapter Twenty-Two

We are never as kind as we want to be, but nothing outrages us more than people being unkind to us.
Leo Tolstoy

MY ASSOCIATION WITH THE RED CROSS IS AS OLD AS feeding from my mother's breast. My father and grandmother would have been slaughtered on the train from Pakistan, during *Partition*, had it not been for the valiant young Red Cross staffer who guarded their journey.

That man, who stood between them and the blood-thirsty mob, epitomised all that the Red Cross Red Crescent stands for. He was unarmed, impartial and acting on no one's side but that of humanity. These qualities are the armour the Red Cross Red Crescent wears when its people head into the most dangerous places on earth. At times like this, when normal society has been degraded beyond all recognition, this is where you'll find the Red Cross and Red Crescent people, where no one else dares to tread.

I had always held them in very high esteem, so much so that when I was working for DFID I had identified the ICRC[1] as the first organisation I wanted to collaborate with, when launching a brand-new UK Government initiative I named as "Institutional Strategic Partnerships".

---

[1] The Red Cross Red Crescent have a presence - known as National Societies - in almost every country in the world. These come together under the International Federation of Red Cross and Red Crescent Societies – IFRC, headquartered in Geneva. The International Committee of the Red Cross - ICRC - is a little different. This is an independent body, also based in Geneva with special status under the Geneva Conventions. The National Societies, IFRC, and ICRC together constitute the International Red Cross and Red Crescent Movement - the world's largest humanitarian network.

In those days, donors like us would grant money to organisations on a project by project basis. If a famine hit Ethiopia, the British government would contribute to the World Food Programme in order to feed the starving people. If there was a drought in Namibia we would pledge to Unicef. These bodies would also use a percentage of these donations to fund the day to day running of their administrations.

This kind of contract funding was sensible to a point, yet it made it very difficult for the organisations involved to develop themselves. All the money that came in was linked to disasters, leaving their futures very unclear. While their efforts went into dealing with unfolding emergencies, there were few resources left to invest in bettering their working practices.

I wanted to incentivise these agencies to refine their methodology and develop more effective, smarter ways of operating that would ultimately benefit people in the field. I devised a scheme where we would partner with an organisation for an extended period of time. In return for improvements in their general delivery, we would guarantee them a block of money every year. This would not be tied to any particular project but instead would be used to upgrade the organisation's management, update their equipment, invest in advanced technologies, and so on.

The advantage to this was that a strong, well-functioning institution would develop more effective and efficient projects. Investing in this way also showed respect for our partners. Rather than just contracting them to do a job, we wanted to show our belief in the good work they did and help them to do more and do better.

I proposed to invest fifteen million pounds into ICRC every year, over five years, in order for them to improve their ways of operating. There was one obstacle to this plan however, and that was that the ICRC had always been highly secretive about the details of their work.

They would not share the results of their activities. Their people were often the only ones allowed into incredibly volatile areas, thanks in part to their reputation for impartiality and confidentiality. They argued that they could not share the information we requested, in case it endangered the security of their representatives in the field or compromised their access to highly sensitive situations.

In their defence, they did hold a very unique place in the aid world. There is nobody else quite like the ICRC. They have special international status and they surpass all others in their commitment to humanitarianism. Maintaining that mystique was a crucial part of their identity and role.

They believed that their reputation should be enough for donors. We should give them money without question so they could get on with their important work. I understood this to a point, but I couldn't invest seventy-five-million pounds into any one organisation that refused to tell me what they were up to.

That style might have worked in the past, but modern times called for openness and accountability. I made it my mission to cajole the ICRC, commanded at the time by the formidable Cornelio Sommaruga - a prominent Swiss humanitarian - into becoming more transparent. I went for many meetings in Geneva in the hope of building a mutually respectful and trusting relationship. While they still refused to divulge much information, they invited me to come with them to see for myself how they operated in the field. I accepted.

I spent a fascinating week with them in the north of Sri Lanka, then a nation embroiled in a vicious civil war. I stayed in the ICRC's guesthouse in Batticaloa and spent day and night with their delegates there. At that time the Tamil rebels of northern Sri Lanka were fighting the central government. The Red Cross were operating on both sides of the frontline. Thanks to the bond of trust we were forming, they allowed me a level of access that they had never permitted before. They showed me how they rehabilitated landmine victims; supported food production through local farming; and tended to the needs of prisoners of war on both sides.

Education was always highly prized in Sri Lanka and provided a valuable bridge between the warring sides. During the worst of the fighting, the ICRC had even arranged ceasefires for students to take their public examinations, and then transported the scripts from rebel areas to be marked by the central education authorities in Colombo. I found it remarkable that while the rebels fought tooth-and-nail with the central government, they were keen for their pupils not to miss out on their diplomas from the universities on the "enemy" government side.

I accompanied one ICRC delegate - a typically dedicated, straight-talking, Swiss man named Max - into a government prison, to observe how they protected those captured during the war. We were ushered inside the thick-walled building into an inner courtyard. Around the perimeter were detention cells containing captured rebel Tamils; all tough-looking soldiers, sitting or lying around in their cells. They seemed well-fed and well-cared for. None were very talkative, but Max visited each cell to deliver letters from their loved ones and to ask if there was anything they needed.

"What's your name?" he asked, checking an official list he'd been given by the guards. It was important to ensure that each prisoner was recorded by name and number, so that they could keep track of what happened to each.

"G…," a man muttered in response. He was broad-shouldered, muscular and mean looking.

"What's your story, G…?" I enquired. I had heard much about the infamous Tamil Tigers, who were fighting the government in an attempt to create an independent state, *Tamil Eelam*, in the north of Sri Lanka. The war had been characterised by horrific human rights abuses on each side. This was partly why ICRC was playing such an active role here.

"I fought for Tamil independence. I murdered. I raped," he told me, in a surprisingly off-hand tone. "I was planning to commit suicide on capture but they took my cyanide capsule away from me."

Max shot me a loaded glance and I didn't ask any more questions after that. I was shocked to hear G… speak so plainly of such terrible deeds and his readiness to take his own life. The conflict had brutalised the people so much that to speak of such things was no longer taboo.

ICRC's core mandate was to make sure that captives like G… received humane treatment. They attended to prisoners of war on all sides to ensure their safety and welfare. Max checked that the prisoners had soap, healthcare, enough to eat and that they were not tortured or beaten up. Most importantly, he made sure they knew they were not forgotten. Even though they had been thrown in gaol, with no idea when they might be released, the ICRC was there to bear witness to their existence and to their humanity, despite the loathsome crimes they had committed.

As I watched Max interact with the gaolers and the prisoners alike, I was incredibly impressed. He behaved totally impartially, showing no judgement on either side. He was there simply to ensure that no human being, no matter their crime, was treated inhumanely. Nobody but a representative from the Red Cross, with all the loaded symbolism that represents, could have achieved this.

Normally, when I would go and visit a programme in the field I would write a long mission report detailing everything I had seen and done, my thoughts and opinions, my criticisms, and so on. In the case of the ICRC I did no such thing. They were right when they claimed that their reputation for confidentiality was vital to their work. To jeopardise that would be to disrespect the unique place they held in the world, holding a candle for humanity when all around was in shadow.

The fact that I had seen this for myself was enough. I appreciated the trust they were bestowing in me by taking me into these places. I had come to this project hoping to force them to accept more accountability, but when I saw how professionally and compassionately Max and the others conducted themselves, I changed my mind. I was satisfied that not only did they have integrity but they were committed to self-improvement. I was delighted for DFID to give them seventy-five-million pounds to continue their good efforts.

I had also learnt that when I could trust the people of an organisation, I didn't need to know all the details of how they used our funds.

***

So, when I received the call from Markku Niskala inviting me to join ICRC's sister body, the International Federation of the Red Cross and Red Crescent Societies (IFRC), I was excited.

"Come and work with us," he urged. "I need someone of your background and experience to be my special representative for AIDS work."

The general assembly for all national Red Cross and Red Crescent Societies had met in Seoul, the previous year, and had made a policy decision that they needed to scale up their work in HIV and AIDS globally. They had created a new position - Special Representative of the Secretary General - to supervise this area.

"You want me?" I asked, in disbelief. "I mean, thank you, but I must ask, do you know who I am? I have made myself hugely unpopular with many international organisations and governments. I am quite notorious. Do you think the Red Cross really needs someone like me?"

"We know all about that," Markku replied. "You are well known for your outspokenness over Sudan, but it's not a problem for us. In fact, we admire your commitment and passion."

I was quite taken aback, but agreed to go and talk to him right away. I walked the short distance between my office at WHO and the headquarters of IFRC in Geneva. To my surprise, when I arrived there was a room full of people waiting for me. I had not realised I was coming for a job interview, because I had not applied for any job. Nevertheless that was clearly the situation I now found myself in.

***

I must have done okay as a few weeks later I began my new position at IFRC. This move was a huge culture shock. There was none of the stuffy, stultifying formality that I had got used to in the UN and WHO.

People here were passionate and argumentative and the corridors rang with lively discussion. This was an organisation with zeal. With a mission. With a purpose.

I was now part of the world's biggest humanitarian network with a presence in every country. I was in charge of overseeing all their HIV and AIDS work across the world. This in itself presented a challenge because the AIDS crisis affected people differently from place to place.

The main problem in Southern Africa was that a whole generation had been wiped out, leaving child-headed households. I had seen this during my time in Malawi. These young people had lost a generation's worth of knowledge and were trying to adapt themselves to the adult world with none of the necessary skills. They needed support to raise their families.

The main problem in Cambodia, Thailand and India was sex work. From my experience with the women of Sonagachi, I knew that we needed to provide information about HIV and AIDS, sex education, access to condoms and the promise of ending the trafficking and exploitation of vulnerable people.

Conversely, in Russia, HIV was prevalent mainly in intravenous drug users. Here we needed to implement needle exchange schemes, as we had done in the UK in the 1980s, to prevent the virus spreading by sharing needles. Drugs use is illegal in Russia. So was helping people to take drugs. First we had to overcome the very real problem of Red Cross staff and those they worked with getting arrested for implementing needle-exchange schemes.

Applying a blanket approach globally would not be effective here. There was no one-size-fits-all answer to the myriad problems of HIV. In the world-wide Red Cross Red Crescent family, what we needed was an idea that would fire people up and motivate them to confront HIV everywhere, and in the right way. How could we compel people to grapple with the underlying causes of the epidemic - be that lack of education, stigmatisation, corruption - and work to elevate those causes to real action?

My answer was the *"Global Alliance on HIV and AIDS"*. This was an intellectual and practical framework for key strategies, policies, and do's and don'ts, on how to tackle the problem. I packaged the seven elements into a framework that I christened as the *"Seven Ones"*. This was put out as posters, videos, and other communication and training materials in many languages. It fired up the Red Cross Red Crescent network to unite behind a common goal.

Our overall message was that no matter where you were in the world, or what your situation, under our new *Global Alliance on HIV and AIDS*, our ambition was to do "twice as much good" within three years.

Thus, we adopted the target of doubling everything. Doubling beneficiaries, doubling the number of programmes, doubling the resources being applied. Regardless of how our HIV prevention strategy looked when we started, within our three-year timeframe it would receive twice the investment and aim to expand twice the reach. We made this a universal programme, but one implemented according to local circumstances. The localisation was important, because humanitarianism is still ultimately a personal act, and we didn't want our worldwide scheme to bury the individual, as the personal altruistic desire to relieve suffering is what the humanitarian world is founded upon.

Thinking back to the vow I had made to myself, decades earlier, as I had stood on the edge of Victoria Falls - promising to bring practical hope to people with HIV and AIDS and to communities torn apart by the virus - I felt I was now achieving it, via my new IFRC initiative.

***

At its core, the Red Cross Red Crescent embodies the basic human instinct to help another who is in distress. This selfless impulse was truly epitomised by one Red Cross volunteer I met in Zambia.

As I well knew - to near-tragic consequences from my road tour with Marianne - Zambia is a vast and sparsely populated country. It had been many years since I had first seen the pioneering treatment of AIDS patients by the Quaker doctors in their hospital in Zimbabwe. Since then, our dream of making antiretroviral treatment available to all across Southern Africa was becoming a reality.

Thanks to millions of pounds in donor aid, much of which still came from DFID, treatment was widely available. However, standard distribution methods came with limitations. Often drugs were delivered only as far as the few hospitals and clinics, with no way to bring them to the scattered remote populations.

This is where Mary came in. A typical Zambian Red Cross volunteer in her forties, she took care of a dozen people with HIV. She lived in a very remote rural district, where her role was "to walk the last mile." Her patients were all either too isolated, too ill, or too dejected to travel to the clinic to collect their medication. So Mary would travel to each on foot, often walking over thirty miles every week, to deliver their drugs and check how they were doing.

Committed to my purpose of bringing health to the unreachable, I visited Mary to see how we might help her under our *Global Alliance on HIV and AIDS*. I drove four hours from Lusaka, the nation's capital, to reach Mary's neighbourhood, before accompanying her on her rounds by foot.

A two-mile walk brought us to the first of her charges, an HIV positive teenage orphan who was caring for her baby sister alone. Like so many others, their parents had both died of AIDS. Mary handed over the medicine and watched her take it while the baby crawled around at her feet. There was a black-market trade in HIV drugs, and the poorest often sold their stock in order to buy other essentials, so it was imperative for Mary to observe each patient swallowing their pills.

Mary checked there was enough milk powder for the baby, before we set out to walk another mile across the rocky terrain to her next destination. This was the home of a farmer who had been recently diagnosed with HIV. Mary listened as he ranted about his corn crop.

"It has to be brought in or they will all starve," he declared, gesturing at his wife and five children who sat in a morose circle on the floor. After ensuring he had taken his medicine, Mary discussed with his wife whether they had any relatives who might be able to help with the harvest.

Our third visit required a rough uphill scramble to reach an older woman living alone. Mary told me as we climbed that she had refused testing for HIV. As soon as I saw her, my heart sink. Frail and emaciated, she was certainly dying from AIDS. Mary cooked her some porridge and gave her paracetamol for her headache - ensuring, as Max had done with the Tamil prisoners, that she knew she was not forgotten.

Our afternoon's mission complete, Mary set a brisk pace back to the clinic. Her day's work done, she wanted to get home to look after her own family. I was relieved to get back into my Land Cruiser, my legs aching from the unaccustomed exertion. But before I left, as was my custom, I asked her if there was anything she needed.

"There is one small thing, sir. Do you think that the Red Cross could give us umbrellas? Our heads boil under the sun and when it rains we are drenched. Then we get sick ourselves."

I was stunned. "Is that all…" I muttered sheepishly, lowering my eyes to her bare feet. "Yes, of course, you can have an umbrella and also flip-flops or shoes, if you prefer?"

I felt humbled. Every day, in every part of the world, there are people like Mary, unpaid and unrecognised, bringing comfort to neighbours in distress. Mary exemplified the Red Cross's belief in reaching out, to bring hope, going the last mile.

***

By the time that the *Global Alliance on HIV and AIDS* was well under way, IFRC had come under new leadership. The new Secretary General was a former Ethiopian diplomat named Bekele Geleta, who had previously been imprisoned in his home country for his political beliefs.

Bekele had headed the Ethiopian Red Cross, and as such had a lot of fresh ideas about the way National Societies should be managed. In theory the IFRC was a family of equal organisations; whether you were Namibia or Norway you were considered equal players guided by the same ideals. In practice colonial attitudes predominated, and as such it was the wealthier National Societies who called the shots.

Bekele believed that everyone should be on the same footing. His idea was that the rich should give to the poor, as was their social obligation, but that didn't give them the right to dictate terms. He felt each National Society should be able to prioritise and design its own work according to its circumstances, without fear of angering influential donors.

I agreed with him wholeheartedly. Working in ODA under the Conservative government and then DFID under Labour, I'd learned that the true purpose of aid should be to help the recipient grow and flourish, not to serve the interest of the giver.

I supported Bekele totally in his mission to create a more egalitarian Federation. In addition to my HIV and AIDS responsibilities, I was now working in a more managerial role. This meant that together we could challenge the western hegemony and the power relationships within the Red Cross Red Crescent network. As predicted this really shook up the status quo and didn't make Bekele or myself very popular, though I was past caring about my own popularity by this point.

All I cared about was implementing the courageous work the Red Cross and Red Crescent were doing in the world's most forgotten or dangerous places.

***

I visited one such endeavour in the *favelas* of Rio. This shocked me, as I had never seen such a stark division of wealth. I was there to look at the situation in the slums, yet I was staying in a lavish hotel on the famous Copacabana beach. Here I saw the beautiful elites of Brazil parading their bronzed bodies along the wide boulevards. As the sun shone down upon an intoxicating landscape of blue sea, luxurious high-rise buildings and rippling green mountains, people enjoyed a life of extreme privilege.

Yet the *favelas* lay only a few kilometres away from the affluence of Copacabana. They are the largest slums on earth and some of the most violent. Miles and miles of shanty houses, patched together from concrete, tin and wood, made up the urban landscape that many called home. Every evening this was where the cleaners, taxi drivers, hot dog vendors and road workers would return to, after a day serving the elites in the glittering part of town.

A policy of containment was used by the authorities: keep the poverty within the *favela*s, out of sight and out of mind, and by any means necessary. Inside, the *favelas* were governed by their own laws. They were a no-go area for police, and those civilians who lived there had to fend for themselves. Life centred around survival of the fittest. Rape, murder and even child abuse flourished. Rival criminal groups were the only jurisdiction, and gangs battled one another with the kind of heavy weaponry you'd expect to see in a war zone.

The situation was so violent that the ICRC who normally operated in conflict zones with warring armies were there, just a few kilometres from Copacabana beach, adopting the same ways of working as they would in Afghanistan or Syria.

ICRC's main aim there was to protect the most vulnerable. They were trying to get the criminal gangs to honour the rules of war and respect unarmed civilians. Yet how could you educate gunmen - many of them on drugs and plagued by paranoia - to understand the Geneva Conventions and apply them to gang warfare?

One method ICRC succeeded in was setting up an ambulance service. It was created by agreement amongst the gangs and facilitated by the Red Cross. It meant that if anyone was wounded in a gun fight, an ambulance could be called to ferry the casualties to safety. When the ambulance came screaming in, sirens blazing, the unmistakable emblem of the Red Cross daubed on its side, the fighting would cease. The gunmen would halt their hostilities just long enough to load the injured from both sides aboard. Then it would go tearing off to the hospital and fighting would resume.

This may not sound like much, but it meant a lot to the casualties and their families. Gang members respected this agreement, because they knew that they might be next. At any moment they could be cut down, bleeding from bullet wounds. Should that happen, they would want an ambulance to come for them. By inspiring this kind of interdependent empathy, ICRC was able to create small islands of humanity where everything else had been brutalised.

They did not preach about bringing peace or finding solutions, when there were no clear answers and no peace was in sight. Conflicts must be ripe for solving, and when generations of inequality and rapacious capitalism had created such extremes of winners and losers, and so much discrimination and separation, there were no easy fixes.

All that humanitarian organisations like the Red Cross could do in a dysfunctional society like this, was to work to keep humanity alive. They did this with the dream that, at the right time, peace might become possible.

It was surprising to me that deep in the heart of this very frightening, insecure place, people had started schools. I went to one, which appeared much like any other anywhere in the world. The one difference was that this school was encased in a metal cage to help protect those inside from accidental gunfire. Thanks to the Red Cross training on humanitarian law, the gangs had learned not to purposefully shoot at the students or teachers.

The presence of these schools gave me hope. If you send your child to school, even in the midst of violent gang warfare or in the centre of a war zone, you are sending a message of optimism. To educate a child is to declare that you believe there will be a future for that child; that no matter how awful things get or how much tragedy you have faced, life does go on and hope endures.

My next mission showed me this kind of optimism can prevail even in the most terrible places, where I feared all hope had perished.

Chapter Twenty-Three

The weak can never forgive. Forgiveness is the attribute of the strong.
Kasturba Gandhi

I WAS OFFERED THE OPPORTUNITY TO RETURN TO Rwanda by James Smith and David Brown of Aegis Trust, an NGO working towards the prevention of genocide. It was not the first such offer: I could very well have returned sooner, but I had always made excuses not to do so. Until now.

I had thought of Rwanda often. Now, after so much time had elapsed, I felt better equipped to deal with those traumatic memories. I accepted the Aegis Trust's offer, but my heart still raced as I flew into Kigali. I tried to banish the images of my last visit from mind, and as my car navigated the busy streets, I was struck by the difference between then and now. Kigali was unrecognisable. I could not believe I was in the same country, where I had experienced such barbarism only two short decades before.

I spent several days exploring Rwanda, meeting with whoever I could - survivors and perpetrators of the genocide alike - to understand how the country had made such a remarkable turnaround. Everywhere businesses were thriving and the people seemed peaceful and happy. Yet they had not swept the evidence of the genocide under the carpet. Most towns had genocide memorials, solemn tributes to those who had died, serving as reminders that this must never be permitted to happen again.

After a short tour of the country I returned to Kigali. I had agreed to meet with Lauren, a young Canadian journalist. She was writing a piece on Rwanda's regeneration and wanted to interview me about my experiences in 1994 and now, on my return. I waited for her at a table outside a roadside café in a bustling Kigali street. I ordered a locally brewed sorghum beer and sipped it, marvelling at the transformed cityscape. Birds were chirping, traffic was buzzing and people were laughing as they engaged in all manner of enterprising activities.

This was a far cry from the packs of dogs eating the dismembered corpses of murdered civilians in 1994. Luckily Lauren arrived before I had more chance to wander too far down memory lane. A smiling, dark haired young woman with a direct, open demeanour, Lauren introduced herself, ordered a beer and joined me at my table. After the usual polite introductions, she began the interview.

"Before we begin talking about what you're doing in Rwanda now, I think it would be good to get a recap on what you were doing last time you were here and why?"

"Sure," I said. "My first trip to Rwanda, was in July 1994, a couple of days after Kigali was liberated. I was the first member of the British government to set foot inside immediately after the April genocide. So my job then was to reconnoitre what was going on..."

I told Lauren as much as I could remember from my harrowing first visit.

"I travelled in and out of the country for a year or so, and then I went away and never came back until this week."

"So you hadn't been able to come back?" She asked. "Has that been a coincidence or something more? I see that you've been busy, but what has kept you away?"

"Well yes, I have been very busy. My subsequent jobs for the UN and the Red Cross among others have taken me into many more crises and disasters and so on..." I began, "but that's not really the reason I did not return earlier."

I picked at the label on my beer bottle distractedly. "I really did not think I had the nerve to return. Of course I wanted to, but what I saw in those early months here immediately after the genocide... well it seared itself into me, not just into my head but into the very core of my existence. It was just too painful to contemplate.

"One of the worst things was the smell. The stench of dead bodies leached through the whole city. Everywhere I went would be the sickly-sweet smell of decaying flesh, and to this very day when I think about it, I get that metallic taste in my mouth, and that's nearly twenty years ago now."

I took a swig of beer to try and obliterate the taste of that memory. "It was as if the whole world had gone mad. The same in village after village, town after town. I travelled up and down many, many places large and small and everywhere it was the same. I saw the evidence of killing on an industrial scale, which was beyond any feasible human imagination.

"You know it was so bad that I could not even bear to take photographs?" I added. "I wish I had photographed more but I just couldn't bear to do it. I felt it was somehow sacrilege to record what was going on. Subsequently I tried hard, very hard, not to think of

Rwanda at all. Many others were involved, you know? Many, many others were helping and the country was making progress. That was enough for me."

"Yet you're back now?" Lauren queried.

"Well, time passed. I saw what happened in Srebrenica. When I worked for the High Commissioner for Human Rights I went to Cambodia and saw the evidence of the genocide there. I then witnessed the bloodshed in Darfur under my own command as head of the UN. I realised I could not deal with the worst of the world's injustices until I had exorcised my own demons. Until I also came back and confronted what I'd seen here."

Lauren nodded, her face full of concern. I felt I needed to clarify.

"Much of my subsequent work with the Red Cross Red Crescent has been about confronting the brutal side of human nature, searching for humanity in the very worst situations, and trying to mitigate suffering. I am not an overly sentimental person. I have seen too much around the world to have that self-indulgence. Yet what happened in Rwanda in 1994 was unprecedented. Even the Nazis asphyxiated their victims quickly in gas chambers. In Srebrenica when they machine-gunned the Muslim Bosnians into mass graves, it was quick. Here, as you go around and see for yourself - it's well documented - the very nature of the killing is unrivalled anywhere in the world. Gangs of men, filled with blood lust, cutting people down with axes and machetes... the sheer inhumanity of it...". I trailed off.

"So for me coming back to Rwanda was very personal. It's not a mission but a pilgrimage. To go back to the places that have haunted me for many years and by seeing them again - thankfully in much better condition now - to lay my memories to rest in a proper place."

"So how did you know you were finally ready to come back?" Lauren asked. "Why now?"

"I think the principal stimulus for overcoming my own reluctance to return was the realisation that these kinds of situations were occurring elsewhere. I realised that I mustn't be selfish. I see that, for whatever reason - accident or misfortune or fate - my career has taken me from one trouble spot to another. I was present at, for example, the last genocide of the twentieth century, here, and I also presided over the first genocide of this century, in Darfur. That makes me fairly unique.

"So I felt that somehow I have a special duty. That duty is to connect the past with the present and to think of the future. I couldn't do that without returning to make peace with the ghosts of Rwanda. That is my compulsion: to visit, to remember again, and through that process to distil whatever lessons we can learn from the past and apply them today in a much-changed world."

"And what are those lessons?" Lauren probed. "What has impressed you the most on your return?"

"What stands out for me here is that I see civilians walking in Kigali, day or night, with no care in the world. It feels so safe on the streets now. What's more, there are ordinary Rwandans - teachers and nurses and small business owners - leading fulfilling lives and contributing to the growth of their country. The people here that I have spoken to are articulate and educated. This is an amazing accomplishment in such a short time.

"It's been only twenty years since the genocide and this is now one of the least corrupt countries in the world. That is an extraordinary achievement. They even abolished the death penalty a few years ago. I find it remarkable for a country that has experienced such massive violence to do away with the death penalty. Meanwhile, our friends in the United States, who by now should have arguably achieved a higher level of sophistication, still commit judicial murder. It's an incredible turn around.

"I must also mention the transformation of the Rwandan army." I added "This is not just an army of the victors. Many of the old Hutu soldiers who committed the crimes have been rehabilitated. They are now proud members of the new Rwandan defence forces, serving alongside their old enemies. They even provide peace-keepers for other countries, including in Darfur, so they are playing an active part fighting against genocide elsewhere in the world.

"So, I think Rwanda has truly come of age. It has not just recovered as a country, but it has created for its citizens a new humanity Now that legacy is slowly spreading into the wider world. Rwanda is contributing much to this continent and to the world in a way that was inconceivable before. That's the progress that I see."

I ordered us another drink. I felt elated discussing all the incredible things I'd encountered here. Lauren brought me back down to earth with her next question.

"All that is great," she agreed, "but does it signify a change in beliefs of the people here? Could genocide reoccur in Rwanda?"

"Only time will tell," I hesitated and pondered for a long moment. "I think that there are two main factors that will require continued attention, to change hearts and minds to prevent something like the April 1994 events from re-emerging. To prevent crimes against humanity we primarily need two things: strong people and strong institutions.

"Through all my experiences in Rwanda, Sudan and elsewhere I have realised that genocide is committed by governments. In every instance, genocides have been accomplished by the controlling authorities, because the nature and magnitude of the killing is such that it can only be done by an organised institution.

"So in order to ensure that future leaders do not do what their predecessors did, we need strong and right-thinking governance. In my opinion, they have made very good progress in institution building in Rwanda since nineteen-ninety-four. From the ministry of defence, to the social agencies to the justice and correction centre, they have built very capable organisations. All are established on a basis of law and order, without gender bias and with equal representation. So that side is going well.

"The parallel to strong institutions is strong people. Here too I think the country has vastly improved. I have spoken to many, both the victims as well as the once-violent killers. There is of course a residual tension. That tension cannot be air-brushed away, nor can it be wished away by good intentions. Yet I think that provided the rule of law applies, provided the leadership is seen to be a government of all the people and provided that it treats all its people as equal citizens, these challenges will be overcome.

"However, Rwanda's internal social capital is still being built. It's work in progress." Lauren looked puzzled, so I elaborated. "By this I mean the people's ability to conduct themselves in the right manner. To do right because they feel it is the right thing to do, on their own, not because someone in authority tells them what is right."

Lauren was a captive audience by this point, so I went on.

"One important element for rehabilitation after genocide is the capacity of society to think for itself. Different groups within the country have to be able to express their thinking and to hold divergent opinions, without that descending into violence. That capacity building is still going on. Education is a good way to start, as we've seen, but education alone is not sufficient to permanently immunise the population from the kind of evil thoughts that led to the nineteen-ninety-four massacres.

"The key thing here will be the younger generation. It is in the hearts and minds of the youth that the cycle of violence is either terminated or perpetuated. By all accounts, I think this is heading in the right direction."

"So you say education is a good place to start but it's not sufficient on its own," Lauren queried. "How else would you suggest the Rwandans act to ensure this never happens again?"

Here I paused. I was wary of inflicting my own beliefs onto others. Perhaps if I evangelised too much on the way Rwanda should conduct itself, that made me no better than the rich, bullying National Societies that Bekele and I were battling in the Red Cross.

"I think coming from outside, especially representing the wider world that failed this country so completely, we have absolutely no basis for preaching to Rwandans. We have no right to dictate the way the people of this country go about their business. We can advise them, we can express some concerns, we can protest if worrying things are happening, but we cannot preach to them.

"With that in mind I do think it's important for the people here to remember the past. To remind ourselves what took place physically and emotionally in a very visible way. I think it would benefit every Rwandan to make a pilgrimage the Kigali Genocide Memorial at least once every five years. Each community should commemorate the genocide yearly as well, more locally, in order to make sure it is not forgotten. That must continue forever. I believe genocide prevention is a permanent task. It's not something you do once. Every generation has to continually commit to it, otherwise it can reoccur.

"The Rwandans are not the only ones who need to remember. Let us look back to our own experiences. Let's remember how the international system failed to prevent genocide. The blood is on our hands also. Not only did we not stop the killing but, by pulling out of the country at the worst moment, we made the death-toll worse.

"Personally I find it extraordinary that Rwanda, instead of bitterly hating the world, is so outward looking. Rwanda is a positive influence. Not only does it lead by example but engages marvellously with the wider world. After the way the international community betrayed the Rwandan people, they could have closed their doors on us forever. Yet they chose to forgive. It's this incredible capacity for forgiveness that has impressed me most."

Lauren smiled. "Other than forgiveness, what will you take away from here to teach the outside world?"

"I've been thinking about that, as I reflected on my first few days here. There are a number of lessons. First, the propensity to commit evil is present in all communities, all races, all cultures. I have seen it whether in Africa, whether in Europe, whether in Asia or the Americas. We must not pretend that anyone is immune to this.

"Second, the experience here indicates that constant vigilance is required. If one becomes careless with aspects of civilised behaviour by ignoring small transgressions, then evil can escalate.

"Thirdly, I have learned that it is not possible to move forward without accountability and justice. We cannot recover from genocide without the wrong-doers admitting they have done a wrong and serving the appropriate penalty. By this I do not mean locking people up, or executing them, but for them owning up to their responsibilities.

"It means saying: "I did wrong. I want to do right now. There is nothing I can do to erase the wrong, but I can do something for the future. Through this I can show that we can live better together." This is the only way to counteract impunity. Do you see?"

"Absolutely," Lauren agreed. "Now I think I have exhausted you, and you have exhausted my list of questions. Unless there is anything else you want to touch on?"

I thought this over. Rwanda had stirred so many feelings in me. The country's past and its transformation spoke of an optimistic future for the people. I was overjoyed to see this, yet I felt that if peace and progress were possible for Rwanda, could the same not be found elsewhere?

"All I would say is that I hope we can look at what happened here to influence global policy in a more proactive way. The sad reality is that even the superficial lessons of Rwanda have not yet been learned elsewhere. I know this from my own observation and at my own cost. The UN in Sudan made exactly the same mistakes as they did here. History keeps repeating. So we know already that we have not taken on board the lessons of Rwanda. I hope we really can do that in time."

"I do too," Lauren finished with a smile.

She had a flight to catch back to Toronto, so she packed up her sound recorder, shook my hand and thanked me for my insights before heading off.

I remained behind at the café ,deep in thought.

I had dreaded the prospect of returning here. As I told Lauren, there had been no pressing need for me to come back. The Rwandans had made incredible progress and were well on their way to an unprecedented recovery. Much work had been done to get them there and part of me felt guilty that until now, I had not been more involved. Yet Rwanda had received assistance from outside. Admittedly, it had come too late to stop the killings, but the world had responded to help them rebuild their country in the wake of the violence.

The same could not be said for Darfur. They were not receiving the same kind of help the Rwandans had. Plus I had failed to bring further attention to their cause, constricted as I was first by WHO and now by the institutionalised impartiality of the Red Cross. I felt as if I had somehow turned my back on Rwanda for twenty years. Would I do the same for Darfur?

***

Nevertheless, my work with IFRC was incredibly rewarding. I had recently been tasked with a new job, the formulation of *Strategy 2020*. This would provide the blueprint for the next decade for the whole of the global Red Cross Red Crescent Movement, reaching the 189 National Societies at that time. I was given a blank slate upon which to draw up my vision for IFRC's future action. This was a chance to affect the direction of the largest humanitarian network on earth. It was an opportunity to be imaginative and creative and also to challenge the status quo.

I was allocated a budget of half-a-million Swiss francs to hire outside consultants, but ended up spending hardly any of it. I believe that an organisation that contracts out its core thinking is intellectually and morally bankrupt. Instead I turned to our greatest asset: our own people.

I spent six months travelling all over the globe to ask each National Society what they wanted to see included in the new policy. I wanted to implement a bottom-up redesign, rather than imposing ideas from the top-down. I took this one step further and consulted the people of the world over the internet. We set up a *Strategy 2020* Facebook page where I asked what changes people would want to see implemented over the next ten years. This resulted in a lively debate. Some of the opinions generated were quite radical and many were certainly controversial. One volunteer from a Red Cross branch in rural southeast Asia thanked me for including them in the conversation.

"It's amazing to be consulted," he wrote. "Usually nobody listens to us. We are being let down badly by our National Society leaders who are so domineering and set in their ways. We have a lot of ideas to change and improve our working methods but we are not allowed a voice."

That really touched me. These were the real feelings of our workers that I needed to hear, and I would have had no access to them otherwise. After all, wasn't the Red Cross Red Crescent about giving "voice to the voiceless"? After about a week of such lively, online conversation involving many, many opinions from across all continents, I received an email from Bekele telling me to shut down the Facebook thread. Apparently, other high-ranking members of the organisation were not happy with such democratisation of policy making.

I was reluctant to shut down such a rewarding forum for direct engagement with the very life force of our Red Cross Red Crescent. I was also suspicious. Lately, Bekele had seemed different to me somehow. Though we still shared the same beliefs and I respected his ideas and his commitment to reshaping the organisation, I found his leadership style increasingly jarring. The way he shut down that Facebook debate was indicative of an increasingly arrogant attitude.

Strategy 2020 was still a resounding success, particularly with the small nation states. They usually felt ignored when it came to making the big decisions, so to have their viewpoints considered meant a lot to them. They saw the impact their small yet important voices had made and knew that their good work was valued.

Thanks to this I was promoted. I was now Under Secretary General for National Society and Knowledge Development. This meant I could stick around to oversee the implementation of the progress I'd envisaged. I had more grand ideas.

We created an academic network to bring higher thinking to the Red Cross Red Crescent leadership. We worked to close the digital gap, ensuring all National Societies around the world were IT-connected. We developed a novel methodology for assessing the organisational capacity of National Societies so as to benchmark and track their progress. We prioritised local capacity building. Instead of trying to control the independent National Societies, I encouraged them to be more collegial and transparent, by sharing their targets, budgets and achievements. In this way I hoped to lift up the performance of this huge network of millions of volunteers.

It was exciting, challenging, rewarding work. Now I could finally put into practice all I had learned over the years. Yet all was not entirely sunny for me.

Certainly, returning to Rwanda had been a healing act for me. While I was exhilarated by the changes the nation had made since the genocide, my soul wept that no such peaceful solution was in sight for Darfur. The Aegis Trust had approached me to do more work with them in genocide prevention and I felt I could not ignore the pull of Darfur much longer.

I had also seen Bekele in a new light. The tipping point for me came during a *Red Talk* session. *Red Talk* was my initiative to make the Red Cross Red Crescent into a world leader in humanitarian thinking.

Every couple of weeks an influential individual would come and speak on relevant topics of the time - food security, the laws of war, refugee rehabilitation, etc. We invited them to speak, asked questions, and encouraged audience participation.

These talks were open to the whole of the Geneva humanitarian community, so people could come together and debate their ideas. They were also broadcast live over the internet so a wider world could participate. Often, we had tens of thousands of people who connected in this way.

There was a lot of excitement and buzz around *Red Talk* and as I usually chaired these discussions I received increased visibility. Bekele did not seem to like that at all. Perhaps I should have pandered to his ego by including him more, but in truth he had become an uninspiring speaker, full of his own grandiosity. In the middle of one of the *Red Talks*, unbeknownst to me, he instructed our technical team to cut the internet connection. The talk continued in Geneva but we were no longer being webcast.

Bekele argued that we were wasting too much time and taking people away from their desks. I was shocked. Where had our inspiring leader gone? Where was the man who had revolutionised the organisation with his fresh-thinking and courage in the face of the domineering, rich National Societies? It was hugely disappointing.

This coincided with my conversations with the Aegis Trust. My conscience longed to help the people of Darfur. As I considered what to do, I thought of Rwanda's healing process, and to the interview I had given on Radio Dabanga shortly beforehand. Radio Dabanga is a shortwave station based in the Netherlands and broadcast across Darfur. It is run by Sudanese journalists in exile and often features interviews, call-ins and question-and-answer sessions, aimed at keeping the displaced abreast of current affairs and to boost their spirits.

I had been asked to appear and answer some questions. One brave refugee had called from an IDP camp inside Darfur. She risked dire retribution doing so - it was illegal to listen to this clandestine radio station inside Sudan.

"The blood of our menfolk has soaked into the desert sands, and for what?" she asked me. "Are we now to accept the theft of our lives and our land? Has the struggle been for nothing? We must continue to resist by all means, to the last woman if needed, until we get our livelihood, our pride and our dignity back.

"Thank you for what you did in speaking out - you gave us hope.

But what now? We are still here suffering. Our struggle is not over. Mr Kapila, your job is not done."

I realised then that she was right. My job was not done. I began drafting an email to Bekele informing him of my resignation.

Chapter Twenty-Four

Failure comes only when we forget our ideals and objectives and principles.
Jawaharlal Nehru

I WANTED TO SOMEHOW GET BACK INTO DARFUR, BUT I knew it would be dangerous. I was among the Sudanese regime's top enemies and I had endured many death threats. These made me even more determined. So, when The Aegis Trust, the British NGO dedicated to ending genocide, invited me to visit a refugee camp on the border of Sudan and Chad, I jumped at the offer.

The refugees from Darfur had been eking out an existence in the desert for the last ten years. I could hardly believe it had been so long; that I had stayed relatively quiet, and more or less totally inactive over Darfur for so long.

I knew I could not remain at the IFRC. The Red Cross is built on impartiality, and its neutrality is part of the reason it is granted access to highly sensitive situations when no others are. I could not let my actions undermine that reputation. But if I was going to throw away my high-level career, once again, to speak out, I wanted to ensure that as many people as possible would hear me, as I had done in my original whistleblowing over Darfur in 2004.

I approached David Loyn, the BBC World Affairs Correspondent, to ask him to cover the story. He agreed and we devised a plan. We would reveal *"The Story of Darfur: The World's Most Successful Genocide."* We would fly into N'djamena, the Chadian capital, before catching a UN flight across the thousand kilometres to Abéché, a town in the east of the country. From there we would drive to Gaga refugee camp, close to the border of Darfur.

He would film me speaking to the displaced Darfuris, witnessing the conditions they live in, learning what their lives were like and what we could do to help them now, ten years after the genocide. Our transportation booked and team assembled, there was just one more task to complete. I had to send the email I'd been painstakingly preparing, informing Bekele of my resignation from an institution I had come to love, the IFRC.

***

As my finger dithered over the "send" button, a memory from my British boarding school came unexpectedly to the forefront of my thoughts. Once I had settled in to school life, I made some friends who

I liked very much. They were kind and sensitive people who did not share the other boys' pleasure at ridiculing me, and were happy to make space in their world for a stranger who found himself so far from home.

My loneliness lessened and I was determined to make the very best of the experience of Wellington College. I had not come so far or climbed so high to be shot down by bullying, and I vowed I would get absolutely everything I could from the opportunity. I already excelled in my classes, but the school had a strong sporting tradition and every boy was expected to do at least some kind of physical exercise. My natural inclination was to hide behind a bookshelf at the first mention of exercise, but in my new-found resolve to embrace whatever this glorious institution had to offer, I decided that I too would take up a sport.

I ambled down the corridor towards the sports hall, feeling self-conscious in this unfamiliar part of the campus. I was sure everyone was looking at me as I edged along the mouldering red-brick hallway. I could imagine their thoughts: *You don't belong here four-eyes. Go back to the library.* Yet I was determined. I fixed my gaze on my shoes as they stepped resolutely forward across the cold flagstone floor. I didn't look up until I had reached my intended destination: the sports notice board.

I surveyed the large, imposing cork-board, framed in dark polished wood, with the school's motto emblazoned across the top in Latin. "*Virtutis Fortuna Comes*": Fortune Favours the Brave. I gulped and stood a little taller in my Wellington uniform to better see the posters and notices pinned beneath those portentous words.

Here, tacked to the pin-pricked cork, stained from decades of sweaty teenage thumbs, I felt sure I would find the answer to my sporting aspirations, if only I knew what I was looking for. I scanned the posters of clubs, notes about lost property and lists of rugby match dates, searching for some kind of game or club that might appeal to me.

For just about every posh boy from England, rugby is the game of choice. The boys from the rugby team marched around the school like minor celebrities and everyone knew who they were. Even I knew who they were, although I wasn't exactly sure how one even played rugby.

There was no point even trying for the rugby team. Being crushed to death by huge, testosterone-fuelled boys in gym shorts was not high on my list of aspirations. There were clubs for wrestling and boxing, but I bypassed those too. I did not want to give my bullies the chance to punch me in the face. Sailing and rowing were both out of the question, for I couldn't swim, and while fortune may favour the brave, I doubted it was the companion of the drowned.

I kept looking. Cricket? Hockey? Nothing seemed to jump out at me and I was beginning to lose my nerve. The longer I stood frowning up at the notices, the more of a target I became for potential snide remarks, slung like mud from a passer-by regarding my perceived sporting prowess.

Then I saw a small hand-written flyer titled simply: "Fencing Club." It started the following Thursday, after class, promising to cover foil, sabre and epee styles with an instructor from the nearby Sandhurst Military Academy. I wasn't sure exactly what fencing was, but I knew a sabre was a kind of sword, and sword-fighting sounded promising - kind of cool in a way, like something from a story book.

At any rate the list of names on the sign-up sheet was not very long, so if I proved to be a ghastly fencer at least not many people would know. I scribbled my own name below the list of others, made note of the room number and meeting time, and scurried away as fast as possible.

The following Thursday I showed up at a small portacabin which housed the fencing club. To my surprise I felt strangely excited. I had no real idea what I had signed up for, but I was proud of myself for getting this far. The instructor, a very upright yet friendly and surprisingly patient man, began to explain the ins and outs of the noble sport of fencing. Clambering into our white padded breeches and jackets, I learned that hardly any of the other boys had fenced before either. We would be on a level playing field for once.

From that first day, I loved the sport. I found out rapidly I was good at it, too. I liked the one-on-one nature and the fact that it required mental agility as well as speed and skill. While it was very fast moving and tough on the body, there was a logic and strategy to it, and brute strength was not necessarily the key to winning a fight. I found it a therapeutic and relaxing pastime after a day's hard studying.

I soon became good enough to join the school fencing team. This meant I got to travel around England for inter-school tournaments. Before long I was made the secretary of the fencing club. I also got my "colours" for it, a privilege distinguishing the school's top sportsmen, which meant I could wear a special tie. Now the whole school could see I was no longer just a swot, but a sportsman as well.

This was crucial at Wellington, where physical achievement was so highly prized. Fencing helped to build up my self-esteem and filled me with new confidence. As this grew, I felt the weight of my personal destiny pulling me onwards. The positive experiences were for a purpose and the negative ones didn't matter. I felt I was meant to go on to do important things, as the eldest son and a descendent of the ancient Kapila clan. With my aim of becoming a doctor, I could fulfil Brother Drew's and my family's hopes for me. Destiny awaited.

Yet that destiny had now led me here, to this moment, about to throw away a high-level career with an institution I loved, in order to be true to myself and Darfur. My well-paid sojourn amongst the lofty institutions of Geneva would be well and truly over. But for me the one thing harder than clicking "send" would be to not resign and to abandon my calling.

I took a deep inward breath and sent the email. With that I closed my laptop, stowed it in my bag and went for a walk past the gleaming white offices of IFRC. I felt a pang in my chest I had not been expecting. Was I making the right choice? Only time would tell.

I mentally fortified myself for the task ahead. *"Fortune favours the brave,"* I reminded myself, ruefully....

***

When I had left Sudan, the government of neighbouring Chad had been an ally to the Darfuris, funding their resistance against Khartoum's oppression. They had subsequently made space for the displaced civilians in refugee camps in their country. Ten years later that dynamic had completely changed. The Khartoum regime, adept as I knew they were at ingratiating themselves with international powers, were now firm friends with Chad.

The Chadian president had even married the daughter of Musa Hilal, the notorious *Janjaweed* leader who had orchestrated much of the genocidal violence in Darfur, including the attack on Aisha's community in Tawila. None of this boded well for the refugees. The Chadian authorities were now working with the Sudanese military to harass survivors. Combined with the world-wide indifference to their plight, the Darfuris were alone and friendless, marooned in the desert.

My visa for travel had been approved long before the trip, yet when I arrived in N'djamena I received a shock message from the government. There was a problem with my travel documents. I would not be permitted to fly on to Abéché and should in fact leave the country at the earliest opportunity.

I couldn't believe it. I had applied for all my travel permits in the usual way. Everything had been processed and approved without a hitch. What had caused them to change their minds?

It turned out that one of the UNHCR staff members in N'djamena had been scrutinising the passenger manifest for the flight and came across my name. I was familiar to him because he had previously worked for UNHCR in Sudan. He had shared that information with the Chadian government's security agency and strongly advised that I should not be allowed to visit the displaced Darfuris.

It was all too familiar. Here was the UN blocking me over Darfur again, preventing access for me to see the refugees that their own failure to act had forced to leave their homeland in the first place.

I argued with the Chadian authorities that I was planning to visit the refugees so as to ask the aid world for more money. Chad had been requesting funds to support the three-hundred-thousand displaced Darfuris in camps along its eastern border. Really they should welcome my trip to bring attention to this problem, I explained. Yet this line of reasoning seemed to do little to help my cause.

We decided that David Loyn and his BBC team should continue as planned to the refugee camps. I would remain in N'djamena as long as possible and await his return with the footage. Luckily, my plane ticket had restrictions so I could argue for a few days leeway.

We would have to spin the story differently. Now it was all about the ex-head of the UN in Sudan being denied access to see the Darfuri refugees and forcibly expelled from Chad. If anything, it was a better angle, as it implicated the government in shady underhand dealings.

When the BBC film crew arrived at the camp, the scenes they covered were bleak. The majority of the shelters were constructed from tarpaulins suspended between structures of slender tree branches, bleached white by long exposure to the sun, the edges weighted down with rocks or whatever they could find. The camp border was marked by a fence of coiled razor-wire and the peacekeepers guarding this perimeter were effectively prison wardens, keeping the Darfuris inside their desert gaol.

Here they sat waiting, day in and day out, for their freedom to come. They had been here ten years already. How much longer would they remain? Once they had filmed this, it was imperative the BBC crew return to N'djamena as swiftly as possible, to capture the interview with me before I was banished from the country. The next flight out of Abéché would get them back far too late. So, ignoring the warnings of night-time ambushes and marauding bandits, David's team embarked on a two-day drive across the desert.

Meanwhile, the refugees in Gaga camp had heard of my detention in N'djamena. They were roused to action. One brave woman, a

Darfuri widow named Noresham Hasaballah Osher, vowed that if I could not come to visit the camp, then she would come to talk to me.

Noresham convinced her camp guards that one of her children was sick and she must get to the hospital for treatment. Both her own and her child's acting skills were excellent, and they were able to slip out of the camp without arousing suspicion. We had a car pick them up to bring them the thousand kilometres across the desert to meet me in the capital. It was a race against time before I was bundled onto my plane, probably never to return to Chad again.

David Loyn came screeching into N'djamena, covered in dust and on their last few litres of fuel, just a couple of hours before my flight was due to depart. His team set up their cameras in the living room of the accommodation we had rented and they filmed my reactions to the footage from the camps.

I saw emaciated children. Born in exile, they had known no life other than this state of limbo. Desert winds blew through the scrappy tarpaulin shelters - "homes" that were woefully bereft of even the most basic of comforts. The refugees were starving and seemingly forgotten by everyone. It was a horrendous thing to behold.

Noresham, my brave envoy from the camp, was still a few kilometres short of N'djamena when I had to leave for the airport. We resigned ourselves to speaking over the phone.

"Nobody comes to help us anymore," she confirmed. "We want the international community to come back. To bring us food and medicine and education for our children, like they did before. We have been forgotten, but we are still here."

It broke my heart to hear her words. "What do you want to happen most?" I asked her, my voice heavy with regret.

"The Darfur problem is far from finished. The problems are still going on at home even worse than before. The killings and the rapes. I want the world to stand up and find a solution, because my people and I are imprisoned."

Time was running and I had to make my flight, or who knew what might befall me at the hands of the Chadian security forces. Before ending our phone call, I left Noresham with this message: "Please do not lose hope. It is with you, with the brave people like you in the refugee camps, that we have hope that peace and justice will come and you will be able to return to your homes."

David filmed my reactions to the footage and my entire conversation with Noresham. He would skilfully edit the piece together, ready to broadcast when I was safely in the air and off Chadian soil. And that is what happened. The BBC report went around the world, and Darfur was back in the news after so long.

***

As soon as my plane landed back in Europe, I received an incensed call from Bekele. It seemed all hell had broken out at the IFRC. I was still associated with them, so the world wanted to know why their high-level representative was speaking out against the Chadian and Sudanese governments, when the Red Cross by its very nature had to be politically neutral.

"How could you do this?" Bekele demanded sorrowfully.

"Did you not receive my email?" I countered. "Declaring my immediate resignation and that whatever I said or did in Chad in relation to Darfur was entirely in my personal capacity and nothing whatsoever to do with the Red Cross Red Crescent?"

Bekele insisted that he had received no such email. I doubted that this was true. I suspected that he had received it, yet he did not want to believe that I really had resigned. Whatever our recent disagreements, he genuinely did not want me to leave.

My heart was also full, even as it was broken. No one had asked me to leave the Red Cross Red Crescent where I was at the height of my authority and influence. I was respected and even loved, and had made friends all over the planet. Yet I felt forced to leave the most humanitarian of all institutions for following the most basic of humanitarian instincts: to stand up for those who were in the greatest need, the forgotten victims of Darfur.

I had chosen to do the right thing, yet it was a bitter-sweet reality. Ultimately, the neutrality of the Red Cross, although necessary for much of their work, meant that our paths had to diverge. I resigned myself to this reality, but I was gutted. Why could I not have both the worthwhile humanitarian career and the freedom to speak up?

My old friend Mukul came to my office at midnight to help me pack up my books and personal belongings. I put my IFRC ID, building access pass, and Swiss diplomatic accreditation in an envelope, and dropped them through the letterbox on the way out.

Of all the jobs that I had done in my life, in so many places and for so many institutions, it was at IFRC that I had found the most fulfilment. The deepest meaning. It was my spiritual and emotional home. Yet here I was, stealing out of the building like a thief in the night.

Mukul sensed my sadness but was silent. What could be said?

Chapter Twenty-Five

I am not a saint, unless you think of a saint as a sinner who keeps on trying.
Nelson Mandela

AS MY PLANE CLIMBED ABOVE THE CLOUD LINE, breaking through the layers of grey to the blue sky beyond, I felt surprisingly positive. Though I was headed to the war-torn borderlands between Sudan and South Sudan - some of the most insecure and troubled terrain on earth - I felt strangely free.

With my Red Cross career over, all I cared about now was doing something to redress the wrongs in Sudan. The international community had failed us over Darfur and I had lost faith in them. I vowed that I would no longer allow myself to be hamstrung by them. I might tread on a lot of toes and make many enemies - but what did I care?

Unsurprisingly, getting to Sudan via Chad for a second time had proved impossible, so this time we planned to enter though newly independent South Sudan. At least I was among friends there. The South Sudanese were well aware of my interactions with the widely-revered founder of their nation, John Garang, and my own efforts for the region, during my time as UN Coordinator.

On arrival we hired the best vehicle we could find - an old, white Land Cruiser with a busted suspension - and set off on our somewhat unorthodox mission. Our first stop was a refugee camp at Yida. It was still in South Sudan, but very close to the border and had become home to refugees from the Blue Nile State, Nuba Mountains and Darfur. These three regions were populated by black African Sudanese; hence they were targeted by Bashir's campaign of terror. Our plan was to visit these areas, seeking evidence of Khartoum's wider genocidal crusade and bringing their war crimes to the attention of the world - once more.

The camp at Yida was crowded with women and children. They told us that most of their men were still fighting for control of their homelands. When the predominantly Arab North Sudan separated from the largely black African South Sudan, the north took nominal control of these disputed territories - Blue Nile State, Nuba Mountains and Darfur. The back Africans who had lived there since time immemorial faced losing their ancestral lands and livelihoods at the hands of the invaders. They fought back, and they fought valiantly.

Despite the government of Sudan's obvious wealth and fire power, the rebel fighters took back control of much territory, battling against Khartoum's presence on the ground. With his ground forces pushed back, Bashir mounted a war of attrition from the air. Under the guise of quashing the rebel fighters, Khartoum continued its campaign of ethnic cleansing, purposefully targeting civilians to kill them, destroy their villages, and force the people from their homelands.

We crossed the disputed border into Sudan - nothing more than a rope strung across what passed as a road in these parts - to find some of those villages. As our battered vehicle bumped and jarred its way through the countryside, we pieced together a picture that was all too familiar. Market-places had been bombed, grain stores destroyed, and gangs of raiders had attacked innocent civilians, torching homes, stealing children, raping and murdering.

In many ways what I was witnessing now was even worse than I'd seen in Darfur. In the ten years that I had been away, the Sudanese government had streamlined their deadly methods. Now they used sophisticated weaponry to facilitate their programme of ethnic annihilation. We came to one village in the Nuba Mountains region that had until recently been under Khartoum control. It had been retaken by the rebels - called "SPLM North Army" - in a frenzied battle.

A local man named Paul, a sometime rebel fighter, showed us around. We saw the charred remains of destroyed homes; abandoned heavy artillery; craters where bombs had fallen amidst the houses; a pit where the villagers disposed-off unexploded cluster bombs; and dugouts where people would hide from the Khartoum regime's Antonov bombers when they came rumbling through the sky.

Paul led me between two flame-blackened houses where Khartoum's raiders had left crates of anti-personnel landmines. They had abandoned these Iranian-designed devices in their hurry to retreat. I examined the fiendishly simply yet deadly contraptions. Nothing more than a small metal box packed with explosives and a simple pressure release system. It was chilling to see how something so unassuming could cause so much death and maiming.

During my time in Kabul under the Taliban, I had seen the damage landmines could do. Everywhere I had encountered men, women and children hobbling along on crutches with legs truncated at the knee or with arms ending in a blunt stump. Afghanistan was littered with landmines, thanks to the long civil war. Retreating militia would often lay minefields in their wake, to make the terrain uninhabitable.

Here in the Nuba Mountains, the Khartoum military were planting mines around villages and water wells. They were not setting traps to deter enemy soldiers. Their aim was to make it impossible for the black Sudanese people to ever return to their homes. Landmines spread fear and anxiety. Their hidden presence transformed an entire landscape into a potential death trap. People were scared to return to their old lives, lest they lose a limb, their livelihood or their life.

Anti-personnel landmines are illegal. Sudan had signed the Ottawa Treaty that prohibits their use under international law. I was certain of this for I had had a hand in pushing for the creation of this treaty, during my time in the UK Government. Their use was a flagrant disregard of the rules of war, and targeting non-combatants was sheer barbarism. It was clear to me now that the Khartoum regime were committing crimes against humanity, targeting their own people on a wider scale than ever before.

Paul introduced me to his nephew, a small, smiling boy of about six years old named Joseph. He played and laughed along with his friends, despite the fact that he used a crude wooden crutch to get around, because one of his legs had been blown off at the hip. I watched him hobbling about, seemingly undeterred by his disability. He, like so many others, was forced to adapt to the realities of life in the middle of a war zone. These innocents were the ones paying the real price for Khartoum's bloodlust.

Joseph would very likely have died from his injuries, if it hadn't been for the actions of the one and only doctor who remained in this area, an American missionary known affectionately as Dr Tom. A family practitioner by trade, Dr Tom Catena came to Sudan as a volunteer with the Catholic Medical Mission Board. He is the closest I have ever come to meeting a living saint. I had heard Nubans compare him to Jesus Christ for his talent performing medical marvels and I could understand why.

He would help the lame to walk after being injured by landmines. He would restore sight to the blind after explosions and smoke from bombs meant they could no longer see. He was dealing with biblical levels of suffering on a daily basis, often with little more than biblical-era technology, and doing it all in the midst of a war zone.

Dr Tom cared for upwards of seven-hundred-and-fifty-thousand people across the Nuba Mountains. When everyone else had pulled out due to terrible instability, he had refused to abandon his patients.

Now he was the sole doctor remaining at the Mother of Mercy Hospital, the next stop on our tour of this benighted region. We arrived at his hospital just after sunset and were able to catch Dr Tom in a rare moment of rest, although he was always on call, twenty-four seven, every day of the year.

"Welcome to the Mother of Mercy," he greeted us warmly. The hospital compound was nothing more than some low brick-built wards, nestled in the dusty bushland.

"Dr Tom, what an honour to finally put a face to the legend!" I said, presenting him with our gifts; a wheel of mature English cheddar, a box of red wine and my favourite McVitie's digestive biscuits.

"Thanks so much," he said in his fast-paced New York accent. He gestured for us to join him at a table on the hospital veranda, to share some cheese, wine and conversation.

Tom was a tall man with strong features. I had researched him online prior to our trip and learned that he'd been an American football player in his youth. That was before he became a missionary doctor and moved first to Kenya and now to Sudan. He did not look like a football player anymore. His formerly broad shoulders were now bony and his strong cheekbones protruded from hollow cheeks.

It sounds dreadful, but I had become used to seeing emaciated looking black Sudanese. Hunger and malnutrition were a sad reality of life here, thanks to Khartoum bombing crops and grain stores. Yet it was only after seeing Tom's once athletic frame so altered, that I realised the true magnitude of the food shortages.

It was hard to place his age. I suspected his bald head and lean body made him appear older than he really was, not to mention the strain of dedicating one's entire life to the care of wounded civilians while bombs fell overhead. Yet, when he smiled his straight white American smile, he had an air of eternal youthfulness about him.

In these moments the man seemed to glow. He was universally revered across the region, but maybe this really was the light of Christ shining out of him. Who knows?

"Did you train as a surgeon?" I asked, as we sipped wine in the warm evening air.

"At med school? No," he told me. "I trained as a family doctor."

"Same as me," I said, "though more years ago now than I would like to admit. I could never do the amazing things that you do."

"Oh, you could," he remarked. "You mustn't talk like that. I worry that other people see me as some kind of super-human-doctor who can do anything. They fear they wouldn't measure up, so they don't give volunteering a try. Truth is, I didn't know a thing about surgery until I lived in Kenya. I learned from some amazing surgeons there - but I learned as I went along. On the job. Don't get me wrong - it's far from ideal - but when there's no other option and lives are at stake it's amazing what you can do if you put your mind to it."

"That's what I wanted to ask you," I said. "Here in the bush miles from anywhere with the Sudanese government blockading all imports, even medical supplies and humanitarian aid, how do you manage to run a hospital? Surely it just shuts down once you run out of supplies?"

"Well, people smuggle me things. They come in the same route you just came by, and they bring us hospital materials. Risk their lives to do it. So brave. So that's one way. But we've also been studying historical medical practices like they used in field hospitals during the American Civil War to set bones and the like, when they were working in tents with limited resources. I've also had to diversify. I've had to learn complicated surgery from books."

"Wow," I said. "That sounds very frightening to me, but then anatomy was the class I failed, first year at med school."

Tom chuckled, but his face then fell serious. "No, it is frightening. In fact, it's terrifying. To undertake a procedure that I don't feel confident in, when I'm really out of my depth, but knowing that if I don't at least try then the patient will die for sure, that's the most nerve-racking stressful thing ever. I have to be really careful to weigh up the risk against the potential gains for the person. If there is no other option then of course I must try. Sometimes what I try doesn't work and we lose them anyway, but often times it does. I am always so thankful whenever it does, and I am continually surprised by what God can do, and allows me to do. We are often caged by our mind's limitations, but it is amazing what mankind is capable of when we put our hearts and minds into it.

"More than anything it's just showing up and being here for the people that means so much. That simple action says: 'I'm here because I care about you and I will help you if I can.' In a traumatised community like this one, often that is what really matters most."

I remembered the Drs McAlister in their beautiful Quaker hospital in the rolling hills of Zimbabwe. Maybe it wasn't too late to fulfil my dream of returning there as a community doctor after all.

"What help would you most like to see?" I asked.

"I'd like the government of Sudan to stop bombing us for a start," said Tom. "They know very well that we are a hospital. Khartoum have been informed of our GPS coordinates and there is a Red Cross on the roof to indicate our status. Yet we've been bombed many times. Really I would like the international community to intervene and force Bashir to end the ethnic cleansing in the area and stop bombing civilians. Or at the very least lift the blockades and allow relief to come in.

"Then I could get the medicines and vaccines I need to protect the people from disease. We have very serious outbreaks here – inevitable, as everyone is living in such close quarters, often hiding in caves, with no sanitation at all."

***

At this mention of vaccines, I remembered a concept that I had worked on, earlier in my career. The idea of using health as a bridge for peace. Before the Taliban took control of Kabul, the civil war in Afghanistan had raged unceasingly. Except for one week a year. During the early nineteen-nineties Afghanistan was one of the only countries left where polio still flourished and it was a major cause of disability.

At the behest of WHO and Unicef, the warring factions declared a ceasefire for one week each year. There would be a pause in the exchange of fire so that children could be immunised for polio. During this week, the fighters would be deployed to deliver the vaccines to remote parts on the country. Normal vehicles couldn't reach these distant, mountainous places, but the Taliban had tanks which could go virtually anywhere.

So in the middle of the war the fighting would stop and you'd see the gnarled old Taliban militia with long beards and AK-47s slung over their shoulders emerging from their armoured vehicles, clutching their thermos flasks of vaccines as if they were some precious elixir, which I suppose in a way they were.

Fighting resumed as soon as polio immunisation week was over, but maybe for a short while it was not as intense as before. The theory behind this scheme was that in a protracted conflict, if you could remind people what peace was like, maybe they would be more reluctant to go back to war. If you could make people connect through co-operating over the provision of healthcare, you could maintain a bridge of humanity between otherwise fiercely antagonistic parties.

Ultimately, I had decided that healthcare provision should not be subjugated to politicised objectives, and could not create peace unless other issues were addressed and the conflicts were ready to be solved. Nevertheless, these initiatives could help to create islands of humanity amidst oceans of senseless brutality. An important driver of sustainable peace is realising the self-interested mutual interdependence of both sides. Preventing polio was in the best interests of everybody.

Sadly, not so in Sudan. There was no shared interest in keeping the population healthy, if the government's goal was to eradicate their black African citizens from the face of the earth. No wonder Khartoum was enforcing the border blockades so ruthlessly.

"I guess there is no hope of that for some time," Dr Tom commented, after I'd shared my Afghanistan experience with him. "But what I would really like to work on is some lasting development, rather than patching up kids who have been blown apart by shrapnel and landmines."

At this I mentioned Joseph, the little boy with the amputated leg I had met earlier. Tom smiled apologetically. "It's dreadful, 1 but I see so many child amputees it's difficult to keep track of the individual cases. Is he doing OK? Who was it… Joseph?"

"Seems to be," I told him brightly. "He was very happy and playful."

"Oh, I'm glad." Tom smiled. "That's the best part of the job for me. Usually the children who have lost limbs do recover their mischievous side somehow, despite the trauma. When they're getting better and want to play and joke with you, well that makes it all worthwhile. Those little moments."

"Does it ever feel not worthwhile?" I asked, unsure what his answer would be. He seemed like a bottomless well of selfless patience and generosity, and I wondered if he ever had doubts.

"Yes," he said. "Most days it feels too much. Not all day every day of course, but a couple of points through the day I usually think: "I can't do this anymore. I can't go on. It's too desperate, too hard, too unfair, too sad." But then I look at all the blessings I've had in my life and what a privilege it is to be able to come here and care for these people every day in the grace of God. That keeps me going. It's not that I hate it here either, by any means. I love my life here, but some of the tragedy and the hardships I've seen can be hard to bear.

"I'm sad I don't remember Joseph. I feel like the ones you really remember are the ones who don't make it. The kids who struggle through inconceivable suffering for months on end, but you lose them anyway. Those worst cases… well… I remember all *their* names. One little boy, Benny, was hiding in a fox hole when a fire bomb dropped in his direct vicinity. His parents managed to drag him out but not before he was terribly burned, right through to his hypodermis and across large areas of his body.

"They rushed him here, blackened and bloody, and we did what we could for him. My team of nurses are incredibly dedicated. They did most of the work in Benny's case, keeping him clean, changing bandages and dressings, talking to him and keeping his spirits up through months of unimaginable pain. For a while it looked like he was going to make it, until the maggots got to him."

Tom's anguish was visible on his face as he told this story. "It's the patients like that I can't forget. The only thing you can do is try to move on. There is always someone else who needs your help. For your own sanity, you have to try and keep these thoughts out of your mind and pray that kids like Benny find peace."

At that point a Nuban nurse arrived at Dr Tom's elbow. A patient was in need of his attention. As he went to tend to his charges I considered the last thing he had said. Funnily enough I felt as if I understood, at least in some way, exactly what he meant. I'd felt the same thing during my own medical career.

***

I completed my three years' vocational training as a resident physician at Cambridge University's world-class Addenbrooke's Hospital. Naturally I chose Cambridge for my postgraduate study. After Oxford where else was there for the aspiring young Mukesh.

There are not so many patients who stick out in my memory, but there are a precious few I will never forget. I believe this is because they taught me lessons on the kind of life I wanted to lead; the kind of man I wanted to be. One of these, Siobhan, was a beautiful baby girl of only eighteen months old. She was suffering from leukaemia, a blood cancer, and had been referred to Addenbrooke's because we had the latest medical technology that might enable her to beat the disease.

Her parents lived over a hundred miles away and had other children to take care of, so while they came to visit her at every chance they could, for most of the time she was left in our care. It was terribly hard for them to be away from her but they wanted her to have the best chance. We were the only hospital that could offer that.

Somehow, she bonded to me. I would get teased by my colleagues on the ward because she had taken to calling me "dada". Perhaps it was because I spent so much time with her, picking her up and cuddling her in between trying to insert drips and needles into her tiny veins. We were a specialised hospital with the latest technology. When the usual therapy had no effect against the cancer in her white blood cells, we turned to more experimental drugs, trying everything we could to try and save her.

She was covered in bruises from my frequent injections, but she bore it all with an incredible stoicism. She didn't yell or scream like I fear I would have done in her place, injected with poisonous chemicals that made all her hair fall out. She remained quiet and calm, even as she grew sicker and sicker, and was punctured and poked by me day in and day out.

When she eventually died I was terribly upset - but in some way I also felt relief. Her little body resembled a pin cushion by the end, and though she had faced it all with courageous spirit I was grateful at least that she no longer suffered. As they cleared her cot, preparing for the next admission, there was a forlorn little grey elephant left behind. It was a hospital toy but she had made it her own.

There it lay. No one wanted it. Nobody wanted to give it to any of the other children because it was hers. She had been inseparable from it, but also it had such a sad story attached to it now, because the baby who had so loved it had died from leukaemia.

I couldn't stand to see this little creature abandoned when it had brought so much comfort to Siobhan, so I took it home. I put it in the washing machine, hung it out to dry, and gave it to my young children. I cherished it as a token of Siobhan's stoicism and bravery. Her innate courage in the face of such a monstrous disease and difficult treatment, even at such a young age, meant I have never forgotten her.

Some lessons never leave us. Mostly these are not the lessons we learn at elite schools or high-minded universities, they are the lessons we learn from those people we encounter who embody great fortitude in their spirit or character. Little Siobhan really imprinted on my brain: she was the spirit of endurance in the face of adversity. She had great strength within, despite her life-threatening sickness and pain. She was suffering but she did not give up her dignity.

In the years to come I would remember her and when I came across traumatised people in one crisis or other, I would not see the sick patient or the starving person or the frightened one - I would remind myself to see the human being inside who was much more than just the sum of their suffering. This ability to see the person behind the problem lent a human face to the staggering statistics of atrocities in Sudan. They were not statistics. These were dignified people and they needed our help.

***

I bid adieu to Dr Tom. The next leg of our odyssey took us to the Blue Nile State, on the opposite side of the country to Darfur and something of a refuge for the black African Sudanese. Here the people recounted tales of the same genocidal violence from government forces. The stories were much the same, yet it was important for me to hear it from the lips of the people.

One man's account remained with me due to his incredible grace and nobility. We had travelled to the town of Wadega to see the site of a mass grave. This was the final resting place of the dozens of victims of an Antonov attack on market day.

Here we met an old man named Samson who had lived in the Blue Nile all his life. His skin was so black it was almost blue and though age-worn and wrinkled he glowed almost luminescent. Yet the impression his gnarled features wore, when talking about the destruction of his people, betrayed a heart-breaking sorrow.

"We tried to figure out why they were bombing us but we have no idea. We are poor people," Samson told me sadly. "We thought the government would do good things for us but they just keep bombing us. I am an ordinary person. I don't know why they keep bombing me."

His anguish was clearly visible. He was right too. After so many years of bloodshed, I had almost forgotten that the Khartoum regime had a social contract to protect all its people, including their black citizens. They had been enemies for so long now, but once Samson would have looked to Khartoum in the hope of help and fairness. Bashir had broken this trust beyond any chance of repair.

Our experience in The Blue Nile confirmed that Khartoum's "*final solution*" was *nationwide*: it did not just refer to the Darfuris, as I had first feared, but was in fact a campaign to rid the entire country of the indigent black population.

The international community were still failing to act. They were negotiating humanitarian access with the government of Sudan, who kept stalling for time before reneging on any agreement. Why did the UN not come anyway, the people here were all asking? When would their longed-for help arrive?

I was re-witnessing what I had seen earlier in Darfur and even Rwanda before that. I realised that if the UN cannot protect people - either because they don't have the means to do it or they don't have the will to do it - then the most decent thing to do would be to admit it and say so. To stand up and say: "Sorry, we can't help."

If the UN would at least admit that they weren't coming, these people would know that they had only their own selves to rely upon. Without false hope, they could take care of themselves to the best of their abilities.

I have no doubt that many more people were killed in Rwanda because they believed the UN presence would protect them. The Tutsi ran to the peacekeepers for help and many did receive temporary protection. Then UN Headquarters ordered their peacekeepers to leave because it was dangerous, leaving the Tutsi unprotected and helpless. If the UN had not been there in the first place, many of the Tutsi would have dispersed and at least some would have survived the violence. Instead, as the UN departed from the so-called safe havens that had lured the Tutsi, they were rounded up and murdered as if in an abattoir, ten- and twenty-thousand at a time.

I remembered the time I had pulled our UN workers out of Darfur in 2003. Though my remit was purely humanitarian, and I lacked the means to send in forces to make the area secure, I wondered how much their leaving contributed to the destruction. I had removed our eyes and ears from the ground and enabled Khartoum to slaughter the Darfuris, who had put their trust in our system and been let down in the worst imaginable way.

I felt that the same was happening again. Nobody was standing up to Bashir or interfering to stop the violence. Instead, they were moving the local people to refugee camps, abandoning their lands, and enabling the Arab settlers to move in and complete the ethnic cleansing.

The refugee camps like the one I had seen at Yida were usually only a little more secure than the homes the refugees had left behind. They often had little in terms of sanitation, no education opportunities for the children and were still bombed by the Sudanese air force. I was aghast that more was not being done in the face of this blatant ethnic cleansing.

If white people were being murdered by their own government, day in day out, I wondered whether the west would sit up and pay attention. Whatever the reason, it was clear that the UN were not coming. It was up to the local people to defend themselves and resist the Khartoum regime however they could.

The spirit of one woman embodied this resistance. Hami was a statuesque grandmother I met in Blue Nile State. She had a rebellious energy about her. We spoke at length about the hardships she and her family faced. Before I left, I asked what we could do to help her and her people. She paused for a long moment before fixing me with her direct, penetrating stare.

"What can you do? Thank you for coming. Thank you for listening. Thank you for caring. But you will go away. Because you can go away. I will still be here."

With those words she gathered herself up to her full height and ordered my cameraman to come closer.

"Bring your camera here and look well at me. Show my face to the world. Tell the world my story. My greatest fear is that I am born here, I have lived here, I suffer here and I will die here. And no one will know. I will be gone and no one will know. I know that you can't do much here for us. You have no army and no other means to relieve our suffering. But go and tell the world my story. Tell them that I am still here and I am fighting back."

***

I did tell her story. I related the tale of my time in Sudan as UN chief in my first memoir, *Against a Tide of Evil*, which served to bring some attention back to the genocide. The book gave me a chance to tell my own story, but more than that it provided a forum to speak about the issues people like Hami and Samson still faced a decade later.

As I embarked on my book tour, speaking at many literary festivals and humanitarian events across the globe, I learned that the book had done something else too. It had helped the Darfuris to understand more of their own recent history.

I met many Darfuris and their thanks and appreciation was deeply touching. I had not managed to save them or their people, but the fact that I had tried was important. Their gratitude helped assuage my guilt. I had written the book to tell my story, to name and shame those who had orchestrated and abetted the evil, and to highlight the problems still rife in Sudan. Yet the personal impact the book made on the lives of the diaspora was the most fulfilling aspect of all.

The North American leg of my book tour took me to Phoenix, Arizona. Here I was met at the airport by a Sudanese man named Madut who had arrived years before as a refugee.

"I was in a refugee camp in Darfur when I heard you on the BBC," he told me. "Now I have asylum here and have grown a prosperous taxi business." Madut placed one of his taxis at my disposal for the length of my stay and drove me around everywhere. "We will look after you, Dr Kapila. There are many Sudanese in Phoenix who are grateful to you for what you did."

Madut was warm and friendly, thriving in his new life in America. He had a lot of friends and introduced me to many other Darfuris. First we went to a café owned by a fellow Sudanese refugee. Then I met many more packed into the book shop where I was to give my lecture. In the evening some of these survivors took me to dinner in a Sudanese restaurant and later put me up in a hotel they had clubbed together to pay for. I didn't spend a single cent. I was looked after in every conceivable way and welcomed into the homes and hearts of the Dafuri population here. The following morning Madut drove me back to the airport in his taxi.

"Thank you, Madut, for all your kindness. It means more to me than I can say," I began, but he cut me off.

"No, Dr Kapila, thank you. You spoke up for us when nobody would. You gave us hope for freedom and a better life."

***

I was moved by his kindness, as I was by all the Sudanese I encountered wherever I went. But none more so than Talia, who I met when delivering a lecture in Vancouver, at the invitation of an NGO called PeaceGeeks. After my talk was over, a young woman shyly approached me for a conversation. Though she had classically black African Sudanese features she was clearly well-accustomed to life in Canada. She wore jeans and trainers with a dark green scarf wrapped over her head.

"Hello," I said, and smiled at her to dispel her obvious nervousness.

"Hey," she replied, clearly having picked up the north American linguistic idiosyncrasies as well as the fashion sense. "My name's Talia."

"Pleasure to meet you Talia, I'm Mukesh," I said, shaking her hand.

"I know," she replied shyly. "Please, can I talk to you about something?"

"Of course. I think I saw a *Tim Hortons* across the street. Let's go and get a coffee."

Over coffee she told me her story. She was from a village near Korma in north Darfur. She had fled as a young teenager, through Libya to Italy and finally managed to make her way to Canada. Now she earned a few hundred dollars a month working as an undocumented cleaner.

"I want to help my country, but I don't know how," she explained. "There are so many Sudanese charity groups now, but they are all quarrelling with each other. I don't know who to trust. But you seem to be a good man." With that she pulled a crumpled ten-dollar bill from her pocket. "Please take this money. I know you will do something good with it. For my people."

I thanked her solemnly and assured her I would do what I could for her people on her behalf. I managed to hold back my tears long enough to wish her a heartfelt farewell, before bursting into uncontrollable sobs into the dregs of my coffee. Talia's ten dollars, saved from her pitiful income working as an illegal migrant cleaner, were more precious to me than a million dollars from any philanthropist.

I was trusted and thanked by the Sudanese diaspora, applauded and commemorated by them even, yet in my heart of hearts it still rang hollow. I did not deserve their praise. Whatever they might say, I had failed to prevent the genocide. I was still failing. We were still failing to bring redress and justice.

Reflecting upon these brave Sudanese women - Hami in the Blue Nile and Talia in Vancouver - if they had the courage to carry on struggling, if they refused to give up, then what right did I have to stop?

The fight had to continue. Even when we have failed on the ground, the struggle in the hearts and minds could yet triumph. That was what kept me going. Even as I have meandered in and out of my numerous careers, I have always come back to this.

Chapter Twenty-Six

He who opens a school door, closes a prison.
Victor Hugo

THROUGHOUT MY BOOK TOUR, I WONDERED WHAT I should do next. One of the paradoxes of my life had been that, despite my rebellious nature, I'd always been closely associated with institutions. Now, for the first time, I was cut adrift. I felt somewhat rudderless and unsure of myself. I knew I could not return to any of the lofty organisations of Geneva: those bridges were burnt beyond repair. But what institution would take me now, with yet another outspoken controversy attached to my name?

Then came a job offer via Tony Redmond with whom I had collaborated during the siege of Sarajevo and who had gone on to establish the pioneering Humanitarian and Conflict Response Institute at Manchester University. Manchester had what they dubbed a "diamond scheme." They plucked inspiring people from different industries who had exciting, provocative things to say, and made them professors at the university.

I had never considered myself to be an academic. I wasn't sure I was even qualified. I didn't have a lot of published papers pontificating on health or humanitarian theories. Manchester assured me that this didn't matter, averring that I clearly had an academic mind.

I agreed to meet the vice chancellor of the university, Dame Nancy Rothwell. I'd met her once before at an event with the IFRC. I liked her no-nonsense style and admired her keen scientific mind. I had never considered the possibility of teaching before, though in a way I did like the idea of it. I have always been passionate about the power of education. As a university teacher I could influence intelligent young minds and inspire the next generation of radical thinkers.

I thought back to Brother Drew, puffing cigarettes in his kitchen, and his dedication to the tutelage of children like myself. There were few people in my life whose kindness had such a deep and profound effect on me. Could this be my chance to inspire others in the same way?

I flew to Manchester on a typically grey morning. This city was a far cry from the exalted spires of Oxford where I'd had my own university experience. Yet, as I took in the grittiness of the city I was excited by the cosmopolitan starkness. After Geneva, the concrete jungle of Manchester was somewhat forbidding but perhaps I could do something useful here.

I expected my meeting with Dame Nancy Rothwell to be a casual one-to-one chat over a coffee. Yet when I arrived I was ushered into an elegant boardroom surrounded by various other professors and dignitaries, with Dame Nancy presiding over everything. I sat down opposite her, was served tea in a bone china cup and offered a fancy looking plate of biscuits including my favourite McVitie's digestives, I noted.

Much like when I had been recruited into the IFRC, I had not realised I was coming for a job interview, but clearly that's what this was. After the exchange of niceties and the usual questions, Dame Nancy offered me a full Chair - the professorship in global health and humanitarian affairs - right then and there. I think they must have already decided they wanted me and this interview was something of a technicality. I was a little taken aback at the path my life was taking so unexpectedly. It seemed that fate was taking care of me yet again.

"Oh there is one other thing," she added. "We know that you are very outspoken and you are known for your candid utterances..."

My body went rigid with tension at these words. I was sure they were going to tell me to be less publicly critical of the UN or Darfur and so on.

"Yes?" I said defensively.

"Well, next time you go on TV for an interview or anything, please will you make sure they credit you as being a professor here?" she asked politely.

I broke into a wide smile. I couldn't believe what I was hearing. For the first time in my life, I was being offered a job where they wanted me to be myself. I felt like weeping with joy. Here was an institution that really understood the kind of man I was and did not only accept it, but valued me for that.

I realised what this position meant. University professors have freedom of speech so I could speak openly about anything. What's more I could teach and inspire those who would build our world's future, a future where - with luck - whistle-blowers like me were not to be punished, and more people would act with courage in the face of injustice and unfairness.

In Manchester I hoped I had found an institution where I could have a fulfilling role, yet still advocate for the human rights causes I felt strongly about. I accepted the post immediately. I soon discovered that my students - undergraduates and masters students in medicine, heath, and humanitarianism - were less interested in my formal lectures and cared more about my stories. They wanted to hear about my experiences, what I had learned and what advice I could give them as they started out on life's journey.

I specialised in running seminars with small groups covering international development and health issues. I very much enjoyed being surrounded by young, keen people. My office soon became a centre for argument and discussion, as students dropped in to ask a question or discuss a project. Their enthusiasm was infectious. Life felt so full of possibilities.

***

While I enjoyed my teaching work, I was still approached often for international roles. I agreed to chair the board of Minority Rights Group International, and subsequently, also the board of Nonviolent Peaceforce. An old UN colleague, Gerhard Putman-Cramer, who had stuck loyally by me through my down times, persuaded me to join the scientific board of DIHAD - the trend-setting annual Dubai International Humanitarian and Development Conferences. I very much enjoyed these interactions which gave me the opportunity to shape global thinking on critical humanitarian matters.

But mostly I turned down various job offers. That was until the most unexpected development happened - the UN came knocking on my door. I was asked to become their special advisor for the World Humanitarian Summit in Istanbul, in May 2016.

Perhaps the bridges I had burned were not irreparable after all. I'd seen positive changes in the UN since Ban Ki-moon from South Korea had become the new Secretary General. We had met in private some months back in New York, when I had presented him with a copy of my first book and asked him what he hoped his legacy was going to be.

I told him plainly about my disappointment with his predecessor. Kofi Annan had done much for the UN system and the Millennium Development Goals for which he was widely adored. But regrettably, *his* legacy was, in my opinion, tainted by failures in Srebrenica, Rwanda and Darfur that had taken place on his watch, badly letting down people who had put their faith in the ideals of the UN.

As was his way, Ban Ki-moon did not say much but he listened closely and our meeting went well over our allocated time. He showed me the courtesy of personally accompanying me out of his office, where he warmly shook my hand, posed for a photograph to accompany the official UN press statement reporting our meeting, and said quietly: "Thank you for your service, Dr Kapila."

A short while later I heard him speak at the twentieth-year commemoration of the Rwanda genocide in Kigali. Ban Ki-moon, despite his many redeeming qualities, was not known for his public speaking prowess. However, when he took to the stage, his voice was clear, loud and impassioned.

"The blood spilled for one-hundred days. Twenty years later, the tears still flow," he said, and I could feel he was very angry. He could barely control his emotions as he apologised to the Rwandan people for the UN's failures. Then he uttered the words that I had hoped to hear from the UN since my first experiences with genocide, there in the Rwandan capital.

"I have sent my own signal to UN representatives around the world. My message to them is simple: When you see people at risk of atrocity crimes, do not wait for instructions from afar. Speak up, even if it may offend. Act first...."

I nearly fell out of my chair, particularly when he went on to say that he would always back up and support UN officials who did their duty to the victims of such atrocities. This was completely contrary to what I had experienced as Head of the UN in Sudan. I had been pilloried for speaking up, and obstructed at every turn in my attempts to protect the victims in Darfur, and all before I was ejected from my position with little ceremony.

Ban Ki-moon's new policy of "Human Rights First" was bold and courageous. Even though there were many detractors and cynics who said nothing would change, I did feel that there was a new wind blowing though the fusty corridors of power.

At around that time I was invited to appear on an Al Jazeera programme about whistle-blowers. I was pitted against a spokesperson for the UN Secretary General. After a lively debate based on my own experience in Sudan, he said, quite to my surprise: "I am sorry for what happened to Dr Kapila. We like to think that if this were to happen now we would be able to give him better backup."

I was startled. This was the nearest thing to an apology from the UN for the shabby way in which they had treated me over Darfur. Perhaps there really was some commitment to change.

So when I was invited to become the UN's Special Advisor for the first ever World Humanitarian Summit, I accepted. It was to be Ban Ki-moon's final act, as his term of office was soon to end, and I felt fortunate to have the opportunity to help him realise his vision.

The flagship concept I developed as part of the World Humanitarian Summit was the idea of a global compact for health. The theory was that, while we may not be able to prevent all disasters and wars, we could certainly prevent the unnecessary suffering and illnesses that come along with them.

I took my inspiration from military medicine. On a modern battlefield if a soldier is not killed outright, the military medical apparatus is able to quickly stabilise the injured, and provide any care and attention they needed. Thanks to this system, nearly all seriously-wounded servicemen and women survive nowadays.

Our science, technology and medical knowledge had advanced in leaps and bounds in recent years, as had our own wealth and capabilities to help people. Why couldn't we create the same for civilians caught in wars and disasters as for soldiers? Surely, we have the capacity and the duty to at least try? Soldiers, after all, sign up to put themselves in harm's way. Civilians caught in warfare have no such choice.

The World Humanitarian Summit was attended by several heads of state and government and supported this concept of creating a systematic arrangement to deliver all the essential elements of healthcare whenever misfortune struck. Yet the World Health Organisation, which was at the forefront of global health, remained ambivalent. Perhaps this was because it would mean more work for them? Or more likely because they would finally have to stand up and take a strong position in terms of assistance and protection for people caught up in conflicts and disasters. I knew from my own experience that WHO was very skilled at turning a blind eye to injustice, and appeasing the political status quo.

I was bitterly disappointed that WHO had let us down again.

***

Hence, when it was announced that there was to be a new Director General of WHO, I felt I must agitate for a real shakeup.

One candidate, the former Ethiopian health and foreign minister, Dr Tedros Adhanom Ghebreyesus seemed like he could be the right man for the job. I did not know him personally but I was impressed by his track record. He had greatly strengthened the health system of his impoverished country and now wanted to do the same for the world through his vision of universal health coverage for all.

He promised to reform WHO and so I wanted to support him in his campaign. But his main competitor was my old compatriot David

Nabarro. David was responsible for hiring me into the British government at the beginning of my career. He also threw me a lifeline after I left Sudan. When I had blown the whistle on the genocide and nobody else would touch me, David was the one who did.

Yet he had taken advantage of my vulnerability and extracted a heavy price from me. At WHO, I had been banned from speaking on anything to do with Sudan. I had swallowed that - I had no choice - but what I could not stomach was the way he had used his high position to stop WHO from discharging its moral duty as a guardian of public health to protect the health of the people of Darfur. Instead, the extensive data on the increasing toll of disease and death trickling out of Darfur was brushed under the carpet or manipulated to appease the authorities. This was a grossly unprincipled betrayal of the desperate survivors of the original genocide.

I knew that under him WHO would never become the dynamic and honest agency the modern world needed it to be. This conclusion was reinforced when I went to help during the Ebola epidemic in West Africa and witnessed WHO incompetence there, even as David Nabarro defended this from his vantage point as the UN's special envoy there.

***

During the Ebola epidemic in West Africa in 2015, the well-known American NGO, International Medical Corps (IMC), had asked me to join them. A few hours up-country from Freetown, the Sierra Leone capital, was IMC's big Ebola treatment centre.

Martha was my guardian angel there. As the nurse-in-charge, her job was to keep me safe when I entered the "hot zone" where the desperately sick got clinical care. She giggled as she dressed me in the special protection gear. It took a good twenty minutes, as I am not known for my physical coordination skills. Boots, two layers of gloves, impermeable gown, mask, goggles, and helmet: the outfit cost a hundred dollars, and most of the bits were used only once and then burnt.

Her final flourish was to scribble my name on the helmet to identify me among the others wearing similar "space suits". And the time of donning my suit was also inscribed - so you didn't stay in the "hot zone" for too long.

The heat rapidly built up and sweat streamed down on the inside, my visor fogged up, and I could hear my foul breath rasping in my ears. I lasted only forty minutes - the experienced managed more than an hour - during which time we had to do all we could for the desperately sick.

Taking off the gear was the most risky part as a strict sequence had to be followed along with the copious spraying of chlorine to ensure that contamination on the outside layers was not transferred to your skin. Only when Martha had washed me down thoroughly and given the green signal, did I finally hop back over the painted red line on the floor that demarcated the "clean" from "dirty" areas.

I was just a temporary helper, but crossing that red line was done every day by local Sierra Leonean health staff. Dozens of beloved local health workers had already died caring for their patients during the Ebola epidemic. And yet, the world media had only focused on the handful of foreign workers who caught the virus, most of whom survived.

As with the early days of AIDS, there was also no cure for Ebola Virus Disease at that time, and the vast majority of patients died. As also with HIV, the Ebola virus flourished on fear, prejudice, and anger. Burial teams and public health workers were attacked and the sick hidden away. That simply spread the epidemic.

I went on to Liberia where the director of the IMC treatment centre in Bong walked me to the nearby graveyard. Recently turned mounds stretched into the distance under tall trees, each with a rough wooden cross. One of them read, "In Loving Memory of Mammie Juah, Sunrise 1982, Sunset 2014".

Sensing my melancholy, the director took me next to the Survivors' Wall. "It's growing," she said proudly, indicating the collage of multicoloured handprints - each one from a winner in the Ebola lottery as IMC's treatment protocols improved with practice.

I watched the discharge ceremony for John. Declared Ebola free, he was given an impressive-looking certificate to say so - useful to get his job back and reassure his family and friends. He took a shower and donned brand-new clothes. After all, he had been miraculously re-born.

But John insisted on keeping his old mobile phone - so it had to be dunked in chlorine for 30 minutes. Another miracle: it still worked. I wondered if my latest-model iPhone would have survived this treatment.

The attending staff lined up to dance him off the premises, along with some money and food. After, of course, he had imprinted his palm on the Survivors' Wall. This rite of passage was important - signalling gratitude, defiance, and optimism. Survivor John was now a cherished community resource - to educate and bring hope to others, and maybe also to care for the sick because he was immune now.

Meanwhile, the psychological trauma across the region was profoundly visible - a mixture of shame, guilt, fear, and isolation. Mothers couldn't cuddle their sick babies; the dead could not be seen-off in traditional ways. "No Touching" and "No Handshaking" posters were everywhere. This was hard for West Africans who are a warm and affectionate people.

Ebola also obliged me to better know my own body. Inspected every few hours along my travels, I had not realised that one's body temperature can fluctuate so much. Passing through roadblocks brought micro-frissons of anxiety when the sanitary inspectors pointed their temperature scanner at me. What if - *this time* - it was raised?

Once, this was indeed the case. Thirty-eight degrees! But common sense prevailed. "You have been walking too long under the sun, haven't you? Drink this water and rest," said the kind-looking nurse. Ten minutes later I was relieved to be declared "normal" again.

At Monrovia airport departures there was a final ritual. The gloved gate attendant peered at the thermometer. A hint of a smile failed to be obscured by her mask as she announced, "Thirty-six-point-two. You are good to go".

***

I felt that Dr Tedros was also "good to go" with his sincere intent to bring radical change to WHO. So, despite owing my career to David, I decided to support his competitor, Tedros, and threw in my efforts alongside his key lieutenants, Senait Fisseha, and Peter Singer.

I wrote articles for *The Guardian*, spoke in the media and was a proactive user of social media to promote the Tedros candidacy. Many of my friends were appalled and shocked by my strident political advocacy.

My motivation was simple: the world deserved better and changing the World Health Organisation was literally a life and death matter. Old personal ties could not be permitted to take priority over the wider public - in this case global - good.

The campaign got very dirty. The Conservative British government weighed in, using its full diplomatic and financial muscle, including bullying some smaller countries in support of Dr Nabarro. Yet the looming Brexit vote and Britain's increasing unpopularity on the world stage ultimately counted against them. Meanwhile the African Union put its full backing behind Dr Tedros. I even went to Delhi to lobby the country of my birth, on his behalf. Many Asian countries also lined up to support a candidate who was not the typical choice from a powerful, western, donor country.

I used all my contacts and sway in every way I could and was delighted when he won the election at the World Health Assembly, in May 2017, by a two-thirds majority of nation states. Amid scenes of jubilation in the *Palais des Nations*, Tedros gave his acceptance speech. A central feature of this was a commitment to universal health coverage. He had a dream that every person on the planet should have access to healthcare as a basic human right.

With Tedros in charge of WHO and global healthcare a real priority, I wondered how I might use my own skills to serve the cause. Despite the gossip put about my detractors, I had no desire to return to a WHO job.

***

Sometime earlier, I had invested in a set of golfing equipment. Perhaps my North Korean experience had deluded me to think that I could have some talent in this area. Anyway, now I had the time to check this out and pass the bags of free time that I suddenly had.

But it was not to be. My long-standing associate, Mukul Bhola, introduced me, over a drink at the Intercontinental Hotel in Geneva, to Soraya Ramoul and Anna Mølgaard Thaysen, from the Danish pharmaceutical company, Novo Nordisk. They asked me to lend my skills to the problem of noncommunicable diseases.

"NCDs, such as cancer, diabetes, and cardio vascular disease, are now the biggest killers on earth," Soraya told me.

"But why do you want me?" I asked. "I have never worked in this field. I deal mostly with disasters and emergencies."

"That's precisely why we want you," Anna explained. "We need someone with your experience of crises like AIDS and Ebola, to bring passion and urgency to the fight against NCDs."

I considered this for a moment and realised that maybe they had hit upon something. Mukul and I had recently been to Tajikistan and understood the severity of this crisis. Tajikistan is by far the most impoverished of the former Soviet republics. One of the last countries to declare independence, its transformation from the old communist system to a modern, cut-throat, capitalist economy had also led to a breakdown of its social welfare system, with devastating impact on the poor.

Healthcare had been hit incredibly hard. Under the Soviets, everybody got their medical care for free. All basic services were covered by the state - immunisations, surgery, maternity care - anything the people required. Now all that had crumbled away. I was shocked to learn that a shortage of insulin meant that desperate people with diabetes were spending their life savings to get it on the black market, or just dying when they couldn't.

One common complication of untreated diabetes is the narrowing of blood vessels to limbs, ultimately causing gangrene, and requiring amputation to stop the rot from spreading.

I visited a Tajik hospital and saw the surgical ward half-full of amputees. These were ordinary people - a farmer, a housewife, a teacher - who had gone in with diabetic complications and ended up without a leg or a foot. I imagined them in wheelchairs trying to cope with the daily struggles of life, losing their livelihood and plunging their families deeper into poverty. This was even more serious in a poor country with limited infrastructure for disabled people.

In the West, amputations and blindness or kidney failure - other secondary effects of diabetes - are uncommon due to readily available medicines and diagnostics. It was shocking that the Tajiks were suffering so much so unnecessarily.

***

As an insulin-dependent diabetic myself, I understood all too well how frightening it must feel to have an unreliable supply. Over the twenty-five years that I have lived with diabetes, my condition has worsened. But this is largely my own fault. My peripatetic lifestyle of frequent travel across time zones, war zones and disaster zones meant that I was often too busy to test my blood sugar, take proper exercise or monitor my diet properly. The truth is that I have become careless over time. My little stress-relieving indulgences such as a beer or biscuits or chocolate have multiplied.

My self-neglect has meant the disease is impacting more on my life. I had the fright of my life when a routine ophthalmic check showed that I had retinopathy in one eye, which was just millimetres away from the optic disk and could blind me unless it was immediately treated. I got laser surgery and resolved to become more diligent in my self-care. Paradoxically, the resolve to tighten my sugar control causes me other, even more serious problems.

Not infrequently, I can awaken at 3am, sweaty and shaking, with the symptoms of low blood sugar. My vision diminishes to a narrow tunnel as the edges of my sight fade into darkness. I stumble down this tunnel to the kitchen to find sugar - in the form of my emergency stock of *Kit Kats* - with my heart racing as the adrenaline response propels me before I black out completely and crack my skull or fall into a potentially lethal hypoglycaemic coma. Gobbling down a sugar-laden

Kit Kat does the trick and I am right as rain a few minutes later. (Of course, keeping the chocolate next to my bed, precisely for such emergencies, would make sense, but I could not trust myself to not eat them when not required).

But the following day I feel washed-out through a combination of lost sleep and rapidly fluctuating blood sugar levels. These experiences are frightening enough but I have access to healthcare and a predictable supply of insulin. I can imagine the insecurity a Tajik diabetic must feel, not knowing where their next shot was coming from.

This was the anxiety of a group of juvenile Tajik diabetics. I met them on their eighteenth birthday which would normally be a moment for celebration. But it was also the day that their insulin supply was being cut-off. Officially, they were now adults and no longer eligible to get their injections from the children's charity that had kept them alive since birth. "Where will I get my insulin tomorrow? Must I die now?" asked Afsoon who was head girl in her school, and aspired to be an engineer. I had no answer.

That night, I could not sleep. "How could any responsible agency play god like this? It was downright unethical and immoral. And why had nobody developed a programme to do something about it." There and then, I decided that I would try to do so.

***

This problem of NCDs is growing across all countries. The Tajik youth had inherited their condition, Type I diabetes. But another form of diabetes - Type II - is now more and more common due to lifestyle changes such as unhealthy foods that are more easily accessible and affordable. That is especially so for poorer people and developing countries who bear the brunt of this new pandemic.

However, diabetes is not the only chronic killer growing in prevalence. An Unicef colleague reminded me that raised blood pressure is the major cause of maternal and perinatal mortality in Africa. Meanwhile, closer to home in Manchester, a cancer specialist colleague told me about his special programme to tackle the accelerating rates of breast cancer in Asian women. All too often, because of shame and stigma, these women present far too late for effective treatment.

Visiting the Kibera slum in Nairobi with the Kenya Red Cross, I met John, a hypertensive labourer who lugged heavy loads for casual earnings. He took me to the roadside café where he took his meal break. "For the twenty-five shillings I have today, I can have either a bunch of these nice greens you say are good for me, or that salty fatty stew that you say is bad but which will give me strength for the afternoon. What would you eat if you were me?"

As my awareness grew, I saw more and more evidence that noncommunicable diseases really are the most serious health problem in the world today. In a very short time I had crafted a global strategy and with the strong backing of Novo Nordisk, Mukul and I had organised a new global health venture that we called *"The Defeat-NCD Partnership"*.

I cajoled my old associate from Cambridge, Dr James Hospedales, a renowned expert on NCDs, to chair our board. I was delighted when Michael Møller, the Director General of the UN in Geneva, agreed to be our honorary president, as this would help reinforce our credibility. I consulted Dr Tedros. He was keen for us to proceed and start helping to advance his vision for universal health coverage in a practical way even as he struggled with his initial efforts at WHO reform.

***

When I was least expecting it, I had stumbled onto this opportunity to use my lifelong international experience, my medical expertise, and my personal insights from living with diabetes, to create something new from scratch. We positioned *Defeat-NCD* as a public-private-people partnership, bringing on board the UN, WHO, governments, private sector and NGOs. But above all, we involved the people with NCDs who must take more control of their own treatments.

Most of all, we wanted to make a programme that would not be strangled at birth by the self-serving bureaucracies that I had spent most of my life battling against. As we pressed forward, we came up against the familiar institutional turf battles, personal rivalries and egos, along with an additional financial dimension that I had not seen before.

This concerned the availability and affordability of life-saving NCD medicines, and the related diagnostics and equipment. In impoverished Haiti, I discovered that it cost the equivalent of a daily wage to buy just the test strips essential to check your blood sugar. And the actual insulin was totally unaffordable even if you could find it.

In Myanmar, I learnt that the government procurement system paid twice the world market price for essential medical supplies for NCDs. Meanwhile, I saw from a visit to the Rohingya refugee camps in Bangladesh that hypertension was a leading cause of adult mortality there. Humanitarian agencies were too busy tackling the other traditional problems of refugees to spare a thought for what was actually killing so many people. On a visit to Tanzania, the health minister asked me why it was so difficult to get simple blood pressure machines for their health centres that were not always breaking down.

Could we do something?

Of course, we could. But it would require disrupting the global marketplace to reduce the price of essential NCD medicines, diagnostics, and equipment. If we were to do that, would the manufacturers and middle-men who were profiteering so obscenely at the expense of sick people, tolerate us?

Someone from a pharma company asked me during our meeting, "Have you considered getting a bodyguard?" He was joking, of course, but was there an underlying hint of menace? "Don't be absurd," I laughed, but my thoughts flashed back to the post-Darfur death threats I had received. After all, the medicines market we planned to disrupt is valued at tens of billions…

But then, no one should die in the world because they can't afford insulin and no one should go blind or have a leg chopped-off for the same reason. After all, is this not what Tedros meant by his dream for universal health coverage?

We must get ready for the necessary battle ahead.

Chapter Twenty-Seven

To help, without asking whom!
Henry Dunant

THE UNITED NATIONS PUBLIC APOLOGY TO ME, FROM ITS highest levels for the way that they had treated me over Darfur, and then, nailing my colours to the cause of getting leadership change at WHO followed-up by my new work on NCDs, saw me getting closer to the multilateral system, once again.

Of course, I would never be fully welcomed by them and neither would I ever make the mistake again to be fully co-opted by them. I had learnt painfully that even our most revered institutions are only as good as the people in them. And such good people always go when their time runs out. So it is wiser for me to remain a little apart - and free.

However, there was one more institution left to make peace with - the one that had been closest to my heart and the hardest to let go of. Luckily for me, when my opportunity to return to the Red Cross Red Crescent family came, it also invited me to embark on a personal journey into my own cultural identity.

I was approached by the Secretary General of the Indian Red Cross Society, Dr Veer Bhushan who informed me that the society would soon be one hundred years old. I was still well known for my work on the IFRC's *Strategy 2020*. So, Dr Bhushan asked me if I would help the Indian Red Cross to create a new strategy in time for its centenary.

The Indian government - their national Red Cross included - were wary and suspicious of foreign interference. They abhorred the arrogance of the western powers telling them what to do. This was hardly surprising given their colonial and postcolonial aid-dependent history. Yet the venerable, one-hundred-year-old Indian Red Cross establishment lacked the capacity to craft its own redesign, mostly because it was riven by internal disputes.

I was respected as an internationally well-known personality but, more important, I was of Indian descent, with a useful grasp of Hindi and a couple of other Indian languages. They hoped that by combining my skills and credibility with the legitimacy of my Indian heritage, I would be able to formulate something that would bridge the different warring factions of the Indian Red Cross.

Though I had gained British citizenship in the 1990s, in my heart I still consider myself to be Indian. The more I have achieved in the western world, the more I have felt Indian inside. No matter how much time I spend in Europe, despite the accolades I have received there, I feel that I will never be truly assimilated there.

I feel obligated to the west. I am thankful for all the time I have spent there and all the benefits and privileges that have been bestowed on me. Yet more and more I have felt drawn back to the country of my birth. I yearned to return to my roots. It's difficult to know why. Perhaps this is just an innate instinct in all of us, especially as we get older.

Despite my desire to take on this assignment I was not sure I'd be allowed to. IFRC was under new management now as Elhadj As Sy had replaced Bekele as the Secretary General. But I was concerned there would still be plenty of people at IFRC HQ in Geneva who were jealous or wary of me. I checked with him, and with Xavier Castellanos, the regional director for Asia Pacific, and the country office in New Delhi headed by Leon Prop. They were all surprisingly receptive and offered to invest IFRC funds into my strategic planning exercise. The British, Italian, and German Red Cross Societies also pitched in with more money. As had also been the case with the *Strategy 2020* exercise, I never managed to spend all the money they made available to me.

Before I accepted the task, I met with the Chairman of the Indian Red Cross, who was also the Minister of Health and Family Welfare in the Government of India, Shri J.P. Nadda. This encounter was brokered at the margins of the World Health Assembly by Rajiv Chander, the Indian Ambassador to the UN in Geneva, and my original purpose was to lobby to get the Indian vote for Tedros. Minister Nadda was receptive and with that done, we moved on to discuss his other views over coffee and Indian sweets. As I tucked into a pistachio flavoured treat, the minister addressed me urgently in Hindi.

"*Kapila-ji karo, kuch karo, achcha karo, abhi karo, jaldi karo.*" In other words: "Do something. Do something good. Do it now, do it quickly." He was referring to his frustration with the Indian Red Cross because he wanted to see change. "The only time they ask me as chairman is to cut a ribbon, open a conference, or flag off a relief supply truck," he grumbled.

"What's your ambition for change in the Indian Red Cross?" I asked.

He sipped his tea contemplatively before answering. "I would like to project a vision of a humanitarian India, not just an economically and industrially advancing India. Not just Bollywood and IT and doctors and factories, but a kind and caring nation that is in line with India's historic, cultural and religious beliefs that reach back thousands of years. Let's call it *Humanitarian India!*"

He wanted the new strategy for *Humanitarian India* to reflect these ancient values, enabling them to flourish under the banner of the Red Cross. He was right about the Indian nation's disposition towards benevolence. Indians are by nature a warm-hearted, deep-thinking people. Four world religions were born on the Indian subcontinent - Hinduism, Buddhism, Sikhism and Jainism - all of which champion ideas of altruism and a love of humanity.

Naturally, I jumped at the chance to revitalise this institution. I would be working for a cause that I loved, and also for my country of birth where the Red Cross had so much potential for success.

Nine months of intensive work followed with several trips to India. I put into place my usual methodology of evidence-based analysis by consulting with everyone I could. By listening to all and keeping an open mind, I used numerous such conversations to energise a wide-ranging debate. They fed the fire of my future ambitions for the Indian Red Cross.

I was granted free access to everything: premises, papers and people at all levels. It seemed as if they trusted me, and I worked hard through honest communication and transparency to strengthen that trust further. Everyone knew that I had no career ambitions. I was an outsider who brought wider perspectives, but at the same time I was one of them, so they felt that I understood and that I cared.

When I had arrived at the national headquarters in New Delhi, I began to see how awry this one-time power-house for good had become. The address of the main office, a stone's throw from the Indian Parliament is *Number One, Red Cross Road*, which shows the prestige the organisation once held. I saw that the large, imposing building had a gloomy, run-down air about it. The extensive grounds were littered with broken vehicles with unkempt long grass growing through their wheels. The once white paint was greying and peeling off the walls.

When I entered the building the situation was not much better. Various clerks listlessly moved files from one office cubicle to another, collecting endless signatures. I was shocked to see that these files were all secured with strips of red string. This was a literal red-tape bureaucracy, introduced by the British colonial masters, that was still in full swing.

As I explored more of the building, it became clear that the Red Cross here represented the antithesis of all that was going on in the rest of India. The nation was modernising at top speed, but the same urgency had not extended to these fusty offices. No wonder they needed help.

I located the man in charge of all this, Veer Bhushan, who had asked for my input in the first place. He was sitting behind a large wooden desk in a claustrophobic office, almost totally obscured behind stacks of files and paperwork. Across from him were two rows of straight-backed chairs where people sat, waiting for a moment of his time.

We began talking about the problems he saw and potential ideas to rectify them, yet we were interrupted every few minutes by assistants who came and went, asking him to sign papers or answer questions. It was impossible to make any progress. It became clear to me that the head of this Red Cross was more of a general secretary than a Secretary General.

Yet he was a very good man. Once I had managed a proper conversation with him, I discovered he was a thoughtful, dedicated professional. He had been a renowned surgeon before he took this job, on the death of the previous leader. A portrait of his predecessor, Dr Satya Paul Agarwal, glowered down from the wall behind his desk. I had known him well. He had also been the former Director General of Health Services of India and I had done battle with him many times during my stint as Special Representative for HIV and AIDS. I'd wanted the Indian Red Cross to scale up their work in this area, particularly by ending discrimination against people with HIV, drug users and sex workers.

Dr Agarwal had been highly resistant. A staunch conservative he was unwilling to extend our benevolence to people on society's margins. I had finally managed to persuade him to allow the HIV programme to scale up, by speaking a language he understood. Once I realised that I could not appeal to his compassion, I petitioned his scientific mind instead. I reasoned that if he didn't control the spread of the virus in these groups, then the general Indian population would suffer. By arguing from a purely epidemiological perspective, I managed to convince the old traditionalist to do the right thing.

I could tell that Veer Bhushan was different. He wanted progress, change and modernisation but he was a victim of the system he had inherited. He seemed to lack the confidence and authority to break through the red tape, both literally and figuratively. I saw now why he had asked for help, hoping that my role as an independent facilitator might provide the catalyst for change.

I was not sure I would be able to manage such a task. As I walked around the corridors I felt increasingly downhearted. Was this really India's leading light for humanitarian action? In which was vested the spirit of humanity and the hopes of all who suffered from disasters or crises across this vast land? What could writing my report actually achieve? Could I do any real good here, or was my strategy for improvement simply a way for these bureaucrats to paint over the cracks in a fatally flawed edifice?

My despondent trudging eventually brought me to the building's basement. I sighed as I regarded the decades' worth of junk that officialdom refused to dispose of. I wandered about between the piles of old car parts, broken chairs and faded office supplies until something caught my eye. Propped against one wall stood an old photograph. It appeared to have been there for decades judging by the cobwebs, yet even through the dust I recognised the iconic figure of Mahatma Gandhi.

In the photograph, the legendary leader of the Indian liberation movement was handing over a giant cheque for four-thousand eight-hundred rupees made out to the Indian Red Cross. The date on the cheque said 29th of August 1947, just two short weeks after India became independent. I smiled as I rubbed away the grime to see that he was handing the cheque to a serious looking young woman with thick glasses. Her identity is lost in history, but I guessed she was a Red Cross volunteer.

With this discovery all my doubts disappeared. The country's National Red Cross Society, originally established in 1920 by an act of the colonial parliament of that time, predated the Republic of India itself. An institution so entwined with the history of this ancient land, bringing help to thousands over the past century, could not be allowed to calcify under out-dated notions.

Full of renewed hope, I embarked upon a mission to visit as many of the Red Cross branches as I could across India. For me it was a pilgrimage, rediscovering the land of my birth. I connected once more with the diversity of beliefs and cultures. Everywhere I went I found delicious food, divergent cultures and languages, and above all else the irrepressible Indian spirit. This was the life blood of what I saw to be an unruly and tempestuous, but highly exciting democracy.

NO STRANGER TO KINDNESS

I also found that the ancient humanitarian instinct that Minister Nadda had talked about at the Intercontinental in Geneva was very much alive and flourishing across the land, in the actions of ordinary people.

***

Outside one Red Cross branch in Andhra Pradesh, I came across a statue that looked oddly familiar. On closer inspection I realised that it was an Indianized version of Henry Dunant, the Swiss founder of the Red Cross. The sculptor had obviously crafted the bust from available pictures and added Indian features.

In front of the statue flickered a *diya* - a traditional tear-shaped oil lamp the likes of which you find in countless temples up and down the country. Around the bust, was a garland of vivid orange marigold flowers. My guide explained that the statue had been erected on the founding of this particular office, some forty years previously. She recounted how every day the lamp was lit and the marigolds freshened in tribute to the organisation's founding father.

This was a quintessentially Indian expression of respect. There are many, many religions practiced across India and I could tell from the names of the volunteers in this branch that they came from different faiths. So, they had just incorporated Henry Dunant into this pantheon of Indian gods.

I realised how interconnected we all were by the great web of the Red Cross Red Crescent. Here I was in India, the land of my birth, looking at a statue of Henry Dunant whose home city of Geneva was now my own home. I appreciated this symmetry.

I ventured inside the building where I met an elderly gentleman with dark, twinkling eyes, tufty grey hair and a stooped posture who introduced himself as Dr Parth. He sat in the centre of a small room perfectly kitted out as a dental surgery. He must have been at least seventy-five years old, but clearly still possessed a very sharp mind. Dr Parth explained to me that he'd been retired for the last twenty years, yet he came twice a week to run the dental clinic to serve local people.

"The Red Cross raised money from the neighbourhood to equip the surgery with all I need," he told me. I was impressed to see that it appeared to contain all the very latest in dental paraphernalia. "The poor deserve the best and they should be first, and not last in the queue for latest treatments," he affirmed. "And, of course I volunteer my experience and time for free."

"What kind of services do you provide?" I asked.

"Oh, you know," he shrugged, "pulling teeth, doing fillings, lecturing on dental hygiene. I make sure the teeth of the poor are well taken care of." He smiled at me with his own set of pearly whites.

Dr Parth explained that across the corridor was a medical centre that operated in a similar way. This was run by three junior doctors from the nearby private hospital.

"A dozen young men and women come by on a rota system weekly," he told me. "Each of them does a session a week to treat the ailments of those who cannot afford to pay for healthcare. All for free of course, the Red Cross again providing equipment and supplies."

Everything the clinic needed was purchased from donations. It was clear that this was very much a Red Cross of the community, for the community, with very little to do with the distant headquarters in Delhi.

I questioned Dr Parth about sustainability. "How do you keep your work going and pay the bills?" I enquired. He seemed puzzled at this, like he couldn't understand what I was talking about.

"We have no financial worries," he said. "When the people have a need, they come to the Red Cross to propose a project. The Red Cross then asks nearby businesses and companies to contribute funds. They do so because we are serving the community. With the money raised we provide a service for whatever problem the people have brought to our attention. When the need has been fulfilled the project finishes and we stop. Then we make new projects for new issues and these are then supported in the same way, and so we have been going on for forty years." He told me all this, as if it was the most obvious thing in the world.

I had spent several years in my big office at IFRC in Geneva, anguishing over the problems that Dr Parth and his people had solved decades before. I was busy devising resource mobilisation strategies, running after donor funds, dreaming up schemes for organisational improvements and generally fretting over how to get support to expand our work, while the answer was right here all the time.

The Red Cross's true strength lay in its community base, its localised ownership, and each branch's self-initiated motivation to deal with their own problems themselves. Dr Parth had shown me that this was a self-sustaining concept. It fostered responsibility and grass-roots cooperation. They were bringing people together and creating harmony through mutual help and interdependence. These were the truest of Red Cross principles in daily action.

I thanked Dr Parth for his insight. On my way out I paused at the shrine to Henry Dunant. I recognised that this Red Cross branch was a modern temple to humanity. Outside sat this secular god, garlanded with marigolds, epitomising the founding ideals of the Red Cross's noble sentiments. Inside the prayers of the people were answered; salvation executed through services to the poor and needy who came through the doors. No one was turned away. It was all done by these people for their own people.

I added a flower of my own to Dunant's shrine, and went away with an idea. It was clear that this grass-roots charitable action was alive and well in India, regardless of the sclerotic officiousness of its distant headquarters in New Delhi. My vision for Red Cross resurrection was to focus on enabling and magnifying the many acts of kindness that were already occurring every day, to provide a beacon for hope to the country's impoverished.

This meant a bottom-up network of branches as opposed to the prevailing culture of top down management. The inertia of the headquarters was stifling the national humanitarian spirit, even as it struggled to stay alight in the hearts and minds of the kind-hearted volunteers.

Before I left India, I visited a Red Cross branch in my own district of birth: Sambalpur, in Odisha State. Here I met a young volunteer named Rachit. A diminutive but determined young woman, she could have been no more than twenty years old. In a brisk voice she told me about the initiative she'd designed.

"I started collecting unwanted clothes for the homeless," she said. "Just from my friends and neighbours at first. With the help of my siblings and a few friends we would collect old clothes and distribute them to those in the area who could make use of them."

Rachit had thought of the project herself, developed it with the people she knew, and brought it to the nearest Red Cross branch when it had outgrown her bedroom, not least because she wanted to use their warehouse to store the goods she procured.

When I talked with her further she told me that she wanted to be a member of parliament for her district one day.

"My goal is to fight against corruption," she said. "It is eroding society here so badly. I want to make a difference against that. Providing clothes for the homeless is one thing, but I don't want to just give them clothes. I want to confront the underlying causes of people's suffering and injustice."

I was struck by the juxtaposition of her charitable work and her obvious political activism. Here, back in my home district of India,

Rachit confirmed to me that although it was important for the Red Cross to be impartial, that did not mean that we had to close our eyes against social ills and all that was wrong in society. It was possible to address both.

Over the following months of vigorous consultations, I asked how we could scale-up these every-day acts of kindness to combat the nation's big problems. For the first time in decades, volunteers and staff from across India came together to seek answers. We talked, learned, shared inspiration and began finding solutions. Together we worked on establishing a solid, inter-connected network that would rejuvenate the broken relationship between the national headquarters and its scattered field offices.

Many, many innovative ideas were offered from across the Red Cross network of over one-thousand autonomous branches. For the first time this network of dedicated humanitarians felt that they were being given the chance to shape their future. This open consultation meant the workers felt empowered to put the new strategy into action for change and transformation.

I was delighted when the Indian Red Cross proudly presented their new *Strategy 2030* to the whole world at the General Assembly of the Red Cross Red Crescent in Antalya, Turkey, later that year.

A couple of months later, I returned for a final visit to *Number One, Red Cross Road* in New Delhi. The transformation was remarkable. Gone were the stacks of files, red string, cluttered offices, dirty damp basement, broken furniture, long grass and abandoned vehicles. There was fresh paint on the walls, computerisation, and everywhere the staff seemed more energised. Seeing all this redoubled my faith in the capacity for change and revitalised my hope for their transformation.

On the wall of the chairman's office, cleaned up and installed in pride of place behind his desk, was the rescued picture of Gandhi handing over the giant cheque that celebrated the birth of the nation of India. It was by rediscovering the public-spiritedness of the past and recognising the eternal benevolent values that are both Indian and universal, that the Indian Red Cross could reimagine a dynamic future on the approach to its centenary year.

Enabling this metamorphosis was incredibly rewarding for me. I felt blessed to connect with the Red Cross once more. Here, in the biggest and most compassionate of institutions, I rediscovered my own humanity and personal identity. I was able to explore my own country and my people once again, experiencing all the spontaneous good and kindness in their hearts.

Epilogue

The real voyage of discovery consists not in seeking new landscapes, but in having new eyes.
Marcel Proust

I HAVE VISITED MANY PLACES ON THIS LONG VOYAGE, starting out from my adopted country of Britain that generously granted a young Mukesh so much opportunity, and returned eventually via the warm heart of my nation of birth, India, to the real home inside my own self.

It has not been a straight path but one with many forks. The dilemma of my life has been about which turning to take when the path diverged. Can I claim, in the paraphrased words of the poet Robert Frost that *"I took the road less travelled by, and that made all the difference?"* I am not so sure. It might be equally correct to say, in the words of his critics, *"whichever way I went, I am sure to have missed something good on the other path."*

***

However, as I reflect back on all I have done and dream forward of all I have left to do, there is one realisation that stands out more clearly and consistently than any other. It seems that the propensity to commit evil or do good is present in all of us; they are the opposing sides of the same coin. We are engaged in a perpetual battle between the two forces, and the outcome can't be taken for granted. Neither is it pre-ordained. We have every possibility to shape the world we want.

My life has been an unintended witness to the evil side. These include both *'big'* and *'small'* evils, and I have learnt that no continent and culture is immune to them. I had a ringside seat at the *big evil* of genocide in Rwanda, Srebrenica, and Darfur, and although these were orchestrated by truly horrible leaders, the real shock was that they were successfully implemented, in practical terms, by ordinary people like you and me.

"Never again" has happened *"again and again."* Because people who are ordinarily good, find it easier to make small concessions to tyranny, as that is less trouble than taking a principled stand. Thus, small concessions can cascade into a full-blown *tide of evil* that can overwhelm everyone and everything.

Perhaps it is also my lifetime of exposure to *small evils*, as part of my humanitarian and development career, that has shaped my attitude towards the *big evil*. Knowing how my baby brother Bunty died of ignorance; watching helplessly as Saif's teenage sister perished in childbirth in Moudubi; seeing the hundreds who expired from AIDS in Lilongwe hospital; hearing how Ambi was serving her life sentence of sexual slavery in Sonagachi; inadvertently sending my interpreter Hwan to his execution in North Korea; understanding the pressure on young Tsunami women survivors to marry fast; or realising that a fellow diabetic in Tajikistan was suffering a leg amputation because he could not afford insulin - these experiences have left indelible imprints.

Yet, in a lifetime spent at the frontlines of misery and misfortune, I have also witnessed myriad acts of extraordinary courage and compassion in the most desperate contexts. It seems that for every act of cruelty, there is available, right next to it, the antidote of humanity.

These are the people like Elias caring for Syrian refugees on his muddy field or the talented but stateless Bushra treating autism in Lebanon; Dr Austin in Bangladesh, and the Drs McAlister in Zimbabwe for whom service was a lifetime commitment; the septuagenarian Dr Parth tending to the teeth of the poor in India, come rain or shine; Mary walking the last mile to deliver life-saving anti-HIV pills in Zambia; or Talia, an undocumented refugee in Vancouver, sharing her meagre income with her brothers and sisters still suffering in Darfur.

Every one of these acts of kindness - often small, random, and unrecognised - brought hope to someone in their darkest moments. And when kindness is combined with courage, the power of evil can be blunted in surprisingly effective ways.

Such as by the unknown ICRC delegate saving my grandmother and family in the Indian Partition, or his modern successor Max prison-visiting in Sri Lanka; Fatima criss-crossing the Syrian militia frontlines to ensure that none of her grandchildren were left behind; Ajša defying the snipers of Sarajevo with her lipstick, to ferry tampons and toothpaste for the dignity of her sisters; Dr Tom refusing to be bombed out of the Nuba Mountains; Aisha, enduring terrible personal insult and injury to travel so far to demand action against the crimes in Darfur; Nina standing up for all mothers whose sons had been disappeared in Guatemala; Emanuel taking daily risks as a human rights defender in Burundi; Noresham daring to escape so as to give voice to the incarcerated refugees in Chad; Baby Siobhan smiling to the last against cancer in Cambridge; or Rachit, fighting against corruption, when distributing clothes to the homeless in Sambalpur was just not enough.

***

Finally, what of myself? The same ordinary - and yet extraordinary - people have also given me the courage to persevere along the path that I have found myself on. That has meant not being afraid to speak up when necessary. I have come to realise that the platforms I have been fortunate to occupy during my diverse career have come with the special responsibility to use them.

Yet that was not always so. There was a time when I had doubted whether speaking out was the right thing to do. I was warned on this by all the great institutions that I have held high office in, and where I have always ended by becoming a pain in the butt for them.

It is the same with my friends who, in their well-meaning exasperation with me, have told me that my outspokenness was not a good quality; it would lead to my own ruination and ostracism. So it has proved to be; I have few real friends now. But this has also been liberating. It is often necessary to jettison the people who hold you back. And those few who remain with me are all the more precious for it.

I know myself better now and, at last, I am at peace by giving up the struggle to become someone I don't want to be. I know I am not the type of person who can keep quiet. Once I feared this would be my ultimate downfall, but now, I have realised that this is my greatest strength.

Printed in Great Britain
by Amazon